The Ecology of Higher Education

Perspectives of an Ecologist as Educator

ANDREW MARTIN

EU GPSR Authorised Representative:
Logos Europe, 9 rue Nicolas Poussin, 17000, La Rochelle, France
contact@logoseurope.eu

For information, contact State University of New York Press, Albany, NY
www.sunypress.edu

Library of Congress Cataloging-in-Publication Data

Name: Martin, Andrew (Andrew P.), 1961– author.
Title: The ecology of higher education : perspectives of an ecologist as
   educator / Andrew Martin.
Description: Albany : State University of New York Press, [2026]. | Includes
   bibliographical references and index.
Identifiers: LCCN 2025024504 | ISBN 9798855805055 (hardcover : alk. paper) |
   ISBN 9798855805079 (epub) | ISBN 9798855806908 (PDF) | ISBN
   9798855805062 (pbk. : alk. paper)
Subjects: LCSH: Education, Higher—Philosophy | Ecology
Classification: LCC LB2322.2 .M36768 2025
LC record available at https://lccn.loc.gov/2025024504

Dedicated to students and teachers everywhere

The principles of ecology, if we take them to heart, should keep us aware that our lives depend on other lives and upon processes and energies in an interlocking system.

—Wendell Berry (2021)

The problem of how to transmit our ecological reasoning to those whom we wish to influence in what seems to us to be an ecologically "good" direction is itself an ecological problem.

—Gregory Bateson (1972)

Contents

Acknowledgments

I am indebted to many of my colleagues who have shaped my perspectives and abilities as an educator, especially, in alphabetical order by last name, Nichole Barger, David Budd, Kendi Davies, Emily Fairfax, Anne Marie Hoskinson, Gabrielle Katz, Mike Klymkowsky, Jenny Knight, Abe Lo, Brett Melbourne, Diana Nemergut, Valerie Otero, Abbey Paulson, Steven Pollack, Sarah Seiter, Betty Stennett, Sierra Love Stowell, Paul Strode, and Sarah Wise. Raphael Sassower and colleagues of the Presidential Teaching Scholars program expanded my perspective about why and how to teach. I thank the dedicated individuals who were part of the Science Education Initiative spearheaded by Carl Wieman, including Carl, Cathy Perkins, and especially Stephanie Chasteen. My graduate students (chronologically ordered) Jennifer Wilcox, Jessica Metcalf, Ryan Jones, Eric Dechaine, Loren Sackett, Mitch Eaton, Sean Streich, Spencer Buck, and Micheala Seaver pushed me to be a better scientist, educator, and mentor. Cori West provided feedback. Eva Corral produced figures 1.1 and 1.2. My in-laws Carol and Ramon provided a place of solace and unbridled ecology in northwestern Georgia, where much of this book was written. The University of Colorado–Boulder provided me with the academic freedom and resources supporting a life full of exploration. My wife Cindy has been a constant companion and shaped my ability as an educator. My two sons, Dylan and Owen, and their partners, Kat and Ari, have shown me what matters in the world, fine-tuned my values, and set my sights on the future. I appreciate the thoughtful and constructive anonymous reviews of my manuscript; remaining rough patches reflect my shortcomings. And I am forever grateful to thousands of students for opportunities to learn together about ecology, evolution, and ways of thinking like a scientist.

Introduction

I have been working for years to advance the educational capacity and abilities of myself, my colleagues, and my university with measurable positive effects. I have served as a Presidential Teaching Scholar for the University of Colorado (CU) system, led a productive research program in ecology and evolution, mentored more than three dozen professors across a range of disciplines, and taught thousands of students. I have served on innumerable university committees and have seen and experienced, as a faculty member and administrator, how the university functions. It has been a privilege. At the same time, I count myself among the many who have joined the chorus singing that change needs to happen.

The CU system includes three college campuses and a medical school populated with over 67,000 students and nearly 25,000 employees. The University of Colorado at Boulder (CU–Boulder), where I work, is a Tier 1 research university. It is recognized as the state's flagship institution of higher education. The stories in this book come mostly from my experiences teaching at CU–Boulder embedded within a disciplinary population of students, staff, educators, and scientists in the Department of Ecology and Evolutionary Biology. I feel immense gratitude to have served as part of an institution of public good. Yet, over the years, I have become increasingly concerned about the purposes of our mission, how the mission is achieved, and what specific actions happen across different contexts. The recent commentary by the National Academies of Sciences, Engineering, and Medicine (2025) rings true in my experience:

> Achieving equitable and effective undergraduate STEM education will require concerted and consistent action by multiple stakeholders within and beyond the higher education system. The changes needed extend far beyond actions that can be taken

by individuals. Undergraduate learning is occurring within a system that undervalues teaching and does not generally prioritize equitable outcomes for students. Instructors cannot be expected to offer equitable and effective learning experiences if they are not trained in pedagogy, provided with ongoing professional learning, and supported with appropriate rewards, recognitions, and resources. While many instructors go to great lengths to serve their students, widespread equitable and effective teaching is dependent on changes to the larger system.

We need to think differently about how to achieve change and sustain shifts in why, how, and what we teach. My contention is that we can look to nature for discovering ways of change, because the wild things in wild places have been continuously changing since the origin of life and the emergence of ecology billions of years ago. Nature has invented remarkable solutions to difficult problems, some of which include myriad ways of engaging in cooperation and collective action and making educated life or death decisions. The scholarly disciplines of ecology and evolution focus on the proximate and ultimate causes of biological outcomes. These disciplines offer ways of thinking that have much to offer educators. In this book I focus on how knowing about ecology can inform us—in profound and deep ways—about how to be, and become, better educators. And how to achieve "changes to the larger system." This book is mostly focused on individuals, especially individuals actively engaged in education. It does not delve into the system-level changes necessary for realizing and sustaining the change envisaged by the National Academies. I leave this topic for another time and place. In this book, the roles and actions of individuals are followed through increasing scales of organization and interaction in much the same way we scale up our thinking when interrogating and investigating ecological phenomena. It is a book about teaching and a perspective on the craft through the lens of ecology. It is more descriptive than prescriptive, and my overarching goal is to instill ecological thinking as a mindset for engaging in education. It is about realizing that education, like ecology, is an outcome of an emergent process. To gain perspective about this emergent process, it helps to become familiar with ecology and the many ways ecology and education are similar.

I have elected not to focus on specific pedagogical and educational strategies mainly because the purpose of this book is to establish robust analogies between ecology and education as a way to bring ecological thinking into the realm of education. There are fantastic, innovative and promising new ways of teaching differently and utilizing technology that align with realizing education as an emergent process in ways that parallel how ecology happens. These include personalized and adaptive learning strategies that leverage the power of continuous formative assessment and machine-learning (Taylor et al. 2021). In fact, the thoughtful chapters in the book, edited by Ryoo and Winkelmann (2021), align well with the inferences about education stemming from analogies with ecology. This book is not a how-to guide but is meant as a definitive and scholarly attempt at establishing constructive analogies between ecology and education for making inferences that may fuel change in how higher education happens. Where I am going is toward a more data-rich endeavor that engages in regular monitoring of the knowledge of students in the same way long-term ecological studies monitor change in the structure and function of ecological communities. It is a reminder to educators involved in higher education to consider looking to ecology for ways of thinking and strategies for engaging in data-based discovery and prediction. I end the book with an appeal for higher education to better implement the capacity of "big data" for better following the fates of many individuals across the infinite knowledge landscape we inhabit, and to use the data for propelling all students toward productive and successful learning goals. In a separate contribution, I will bring ecological thinking into the realm of effective pedagogical frameworks for creating learning pathways with outcomes measured by progress toward expert-like intelligence and cognitive function instead of measured by whether students achieve particular and specific objectives. Because, as Stanley and Lehman (2015) emphasized, education is hampered by the myth that it can be objectified.

I teach differently from many of my colleagues. Students sometimes ask me why I teach the way I do, because my course is often one of the first that students take in their academic journeys that is not content-laden and didactic. The short answer is that I do my best. The longer answer is that I follow where the science takes me. I have never taught a particular lesson in the same way twice, because each time I teach, I learn from students that there are better ways of teaching that stem from what they know rather than what I think they should know. Evidence of why I teach the way I do comes from reflecting about why and how I teach. My teaching changes over time because my knowledge about pedagogy improves, my interest in teaching increases because I more fully embrace the awesome opportunity and the gravity of educating the future, and

I learn by engaging in scientific teaching. "The scientific teaching pedagogical framework provides various approaches for science instructors to teach in a way that more closely emulates how science is practiced by actively and inclusively engaging students in their own learning and by making instructional decisions based on student performance data" (Durham et al. 2017, p. 1). Scientific teaching satisfies my itch to do science and to see whether my hypotheses about why, how, and what learning happens are supported by evidence. The legendary musician Gil Scott-Heron said, "The first revolution is when you change your mind." Enacting scientific teaching has driven change; I am in a state of continuous revolution. My continuous revolution happens within a well-defined pedagogical frameworks called STeLLA (BSCS 2018) and the Next Generation Science Standards.

The seeds of this project were planted sometime in the late 2010s. Mike Klymkowsky and I were asking questions about what happens to students during the time between when they enroll in our respective departments in the College of Arts and Sciences at the University of Colorado–Boulder—nicknamed MCDB (Molecular, Cellular, and Developmental Biology) and EBIO (Ecology and Evolutionary Biology)—and when they graduate or leave prior to graduating. The questions needed data for answers, and we began a collaboration with Robert Stubbs and Ali Oran in the Office of Data Analytics at CU–Boulder. To our knowledge, much of the data was not being used, or at least not used by educators. And most of the data were aggregated and then analyzed, leaving out the individual student stories in favor of easier to interpret summary statistics, like the percentage of students who persist from enrollment through graduation. The data for each student included aspects of their identity (e.g., sex, race, and ethnicity), the courses completed and the courses enrolled in but not completed, the grades for each course, the instructors for each of the courses, the departments in which each course was offered, the numbers of students enrolled in each course, and the student-generated evaluation scores for each faculty member.[1] Importantly, the identities of all students were unknown to me. We followed the fates of anonymous individuals, but their stories were not available. There was a lot of important data missing, including elements related to what each student learned, the teaching modality, whether the rooms where teaching happened were at capacity or not, and whether the pedagogy was multidimensional or not, among other variables known to influence the ability and capacity of individuals to engage productively in whatever pedagogy was being offered across a diverse set of topics and educators. In other words, much of the relevant data for understanding the education mission of our two departments was and remains missing. Despite enormous amounts of data generated by students pouring into digital educational platforms, there is a paucity of available information about student experiences and their gains during their time in college. But we could get answers to some of our questions. Ours was not a research project aimed at achieving inferences relevant beyond the boundaries of CU–Boulder; it was an exercise in enlightenment, in revealing the paths students and educators took through a densely populated forest of structured opportunity. The theories and empirical work in ecology provided a useful framework for making sense of education data and experiences.

Of course, I am not the first person to construct analogical bridges between ecology and education. Likely I will not be the last. My hope is that the bridges I build will hold up over time and won't be swept away in the torrent of change flowing from artificial intelligence, the exponential increase in information, and the continued progression of the neoliberal model of higher education (Olssen and Peters 2005). I am hoping my perspective opens minds in ways that allow us to ask questions and use examples of complex natural phenomena as inspiration for trying new ways of engaging with people toward greater education gains. Ecomimicry is a source of inspiration and innovation.

The book is organized in six main chapters. Each chapter is divided into sections identified by subheadings and each section begins with a brief synopsis of relevant inferences about some aspects of education gained from analogy with ecology. Chapter 1 provides a broad overview of different perspectives and contexts for creating analogies between ecology and education for the purpose of making inferences that will, I hope, improve understanding of the process and practice of education. I first describe direct and emergent processes and make the claim that both ecology and education are naturally emergent processes. I review the properties of constructing valid analogies, briefly reference work on "learning ecology" that precedes and partly motivated this book, I underscore that ecology and education happen in ways that can be partitioned across different scales of perspective and analysis, and I discuss the meaning of success. I end this chapter with a brief discussion of the theoretical context of education and assert I am firmly in the constructivist camp. This last section is admittedly too brief, and it omits explicit development of what might be best referred to as an ecological and evolutionary theory of education. I do all of these things because these are important themes that flow through the many stories useful for exploring the dimensions of education through an ecological mindset.

The rest of the book is organized by scale, beginning with the individual and ending with communities. Each chapter lays out analogies for making inferences from ecology to education: it is a one-way bridge. I begin with individuals in chapter 2, because the individual is the fundamental unit of ecology and education. I explore what I refer to as multidimensional cognitive phenotypes and introduce the idea that, as Bateson (1972, p. 503) asserted, "Ecology, in the widest sense, turns out to be the study of the interaction and survival of ideas." This conceptualization lends itself to exploring the structure of knowledge as individual ideas—the fundamental units—that interact and survive in the minds of students in ways that resemble what happens in populations of individuals in nature. After establishing the Batesonian thesis that ideas have an ecology, I return to compelling issues of the individual student, their differences, issues of persistence and belonging, and finish chapter 2 with description of how ideas exist as ephemeral units that only persist if they, like individuals in ecological populations, are connected to other ideas in the constantly changing minds of students.

Chapter 3 explores the emergent outcome of the niche, that the fundamental and realized niches described as ecological entities exist in educational settings, and I spend most of the chapter exploring the idea of the constructed niche. Niche construction happens as a consequence of individuals taking ownership of educational opportunity wherever and whenever it emerges. Because this is a book mostly written for educators, the plea for enabling niche construction is mainly about how we need to create productive environments for the success of cognitively diverse students. The dimension of constructed niches flows through the focus on the differences between competitive, cooperative, and individualistic aspects of education that depend on how interaction is facilitated and promoted by instructors. The centerpiece of the discussion about interactions (chapter 4) is the dynamics that happen in small groups, and how group size and composition covaries with the difficulty and scope of learning goals. The focus on interactions flows into a chapter focused at the scale of population (chapter 5). It is here that data and perspectives stemming from individuals are aggregated. Instead of emphasizing individuals, there is an explicit focus on general properties of collections of individuals, as part of specific courses or scholarly disciplines. Included in chapter 5 is a focus on recruitment, students' choice of disciplinary focus, switching majors, persistence, and ultimately graduation. Finally, in chapter 6, the scale increases to the level of communities in which there are multiple populations of individuals changing over time across a heterogeneous landscape. A central focus is on the change in the composition of communities, a phenomenon referred to as succession. In this chapter, I explore issues of diversity and productivity, the disruption and value of disturbances and whether we continue enacting education as a direct process that can be effectively engineered in ways that maximize profit and outcomes or we, as a community, pivot and decide that the future depends more on enabling education to be an emergent process with myriad outcomes including collaboration and a sense of shared responsibility and participation in solving the world's most pressing issues. This chapter on communities is, in my opinion, the crux of why ecology helps make sense of education as a process and can help define directions for change that will improve the multitude of processes and outcomes of higher education.

Bateson wrote, "The problem of how to transmit our ecological reasoning to those whom we wish to influence in what seems to us to be an ecologically 'good' direction is itself an ecological problem" (1972, p. 524). Like Bateson's perspective, mine is a view colored by ecology. I have assembled stories about education by invoking the contexts and processes of ecology that, taken as a whole, provide the basis for the claim that there is an ecology of education.

Chapter 1

The Context of the Ecology of Education

Ecology and Education Are Emergent Processes

Education-relevant synopsis: Education is, if we let it be, an emergent process. Achieving greatness as an outcome of the emergent process depends on casting aside our tendency to direct and objectify education and instead pay attention to students and help establish multiple pathways toward success.

A process consists of parts and actions that happen over some period of time with a measurable or describable outcome. There are two contrasting types of processes, described as direct and emergent. Our lives are filled with direct processes. Making a meal by following a recipe is an example of a direct process that happens every day in the lives of billions of people. There are ingredients, the ingredients are mixed together in specific amounts in a particular order and often subject to changing physical conditions (e.g., heating or cooling) with a purposeful and singular outcome: a meal. In the realms of science, designing and carrying out an experiment is a direct process. In education, learning about the components of a direct process and being able to describe a direct process on an exam is a direct process. Direct processes are often subject to optimization for improving efficiency to reduce time and costs and increasing consistency so that the outcome of every iteration of the process is the same. We call this streamlining. Our lives are so full of direct processes driven by purpose that we don't often think about emergent processes; yet, it is emergent processes that resulted in wonderful and amazing outcomes. Evolution is an emergent process. And so is ecology and education despite attempts to

9

assert or assume otherwise.[1] "Emergence is what 'self-organizing' processes produce. Emergence is the reason why there are hurricanes, and ecosystems, and complex organisms. . . . Indeed, the term is positively awe-inspiring. As physicist Doyne Farmer observed, 'It's not magic . . . but it feels like magic'" (Corning, 2002, p. 18).

Emergent processes are everywhere and reflect the fact that life is multifaceted, multidimensional, complex, and subject to randomness, influenced by contingencies and interactions, and the outcomes are often unpredictable and unique. The diversity of life on Earth is an example outcome of the emergent process of evolution. If there were multiple Earths and each one was identical, and if evolution happened on all of them starting from the same initial conditions, the outcomes would be wildly different. "Replay the tape a million times . . . and I doubt that anything like Homo sapiens would ever evolve again" (Gould, 1989, p. 289). Differences in the abundance and diversity of organisms in two different places is an example outcome of the emergent process of ecology. And the variation in abilities, knowledge, and ways of thinking among students graduating from an institution of higher education is an example outcome of the emergent process of education.

And yet, both ecology and education often happen as direct processes due to the investment of energy for controlling and streamlining nature and minds, respectively. I am currently writing on the porch of a house near the edge of a farm in north Georgia. It's early spring. The process of controlling and directing ecology is underway. Roundup-ready, Bt-pesticide-engineered corn seeds were planted in neat rows at the same time the existing plants (referred to as weeds) were sprayed by the Roundup herbicide. Today it's two weeks after spraying and planting and there are thousands of individual corn plants separated by the same distance across many rows and growing up from a chemically scorched-brown earth. The corn grows fast, all individuals grow at remarkably similar rates reflecting genetic homogeneity and uniformity in the amount of controlled-release fertilizer deposited in the ground with each corn seed. And each plant experiences the same local environmental conditions. The field that was once solid yellow from innumerable flowers of ragwort (*Packera glabella*) quickly transformed into a cornfield. The ultimate destination of this field's productivity is for growing cows that ultimately feed humans from milk or meat. Every year the same constrained process happens and there is little room for the effects of randomness, although random events happen. It's hard to see them because they are minimized, to the extent possible, by the mechanization and years of optimization and streamlining. Nonetheless, a few scattered plants may die because of local events; a deer may kill a few plants in a desperate attempt to escape a perceived danger, a burrowing mammal may destroy the roots of one or two plants, and a windstorm may knock down some plants near the edge of the field. But the field, with its neatly organized lines of plants separated by just enough space so that they do not compete much for resources but gain from the protection of having close and identical neighbors, remains intact and delivers about the same yield every year, depending on rainfall. Where we manage and engineer nature, ecology appears to be a direct process with a predictable outcome.

Education has a similar story. Many classrooms in the institution of higher education where I work resemble corn fields. There are desks organized in rows, each desk has the same shape and dimensions and is separated by the same distance from nearby desks, and all desks are bolted to the floor. Much of the curriculum is the same for all students and is delivered in ways designed to equalize access for everyone using a mechanized, digital-delivery system.[2] Instructors know there are differences in abilities and interests and ways of thinking among their students, but they rarely, if ever, reveal the differences or use the differences for supporting and challenging student thinking. Pedagogy often assumes all individuals are the same. Free-response questions have been replaced by choosing-the-right-answer questions, and academic achievement is measured on a single, ranked, linear scale using points or percentages. Students learn that grades matter more than intellectual growth and that studying for the test is more important than being fully engaged in learning. There are exceptions to this generalization of higher education experiences, but, at my institution, we still teach many of our first- and second-year students using didactic approaches in large enrollment classes (Stains et al., 2018). I regularly visit large-enrollment lecture courses just to make sure I know what is happening in required learning experiences for a particular discipline. What I commonly observe is a focus on content, on knowing information. And teaching happens in ways that do not depend on whether students are present or not. When we manage and engineer teaching, education appears to be a direct process with predictable outcomes. And yet, if ecology and education happen more naturally, they are both emergent processes.

It is worth spending a little time unpacking the properties of emergent processes. While there are many properties (Chi, 2005), I want to focus on four: the variability of the individual component parts of the process, how the process happens over time, the dependencies among the component parts, and the outcomes. I will do so by comparing direct and emergent processes for ecology and education using the four categorical properties.

What we know as the discipline of ecology is an outcome of a complex emergent process. Each individual in the world is unique due to differences in genes and the environment during growth and maturation. And each individual interacts with a large number of other individuals of varied species in a tangled web of interactions. Moreover, if we looked closely at two individuals of the same species, even though they may be near each other, the interactions that play out during each of their lives are different and the differences are entirely contingent on where they live, because every place is different. And every place is different because the assemblage of nearest neighbors and the litany of various events that impinge on growth and development of individuals has a large element of randomness. Nature is wildly and magnificently unconstrained. Similarly, education is an outcome of a complex emergent process. Each individual is unique due to differences in genes and the environment in which they develop. And each individual interacts with a large number of other individuals of varied personalities, perspectives, and motivations in a tangled web of interactions. Moreover, if we look closely at twins, even though they may have lived in the same spaces and places, and have the same genetic information encoding functional properties, the interactions that play out during each of their lives are different, and as a consequence, they learn different things and become increasingly different during their intellectual maturation. Every student is different because the assemblage of nearest neighbors through the arc of their lives and the litany of various events that impinge on growth and development is subject to stochasticity. Education and intellectual maturation are wildly and magnificently unconstrained.

Many of the things we do happen in an ordered and sequential way. In the corn field, the process is simple and direct. First, a large truck sprays the field with a combination of a fertilizer, a herbicide, and water. A second machine pokes holes in the Earth and drops a single seed in each hole. Each seed germinates at more or less the same time and the plant begins its development, grows, and matures into a reproductive adult. The cob is the next generation of seeds, each provisioned with resources and a genetically defined program of development. After the growing season is over, five months from germination, another large machine cuts down the corn, strips off the cobs and tosses the cobs into a large truck. The corn eventually turns into cow tissue. Although some seeds hit the ground, most are removed and used in a location remote from where they developed on their mother plant, precluding the possibility of local adaptation. When the next spring arrives, the direct process plays out again, with seeds for the farm outside my window imported from an industrial-sized seed farm owned by a multinational corporation.[3] This rural location far from the busy streets of cities where most of the corn is consumed after it has been transformed by a cow into meat is connected, economically and ecologically, to a world in which large multinational corporations seek to consolidate and control farmers' access to seeds.

Most ecology is different. Seeds exist in the soils—in what is known as the seed bank—from the reproduction of plants that happened during different years from different mothers. Within the volume of soil the size of the hole created by seeder-machine there may be many seeds of the same and different species; moreover, each seed of the same species is genetically different because of the power of sexual recombination. Each seed is primed to germinate by specific local conditions, and the individual emerges through the activation of an elaborate and unique developmental plan encoded in its inherited genome. The germination of the seeds happens at different times, depending on the seed and its immediate environment. Individual plants grow at different rates, and it is sometimes the case that the seeds germinating later than others are at a disadvantage and wither over time due to being constantly outcompeted by a neighboring plant at a more advanced stage of development with better developed roots and a more mature vascular system. It is also possible that the individuals from early germination freeze, opening up opportunities for later germinating plants. There are births, and growth, and deaths happening continuously. The emergent process described as ecology happens continuously and there is no start or finish, and it is impossible to discern whether there is a consecutives series of sequential events unless we pay attention to each individual as it moves through its life cycle. And if we do, we realize that the fate of most individuals in nature is death. It is because of death that birth can be successful, and it is through the continuous processes of births and deaths that ecological communities change.

Despite the fact that education, like ecology, is an emergent process, educators often operate as if it is a direct process. There has been immense investment toward developing benchmarks and objectives that have formed the basis of standardized assessments and ranking systems meant to document progress toward success, assuming there is a single global outcome.

Hursh (2013, p. 605) wrote, "The United States has undergone perhaps its most significant transformation" from being enacted locally to state and federal control. "State and federal governments have introduced standardized testing and accountability" as a direct-process tactic with the rationale that "they are necessary within an increasingly globalized economy, they will reduce educational inequality and they will increase assessment objectivity."

Hursh and an increasingly large chorus of educators, education researchers, parents, and others have reached the consensus that "the reforms have not achieved their ostensible goals." Moreover, the pervasive implementation of objective-centric, standardized assessment is a hallmark of a system that is inefficient and resource-hungry driven by an increasingly centralized command-and-control strategy that runs counter to nature. Resistance to the "reforms" is beginning to emerge from US educators and other citizens. My contention is that one of the explanations for the need for reform is that education is not a direct process; it is an emergent process. If education works well, there is not a single global outcome; there are different outcomes that depend on complex, multivariate, continuous, unconstrained, and local processes. If identical people moved through an emergent process of education, even if attempts were made to achieve identical results, there would likely still be differences between them in what they know, how they interact with information, and the decisions they make based on their intelligence. We make the mistake of failing to recognize that many of the amazing things in this world—from art to ecosystems—result from emergent processes. Putting the emergent process in the handcuffs and shackles of a direct process does not make the process direct; it only constrains the range of possible outcomes, creates a sense of not belonging, and likely eliminates the emergence of greatness.

Because education is an emergent process, our perspective of success cannot be measured by progress toward objectives, because the outcome of effective education cannot be known. Progress should be measured by the distance traveled instead of proximity to a specific and defined objective. For a goal-agnostic process like evolution, change is measured compared with ancestors, and progress (if you can call it that) is determined by whether current (evolved) function is better in the descendants than in the ancestors; indeed, this is the definition of adaptation. This description applies, or should apply, to education.

Stanley and Lehman (2015) described a provocative analogy for achieving a goal in the absence of an objective and a known pathway to success:

You probably don't often face the problem of crossing a lake on foot by stepping from stone to stepping stone but imagine if you did. To make life a little harder, suppose also that the lake is covered in mist. The stepping stones closest to the shore fade gradually as the wind into the fog. As you walk along the course of stepping stones over the water, the shore dissolves from sight behind you even as the other side remains cloaked behind the mist. But here's the hard part. Eventually you come upon a fork where a choice must be made. Because of the fog, you don't know where either path leads. For all you know, one might lead you to a dead end while the other might eventually lead to the other side of the lake. But even if you make a lucky choice, chances are that more forks will appear sooner or later. . . . The fundamental problem of search and discovery is that we usually don't know the stepping stones that lead to the objective at the outset. After all, if we always knew the stepping stones then everything we hope to achieve would be easy. . . .

Deception is the key reason that objectives don't often work to drive achievement. If the objective is deceptive, as it must be for most ambitious problems, then setting it and guiding our efforts by it offers little help in reaching it. However, there is an alternative to focusing on objectives. [The alternative is to collect] . . . stepping stones that create the potential to find even more stepping stones. . . . To arrive somewhere remarkable we must be willing to hold many paths open without knowing where they might lead. (pp. 29–30)

There is a long history of engineering education (the process). And like many human endeavors, education has been objectified and engineered in ways designed to achieve specific objectives. Part of the problem stems from the politicization and gamification of objectives. Stanley and Lehman (2015, p. 65) lament that the growing obsession with defining and trying to achieve objectives "harms society" and "tends to dehumanize and mechanize what was once creative." As Stanley and Lehman emphasize, becoming intelligent is equivalent to achieving greatness, and we cannot objectify greatness, because we don't know, for each student, what it looks like and how to get there. As they emphasize, "The fundamental problem of search and discovery is that we usually don't know the stepping stones that lead to the objective at the outset. After all, if we always knew the stepping stones then everything we hope to achieve would be easy." And if it's easy, the result is unlikely to be great. Thus, our challenge is to enable the emergent process of education to happen and hold open the idea that there are many paths and outcomes that achieve the general and widely variable goal of becoming intelligent and achieving social and educational capital.

The myth of the objective recognizes that defining objectives and creating direct pathways toward an objective often fail to achieve the best results, because the universe of possible solutions is larger than imagined and unknown outcomes resist objectification. In this context, using an adaptive landscape model as an analogy provides a useful context for understanding the consequences of defining objectives and charting trajectories designed to efficiently achieve the objective. Figure 1.1 is an example of an adaptive landscape. The x and y dimensions—labeled knowledge axis 1 and knowledge axis 2, respectively—are dimensions of the possible combinatorial universe of ideas and thinking skills—knowledge—that exists for a particular discipline. There are some combinations that can be categorized as novice-like or expert-like. In this landscape, expert-like is represented by peaks and novice-like is valleys. There is a complex 3D topography

Figure 1.1. A "fitness" landscape conceptual model (developed by Sewall Wright 1932). The landscape shows various peaks and valleys defined by combinations of ideas and skills that can be categorized as novice-like or expert-like. The two predictive axes are labeled pedagogy axes 1 and 2 and the vertical axis is labeled novice to expect. The snake-like lines describe learning trajectories for 12 students that all began their journeys as different types of novices and all converged on a single peak. *Source:* Created by the author.

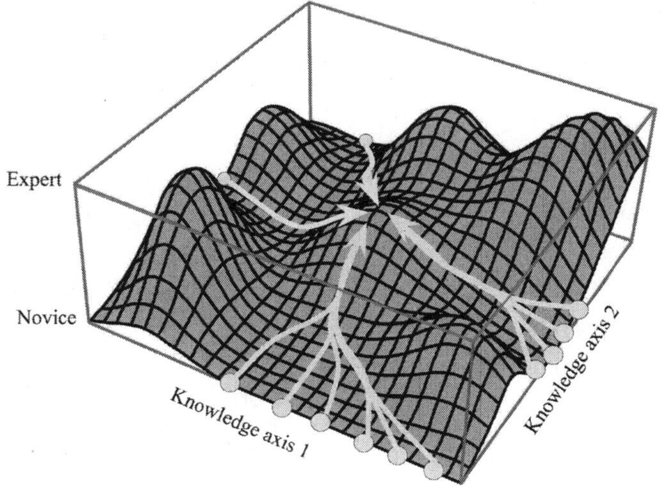

over which education can happen. Imagine, for instance, there are a dozen students, each student possesses different knowledge, and all students are novices. In the context of the adaptive landscape model, students begin their education from valleys. When we implement education as a direct process driven by specific learning objectives and assessed using multiple choice questions, the perceived ideal result is that all 12 students converge on a single peak. This happens even though there are many expert-like peaks, some are higher than others. Most of the landscape is ignored either because the existence of other peaks is not known by the instructor or, more likely, there is a conventional combination of ideas and skills that are emphasized as being more relevant than other combinations. We know, however, that the landscape is complex, with many peaks and valleys, and that where students start can influence where they go. If we embrace that education is an emergent process, recognize the value of achieving gains rather than specific objectives, and allow for the possibility of multiple paths toward success, it is likely students take different trajectories from being a novice to expert, and that they end up on different peaks (fig. 1.2). Teaching as if education is a direct process toward a single defined objective leaves an

Figure 1.2. A "fitness" landscape conceptual model (same as fig. 1.1). The landscape shows various peaks and valleys defined by combinations of ideas and skills that can be categorized as novice-like or expert-like. The two predictive axes are labeled pedagogy axes 1 and 2 and the vertical axis is labeled novice to expect. There are snake-like lines that show learning trajectories for 12 students that all began their journeys as different places on the landscape and end at different expert-like peaks. *Source:* Created by the author.

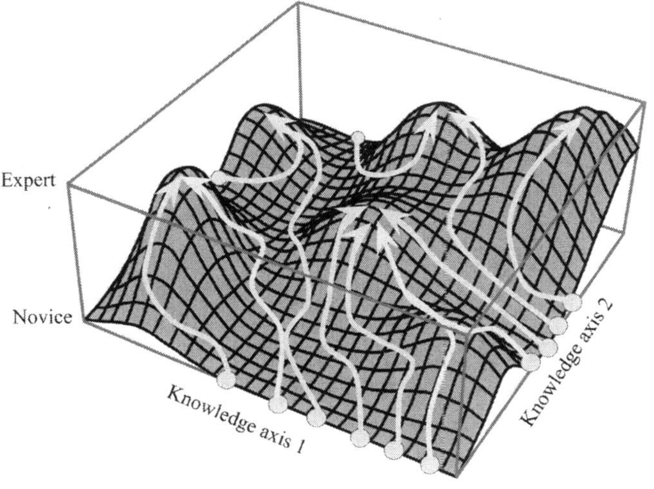

immense and topologically complex landscape unexplored; leaving a large landscape unexplored is antithetical to education. Instead, we should create opportunities to explore the landscape and discover the many peaks of greatness and achievement. One sign of achieving greatness is successfully traversing the novitiate valleys and ascending expert peaks. Which peaks an individual ascends will depend on where the journey starts and the opportunities, resources, and encouragement available along the journey.

The effectively infinite number of combinations of ideas, ways of thinking, and cognitive process skills that defines the topologically complex knowledge landscape is, itself, influenced by the properties of the learners, the characteristics of the classroom, how the students interact with each other and with the instructor, and the varied examples invoked by the instructors designed as ways of making progress toward an intelligence peak. A critical realization is that, contrary to convention of a single starting point for a learning journey, students begin the process of gaining more sophistication in the knowledge and mental models from different places on the landscape. The idea that students proceed along a direct path up a hill toward a peak is an illusion created by monitoring their progress based on assessment designed to determine how far students are from the peak rather than how far they have moved from where they started. Furthermore, the properties of the landscape change as the students change. This is the essence of a dynamic, emergent process.

The myth of the objective also is evident when evaluating the status of institutes of higher education and how these institutes are structured and function. The traditional form of organizational governance is based on autonomy and the guidance of its leaders, with change happening based on what has been called a rational, objective-directed approach to organization change management (Doyle and Brady, 2018). The rational approach facilitates top-down managerialism, emphasizes academic capitalism and higher education marketing with consequent negative effects on the quality of teaching (Franco-Santos et al., 2017; Doyle and Brady, 2018). An alternative model of change is that higher education institutions are emergent entities in a continuous state of change arising from day-to-day interactions between organizational members (Doyle and Brady 2018). In this context, order and organization emerge from human interaction and the institutional structure and function is in a constant state of becoming. Doyle and Brady (2018, p. 308), like Chi (2005), provide a comparative analysis of the organization as a directed process and an emergent process. The comparison is summarized in table 1.1.

Table 1.1. Comparison of higher education as a direct or emergent process

Dimension	Direct process (rational)	Emergent process
Organizational structure	Imposed	Continuously becoming
Perspective	Objective setting Linear causality with predictable outcomes Top-down single organizational structure	Subjective Multiple causality with unpredictable outcomes Bottom-up multiple organization structures
Change	Motivated by objective setting Episodic	Focus on emergent change due to interactions Continuous
Management and leadership	Uses prescribed model Process engineering Leaders play primary role	Make change visible Self-organization Role of leaders is to communicate and make change visible

Source: Modified and simplified from Doyle and Brady (2018).

Organization structure involves how entities are situated in ways that influence interactions, the flow of resources, and ultimately the productivity of actions aimed at supporting and promoting education. In a typical institution of higher education, there are various levels of influence and control; the centerpiece, the place where, as we say, the "rubber hits the road," is the interaction between students and instructors. If either the students or instructors had the autonomy to establish how the interactions happen, the structure of education actions would likely differ from what actually happens. The main reason for the discrepancy is that structure is often imposed on the enactment of education by organizational administrators. A typical class has to have a threshold number of students or, more commonly, needs to meet the student demand that is a response to requirements for graduation. To make this real, I have discovered that class sizes large enough to enable a diversity of student thinking but small enough to maintain cohesion and a sense of singular community are often smaller than the demand and the room capacity for a course. It is often the case that the institution imposes an enrollment that favors more rather than fewer students with concomitant negative effects on community development and learning gains. Moreover, there is a structure of the types of classes offered, when they are offered, whether there are prerequisites, what topics are taught, and other details that each department inherits every semester as a consequence of history. Any change from historical precedent is resisted as a consequence of precedent, national standards, and the bureaucracy required to make changes, and it is resisted by individuals who may feel a strong allegiance to the status quo. This contrasts markedly with an organizational structure that evolves and is continuously emergent because the context, ways of teaching and learning, interests of students and faculty, and the content continuously change.

Perspective encapsulates how the players in the institution imagine and enact their roles. If the perspective is one guided by higher-level administrators in which objectives are set by guidelines and rules at relatively high organization levels (e.g., provosts, regents, state commissions), the results are perspectives and ways of thinking dominated by objective setting, and the engineered process is direct, defined by the assumption of linear causality, and results in predictable outcomes. This happens because of a top-down organization structure. By contrast, the emergent perspective does not emphasize objectives, because the experience for everyone is subjective, there are often unpredictable outcomes, and authentic motivation for action and dedicated work comes from the bottom up; from faculty and students interested in creating better learning experiences.

When change happens in a directed process, it happens as a consequence of objective setting and either the implementation of enforcement or incentives for key players to push toward a singular goal. Because the objectives emerge from a top-down, command-and-control organization structure, change is episodic. Additionally, change happens without being dependent on interaction. New structures and their corresponding function often persist because of enforcement from administrative power. Nonetheless, such change is episodic, because the emergence of new initiatives and objectives take a long time to manifest. By contrast, in an emergent system, change is continuous, often unplanned, and happens as a consequence of interactions among players. Local successes can seep out and spread across institutions as a bottom-up process of innovation diffusion.

Finally, there are clear differences in management and leadership between direct and emergent education institution processes. In the direct model, leadership adopts a prescribed model, sometimes borrowed from a similarly structured university or from the business world. The model engineers the process in ways that direct actions toward objectives. Leaders play a primary role and the rank-and-file, rubber-hits-the-road people are left out of decision making but are essential for achieving objectives. In many cases, the changes are invisible until enacted, and any pushback is quickly dissipated by actions designed to exclude instead of include people. In an emergent process, most management and leadership is local, all changes are visible and emerge from various places within the institutional structure, and there is a self-organization dynamic that reflects that varied context across disciplines. Importantly, in a system defined by an emergent process, leaders situated within departments communicate, share successful strategies, and make their actions and innovations visible and available for adoption by others.

I mention these institution-level aspects of the difference between direct and emergent processes because of the pervasive effects of institutional structure and function on why, how and what we teach. As educators, we seek academic freedom; however, freedom is determined by the context in which the necessary work happens. Institutionalized constraints on how we teach, and the absence of sufficient incentives for achieving greatness in our education missions, limits academic freedom in ways that are often opaque but are no less real. Institutionalized education has taken a free-flowing stream and channelized it; consequently, academic freedom is an illusion rather than a reality. Adopting the perspective that education is an emergent process is a necessary first step toward achieving greatness for individuals and the institution in which education happens.

A profound first step toward achieving a world in which higher education is an emergent process begins with the realization that intelligence in ecology is immensely diverse and its origin, as a thing with value demonstrable by whether individuals live or die, is deep, both within life on Earth and among all people.

The Deep Taproot of Ecological Wisdom

Education-relevant synopsis: Ecology is an emergent process that has been happening since the origin of life and will continue as long as life persists. The deep history of ecology and our ability as scientists to discern why and how ecology happens and the link between processes and myriad outcomes are logical and valuable resources for better understanding other emergent processes, including education.

That there is an ecology of education also stems from the realization that the emergent processes of ecology and evolution explain the existence of intelligence. Ecology is the process that generates the abundance and distribution of organisms across environments that vary in physical conditions and in the types and abundances of resources essential for supporting life, including interactions with other organisms. Ecology originated with the emergence of life. Ever since the origin of life there has been the continuous evolution of individual sensory and response systems that simultaneously sense the world and enact strategies that improve an individual's success: this is sense-making. Making the right decision given a specific context is intelligence. Intelligence has been evolving in changing ecological contexts for billions of years, ever since life originated and began inhabiting the crannies, crevices, and open spaces of Earth.

Of course, today there are many trillions of individuals of myriad types living and dying in interactive assemblages across the planet. This is personally relevant when we consider that each of us is an ecosystem harboring trillions of bacteria engaged in reproduction and metabolism in ways that influence how we feel, our vitality and, ultimately, our intelligence (see Manderino et al., 2017). Each one of the actors has characteristics traceable back to the first life forms through a reticulated common ancestry spanning billions of years. What we have today—and what has existed for a long, seemingly infinite period of time—are loosely organized emergent structures referred to as ecosystems composed of communities of interacting individuals of diverse types called species, each one of which consists of multiple populations of many individuals eking out an existence from a plethora of resources that vary in availability across space and time. If we pay attention to the process and its outcomes, we gain wisdom about the world. And ecological wisdom can help explain the single most important phenomenon in the knowable universe: the structure and function of communities of diverse individuals engaged in edification for the purpose of making good decisions for themselves and for others through cooperative and transactional interactions. This is the most important phenomenon because the rise of human intelligence and its collective consequences influence the function of ecosystems that sustain us and will determine our fate on a planet of limited size and capacity for life. Human intelligence created the existential crisis of accelerated environmental change. Human intelligence will, I hope, provide realizable solutions to the unfolding crisis.

Like the case for the origin of ecology as coincident with the origin of life, the origin of human ecology was coincident with the origin of humans. Human ecology exists as a real thing in nature in which there is a change in the abundance and distribution of resources as a consequence of human activity. Human ecology also exists abstracted from the world as a conceptualization of processes and principles that form the basis for explaining the abundance and distribution of humans and the microbes, fungi, animals, and plants with whom we interact and from which we extract resources for supporting our existence. Ideally, our abstraction of nature and the emergent ecological processes match what happens in the real world; that is to say, our mental models are accurate. We know this is not true, however, although our conceptualization of ecology is becoming more accurate as an outcome of the process of science. Nevertheless, given that our knowledge is incomplete and sometimes inaccurate, we have to become comfortable living with uncertainty.

Contrary to scholars of ecology (e.g., Quinn, 1939, p. 161), human ecology, as a discipline of investigation, did not begin in 1924 with the definitive statement that it is "a study of the spatial and temporal relations of human beings by the selective, distributive, and accommodative forces of the environment" (McKenzie, 1924, p. 287). Human ecology as an abstraction that formed the basis for actively modifying the abundance and distribution of species began with indigenous people. Human ecology began when humans started fires as a means of managing the harvestable productivity of landscapes (Trauernicht et al., 2015), and when humans actively cultivated particular food plants in distributed patches embedded within vast forests.[4] In fact, there is increasing evidence of long-term human activities that have altered the structure and species composition "across even the most intact forests worldwide" (Levis et al., 2018). Roos (2022, pp. 2–3) wrote, "Native peoples . . . maintain oral histories and traditions that connect culture, language, animals, people, plants, and other resources to home landscapes since time immemorial." Ecology has been a subject of study for longer than the word ecology has existed.[5] Stories from indigenous cultures and people suggest that ecological knowledge and intelligence has existed for many thousands of years. Salmón (2000, p. 1327) wrote, "Indigenous people in North America are aware that life in any environment is viable only when humans view their surroundings as kin; that their mutual roles are essential for their survival." Salmón's description of the role of humans in fostering biodiversity underscores the active role humans played in ecology of a region: "It is no accident that the Rarámuri homeland is biologically diverse, as we have managed this region for at least 2000 years" (p. 1328). Given the long history of humans living within and altering their habitats, it is safe to conclude that human intelligence emerged from ecology; thus, there is an ecology of education.

Ecology is the study of the states and fates of organisms within a continuously changing environmental context. A key aspect of the ecology of organisms is knowing the fates and functions of individuals from birth to death in various environmental contexts. Too much heat or cold, too little or too much food, ample or limited space, and a variety of other environmental variables can mean the difference between thriving and struggling and between success and failure. Moreover, the organisms inhabiting a particular environment interact, and the interactions can determine the difference between thriving and struggling and between success and failure. Organisms have been operating within an ecological context for billions of generations. The information for making the correct life-or-death choices is passed down in the combinations of As, Ts, Gs, and Cs that constitute genes. Individuals are hardwired to learn by trial and error. Successful trial and error becomes the ancestral state for future trial and error. Ecological intelligence—the intelligence to know how to make a living from an inhabited world—persists through millenia because of a series of successful decisions. For many organisms, ecological intelligence is hardwired and is manifest as innate behavior. The wasp that constructs a clay pot for rearing its young is an example of a hardwired set of very specific behaviors that solves a particular problem: it is intelligence that has been passed down through millions of generations, hardwired into behavior. There are hardwired ways people learn that stem mostly from our proclivity to engage in trial-and-error and construct stories for transmitting wisdom.

There is a natural connection between ecology and intelligence. Many simple organisms have distributed nervous systems that integrate information gained about the environment and translate the information into whole individual action. There are many other organisms in which the nervous system has become centralized and expanded—a process referred to as encephalization—that evolved in parallel with the increase in number of body parts and their integration as a response and a strategy for taking advantage of resources supporting life in an ecological context.

Intelligence resulted from, and is supported by, ecology. The importance of ecology for intelligence is evident in studies that examine the correlation of brain size—a measure of the degree of encephalization—with ecology. Individuals of species that live in more complex and dynamic environments, due to both social interactions and in the distribution and abundance of resources necessary for life, often have larger brains than individuals of species that do not live in ecologically complex and dynamic environments (see, e.g., González-Forero and Gardner, 2018). Indeed, comparative studies have revealed the existence of variation among individuals in several core processes that contribute to intelligence essential for successful foraging, including spatial memory, value-based decision making, and executive function (Rosati, 2017). Executive function includes the ability to regulate thoughts and actions, express different behaviors and pursue different actions in response to changing conditions, and the capacity to analyze situational information coupled with decision making. Intelligence is an outcome of evolution happening in an ecological context.

The idea that intelligence is an emergent outcome of generations of ancestors navigating a complex environment suggests that differences in cognitive ability among individuals may be hardwired (are adaptations). Intelligence also stems from learning that, itself, is a complex adaptation. Studies of different species of birds and mammals have revealed that species' innovative problem-solving and spatial processing ability can be explained, at least partly, by particular foraging techniques or search strategies, respectively (Henke-von der Malsburg et al., 2020). In addition, we might expect that individuals of species who tend to be habitat generalists have greater cognitive ability and flexibility than habitat specialists, because they are confronted with challenges that require a greater repertoire of foraging techniques and search strategies. By contrast, individuals of species who are habitat specialists may ultimately have lower general intelligence because of a lack of diversity of cognitively challenging diet requirements. This happens presumably because "whenever a fitness-relevant cognitive problem arises repeatedly and predictably over long periods of time in a given species, natural selection favors a genetically based, developmentally canalized ('hardwired') solution to this problem" (Burkart et al., 2017, p. 8). Thus, a lesson from ecology is that education, especially during the maturation of the brain, should be characterized by diverse and sometimes unpredictable challenges in ways that involve general cognitive abilities.

The main take-home message of the reality that intelligence emerged from making sense of the ecology of nature is that we should allow individuals to explore and through cause and effect discover truths that become the building blocks of an individual's intelligence. Education takes patience and the freedom to explore; Montessori (1913, pp. 4–5) wrote, "We should leave as much as possible to Nature; and the more the babe is left free to develop, the more rapidly and perfectly will he achieve his proper proportions and higher functions." Montessori founded a set of principles for educating people from an early age that emphasized individuals self-constructing who they are and what they know through interactions with nature and other people. This is an example of the ecology of education. Intelligence is embedded in ecology. This is a core idea motivating constructing analogies between ecology and education.

Constructing Analogies between Ecology and Education

Education-relevant synopsis: Gaining valid and informative inferences from analogy depends on four intellectual processes, labeled retrieval, judgment, mapping, and inference. Each of these is defined by specific criteria and approach, and all are required for transferring knowledge and theory from one discipline (ecology) to another discipline (education) in ways that yield valid inferences.

Ecology is full of lessons if we have patience and a willingness to pay attention. One of my favorite examples of ecology as a teacher comes from Robin Wall Kimmerer's "Braiding Sweetgrass." Robin wrote near the end of the chapter "The Three Sisters," "Of all the wise teachers who have come into my life, none are more eloquent than these, who wordlessly in leaf and vine embody the knowledge of relationships. Alone, a bean is just a vine, squash an oversize leaf. Only when standing together with corn does a whole emerge which transcends the individual" (Kimmerer, 2013, p. 140).

I have grown the sisters together in my backyard garden. It is an amazing microcosm of nature watching corn, beans, and squash organize themselves in response to each other; the bean crawling on tendrils up the corn stalk, the enormous leaves of the squash protecting the stalks of corn and stems of beans, and the beans fertilizing the soil. What Kimmerer did in the chapter, though, was transformative, because it fused the rational and sympathetic (or empathetic) minds (Berry, 2002) and cultivated a holistic approach to the ecology of food production. The three sisters is a story about mutualism, the value of diversity, and nature being about interactions more than individualism.

If I allow my rational mind and ignore the riotous beauty of the three species interaction in my garden and focus on data from field experiments designed to compare the productivity of monoculture and polyculture agriculture, I come away with a sense that productivity is less for farms practicing polyculture with the three sisters than for monocultures. An analysis of variance—a statistical technique for finding patterns in nature that tell a story—revealed that there are interaction effects between farming practices (monoculture versus three sisters polyculture) and species on productivity. Although there is not sufficient data for a robust conclusive answer (i.e., there is a high fear of being wrong), the most apparent interaction effect shows that the productivity of a squash monoculture is greater than the productivity for squash when it is grown together with corn and beans. Similar comparison for corn and bean did not reveal any statistically detectable difference, although the trend is the same: less productivity when the species are cultivated together (Pleasant and Burt, 2010, table 1; see also Pleasant, 2016). These results, when combined with strategies for harvest that are complicated when there are multiple species with different growth characteristics, would support an evidence-based claim that monoculture is more productive, more lucrative, and better than three sisters' cropping practices. But as a rational scientist, trained to entertain multiple models and consider multiple variables, the focus on productivity, on biomass produced, fails to capture all of the relevant agricultural outcomes. Moreover, my rational decision that might lead me to grow the three species separately ignores contextual details. For instance, if I am a small-scale farmer and have only a limited area for growing food, it may be that I can't produce enough of each crop across a monoculture patchwork of corn, beans, and squash that generates a sustainable harvest for my family or local community: you can't live on corn or beans or squash alone. I may also forfeit the holistic health of a multiple species diet for a single crop; the three species together form the basis of a better diet than a diet based on any one of the species alone. Kimmerer (2013) explains that "the genius of the Three Sisters lies not in the process by which they grow, but also in the complementarity . . . on the kitchen table. They taste good together . . . and also form a nutritional triad that can sustain a people" (pp. 137–138).

There are other reasons for growing complementary species together. There is good evidence that plots consisting of the three sisters have fewer herbivores (Liao et al., 2024) and fewer weedy species than monoculture plots. "Polycultures—fields with many species of plants—are less susceptible to pest outbreaks than monocultures. The diversity of plant forms provides habitat for a wide array of insects. Some, like corn worms and bean beetles and squash borers, are there with the intent of feeding on the crop. But the diversity of plants also creates habitats for insects who eat the crop eaters" (Kimmerer, 2013, p. 139). Additionally, a bean beetle or squash borer that lands on the wrong crop—a bean beetle on a squash plant or a squash borer on a bean—finds itself in the wrong habitat and unable to feed. The time it takes to fly and find the right host plant makes living in a multispecies garden more difficult and less productive for the herbivores than if they successfully colonized a monoculture.[6]

Finally, there are issues stemming from downstream—and future— effects of poly- and monoculture farms. A study of the effects of beans, squash, and pepper cultivation for future productivity under a crop rotation revealed variable effects of each species on the other species. For instance, bean yields were 8% higher following cultivation by squash relative to pepper, squash yields were 15% higher following cultivation by beans relative to pepper, and pepper yields were 11% higher following beans relative squash (Larkin, 2020). The strong effect of beans is likely due to an increase from nitrogen fixation stemming from a symbiosis with bacteria. The positive effects of squash were likely due to the enrichment of the soil from the decay of its large leaves. There are many studies, like the one by Larkin, documenting the beneficial effects of multiple-species agricultural practices that extend the scope of teaching by the three sisters. The multivariate benefits of polyculture agricultural practices would be interpreted by the rational mind as sufficient evidence for discarding monoculture-based agriculture and making multispecies agriculture work in ways that support continued food production into the future. Importantly, it is the sympathetic mind, the mind that thinks about the future and the impact of soil erosion and increasing dependence on chemically augmented agriculture, that motivated questions designed to reveal the full scope of the issues related to differences between monoculture and polyculture agricultural practices; that mind would come down solidly on the side of polyculture. Furthermore, it is the sympathetic mind, together with the rational mind, that asks whether polyculture agricultural practices can promote greater abundance and diversity of other species, including birds, that may be of aesthetic and intellectual interest and serve as predators of herbivores (see Hiron et al., 2015). The upshot of the story of the three sisters is that we can learn from ecology, and, indeed, we have been doing so for many generations, and the effects of doing so have positive effects on our ability to populate the future. In this sense, it may be that ecological thinking is a shared adaptation inherent in all people—whether we know it or not. The lessons from the three sisters transcend ecology, and food production, and tell us about how we interact as people; that the outcomes of what we do are better when we cooperate than if we remain monoculturally individualistic.

There are multiple lessons of the three sisters relevant for education. The most important lesson is that there are often unrecognized and important properties of the system. If the focus was only on short-term harvest productivity and efficiency, there would be a tendency to abandon polycultural practices and ignore interaction effects. Yet, the story is about long-term sustainability, quality of productivity, and an emphasis on interactions. The dimensionality of cultivation for sustaining humans is more than just kilograms of carbon; it is the richness of interactions that fosters the emergence of intelligence through an ecological mindset.

Analogy is one of the key tools for making inferences grounded in coherent models of reality. The story of the three sisters lends itself to constructing analogy for gaining relevant inferences in a time when diversity has been smothered by the allure of productivity. Constructing a meaningful analogy involves the cognitive process of accessing existing understanding of concepts or processes in one discipline or context and transferring specific aspects or elements in order to understand something in a new way (e.g., Gentner, 1983; Holyoak & Thagard, 1996; Christensen & Schunn, 2007). To use a metaphor in support of analogy, Nichter and Nichter (1986, pp. 63–64) wrote "A good analogy is like a plough that can prepare a population's field of associations for the planting of a new idea. If the field of associations is not adequately plowed to accommodate new ideas, it is difficult for such ideas to take root and grow." The value of analogy, described by Colyvan and Ginzburg (2010, p. 172), is that "analogical reasoning between different branches of science is a very fruitful means of generating new hypotheses."

Gentner (2017) defined four key elements of analogy: retrieval, judgment, mapping, and inference. Retrieval refers to the cognitive process of searching through the mind or other sources of information and identifying instances, concepts, or processes that seem related to a particular topic of interest. The retrieved cognitive constructs are then judged based on the apparent similarity to the topic of interest based on some set of objectively valid criteria. Judgment is dependent on mapping aspects of the retrieved construct with the new topic of interest; mapping reveals the correspondence that establishes the analogy. Mapping creates a bridge between the known and the new object that allows the flow of information about one scenario or system to explain the properties of the new topic of interest. This flow of information becomes the basis for inference.

All of these processes are important. Of these, mapping is perhaps the most relevant for understanding the value of analogy. A key aspect of mapping is that the existing knowledge—the information that was retrieved and judged to be useful—is accurate and is connected to the information in a different context in ways that allow valid inference. A failure of judgment results from retrieving information that is not sufficiently similar to permit establishment of correspondence between the analogical source and target. One factor that explains the effectiveness and value of analogical transfer is the difference between the source of information and the thing being designed or explained (Christensen & Schunn, 2007). In ecology, if we were interested in developing expectations for how a new species functions, we might compare it to a closely related species with structurally similar attributes; this exercise might help design experiments or observation strategies aimed at describing structure and function. This is an example of within domain (also called local) analogical transfer. However, if we use the structural or behavior of species to explain the properties of curriculum in education, the analogical transfer happens between domains (Christensen & Schunn, 2007). It's possible that the disciplinary difference is too large, the gap between contexts and concepts is too wide, to build a bridge for effective mapping and inference.

There is broad consensus that analogy is a powerful tool for fostering conceptual understanding. Gray and Holyoak (2021) elucidated strategies helpful for improving the transfer and gain of understanding by inference using analogies. Analogies should have well described and understood sources and fully explained correspondence determined through transfer and inference. Ideally, the elements being used from the source for understanding the target subject are presented intact and with relevant context. Analogies should be developed using multiple modes of communication, including words and visualizations, that emphasize shared elements and structures. It is not enough to reference a concept from one domain (e.g., ecology) and use it with the assumption that its meaning in a different domain (e.g., education) is known and achieves the intended cognitive outcome. When people use the word ecosystem to describe phenomena in domains or disciplines that are not ecology, they often use analogy for achieving a specific message, but without describing sources, explaining the intended correspondence and relevant context, the word can be misleading.

There is a general perspective, based on evidence, that innovation—namely, the production of novel and creative thinking or solutions to problems—happens when there is between-domain analogical thinking. A common example of analogous design is Velcro. It was invented by George de Mestral when he noticed the small hooks present in burrs surrounding the seeds of certain plants have a tendency to grab onto his pet's fur. Maestral transferred this miniscule hook feature to textiles and created Velcro. The dependence of innovation on the difference between domains is likely not linear, however. Fu et al. (2013) studied the distance between domains during engineering design innovation. They referred to difference as a distance that can be estimated by quantifying the structural elements of the model and proposed innovation. They revealed that there is such a thing as too far when the distance between the domains is harmful (counterproductive) to the design process. Thus, one property of analogical thinking is that the degree of separation between the model and subject can improve or interfere with understanding or innovation.

"Analogical reasoning is thought to be a widely-shared human capacity for making sense of the world involved in most domains, although, perhaps most notably, in creative problem-solving domains, such as science, design, and art" (Holyoak & Thagard, 1996, p. 29). A key aspect of learning through analogy is transfer. Perkins and Salomon (1992) noted that there is positive and negative transfer. Positive transfer enhances learning; negative transfer undermines learning. Whether we know it or not, as educators, we assume positive transfer is happening in the minds of students, because analogy is central to learning. The challenge is to enhance positive transfer but it is likely the optimal distance for specific scenarios varies among students, and the optimal transfer distance varies among topics. Most research indicates learning using analogical transfer often does not occur, especially if the distance is far (Perkins & Salomon, 1992). There are two described mechanisms underlying successful transfer. There is "reflexive or low road transfer" that involves transferring "well-practiced routines by stimulus conditions similar to those in the learning context. . . . For example, when a person moving a household rents a small truck for the first time, the person finds that the familiar steering wheel, shift, and other features evoke useful car-driving responses." There is also "mindful or high road transfer." This type of analogy "involves deliberate effortful abstraction and a search for connections. . . . Such transfer is not in general reflexive. It demands time for exploration and the investment of mental effort" (Perkins & Salomon, 1992, p. 8).

Conventional educational practices often fail to establish the conditions either for reflexive or mindful transfer. Various factors may explain the failure of effective transfer, including, but not limited to, distraction, failure to adequately establish a coherent comparative framework presumably due to lack of sufficient investment of time and mental energy, lack of sufficient prompts and clear connections between the domains of analogy, and high complexity of the constructed analogy (Krawczyk et al., 2014; Kucwaj et al., 2022). Complexity is characterized by the number of relations involved when constructing an analogy. Low road transfer is about using what we have already learned to be successful in a new, and similar, context. High road transfer happens when we learn something new. Life is full of taking low and high roads; education exists to make the high roads more attainable. Higher education is about taking the higher roads.

Making the higher roads more attainable means engaging in building robust bridges between domains. In this case, between ecology on one side of the river and education on the other, with the goal of making it clear that the habitats of understanding are more or less the same on both sides of the river. In the process, my goal is to emphasize the value of directed abstraction in hopes of gaining a better appreciation for the complexity, uncertainty, and processes inherent in successfully educating future generations of informed citizens that are capable of recognizing truths from the maelstrom of fake news and deliberately misleading claims. My perspective is that the emergent processes that characterize ecology provide useful analogies for a better understanding of the emergent process of education.

Individuals differ in their capacity for engaging in successful transfer of ideas or ways of thinking and knowing from one discipline or domain to another (Corkill & Fager, 1995). The differences among individuals reflect the effects of experience (environment) and biology (the structure and function of the brain [Green et al., 2012; Parsons & Davies, 2022]). If students are asked to engage in spontaneous analogy generation and transfer for the purpose of solving a problem, the individual differences in ability are evident (Corkill & Fager, 1995); however, training students to construct analogies can eliminate individual differences depending, in part, on the ability of the educator. Thus, knowing how we create analogies as a sense-making strategy and knowing what aspects of the process pose the greatest challenges seems an essential part of being an effective educator. It's not enough to create scenarios that require analogical thinking, because many students will be unsuccessful, depending on the low- or high-roadness of the analogical challenge. What we need to create are opportunities to engage the analogy-making neural architecture in ways that support and challenge students' thinking. Part of this scaffolded approach is to identify connections between elements of the well-known and the unknown (or less well-known). If ecology is being used as a source for analogy, it makes sense to clearly describe the most relevant aspects of ecology that serve as places for making secure bridges that can successfully transfer information and support robust and predictive inferences.

Transfer is evident when we interrogate some of what have been referred to as essential analogies (Sundrud & Hueftle, 2009). One essential analogy comes from a description of homeostasis. Homeostasis is the capacity of an organism to maintain life processes within a narrow range of operational states. In this context, an analogy has been made with the baby bear in the story of Goldilocks: life depends on not being too hot, or too cold, but in being just right. Thus, the concept of homeostasis is made more relevant by creating a scenario that highlights the familiar (Goldilocks) to make sense of the abstract (homeostasis). This is a simple example. As we scale up the sophistication of what we seek to understand, it is important to keep in mind the influence of complexity and familiarity on the success of analogy. Complexity should be built stepwise using simple and familiar pieces. Returning to homeostasis; it is a process dependent on feedback. An essential analogy for understanding positive feedback might be using the statement "Don't laugh at his jokes, you'll only encourage him" (Sundrud & Hueftle, 2009) to get the idea that feedback is a signal that can trigger a modulated decrease or, in the context of the laughing at someone's jokes, an increase in some type of activity or process.

Published Analogies between Ecology and Education

Education-relevant synopsis: There is an ever-expanding subdiscipline within education and the humanities that invokes ecology as an inspiring and organizing ideal. The connections between ecology and education span decades and the proliferation of ecology as a relevant albeit abstract idea with value in the scholarship of education was most influenced by Bronfenbrenner: his work has been cited hundreds of thousands of times. However provocative, Bronfenbrenner's conception of ecology departs from the ecological thinking within the scientific discipline of ecology. This book is in parts motivated by, and a response to, the idealized and abstracted notion of ecology that found its way into the issues related to human development.

There have been innumerable analogies constructed between ecology and education for the purpose of infusing education with provocative and informative ecological properties. My review of the vast literature suggests that most authors that have attempted to transfer the concepts and models of ecology into their own discipline failed in myriad ways. Most of the failure stems from inadequacy of judgment and mapping. Bronfenbrenner (1977, 1979) remains the most influential scholar that promoted an educational model centered in ecology. As of today, his work has been cited more than two hundred thousand times. Despite explicit reference to education being embedded within ecology, his ecosystems theory of human development "ignores . . . human-nature interconnections" and his view is "deeply anthropocentric" (Elliott & Davis, 2020, p. 1120). Additionally, Elliott and Davis (p. 1124) pointed out that "Bronfenbrenner's use of terminology including 'ecology,' ecological systems, and niches is unrelated to ecology's predominant links with nature and natural systems. Of interest is that while the study of ecology is not treated as separate or distinct from humans by ecologists, Bronfenbrenner's use of ecological terms as a psychologist was not inclusive of nature and natural systems." In other words, Bronfenbrenner's ecological thinking is untethered from reality and continued citation to his work propagates bias and devalues ecology and ecosystems as useful constructs for productive analogical thinking. Of particular concern (for me) is the lack of references to original publications in ecology. Publications that use the hierarchical model developed by Bronfenbrenner ignore the vast world of ecological research and are not fully developed analogies that permit valid inference, because the bridge connecting ecology and education remains an idea (albeit provocative) rather than a built reality. The many publications that reference Bronfenbrenner's work provide license for using the words *ecology, ecological,* and *ecosystem* without adequately understanding the context-dependent meanings of ecology, ecological, and ecosystem.

Similarly, there is a lack of validity with Pompea and Russo's (2020) claim that there is an astronomy education ecosystem, with Väljataga et al.'s (2020) conclusion that institutes of higher education are ecosystems, with Abney et al.'s (2019, p. 256) claim for the existence of "social media education ecosystem," with Emery et al.'s (2019) assertion that education ecosystems are similar to biological ecosystems because there are many component parts that interact with one another and affect the functioning of the system, and with van de Heyde and Siebrits's (2019, p. 3) vague idea that there is "an e-learning food chain, and its attendant trophic levels." Aubusson (2002) wrote, "The animals come again into balanced populations . . . the variety of species and their interactions are unchanged" and that there is "slow and gradual change through succession where the ecosystem slowly modifies itself from within and, organisms well adapted to the conditions, succeed each other to create and recreate ecosystems" (p. 33). Aubusson's perception of an ecosystem is naive and lacks sufficient detail, and his promotion of the analogy fails to highlight key structural and functional properties that can form the basis for assessing the match between ecology and education in ways that promote insight and valid inferences. There are many other scholarly treatises invoking ecology when explaining education that fail to establish a valid analogy either by low- or high-road transfer.

Ronald Barnett and colleagues have been productive within a discipline labeled as learning ecology. Barnett's (2017) book entitled *The Ecological University* says, without evidence, that ecosystems are never static, that they can "re-territoralize" themselves, and propagates a term—*ecosophy*—that defines his inquiry: it is "an ecological approach to understanding complex phenomenon, such as the university." When he writes, "aspects of the world possess a loose coherence . . . we may term them ecosystems," it is clear that he is not referring to any ecological systems imagined by ecologists. In fact, in most of what Barnett and many of his colleagues within an emergent discipline described as learning ecology promote is an abstract idealization of ecology absent grounding in theory and empirical evidence, and missing authentic connection to the ecology that exists in the real world. His edited volume *Ecologies for Learning and Practice* (Barnett & Jackson, 2020) includes 14 chapters that span the scope of learning ecology: none of the 26 authors has credentials related to expertise in ecology. Moreover, only one of the 468 citations includes an author—Simon Levin—recognized as an ecologist by profession. Despite the lack of grounding in ecology, my perspective aligns with the expanding discipline of learning ecology in that there is an ecology of education, and it is based loosely on the idea, articulated by Barnett and Jackson (p. 1) that "ecology, after all, breathes a sense of life and living, of relationships, of connectivity and interdependence, of growth and renewal, of sustainability, of evolution and resilience, and of elements being configured and working together to achieve something that the individual parts cannot achieve alone." I do have trouble with the ecological in Barnett's utopian view of the "ecological university," because imagination operates in surreality whereas ecology, and ecological processes, operate in reality. When "the ecological is understood in terms of the ontological, epistemological and ethical interconnections that exist between our mental ecologies, social ecologies and natural ecologies" (Stratford, 2024, p. 1340) and there are as many as eight ecosystems that describe the utopian university (Barnett, 2017) without evaluating whether well-accepted properties of ecosystems apply to educational systems (like a university), the reality of ecology has been fully replaced by an ideal.

After reviewing published scholarly works that create or imagine analogies between ecology and education, it is clear that many bridges between ecology and education are poorly constructed and the structural materials too flimsy to permit much traffic in valid inference. My assertion is that the abundance of papers that have invoked analogy between ecology and education lack rigor and ignore the rich and important ecological knowledge gained from more than a century of scholarly and scientific inquiry. The general approach of this book is to identify particular ideas and concepts where there are opportunities for developing instructive analogies between ecology and education. The purpose centers on interrogating the structure and function of education and also on making predictions about how education may benefit by the guidance afforded from transfer of ways of thinking and general principles of ecology to the task of understanding and evolving education. In this endeavor I am fully aligned with Barnett, Jackson, and their creative colleagues (Barnett & Jackson, 2020). Each chapter focuses on key ideas in ecology and then introduces the relevant educational topic for which analogy can generate useful inferences about the structure and function of education.

The Scales of Ecology and Education

Education-relevant synopsis: Like most complex and multidimensional phenomena, ecology and education exist and play out at different scales of organization and action, from individuals to systems. Because of the importance of scaling in ecology and education, the book is organized by scale; it begins with the individual and ends with the community. I have left a systems-level analysis for another place and time, in part because unlike all other scales, the systems-level scale completely loses track of individuals. This book emphasizes the importance of the individual in ecology and education.

Both ecology and education happen, and are analyzed, at different scales, from the individual to the system. And, as Wiens (1989, p. 385) emphasized, "Acts in . . . the 'ecological theatre' are played out on various scales of space and time. To understand the drama, we must view it on the appropriate scale." Ecological "drama" is being played out at the scale of individuals, populations, communities, and ecosystems; and each of these scales is hierarchical (fig. 1.3). Moreover, events and processes happening at one scale influence events and processes at other scales.

Figure 1.3. The scales of analysis in ecology. The two axes are time (in years) and space (defined as area occupied). The four boxes represent the scales of individuals, populations, communities, and ecosystems. Arrows between indicate events at one scale have effects at other scales. The thickness of the lines is meant to convey the predicted strength of cross-scale effects. *Source:* Created by the author.

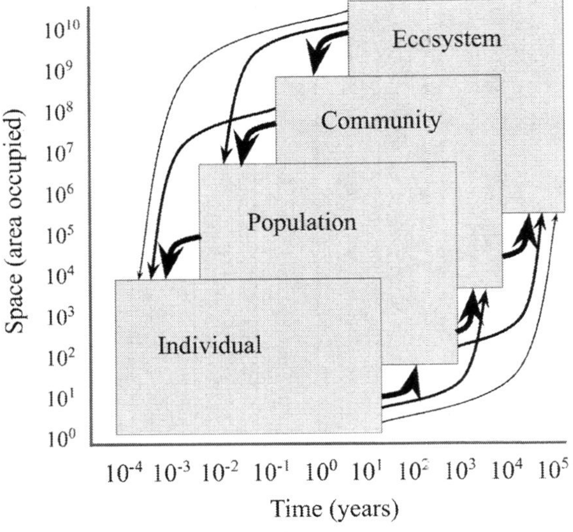

The same scaling framework can be constructed for educational contexts (fig. 1.4). The most relevant scales for both ecology and education range from the individual to the system, and include populations and communities. In ecology, individuals aggregate to form populations, individual interactions form communities, and communities constitute the inhabitants of ecological systems, referred to as ecosystems. The same is true for education. In higher education, individuals aggregate into courses and disciplines in ways that constitute populations, interactions of individuals result in the emergence of communities, and communities constitute the players that comprise educational systems, best referred to as edusystems that exists at the scale of the institution. There is another aspect of education that also exists on different scales: it is the substance of intelligence. At the smallest scale is the individual idea. Ideas are related by context and discipline and can be grouped into disciplinary populations of ideas. Connections among ideas form communities of ideas that can be characterized as knowledge. And the knowledge of many individuals forms the basis of collective intelligence.

Figure 1.4. The scales of analysis in education analogous to the scales of ecology. The two axes are time (in years) and space (defined as area occupied). Left: The four boxes represent the scale of students (individuals), course (populations), departments (communities), and the institution (ecosystem). Arrows between indicate events at one scale have effects at other scales. The thickness of the lines is meant to convey the predicted strength of cross-scale effects. Right: Similarly, there is a scaling of information, from the idea (individual), to a group of ideas that constitutes knowledge (population), to connections among ideas that forms the substance of intelligence (community), to collective intelligence (ecosystem). *Source:* Created by the author.

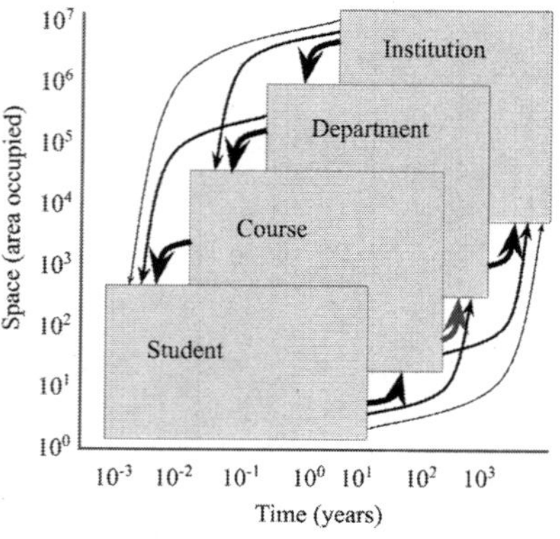

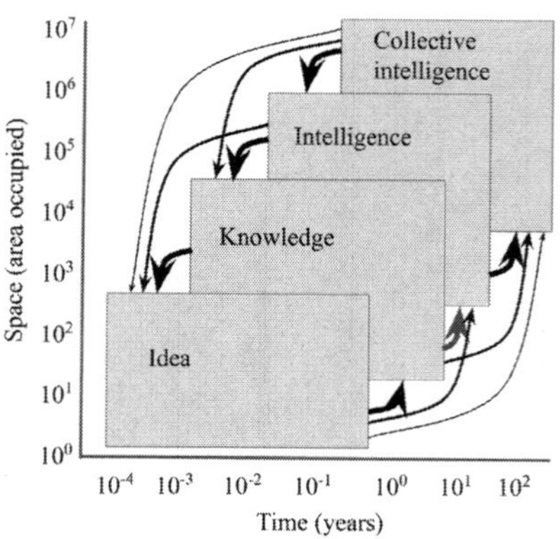

These scales of organization and activity form the basis for the organization of this book. Each of these scales of existence and analysis can be characterized by space and time, although there are also other relevant dimensions. For example, the temporal scale of individuals in an ecological context is defined by their longevity (time) and the spatial scale by an individual's home range size (space). Similarly, the temporal scale of individuals (i.e., students) in an educational context is bounded by a single learning activity that can take place over minutes or from enrollment to graduation (4–6 years) and the space encompasses the home range in which learning happens (e.g., the classroom, the library, the home). Additionally, the temporal scale of an idea is defined by what happens to the individuals that possess the idea. The next level is the population. The spatial scale spans the geographic range of all individuals of the same species subject to study, whereas the temporal scale might be measured in generations and, depending on the species, can range from one to hundreds of years. In an education context, the population is perhaps best delimited as the individual course, because it is a collection of students and instructors who come together with shared interests and it has demonstrable properties that can be used to objectively categorize the assemblage as a population. In terms of ideas, there is a disciplinary collection of ideas—a population of ideas—that constitute some core set of ideas delimited by the properties of a course. Another population-level unit is the disciplinary population (also referred to as the department or the students' major). The scales of time range from a semester (15 weeks) to the duration of time a student is a member of a disciplinary population. This is typically the time between initial enrollment and graduation. The next level in ecology is the community. Communities may change over time frames from less than a year to thousands or tens of thousands of years, depending on the study, whereas for educational contexts, the community level is similar to the population: it is perhaps described as an emergent social network stemming from interactions in the context of a disciplinary population. I often describe the members of a department as a disciplinary population; the network of interactions within a disciplinary population defines the community. A key aspect of communities is interactions. In terms of ideas, the community level is perhaps best described as intelligence; intelligence is an emergent outcome of making connections between ideas in ways that cause the coherence of knowledge. Finally, the ecosystem-level can encompass a landscape (e.g., a wetland) or the entire globe and operate on scales from hours to many thousands of years. In the context of higher education, the scale is the whole institution. For ideas, it seems like collective intelligence exists at the highest hierarchical scale; collective intelligence is the integration, as a consequence of connecting ideas, of information and process skills of a large group of people with shared interests. Importantly, events and phenomena happening at one scale of time and space influence events happening at other scales; moreover, events and phenomena happening at larger scales are aggregates of events and phenomena happening at smaller scales.

It is important to keep in mind that the scaling of ecology, education, and intelligence is an abstraction useful for gaining an understanding of complexity. The complexity is vast. Consider, for instance, that the thing referred to as an individual is, itself, something that can be considered an individual, a population, a community, or an ecosystem depending on the subject of analysis. The fact that I am an individual, but also an ecosystem, stems from my individual body being home to trillions of individuals—mostly bacteria but also including a diverse assemblage of eukaryotes.[7]

Levin (1992, p. 1943) emphasized that "there is no single natural scale at which ecological phenomena should be studied; systems generally show characteristic variability on a range of spatial, temporal, and organizational scales. . . . The key to prediction and understanding lies in the elucidation of mechanisms underlying observed patterns. Typically, these mechanisms operate at different scales than those on which the patterns are observed; in some cases, the patterns must be understood as emerging from the collective behaviors of large ensembles of smaller scale units." In this book, I stopped short of including analogies between ecosystems and edusystems, in part because the focus on systems often fails to consider individuals as central, fundamental players. Instead, systems focus on pools and fluxes of resources. This book is meant to keep individuals as the central player even as we move through higher and larger scales of organization. I develop analogies between ecosystems and edusystems in a companion book.

The scale and units of analysis are critical parts of analogical thinking. This is true, in part, because, as Levin's quote makes clear, processes at lower levels (e.g., at the individual level) influence (or determine) patterns at higher levels (e.g., communities or ecosystems). This has been the subject of considerable attention and debate in ecological literature. Clark et al. (2011) explained why understanding the scale-dependence of patterns and processes is so important: "The processes that control biodiversity operate at a different scale from most of the models and data used to study them. Species do not compete, individuals do. Species do not respond to climate, individuals respond to weather" (p. 1273). Most of ecology is the study of emergent phenomena due to differences in the fate of individuals. Yet the fact that "important mechanisms operate on individuals does not mean that only individual-level data provide insight. Some processes operate . . . at course [higher] scales. . . . Aggregated variables at course spatial-temporal scales contribute perspectives that could not have been obtained from experiments [and observations] of individuals."

A key issue for emergent processes like ecology and education is the importance of recognizing that everything that happens and all measurable properties stem from the existence and actions of individuals. However, paying attention to individuals is often insufficient, because function sometimes is only evident from the aggregated effects of many individuals. In ecology and education, data aggregation is, de facto, the formation of populations. And it is often the case that our information about ecology and education comes from analysis of aggregated data. The challenge, especially in education, is relying too much on aggregated data (e.g., grade distributions, probabilities of success) without paying sufficient attention to the state and fate of individuals. Clark et al. (2011) explained the issue in ecology: "Where possible, the ideal solution is often to 'analyze, then aggregate,' rather than 'analyze the aggregate.' . . . Ecologists have studied . . . individuals for a long time, but the . . . parameters estimated in these studies aggregate over the variation. . . . The individual variation is available and contains critical information, but only the aggregate is quantified. This is a natural tendency, given that we [often] care about species, not individuals" (p. 1274). Clark et al. focused on an example of the recruitment success of individuals for two species of trees (oak and beech) relative to two recorded climate variables—temperature and precipitation—with strong effects on the absence and presence of plant species. Recruitment success is a key ecological parameter because it influences the abundance and distribution of individuals; it is also a key parameter in higher education for the same reasons. Clark et al. showed that the distributions of individuals of the two species broadly overlap. If the data were aggregated and then analyzed, we would come away with the perspective that the process of recruitment is the same between the two species. However, if the distributions for the individuals of the two species are displayed conditionally on whether spring is cold or warm, the story differs from that stemming from the aggregated data. Oak recruitment is higher during cold springs, when there is less precipitation, whereas beech recruitment is higher during cold springs, when there is more precipitation. The key take home message is that the differences among individuals matter and become evident if we ask questions and analyze the data prior to aggregation. Similar issues associated with analysis of aggregated data happen in education.

Education data are often aggregated prior to analysis. One example is the emphasis on retention. Retention is the proportion of individuals that return to college after each semester or year. The average retention of students from the completion of the first year to the start of the second year increased from about 75% to 80% for the US; a similar trend was also evident for CU–Boulder, but the percentages were lower. While these data suggest the collective behavior of individuals is slowly changing, data from individuals are missing, making it impossible to know whether the story from aggregated data reveals an important truth. Based on these data, we can't know why there are oscillations in retention over time, or if trends reflect processes happening uniformly or variably among populations with the CU–Boulder edusystem. As Levin (1992, p. 1943) articulated, "Mechanisms operate at different scales than those on which the patterns are observed; in some cases, the patterns must be understood as emerging from the collective behaviors of large ensembles of smaller scale units." Without the individual data, we are left to our imagination rather than being steered by data to an evidence-based understanding.

Ecologists have invested considerable time, energy, and thought into understanding the effects of data aggregation and how analyses of aggregated data may not accurately represent patterns and processes. Part of the explanation for the pervasiveness of "aggregate then analyze" in education is that our leaders of institutions of higher education are focused on making decisions and implementing policy at the institutional level. They focus on such things as graduation rates and retention from matriculation to graduation. However, we know that the aggregate patterns and processes emerge as a consequence of many individuals making decisions in relation to their unique conditions and perceptions. If we are going to focus on population-scale data, we need to "analyze then aggregate" so that we clearly emphasize that education is an emergent process of things that happen to and by individuals. To make sense of persistence data, educational researchers have focused on various statistics of students' experiences. One is students' sense of belonging. "Students' sense of belonging is known to be strongly associated with academic achievement and a successful life at university" (Ahn & Davis, 2020). There are many factors that influence a sense of belonging. Commonly, students' sense of belonging is described relative to self-declared identity, including racial identity. A simple aggregation of data from first-year students in large biology classes reveals little difference between white and nonwhite students. This suggests that in some first-year courses at my institution there is little difference in the sense of belonging associated with this dimension of identity. However, we also know that whether or not students live on campus influences their sense of belonging; 33% and 42% of first-year students on a commuter campus think about withdrawing from their new higher education environment soon after their arrival (Thomas and Jones 2017). When the sense of belonging is conditional on whether students live on or near campus or far from the university, the statistics change in ways that show differences in students' sense of belonging and suggest that the story may be more complex than simple analyses of aggregated data might suggest. If students live on campus, there is a greater sense of belonging than when they live off campus, there is no difference between white and nonwhite in the average sense of belonging, and there is less variation among nonwhite than white students. By contrast, if students live off campus, there is a lesser sense of belonging than when they live on campus, white students tend to have a lower sense of belonging than nonwhite students, and there is less variation among nonwhite than white students. The conditionality of sense of belonging means that we need to pay attention to the dimensionality of the issue and resist our tendency to aggregate and then analyze data.

The close parallels between the effects of environment on individual well-being and success for animals in nature and humans in classrooms suggests we can learn from studies of behavioral ecology for promoting the development of environments conducive for cultivating a positive sense of belonging. A continuing challenge is how we can collapse negative distance effects and leverage resources for reducing stress responses due to large class sizes while maintaining the value of promoting the social construction of knowledge ideally by teaching in person. Success requires a focus on individuals, because individuals are the fundamental unit that explains emergent patterns and behaviors evident at higher hierarchical levels.

The Meaning of Success

Education-relevant synopsis: Success can be measured in many different ways. There is a natural similarity between success estimated for individuals in ecological settings (birth, maturation, survival, reproduction) and success estimated for students (matriculation, maturation, persistence, graduation). Similar measures of success can also be applied to ideas in the minds of students. This is included as a separate section because the various measures of success are key outcomes of an emergent process.

In this book, I will mention success many times. Success in ecological contexts is very different from success in educational contexts; yet, despite the apparent differences, we can clearly see the similarities and create bridges between them (table 1.2). In ecology, the success of individuals is often measured in several ways. Each is informative and each can be predicted by various attributes of individuals. The same is true for education.

One important unit of analysis is growth rate. Growth rate is the change, usually in size or some physical dimensions, of individuals over a specified period of time. The most relevant period of time is between birth and an individual's age at first reproduction. Reproductive maturity is an important moment in an organism's life, because it means that the effect of an individual transcends self and influences the future. Two other key measures of ecological success include survival and reproductive suc-

Table 1.2. Comparison of different types and units of success in ecology and education

Type of success	Ecology	Education
Growth	Rate of increase of body size	Rate of increase of knowledge and key affective behaviors
Maturation	Gain of ability to reproduce	Gain of individual and collective intelligence
Survival	Surviving to adulthood	Persistence in college
Reproductive success	Number of offspring produced	Graduation
Fitness	Survival and reproductive success	Social capital through academic achievement

cess. Survival is straightforward. It is usually measured as being alive at a particular point in time (when an individual is sampled or observed), and it can be predicted or related to properties of individuals as a means of gaining insight into the factors that contribute to this estimate of success. For example, I studied the effect of genotype on survival for fish living in a spring system using mark-recapture methods (Keepers et al., 2018). The scale was evident in the unit of analysis: the probability of an individual's survival per interval of time. Reproductive success is typically measured as the number of offspring an individual produces during its lifetime. There are other measures of success, including whether an individual increases or decreases the growth rate or success of another individual with whom it interacts, or the extent that an individual gains status or influence within a group of individuals during its life. In a species of bird called a manakin, unrelated males aggregate to form leks. Different males form collaborative alliances on these leks. Whether individuals collaborate depends on their spatial location relative to other males and their social status such that males lower in the hierarchy gain status by interacting with a higher ranked bird, among other factors (Edelman & McDonald, 2014).[8] The point of highlighting manakins is that not all males are reproductively successful and whether an individual is successful depends on its social status. In this context, one measure of success is the gain in social status, which is a form of social capital that can be measured and used to predict an individual's reproductive success. Individuals can gain social capital depending on their interactions with others, and, in general, more social capital is indicative of greater success.

There are similar measures of success in educational settings (table 1.2). There is the growth rate of intelligence and academic ability from the moment of matriculation to the time a student graduates. The ecological idea of survival is similar to persistence in education. Persistence is a measure of whether an individual stays in school or leaves prior to graduation. Success in this context is persistence in higher education through graduation and the gain of a degree. There is no straightforward equivalent of reproductive success. There is, however, the gain of influence or status that is, like the case for manakins, a form of social capital. In academic settings, the units of social capital include access to resources and opportunities that increase the gain of intelligence and skills, development of social networks and establishing connections with people of higher hierarchical rank in ways that increase an individual's academic achievement and increase the probability of graduation, and the gain of experience in different academic contexts that can enhance of the ability of the newly graduated to find desirable employment.

Similarly, in terms of ideas, there are similar measures of success as in ecology. The survival of an idea is estimated by the presence or absence of an idea following its introduction to the minds of students. Ideas can also be characterized as having reproductive success. This is most similar to thinking about the rate of transmission of ideas in similar ways that we have characterized the transmission of viruses among individuals. In the epidemiological literature, viral success is described by the basic reproductive number. "The basic reproduction number (R0) . . . is an epidemiologic metric used to describe the contagiousness or transmissibility of infectious agents. R0 is affected by numerous biological, sociobehavioral, and environmental factors that govern pathogen transmission" (Delamater et al., 2019, p. 1). People talk about memes, ideas, or events "going viral"; they are not referring to pathogens, even in the post-Covid world. They are talking about the spread of information. And interestingly, and disturbingly, analysis of the reproductive success of different ideas has revealed that "fake news"—what we might classify as bad ideas or lies—has a higher reproductive number than the truth (Vosoughi et al., 2018).

The Theoretical Context for Understanding Education

Education-relevant synopsis: There is a rich and voluminous body of theory relevant for understanding the process and outcomes of education. I have deliberately limited my focus to sociocultural theories closely aligned with ecology, especially constructivism. The rest of the book emphasizes what might best be described as an ecological theory of education; namely that education is a natural, emergent process of discovery and sense-making encoded by neural circuitry and continually modified through genetic and environment effects during development and maturation and over generations as a consequence of evolution. A more explicit description of an evolutionary theory of education remains to be fully articulated.

Effective education is built from various theoretical frameworks. There are sociocultural theories of education. Sociocultural refers to the combination of social and cultural factors that influence individuals' experiences, behaviors, knowledge, beliefs, ways of thinking, and interactions within a particular society or group. In many ways, socioculturalism is a set of social variables that exists within a particular cultural context with effects on education and the intellectual and academic achievement of individuals. Vygotsky is perhaps best known for the development of the idea that education happens as a process of individuals constructing knowledge through new experiences within sociocultural contexts. "To do this, Vygotsky's noted that individuals interact with one another in social situations to socially negotiate meaning. To learn, he emphasized the importance of problem solving in this process, which was reflected in his notion of learning by doing. Secondly, Vygotsky believed that peers achieve common understanding by socially negotiating meaning via problem solving activities" (Jaramillo, 1996, p. 140). A key aspect of the sociocultural theory is interactions as a strategy for the emergence of meaning. As we will see, interaction is a core part of both ecology and education. Another important aspect of education is the role of the environment in which it happens. Environment is a core aspect of what sociocultural means. This means that education happens "by controlling the environment in which they [students] act, and hence think and feel. We never educate directly, but indirectly by means of the environment. Whether we permit chance environments to do the work, or whether we design environments for the purpose makes a great difference" (Dewey, 1916, p. 18–19).

In the pages of this book, I emphasize the role of the environment for influencing the success of individuals, both in ecological and educational contexts. As educators, we often ignore the environment and pay attention to curriculum as if it is independent of the environment. We often forget that people are part of the environment. We often teach as if it does not matter whether students are present in person and working together or not. Ecology reminds us that everything happens in the context of the environment, because, in very fundamental ways, the environment determines whether survival and success is possible. And an emergent outcome of putting a group of people in a particular learning environment is a network generated by interactions that happens for the purpose of making sense of information and various process skills.

All of us construct our intelligence through a lifelong process of learning by experience, and in the process we continuously build a large foundation from which we continue constructing our intelligence; that is, until the capacity to do so vanishes under the irreversible process of senescence. My description of education as derivative from ecology is not meant as a theoretical framework or as a replacement for any of the many existing qualitative theories of education. My goal is simply to point out how we might enact constructivism by looking to nature for insights and actionable inferences. One of the reasons for this is that ecology—and its disciplinary companion evolution—are fundamentally constructivist processes that have been incessantly at work building adaptations and ecosystems for billions of years. I advocate that constructivism, as an emergent sociocultural process, should be considered a partner in all educators' pedagogical frameworks used for developing and enacting effective and empowering educational experiences.

Chapter 2

Individuals

The Fundamental Unit

Education-relevant synopsis: All education involves the intellectual maturation and development of individuals. Strategies that aggregate individual data into composition statistics (e.g., persistence and graduation rates) fail to recognize the value of keeping track and meeting the needs of individuals. Current practices ignore the trees in favor of the forest without recognizing that it is the trees that constitute the forest.

A fundamental unit is a thing that is, or is perceived as being, the smallest part of a complex entity that can be subjected to analysis. An atom is the fundamental unit of matter. A gene is the fundamental unit of inheritance. An organism is the fundamental unit of ecology. A student is the fundamental unit of education. And an idea is the fundamental unit of knowledge. An organism, a student, and an idea are all individual entities. All patterns and processes evident in ecology and education ultimately stem from the existence, actions, and intentions of individuals: organisms in ecological settings and students and ideas in educational settings.

The recognition of the value of focusing on the individual is evident from the many studies that model ecological processes using a general approach referred to as agent-based. Each individual is considered to be an agent whose actions are defined by a set of possible functional states during a particular period of time. One example of a possible action is whether an individual moves from one location to another. A parameterized probability distribution determines whether an individual moves, and if they move the direction and distance moved during a defined interval of time. A large number of possible factors affect the average and variation in movement of individuals. Figure 2.1 shows an example of two outcomes of a simple agent-based model for five individuals. In both cases there is a random aspect of each individual's movements for direction and distance. In one case the individuals appear to wander aimlessly across the landscape is if searching for something (fig. 2.1a). In the other case, there is a tendency for directionality (fig. 2.1b). The trajectory of individuals in the real world—whether in an ecological or educational context—is determined by repeatedly monitoring an individual's location relative to the axes that define their possible range of behaviors. For individuals in an ecological context, it may be the axes are latitude and longitude and an individual's movement is recorded using a tag that reports their position at regular intervals. For an individual in an educational context, the two axes may be the content and science process skills emphasized in a course. Individual trajectories are estimated using some sort of assessment implemented at regular intervals. The great value of these individual-based models is the realization that the activity of each individual is unique as a consequence of inherent tendencies and as a response to various external

Figure 2.1a–b. Two different simulations of individual movements using a simple agent-based model with specified probabilities of the distance moved and directionality in a space of an immense number of possible places an individual might exist. For each simulation, there are five individuals that begin moving from the same place. In A, each individual has a unique and divergent trajectory, whereas in B individual trajectories are nearly identical and resemble a directed search. *Source:* Created by the author.

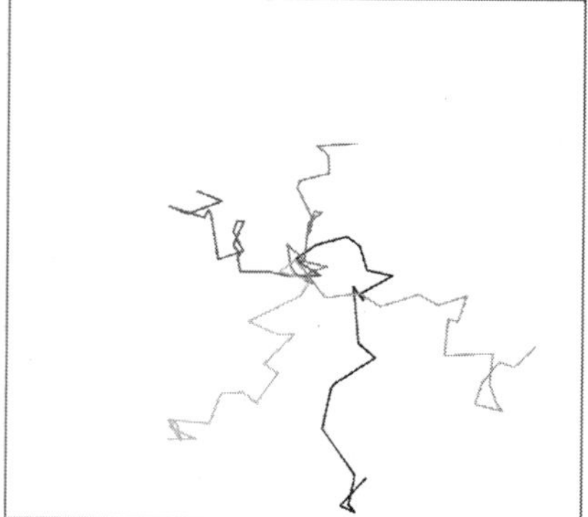
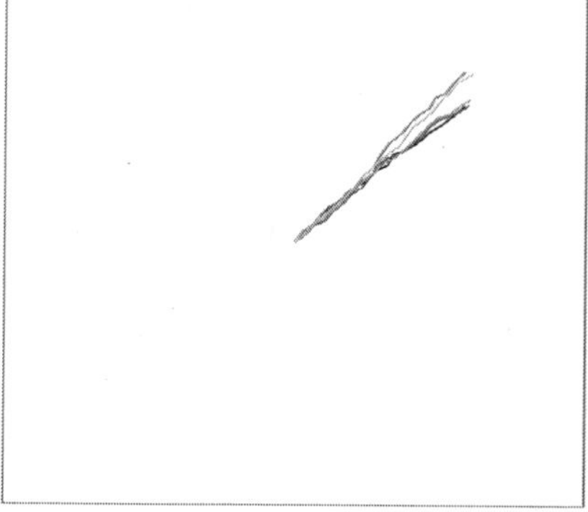

factors—interactions and environment—in ways that generate an enormous range of possible outcomes (DeAngelis, 2018). From the actions of many individuals, the aggregated data permit estimation of tendencies—usually averages—and effects. The focus on individuals in ecology, and that all individuals are different as a consequence of differences across a potentially large number of axes of function, provides a well-developed, transferable, and coherent basis for making analogies with education. Moreover, the importance of individuals in ecology and education underscores the value of following the growth, actions, and fates of individuals in the context of a continuously changing environment.

As emphasized in chapter 1, patterns and processes happening at the scale of populations, communities, and ecosystems stem from the actions and activities of individuals. Our tendency to aggregate individuals prior to analysis, to focus on average effects instead of individual actions, to look for broad patterns that reflect the function of higher-order structures—like a university—rather than analyzing individuals means that we often come to conclusions without knowing the reasons for the observed patterns. As Clark et al. (2011) and others have emphasized, we have a natural tendency to analyze the aggregate and ignore the individual stories, because we tend to care most about phenomena on larger scales. In ecology, the focus is often on species even though species are abstract categories consisting of many myriad individuals. In education, we often focus on institutional-level statistics—including persistence and graduation rates—even though it is individuals that persist and graduate. And, as educators, we often focus on grade point averages and composite scores on exams even though it is individual learning trajectories through a seemingly infinite universe of ideas that matter. When we aggregate data, the stories of individual trajectories are missing even though they are necessary for understanding education. I begin with individuals because it is the individuals—in ecology and education—that have agency.

Individuals and Cognitive Phenotypes

Education-relevant synopsis: Individual cognitive abilities are influenced by many diverse variables such that all students differ, with the caveat that some individuals differ from the average more than others. This fact, coupled with the insights from recognition of the individual as the fundamental unit of analysis in education (and ecology), means student-centered pedagogy is essential and that keeping track of the gain in cognitive abilities of all individuals—estimating cognitive change—is more important than evaluating whether students achieve specific and conventional objectives. This translates into creating diverse opportunities for intellectual gain and enacting innovative personalized and adaptive learning opportunities. The main message is that we should expect differences in ability among students, and we should expect that the differences are likely to be larger and more variable across different aspects of cognitive function than standardized testing, grades, or other simple measures of performance might predict.

Individuals in nature have emergent properties as a consequence of consisting of many cells—in the case of humans, there are trillions of them—that function in coordinated and sometimes conflicting ways. From the perspective of an ecologist (or a biologist), this means that we can think of individuals as collectives or populations of cells united by a common purpose, and because individuals are made up of billions or trillions of living parts, there are myriad ways individuals differ. We should expect all individuals to be different. One perspective is that individuals are "extremely internally heterogeneous. Their states and motions are consequences of many intersecting causal pathways, and it is unusual that normal variation in any one of these pathways has a strong effect on the outcome. . . . Indeed, we may define 'normality' as the condition in which no single causal pathway controls the organism. . . . All attempts to understand causes must necessarily involve the observation of variations" (Lewontin, 2000, pp. 93–94).

Individuals can vary in size and complexity, from a single microbial cell to a redwood tree. In both cases, there are defined and detectable limits to the total mass of a single individual. Individuals can be connected and there may be the flow of information, including genes, or resources between them; one example is aspen trees. Each aspen tree has properties that make it an individual, yet aspen trees are typically part of a larger group of individuals because they grow and reproduce through the production of genetically identical clones from underground structures resembling roots called ramets. Resources can flow between individual trees through the interconnected system of ramets, blurring the lines between the individual tree and the grove. Nonetheless, anyone in an aspen forest can easily distinguish individual trees. I mention this example of the blurry line between an individual and a group because the characteristics of individuals in educational contexts that emphasize interactions and collective intelligence might be more similar to aspen trees that gain some of their resources for growth from others. As social organisms, our success is dependent on interactions with others.[1]

In most natural populations, each individual is unique because of the influence of genes and the environment during growth and maturation. The reference to genes means that different individuals have different combinations of alleles across many different genes in the genome. Genes are the basic units of heredity and are made up of DNA sequences characterized by a connected set of four different biochemical units called bases—labeled A, G, T, and C—that determine—to varying degrees—specific traits or characteristics in an organism. An allele is a unique type of a gene defined by the particular sequence of As, Gs, Ts, and Cs. Each allele contributes some functional property to the biology of an individual, and the differences across all of the alleles add up to differences in measurable characteristics among individuals. The environment refers to the role of prevailing conditions on how individuals develop and function, from fertilization to death. This includes the effects of diet, stress, abiotic factors (e.g., temperature), and other factors that influence growth, maturation, and development.

In general, individual properties are characterized relative to an expected value for a population. The expected value is simply the average individual, where the average is calculated for some particular trait or feature. The average is simply the sum of the particular trait values for a sample of individuals from a population divided by the number of samples (i.e., sample size). Although we often use the average as a description of a typical individual, the average is not real: it is an abstraction and does not exist in nature. The ridiculousness of thinking about something, or someone, as being average is most evident from a joke: "Three statisticians go duck hunting. They see a duck and the first statistician shoots and misses two feet below the duck. The second statistician shoots and misses two feet above the duck. The third statistician leaps up in joy, yelling, 'We got it!' "

What is evident for most traits and populations is that there is a characteristic shape to the distribution of differences among individuals. The average is a measure of the central tendency and the differences depart from the average in a predictable way described as "normal." Recall from the Lewontin quote that "we may define 'normality' as the condition in which no single causal pathway controls the organism." If we collect a large number of individuals and summarize their characteristics, normal emerges as a "bell-shaped" distribution. For example, figure 2.2 shows a histogram that summarizes the trait values—in this case body size—of individuals from a natural population; the average is indicated by a vertical line. The purpose of the average (an abstract representation of an expectation) is that we can use it to compare individuals in a population to an expectation. If the measured trait of an individual is larger than the average, the individual is considered above average; if the measured trait of an individual is smaller than the average, the individual is considered below average. Assessing the effects of genes and environment on the characteristics of individuals stems from asking why individuals are above or below average.

The average is an important summary of aggregated data because it provides a useful way toward understanding why individuals are different. If, for instance, the presence of a particular allele is found in all, or most,

Figure 2.2. A histogram graph of the characteristics of individuals for a sample from a population. The thin vertical dashed line is the average (also referred to as the expected value of a randomly sampled individual). *Source:* Created by the author.

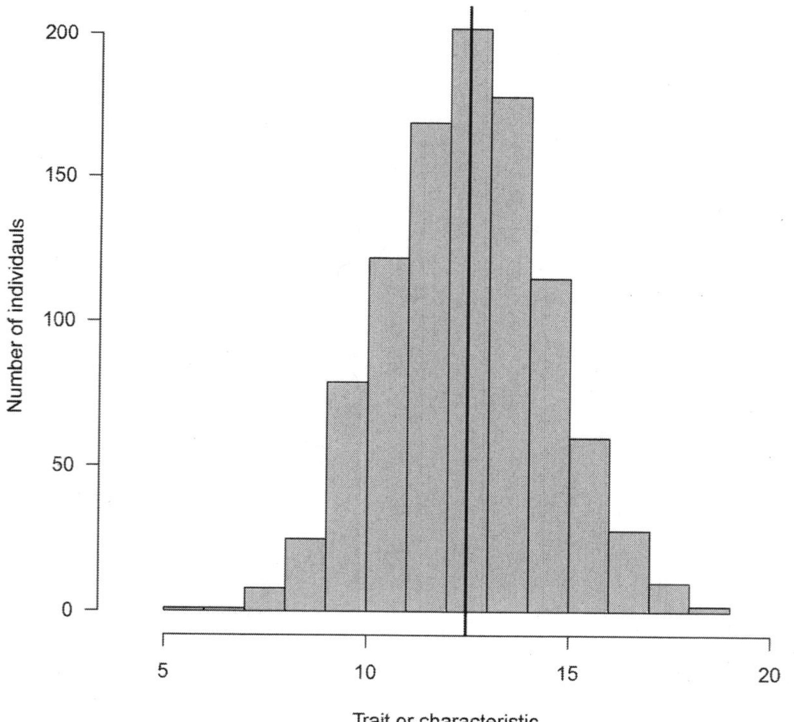

individuals that are above average, it is possible to claim that the allele explains, at least in part, why an individual is above average. This strategy of estimating the effect of particular alleles on the biology of individuals is straightforward and commonly used for understanding the heritable differences among individuals. Heritable differences among individuals are due to the effects of different alleles that exist in different individuals and families as a consequence of ancestry. As figure 2.3 makes clear, the line in the graph indicates we can attribute differences between individuals

Figure 2.3. A bivariate graph showing the dependence of an individual's trait value on their genotype. Each point is an individual. Genotype is represented as the number of A alleles for a two-allele genotype. For this particular case, there are two different alleles (we can refer to them as A and B) and each individual has two alleles because each individual is diploid. Both the A and B alleles have effects on the measured trait. The fact that nearly all of the individuals with at least one A allele are above average (indicated by the dashed horizontal line) indicates the A allele has a strong effect on the measured trait. The slope of the solid line estimates the average effect of the alleles on the trait value of individuals. *Source:* Created by the author.

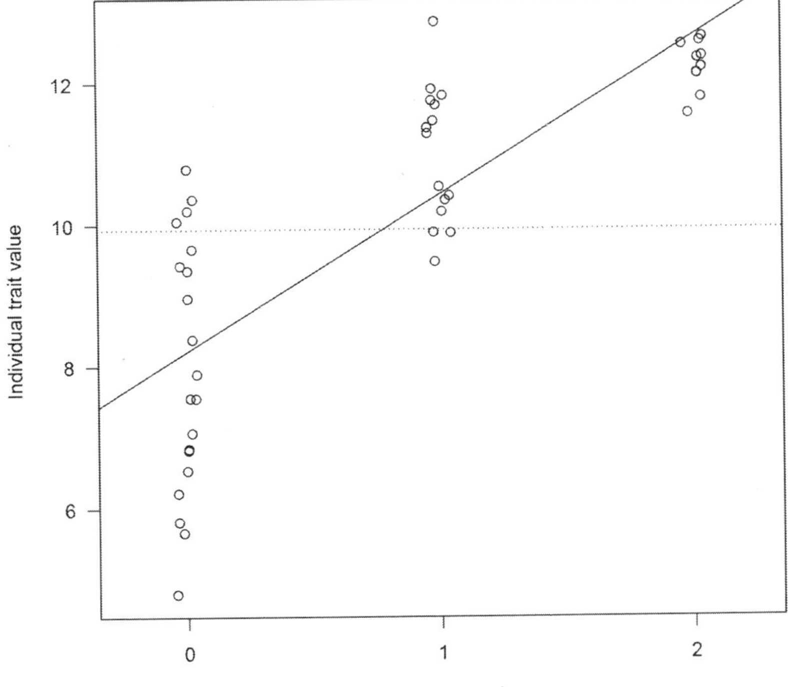

with different alleles to the effects of the alleles and claim genetics matters. What we can't do, however, is use the data to explain all of the variation among individuals, or why some individuals can have different alleles and have the same trait values at the same time differences in alleles explains differences in trait values.

Individuals can be characterized for many different measurable traits, and it is typical that an individual can be above average for one trait and below average for another trait. In fact, on average, each individual in a population will be above average for about half of the measured traits and below average for the other half of the measured traits, assuming the measured traits are independent of each other. Everyone cannot be above average for all traits despite the Lake Wobegon effect—coined by storyteller Garrison Keiller—that describes the tendency for most people to believe that they are above average in intelligence, sense of humor, diving ability, and similar traits (Colman, 2009). We are all above and below average.

A core theme of this book is that individuals differ in their cognitive abilities and these differences matter in ecological and educational contexts. Cognitive ability is a general trait that can be defined by multiple different measures. For instance, studies of general cognitive ability in a type of bird called the southern pied babbler[2] reflects their performance on a variety of different measures of behavior linked to cognition. Soravia et al. (2022, p. 2) measured three different cognitive traits of babblers to gain insight into whether cognitive ability influences an individual's reproduction and its contribution of offspring to future generations. The traits included the ability to "learn predictive contingencies between environmental cues (associative learning), learn new associations when the previous one stops being rewarding (reversal learning), and control prepotent motor response when counterproductive (inhibitory learning)." These three measures can be labeled as learning, changing strategies, and urge control. These three cognitive strategies are also relevant for teaching and learning in education contexts. Soravia et al. (2022) discovered there is variation among individuals in cognitive ability based on the three different measures, and that individuals who exhibited high cognitive function for one trait did not necessarily show high cognitive function for the other traits. The investigation of cognitive ability for individual birds underscores that there is variation among individuals. Moreover, the more traits are measured, the more individual birds become unique entities with unique properties. The idea that an individual is above or below average is context dependent and an abstract representation of an unmeasurable reality. All individuals are above and below average and the average does not exist in nature. This is another reason why focusing on individuals—real organisms with measurable properties—is important.

In addition to the inference that there are differences between individuals due to the combined effects of genes and environment, there is also evidence that an organism can affect the environment. Thus, the environment is not an external thing impinging on individual function, but it is something that individuals can alter based on their actions (Raffard et al., 2017). This issue will emerge in the next chapter when the cognitive niche is introduced. But it should be remembered that organisms, through their actions, influence the environment in which they live, and in which others live. The modifications to the environment can be, on average, beneficial, detrimental, or without consequence in both ecological and educational settings.

The focus on multiple dimensions of babbler cognitive ability is a tip of a giant iceberg of behavioral complexity associated with cognitive ability. There are a large number of different ways of measuring and describing cognitive characteristics of individuals. For example, episodic memory, perceptual speed, processing speed, verbal fluency, working memory capacity, crystallized intelligence, fluid intelligence, executive function, and cognitive control are all descriptors of cognitive characteristics evident in the vast literature about the structure, function, and variation of cognitive ability. Moreover, if we dig into the properties of any one of these categorized cognitive functions, it is clear the characteristics of individuals are emergent outcomes of multiple, interacting processes. For instance, Bunge and Crone (2009, p. 22) wrote that "executive function and cognitive control refer to cognitive processes associated with the control of thought and action" that includes the ability to "selectively attend to relevant information while filtering out distracting information . . . work with information that is currently being held in working memory . . . switch between tasks . . . inhibit inappropriate response tendencies . . . and represent contextual information that determines whether a thought is relevant or whether an action is appropriate." Furthermore, there are aspects of cognitive abilities that intersect with personality, including the traits of being open to experience, experiencing aesthetic sensitivity, being emotionally self-aware and capable of managing emotions, exhibiting a preference (or not) for novelty, being curious and imaginative, conforming to or challenging conventions and expectations, and being introverted or extroverted. All of these dimensions of self have, to varying degrees, neuroanatomical, neurophysiological, and neurochemical correlates influenced by genetics and the environment; some of the factors are listed in the right-hand column of fig. 2.4. And, of course, the dimensionality of cognitive function is much greater than described or imagined. For instance, diet includes what and when people eat (Bellisle, 2004; Economic Research Service, USDA, 2022), environmental toxins include things like lead,[3] sleep refers to whether individuals have predictable and safe places to sleep (Bathory & Tomopoulos, 2017, p. 29; McCoy & Strecker, 2011; Khan & Al-Jahdali, 2023; Owens et al., 2014), digital distraction is the habit of engaging with smartphones (and social media) (Ward et al., 2017; Loh & Kanai, 2015; Wilmer et al., 2019), parental effects include such things as whether they read and tell stories (Bradley et al., 1989) and positively contribute to the social and cultural capital of their offspring (Archer at al., 2015), and so on.

Given the vast complexity of cognition, it should come as no surprise that all individuals are cognitively unique and, moreover, that there is

Figure 2.4. A box-and-arrow model in which a suite of individual variables combined together to form a set of higher-order, mulitivariate variables that all contribute to an individual characteristic labeled cognitive function. *Source:* Created by the author.

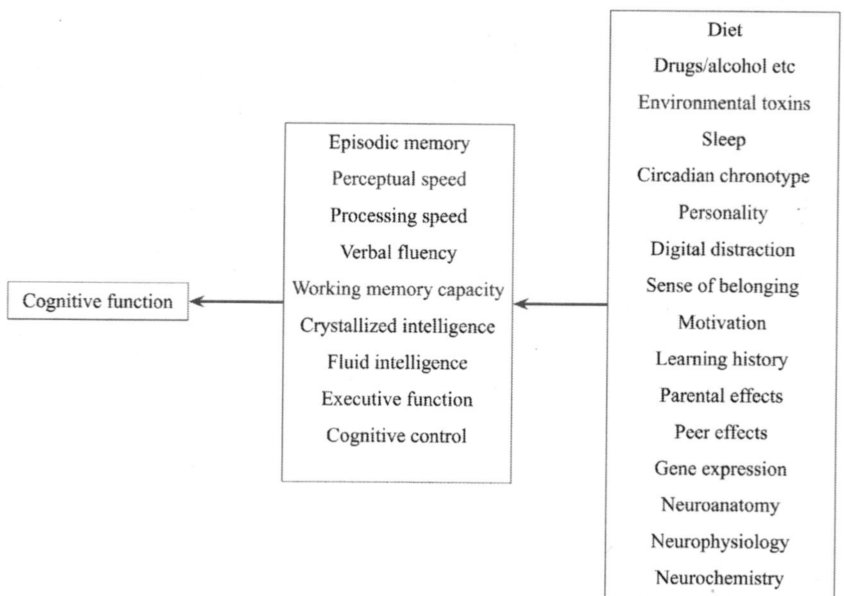

tremendous and often under-appreciated and unknown variation among individuals. For years I had students complete a learning styles survey and every year I discovered the same thing: no matter what axes I used to describe individuals, it was always the case that each individual was unique. This was evident when I plotted scores from one dimension (e.g., whether students were more factual or conceptual) relative to another (e.g., on a continuum from introvert to extrovert). There were no clusters of individuals defined by the two cognitive function axes. For each axis of cognitive variation, the distribution of values resembled the "bell-shaped" curve. The scatterplot of these two dimensions resembled a shotgun blast of points across these two dimensions. The upshot is that everyone is different and some individuals are more unique than others.

The inference that there are genetic influences on cognitive and personality traits in animals does not imply that the differences among individuals are fixed, unchangeable traits. It simply recognizes that some of the variation in cognitive ability among individuals is heritable. The fact that average crystallized and fluid intelligence are positively correlated with amount of education implies that intelligence (and more generally cognitive ability) has a significant learned environmental component. And the ability to learn is a product of both genetically influenced factors and environmental factors, including how frequently teaching and learning happened during an individual's life. In addition to the variation evident among individuals, there is also variation within individuals over time as a consequence of both the effects of genes and the environment. Indeed, most aspects of cognitive function change with age. Increasing age is associated with increases in working memory and fluid intelligence,[4] although the dependence of cognitive ability and age is not linear, but rather parabolic with a plateau instead of a peak.

There is also change of the measurable cognitive properties of individuals over the course of a day due to genetics and the environment. Recent studies have revealed a large number of genes have daily circadian patterns of expression in the brain. With the emergence of light in the morning, there is an increase in the expression of a large number of genes, followed by a decline, a second higher peak later in the day followed by a sustained decline and low levels of expression in the absence of light (fig. 2.5). Note that there is an average (the thick line) but none of the individuals are average; each line, referred to as a chronotype, is unique. If we superimpose scheduled educational activities typical for an institution of higher education like the University of Colorado on the daily

Figure 2.5. Estimated cumulative expression for genes expressed in the brain that exhibit a circadian pattern. The thick black line is the average for many individuals; the thin lines are individuals. Note that there are two peaks during the light hours from 0 to 12 and low levels of expression when there is no light (between 12 and 24 hours). These data suggest there is variation in the genes being expressed in the brain during the course of a day. From Mure et al. (2018). The vertical gray rectangles are times when students might be in class (IC) and when students might do their homework at home (AH) or in some other space. See text for more explanation. *Source:* Created by the author.

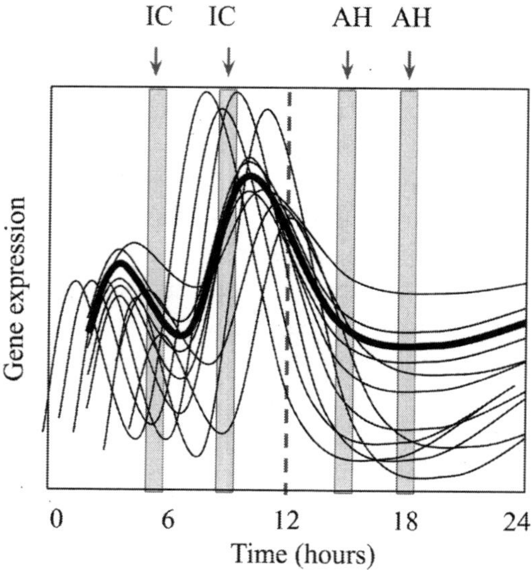

cycles of gene expression in the brain, assuming some of the expression influences cognition, it is likely that gene expression may be declining for some individuals, increasing for other individuals, or at a peak or in a valley for other individuals when a particular event happens. This will be happening whether activities are enacted in the morning or afternoon. If students complete activities designed as homework, expression levels may be low relative to what is happening during the day. This is all to say that we should expect variation among individuals, and also within individuals over time, for emergent outcomes of cognitive ability. One of the things I notice when I teach is when students complete their homework; the time of day is extremely variable.

We might also imagine that profiles of gene expression that influence cognitive ability and personality traits with effects on learning change over time for all students and the changes may be different among students. Some students may be regular and predictable and have low-level fluctuations from hour-to-hour and day-to-day, and others may fluctuate more and perhaps vary wildly depending on the interaction between the inherent properties of individuals and environmental features that trigger or dampen particular behaviors. The expected variation among individuals and within individuals over time is evident from observations of interactions among students working in small groups. Figure 2.6 shows individual trajectories of interactivity for four individuals followed over the course of eight interactive activities during a period of time in class; what stands out is the tremendous amount of variation over time among individuals. We often do not see this variation because seeing it requires allowing students to interact and engage in student-centered learning at the same time educators pay attention to what is happening, including which students are speaking, what they are saying, who is listening, and how long individuals do so. Too often students do not interact, or only

Figure 2.6. The normalized interactivity score of individuals over time during a single semester class. These four individuals represent the range of variation in the mean interactivity—highest (solid line) and lowest (dashed-dotted line) average score over time—and variation in interactivity—highest (dotted line) and lowest (dashed line) interactivity variation over time—from a sample of 30 students working in small groups. *Source:* Created by the author.

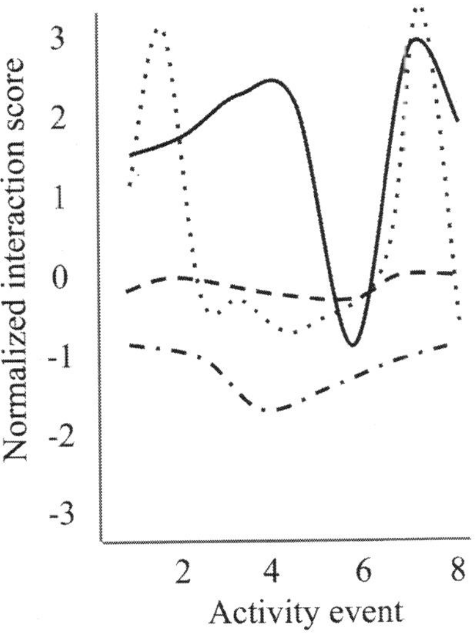

interact for very brief periods of time; too brief for relevant exchange and collaboration.

Schmidt et al. (2007, p. 755) wrote, "Time-of-day modulations affect performance on a wide range of cognitive tasks measuring attentional capacities, executive functioning, and memory. These performance fluctuations are also contingent upon the chronotype, which reflects inter-individual differences in circadian preference, and particularly upon the synchronicity between the individuals' peak periods of circadian arousal and the time of the day" when cognitive performance of individuals is measured or assessed. Additionally, as Dall et al. (2012, p. 1189) pointed out, "not all among-individual variation can be so easily accounted for. One particularly noteworthy form involves behavioural variation among individuals within populations that exceeds the variation expressed by individuals over time or in different contexts. Fundamentally, this is because behaviour has the potential to be very plastic. . . . Moreover, in many cases, such within-population behavioural variation can exceed differences amongst populations in distinct environments." In other words, if we measure an individual's cognitive characteristics today, they may not be the same as yesterday's or tomorrow's measurements. Overall, ecologists and educators, indeed everyone, needs to appreciate the immense capacity for behavioral variation within and among individuals in virtually all aspects of cognitive structure and function that can be imagined and measured, because there are so many variables that make up an individual's cognitive characteristics. This variation plays out every day in ecological and educational contexts.

My goal is not to exhaustively explore the literature about the genetic and environmental effects that cause the variation in cognitive ability among students. My goal is to emphasize that the individual in an ecological setting is very similar to the student in an educational setting: each is influenced by genes and environments, and the ultimate fate of an individual depends on the actions, reactions, and outcomes of daily challenges in a continuously changing environment. Success is measured by survival, growth, maturation, and reproduction in ecological contexts; and by persistence, intellectual growth, and maturation, academic achievement, and gains in social capital in educational contexts. We should expect differences in ability among students, and we should expect that the differences are likely to be larger and more variable across different aspects of cognitive function than standardized testing, grades, or other simple measures of performance might predict.

Ideas as Fundamental Units

Education-relevant synopsis: Ideas are individual units that when connected and assembled into a hierarchical structure constitute knowledge. And like individuals, ideas are born and become part of a community, but can also disappear as a consequence of lack of relevance and importance causing the erosion of knowledge and a decline in cognitive capacity. Connecting ideas with other ideas is more important for creating and maintaining knowledge than "covering the content" of a particular discipline.

Ideas are individual things, like organisms and students are individual things. Ideation theory focuses on the reality and stability of ideas. This brings into focus whether ideas change and if so, whether they change in such a way that they become more closely aligned with an objective reality or not. Many ideas are stable and broadly understood in the same way across multiple individuals, suggesting these ideas exist in the mind and in reality. Ideas can have an abstract and real-world existence. It is also true that ideas in the mind—their abstract existence—may not be evident in nature; they are elements of imagination. Whether an idea is an abstract thing only or ideas exist in the mind in the same way they exist in reality depends on individuals' motivations, perceptions, and understanding of the world in which they live and the meaning of words used to construct an idea.

Carstensen (2011, p. 600) defined an idea "as a web of related elements of meaning." Carstensen further elaborated that uncertainty and complexity characterize the lives of individuals, and, as a consequence, individuals need socially constructed heuristics and interpretive filters that can reduce societal complexity to a level that enables them to act. "These cognitive shortcuts are what the definition refers to as 'elements of meaning' . . . the meaning of an idea does not derive from a stable and coherent core." Instead, the meaning of an idea depends on the particular combination of words used to represent an idea. This perception of ideas suggests ideation is an emergent process. In addition, Carsensten (pp. 602–603) notes "that because people usually want to improve their use of the ideas at their disposal by making them more coherent, more accurate and more relevant to contemporary issues, they often respond selectively to them: they accept some parts of them, modify others and reject still others." Thus, ideas are influenced by transmission from the past to the present in much the same way genes influence individuals. Ideas are also influenced by the cultural environment. One of the fundamental issues underlying the stability and utility of ideas is that they have the property of being able to convey meaning in an uncertain and complex world. Because ideas are dynamic and can vary among individuals and within individuals over time, conceptualizing and delimiting ideas, and characterizing the variation in the properties of ideas among individuals, provides a basis for advancing some general properties of specific ideas useful for the coherency of intelligence. And we might expect the variation of a particular idea increases with its hierarchical level: the more elements that contribute to an idea, the greater the possible variation. I will return to the hierarchically defined "size" of an idea in a moment.

To make ideation more real, like an individual in an ecological setting is real, we can think about the "web of elements of meaning" associated with particularly important ideas in biology. For example, mutation is a real thing in nature and it is also a cognitive construct (an idea). Mutation makes sense in a complex and uncertain world when it is defined, using a set of words, that describes the objective reality of mutation. I might define mutation as a change, by some process, in the sequence of bases that make up the linear sequence of biochemically encoded information in DNA. This is a coherent and widely agreed upon description of mutation. Yet, if I asked students to describe the meaning of mutation (which I often do), they might add information that makes the idea larger—in terms of the number of elements of meaning—than is necessary or sufficient. Commonly, students will refer to mutation as a change in DNA that makes an organism better, or that mutation happens because it was needed for a species to survive. If our goal as educators is to increase the ability of students to make sense in an uncertain and complex world, we should emphasize necessary and sufficient as criteria for delimiting ideas. Necessary is defined, in this context, as the elements essential for a proposition; sufficient is just enough to meet the needs of the proposition. For example, it is necessary to refer to mutation as a change in the sequence of bases in DNA. This is also sufficient because including the elements of linearity, sequence, and biochemically encoded information does not change the core meaning of mutation as a change in the sequence of bases in DNA. Students might be encouraged to include unnecessary elements depending on the context in which the idea is part of making sense of the world. Because ideas are influenced by words, and word choice is influenced by a variety of factors, including connotation, specificity, contextual framing, perspective, metaphor, complexity, and cultural context, we should expect ideas about ecology and evolution, indeed ideas that comprise all scholarly disciplines, to be variable in the minds of students. In fact, it is likely that a single idea, like the idea of mutation, may be different across all students. The variation among students in their particular cognitive construction of ideas is evidence that education is an emergent process.

Size and Hierarchy

Education-relevant synopsis: Ideas are connected to other ideas in a hierarchical structure such that some ideas depend on the existence of other ideas; the size of an idea (like the size of organisms) depends on the number of different ideas on which an idea depends. Recognizing the hierarchical structure of ideas means teaching should focus on explicitly creating the hierarchy and interdependence of ideas. Effective teaching and learning depends on explicit recognition of the size (dependency) of ideas and constructing connections that reveal the size and importance of different ideas.

In any natural area, there are usually many individuals of multiple species that vary in size, body plans, phylogenetic affinities, life cycles, and other ecologically relevant variables. Perhaps the single most relevant difference among individuals of different species or types is body size, mostly because body size is tightly correlated with metabolic rate and metabolic rate predicts many things about the biology of individuals (Brown et al., 2004). In a given population or habitat, body size varies a lot among individuals. This is important, because body size influences the hierarchical position of an individual in the ecological web of interactions referred to as a food chain or trophic structure. In general, larger individuals tend to be higher in the hierarchy of interactions, although there is considerable variation depending on the functional characteristics of individuals (Akin & Winemiller, 2008; Romanuk et al., 2011; Olson et al., 2020). This happens because larger individuals often depend on smaller individuals for sustenance. For example, orca whales eat mostly salmon,[5] salmon eat smaller fish and invertebrates (Duffy et al., 2010), and smaller fish and invertebrates eat even smaller organisms, on down the size-dependent hierarchical food chain. Thus, in ecology, individuals have a place in the hierarchy of nature determined, to a large extent, by their size (fig. 2.7).

Figure 2.7. A generalized hierarchical structure representative of the flow of energy and resources in an ecological system: arrows indicate flow. Each circle represents an individual of a different species, and its size is indicative of average body size. *Source:* Created by the author.

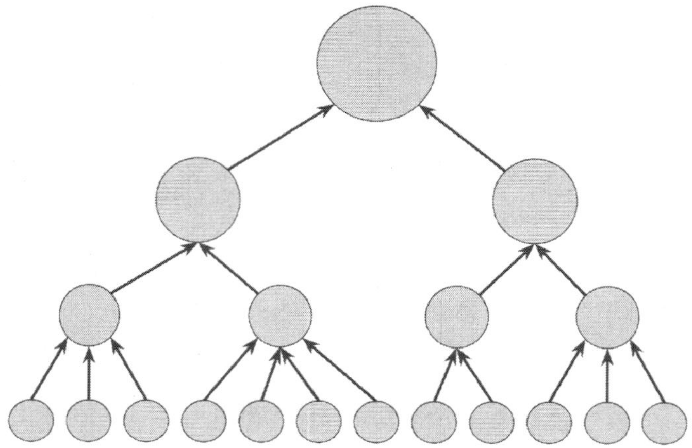

The fact that larger individuals exist at higher hierarchical positions in ecological systems has a parallel in the variation of the size of ideas. Ideas can be simple and small or large and complex. The size of an idea is dependent on the number of ideas that contribute to form another, hierarchically higher idea that has a different meaning from each of its constituent parts. In the education literature, there is emphasis on teaching the "big ideas." It is often the case, though, that big ideas are emphasized without being defined. Twyman and Hockman (2021, p. 803) provided the vague definition that "big ideas are concepts most crucial within a content area; they enable teachers to produce more learning out of less instruction." An even less informative definition is "A big idea is a statement of an idea that is central to . . . learning" (Charles & Carmel, 2005, p. 10). Melanie Cooper's educational research group at Michigan State University has been working on developing big or core ideas in undergraduate chemistry curricula and assessments. A publication from her group espoused that " 'big ideas' will be used in reference to what students stated were take-home messages. The term 'overlapping ideas' will be used to refer to any themes, topics, concepts, ideas, and skills a student might have perceived as a connection between their courses. Finally, 'core ideas' will be used to refer to the list of ideas identified by faculty as being central to their disciplines" (Roche Allred et al., 2022, p. 2). In another paper (Cooper et al., 2017) there is reference to the Next Generation Science Standards that explicitly reference "big ideas" and describe them as being equivalent to anchoring concepts. Cooper et al. (p. 543) noted that a big idea (or anchoring concept) "identifies a set of overarching ideas, typically followed by a hierarchy of ideas that fall underneath the 'big' idea." They provide the following example: "Chemical bonding is a phenomenon that exists because of atomic interactions via electrostatic forces." Immediately below this idea is another idea—what Cooper et al. referred to as "enduring understanding"—that to "break" a chemical bond requires an input of energy. Below this idea is another idea, referred to as a "subdisciplinary articulation": "The energy required to break a chemical bond is the bond dissociation energy." And below this idea are additional, presumably smaller ideas: "Bond dissociation energy is useful at the level of individual molecules; for calculations on macroscopic quantities, the value used is the bond dissociation enthalpy." And "bond dissociation enthalpies can be used to estimate the change in enthalpy for a reaction" (p. 543). The different names (anchoring phenomenon, enduring understanding, subdisciplinary articulation, and content detail) for ideas may be useful, or may add unnecessary cognitive load and confuse what I think is a simple phenomenon: ideas can be of different magnitudes depending on the number of other ideas they are connected to and depend on. This is similar to the idea in ecology that individuals that feed on smaller individuals are larger and occupy a higher level in a hierarchical structure of dependencies. We will revisit this idea in chapter 6.

Cooper et al. (2017) described a big idea (also referred to as a core idea and anchoring phenomenon) in the context of a hierarchical structure. The hierarchical structure is useful because it is representative of an outcome of an emergent process. Cooper et al. constructed the hierarchical branching structure as a strategy for the "construction of assessments [that] involves breaking down core [big] ideas . . . into progressively finer levels of detail" (p. 545). The hierarchical structure of ideas is what I think of as the structure of knowledge. What is useful about this approach is that it provides an explicit definition of a big idea. In this case, a big idea is an idea based on the contribution and interaction of multiple, smaller ideas: the more smaller ideas contribute to a big idea, the bigger the idea. In biology, the size of something is due to the number of parts. For instance, body size of an organism is directly proportional to the number of cells

(Savage et al., 2007). In the case of ideas, the size of an idea is dependent on the number of ideas on which it depends.

I explicitly show students the hierarchical structure of ideas as a map for building knowledge (fig. 2.8).[6] And from structure emerges function. Each idea in the structure requires teaching and learning, as does the process and outcomes of connecting the ideas. Ultimately and ideally what emerges is a structure that reflects the reality that ideas have size and a place in the structure of knowledge. Importantly, different students may have different combinations of ideas that constitute a nested hierarchical basis for a big idea. The analogical inference is that knowledge is organized as a hierarchically nested set of different-sized ideas in the

Figure 2.8. An example of a size-organized hierarchy of ideas giving rise to a big idea about heritable variation. Font size scales with the size of an idea. Big ideas are at the top; small ideas are lower down. The smaller ideas contribute information to the bigger ideas. This hierarchy of ideas provides a template for how to construct knowledge: teach the smaller ideas, connect the smaller ideas to progressively bigger ideas, and create a stable hierarchy of ideas. *Source:* Created by the author.

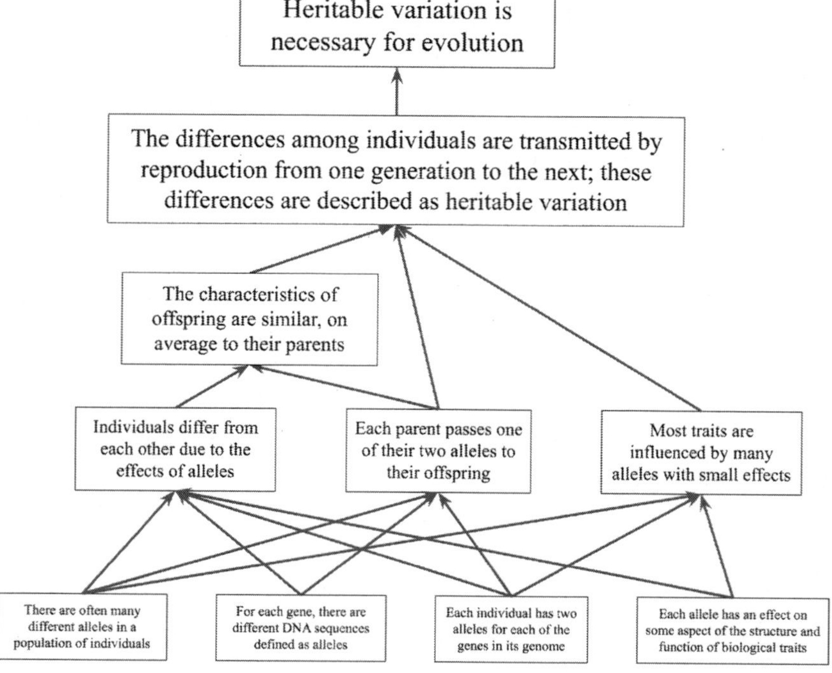

same way ecological systems are organized as a hierarchically nested set of different-sized organisms.

In general, the variation in the size and scope of ideas and their organization into hierarchical structures that form the structure of knowledge provides a natural direction for teaching that mirrors how ecological communities form (see chapter 6). Teaching can begin with the small ideas and build the hierarchy of knowledge by introducing bigger and bigger ideas and making connections such that big ideas are subtended (connected to) many smaller ideas. Intelligence and knowledge stems from connecting instead of collecting ideas. Teaching can also begin with the big ideas and work through connecting progressively smaller ideas that support and are necessary for understanding the big ideas. The point is to enable students to construct the hierarchical structure of ideas that constitutes knowledge. This means providing opportunities for students to create unique and different combinations of connections among ideas, and to evolve their own emergent hierarchical structures of ideas that make the most sense to them.

I introduce ideas and their properties—especially their size—because it is the ideas that are the individual units of thought and intelligence. As a consequence, we need to pay attention to the ideas that make up the big ideas we want our students to learn. If the focus is only on the big ideas—the emergent aggregate of many ideas—we miss the opportunity to construct knowledge that forms the basis for self-efficacy and agency that are necessary parts of educational gain.

Individuals in Heterogeneous Landscapes

Education-relevant synopsis: Students experience very different environments in different disciplines and classes within a discipline; the heterogeneity can have positive outcomes but can also impose stress and cause a decrease in persistence depending on instructor effects. Of particular relevance are density-dependent effects imposed by large class sizes that limit students' access to key resources linked to success, including interpersonal interactions with instructors and opportunities for becoming part of social networks centered in academics.

Individuals that can move across landscapes, whether on legs or wings, encounter different habitats with variable resources, challenges, and dangers.

Individuals have to make decisions about where to be that depend on incomplete information about habitats. Assessing the consequences of individual decisions requires understanding the effects of choices and ignorance (Schmidt & Massol, 2019). Some ecologists assume organisms that move across landscapes have a developing set of probabilities associated with different states of the world. A state of the world might be an area with a stream and a few different tree species of varying heights creating a rich riparian corridor that exists within a matrix of corn fields. Or it might be a continuous forest comprised of many different species. The perceived state of the world provides information. It might be as simple as an internal list of habitat requirements and the individual is "checking boxes" to make decisions. Individuals are assumed to have information and intentionality that manifests as making a decision to be resident in a place for some period of time. This is especially important for making decisions about where to raise offspring.

One model of habitat selection assumes each individual makes the best choice in terms of access to resources and limiting danger. Imagine individuals are colonizing an area—for example, birds arriving to a landscape in spring following the retreat of winter—in which the best sites are occupied first and habitat selection is preemptive such that individuals that take a site prevent others from inhabiting or sharing it. In other words, habitat selection is density-dependent. In this model of the world, the average growth, survival, and reproductive success of individuals is expected to decline with increasing density (Pulliam & Danielson, 1991). In an ideal world, individuals would be able to assess their ability to be successful and they would make a choice about settling in a particular habitat with apparent negative density-dependent effects, or choose to not settle and find somewhere else that may be better. Similarly, the individuals that have already settled may decide to leave after some density is reached with each additional individual that colonizes the site. In this world of effective decision making, the density of individuals would vary depending on resources and dangers. Areas with abundant resources would be expected to have more individuals than areas in which resources are more scarce. Areas with fewer dangers would be expected to have more individuals than areas with more dangers. Thus, we should expect that differences in the growth, maturation, and reproductive success of individuals varies across habitats in direct proportion to resources and inversely proportional with dangers.

In higher education, individuals arrive on a campus in the fall in ways remarkably similar to how birds might arrive in a temperate habitat following the retreat of winter. They settle across a variety of different habitat types defined by discipline based on available information and an internal set of probabilities. Presumably (or ideally), they are "checking boxes" and making decisions that maximize their intellectual growth, maturation, and academic achievement. They also may make choices that maximize some internal set of values related to social capital, including their ability to develop social networks. There are density-dependent effects on academic landscapes. If an individual settles in a habitat that is preferred by many others, and there are already many individuals in the habitat, it is likely they will have limited access to resources because of competition. Alternatively, if an individual settles in a sparsely populated habitat, it may be perceived as dangerous, or lacking in resources, and this may cause them to second guess their decision. There are a variety of ways students generate an internal set of probabilities for acting on available information when making a decision about which of many different habitats to inhabit.

Once in a particular habitat, there are lurking dangers encountered by students. The extent of differentiation between groups inhabiting different scholarly disciplines reflects the topics emphasized and, to varying degrees, limitations on the success of students imposed by instructors and course structures. In one disciplinary department, over a 10-year period, there were 118 different instructors teaching a course that served as a prerequisite for other, higher-level courses. Failure to successfully complete this class means not being able to make progress toward graduation in the next semester. The average DFW proportion[7] across all instructors was approximately 0.33 (1 in 3 students were unsuccessful). There were eight instructors with DFW proportions in the neighborhood of 0.1 (9 out of 10 students were successful), but, alarmingly, there were the same number of instructors with DFW proportions exceeding 0.5 (fewer than 1 out of 2 students was successful). The course enrollments were similar across all instructors and years; thus, the variation in proportion of students unsuccessful was not due to density-dependent effects within each course. While it is possible that the results reflect variation in ability among enrolled students, a more parsimonious explanation is that the differences in success rates of students are best explained by instructor effects. Some instructors are better educators and create more inclusive learning environments than others. Required courses with high DFW probabilities are scattered across the landscape of a student's projected experience like landmines, and they can blow up students' aspirations and schedules of success.

There are also density effects. If a student elects to settle in a habitat with a history of increasing density, each fall they will have access to fewer resources than the individuals in the year before, and, if ecological research is a useful guide, each new cohort of students will grow more slowly, mature later, and achieve less than previous cohorts. For instance, if an individual elects to settle in the discipline population identified as the department of psychology, they will encounter high student to faculty ratios. Between the years of 2020 and 2022, for the 25 highest enrollment courses in this discipline, the minimum class size increased from 70 to 114, and the median class size increased from 118 to 185. Whether it was 2020 or 2022, such large classes limit enacting best-practice pedagogies, like mastery learning (Block & Burns, 1976). Mastery learning was described by Newfield (2016, p. 324) as "teaching [that] adapts to the learning capacities of the students, whatever they are, while also monitoring the progress of each student and giving each student the specific help they need." By contrast, if students had settled in the English academic habitat, between 2020 and 2022 the minimum class size increased from 22 to 28 and the median class size increased from 26 to 31; these are trivially small increases in class size, and the overall class sizes are only a fraction of the enrollments in psychology courses.

I revisit the issue of habitat heterogeneity in the next chapter (focused on the niche). This brief analogy between ecology and education with respect to the heterogeneity of habitats and the choices individuals make underscores that students behave in ways similar to animals in ecological contexts with respect to the phenomena of selecting suitable habitats. And their decisions can have dramatic consequences on the availability of resources and academic achievement. If resources are inversely proportional to the ratio of students to educators, some environments are characterized by abundant and readily available resources, while in other environments, resources are more limited, sometimes much more limited. Thus, we have to assume either that students make decisions based on perceptions of danger or that proximate interests in a particular type of habitat have outsized effects and may be deleterious to individuals' ultimate outcomes measured by academic achievement and the corresponding gain of social capital.

Variation in Survival and Persistence of Individuals

Education-relevant synopsis: Individuals differ in their ability to persist due to a number of different factors. Some differences can be explained by the effect of discipline, which in turn is determined by cultural norms and resource availability. Efforts should be directed toward development of slow-thinking abilities with positive effects that transcend disciplines and increase resilience and persistence.

In ecological settings, individuals are born, live for a period of time, become reproductively mature, and then die. We know this because we can mark individuals and follow their fates over time. If we do this, we discover some individuals live longer than others, some live long enough to reproduce, and some of the individuals that become reproductively mature have more offspring than other individuals. Similar phenomena are playing out in educational settings. We can think of students being "born" into the institution when they enroll and their maturation is complete when they graduate. They can be characterized in a variety of ways. For example, the 2015–2016 cohort of students existed within the CU–Boulder institutional environment for an average of 52 months[8] with a range from 48 or less (44% of students) to more than 120 months (12% of students). If we rank students by the duration of their time in college, and then connect the duration of times across students using a line, we get a picture of the aggregate behaviors of individuals, and we can see that, as in ecological contexts, some individuals persist and exist longer than others. If the data are calculated as the proportion of individuals for a cohort that persist over time, there is an initial early decline in the proportion of individuals that persist until the end of the fourth semester (the second year), a plateau from the fourth to the seventh or eighth semester, followed by a steep decline. This last decline reflects graduation. The decline persists through the fifth and sixth year, and then there is a small tail of survivors that extends past the sixth year.

This picture is similar to many species, including an annual plant studied by Leverich and Levin (1979; fig. 2.9). To make an analogy between ecology and education explicit, I used the graph of survival for an annual plant and replaced the key events (dormancy, germination, growth, flowering, and seed set) with key events in the life of a student (decision to go to college, enrollment, choice of disciplinary focus, maturation, and graduation). The point of the parallel visualizations is that there is variation

Figure 2.9. Left: A graph showing the dependence of survival over time for an annual plant (modified from Leverich & Levin, 1979). Right: The same graph for student persistence from their conception of attending a particular college to graduation. Note that I put one key value on the y-axis scale indicated by the solid horizontal line: the proportion of individuals in the US with a bachelor degree (Schaeffer, 2022). Note the y-axis is on a logarithmic scale. The drop in persistence has a similar shape to the drop in survival for an annual plant (Venezia & Jaeger, 2013; Roderick et al., 2011; Smith, 2004). *Source:* Created by the author.

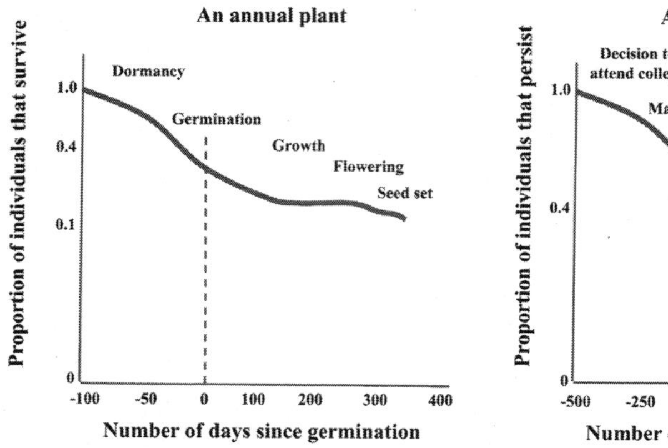

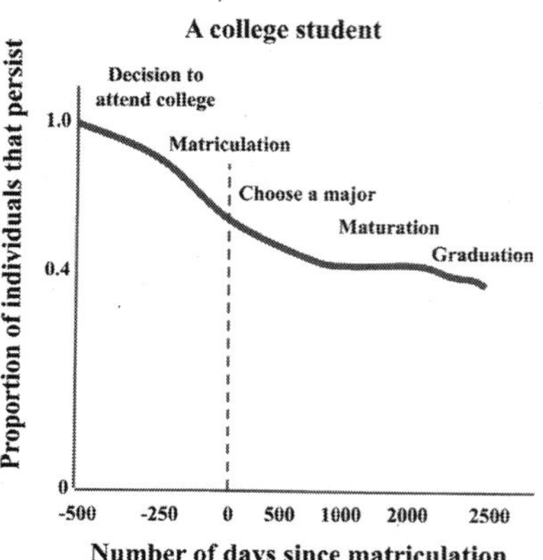

in persistence among students. And the issue of persistence begins well before they arrive on campus in the same way the survival and eventual success of an individual plant begins well before germination because a seed in the soil may succumb to innumerable sources of destruction. Surveys of high school seniors revealed barriers related to finances were the most prominent reasons for not attending college. And college plans of nonwhite individuals were more likely replaced by getting a job or joining the military than for white students (Jimenez, 2011). Additionally, the socioeconomic status and high school experiences of individuals predicted students' perceived likelihood of attending (King, 2013). Hahn and Price (2008, p. 6) wrote, "Despite the increasing importance of higher education, students who are academically qualified for college still face numerous barriers to college enrollment. These barriers range from insufficient financial aid to mixed messages about academic preparation, poor understanding of admission and financial aid application processes, and limited community encouragement." Because the value of college has significant positive effects on social capital,[9] there needs to be a renewed emphasis on making it more accessible and achievable.

"According to the US department of education, only 20 percent of young people who begin their higher education at two-year institutions graduate within three years. There is a similar pattern in four-year institutions, where about 4 in 10 students receive a degree within six years. And these bleak statistics on national college completion rates are averages. In some institutions, the numbers are even gloomier" (Johnson & Rochkind, 2009, p. 2). A variety of factors conspire in ways the limit persistence, including, but not limited to, the challenges of students having to work at least 20 hours a week while attending school, living away from campus that requires commuting, caring for children or other family members, inability to afford education that accompanies the cumulative debt that increases over time, and a lack of sense that the experience is worth the cost (Johnson & Rochkind, 2009). Belkin (2021) reported in the *Wall Street Journal* that "many young men who dropped out of college said they worried about their future but nonetheless quit school with no plan in mind. . . . 'I'm sort of waiting for a light to come on so I figure out what to do next.' " It may be that many men share a similar disillusionment about higher education and academic achievement, because graduation rates for men have been declining over time and their success is eclipsed by the greater success of women. In the US, the percentages of men and women aged 25–34 with a bachelor degree were 20 and 12 in 1970, respectively; today the numbers are 36 and 46, respectively (Parker, 2021). The increases, especially for women, are encouraging; the increasing disparity is worrying. In my disciplinary department, women outnumber men three to two, and the graduation rates after six years since enrollments are 38% higher for women than for men.

In ecological settings, the particular shape of the probability of survival over time depends on the investment of resources by the parents into each offspring, the particular properties of each individual, the variability of the environment, and the interactions of developing individuals with other individuals. There are three distinct patterns when the probability of an individual's survival is plotted relative to time ("Survivorship Curve," n.d.). A type 1 survival curve is characterized by high survival early in life and a drop in survival later in life after maturation and reproduction due to senescence. This curve reflects a strategy of producing few offspring and high parental investment in offspring development early in life; this strategy describes humans and many other species of mammals. By contrast, some species produce many eggs and then leave them alone to fend for themselves armed only with instinct. Not surprisingly, for frogs, and other taxa with similar parental investment profiles, many individuals in early development become food for other individuals. This type 3 survival curve is characterized by a steep drop early in life followed by a gradual increase in the probability of survival as individuals become larger and more adept at escaping predators and finding safe places for foraging, maturation, and reproduction. The difference between success early in life depends on the amount of resources invested in offspring.

We can find similar differences among students inhabiting different disciplinary environments. Figure 2.10 shows the probability of persistence based on multiple cohorts of individuals in two different environments. In both environments, there is an initial drop in persistence following the first time interval, decidedly unlike the case for a type 1 survivorship profile characteristics of humans. The biggest difference between the two environments is the drop in persistence after the second semester (first year). This comparison underscores the effect of the environment on persistence and may indicate a need for greater attention to the allocation of resources. Perhaps resource allocation should be age-structured such that intellectually younger and less experienced students early in their development receive proportionally more resources, on average, than more mature students. In other words, education environments should be creating the conditions emulating what humans do, on average, when they care for

Figure 2.10. Proportion of students persisting in two different environments (disciplinary departments) over the seven semesters (prior to students graduating) based on data from multiple cohorts. Lines are averages. The two environments are both biological disciplines. *Source:* Created by the author.

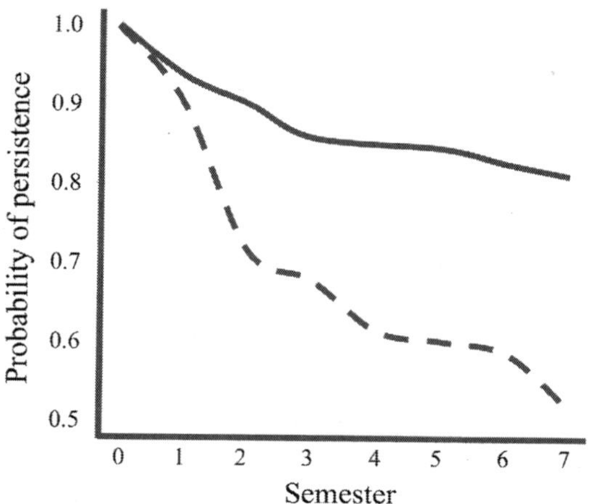

their developing offspring (following the type 1 survivorship curve). One of the anonymous reviewers of this book noted there are efforts toward allocating resources specifically focused on first-year student orientation and transition in the co-curriculum (orientation, first-year programming, residence life live on requirements, meal plans, etc.) and curriculum (first-year experiences courses, faculty mentors/coaches for first-year students, etc.). At the same time, however, there is a continuing emphasis on large class sizes for many first- and second-year courses, especially in the natural and social sciences. These environments fail to develop students' sense of belonging in their chosen discipline. Importantly, the value of large class sizes primarily experienced during early academic development is wholly financial and not pedagogical or personal. Moreover, the tuition resources flow mostly to the institution, away from the disciplinary population where education is happening rather than staying and supporting the students, classrooms, and faculty where tuition revenue is being generated.

There are also clear effects of the properties of individuals on their survival and persistence in ecological settings. Figure 2.11 shows an example of negative density-dependent survival for two different functional

Figure 2.11. Predicted effects of density on the probability of survival for slow (solid line) and fast (dashed line) growing trees. Modified Zhu et al. (2018). The same graph applies to slow-thinking (solid line) and fast-thinking (dashed line) students. *Source:* Created by the author.

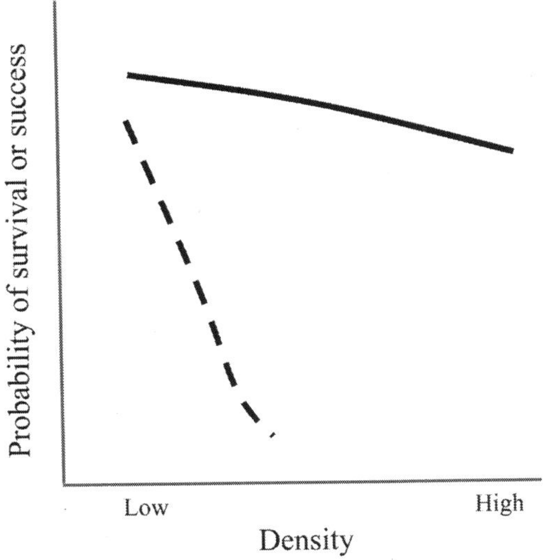

types of young trees (saplings). For both types of trees, the predicted probability of survival of a young tree decreases with increasing density of individuals of the same species. Importantly, though, different tree characteristics strongly influence the magnitude of the density-dependent effects. In this case, slow growing trees survive better—are less influenced by the presence of other individuals—than fast growing trees. I include this example because there are two modes of thinking—slow thinking and fast thinking (Kahneman, 2011)—that are similar in many ways to slow and fast growing. Slow thinking is deliberate, rational, and analytic; results in less bias and error; requires time and energy; and is successful across many different contexts. By contrast, fast thinking is impulsive and intuitive, uses shortcuts and heuristics, is often biased and error-prone, requires little time and energy, and is often only successful in a very restricted set of contexts. We might hypothesize, based on the evidence from nature, that students who routinely engage in slow-thinking strategies have more educational success—measured as the gain in intellectual maturation, academic achievement, and social capital—than individuals who routinely use fast-thinking strategies; moreover, the success of slow-thinking is expected to be evident across diverse academic contexts that vary in density. As emphasized earlier, most of learning, and how our cognitive processes work, reflects the effects of environment and experiences. We can train students to become slow thinkers. In doing so, we imagine that they can achieve the habitus of a slow growing tree and have characteristics measured as persistence in the face of whatever challenges happen.

One way of assessing the effects of the environment on individual performance is evaluated using use of common garden experiments. The experiment involves moving multiple individuals, either as seeds or young individuals, from their unique home environments into a different environment and following the fates of individuals, including growth rate, survival and reproductive success. Differential success among individuals reveals the degree of mismatch between individuals' abilities and the prevailing environmental features (Colautti et al., 2009). In plants, for instance, individuals born and living at elevations higher or lower than their parents are, on average, less productive (Ishizuka & Goto, 2011). Similar results have emerged from numerous common garden experiments across multiple predictive variables of organismal function. In general, individuals are better in their home environments than in a novel common environment. This pattern may explain the saying "Home is where the heart is" and the phenomenon is a consequence of local adaptation. If an individual is successful in a given environment, it is likely the individual benefitted from adaptation of its ancestors over many generations in the same, or a similar, environment. Move away from "home," and the world is more challenging, because the prevailing environment is different and the strategies honed by evolution over generations do not work as well as they do at home.

The discovery that individuals in ecological contexts do best in a set of conditions in which their parents were successful suggests we should see an effect of parental traits on student success in college.[10] College is a giant common garden experiment; individuals (students) come from many different home contexts and begin a new life of growth, maturation, and achievement in a new environment. The effects of local cultural adaptation may be evident in two ways. First, students whose parents successfully completed college are more likely to complete college. Second, students are expected to pursue fields of study that align with their prior interests and strengths, and both prior interests and strengths are affected by an individual's local (home) conditions. Given the pervasiveness of local adaptation in nature, it's not surprising both of these predictions are evident for educational contexts. There is a detectable and strong correlation between the educational attainment of parents and their offspring (Yazedjian et al., 2009; Turcotte, 2011). Additionally, a number of studies have revealed the best predictor of students' choice of disciplinary emphasis in college is prior interest and strengths (Malgwi et al., 2010; Beggs et al., 2008). Prior interest is strongly influenced by the characteristics of an individual's home life, especially parent interests (Kahl, 1953; Goodale & Hall, 1976), although the effect of parents on a students' choice of disciplinary training is more evident for males than females (Goodale & Hall, 1976). The picture is most clear for students electing to pursue a science, technology, engineering, or mathematics (STEM) discipline; of the various factors included when predicting student choice of STEM major (including income, parents education, high school GPA, and ethnicity), the best predictors were whether or not the parents' occupation was in a STEM discipline and whether the student was female or not (Moakler & Kim, 2014). If we think about parents' STEM achievement as an exclusive form of professional (Archer et al., 2015) and cultural capital (Bourdieu, 2020), the parental effects on student trajectory has the effect of promoting the generational accumulation of capital. The value of referencing cultural capital is its explicit recognition of resources inequity among individuals, underscoring the pervasiveness and depth of environmental effects on education.

What general inferences about education can we gain from the apparent evidence of the positive effect of home conditions on student success in college? Importantly, the data suggest conditions on college campuses may be more similar to the home conditions of families in which the parents successfully completed college. First-generation students may be at a disadvantage as a consequence of unfamiliar environmental conditions or expectations. Additionally, the discovery that students are choosing a discipline similar to their local (parental) environment suggests there are limited opportunities and incentives for students to explore alternative disciplines, presumably because of the pressure to complete a set number of courses within a discipline in order to receive a diploma. Also, first-generation students may not have any context from which to make choices of a suitable academic discipline. Evidence that cultural adaptation affects success on college campuses underscores the value of recognizing environmental and social pressures and intervening in ways that limit the challenges students face when they arrive on campuses without career or academic interest convictions. These inferences are not new. However, we can turn to ecological literature for revealing successful strategies for establishing individuals in novel environments. What makes individuals in ecological contexts better able to succeed than others? Can we apply some of the lessons from ecological success to educational contexts? The answer is yes and yes, and one of the main axes explaining variation in success depends on a students' sense of belonging.

Sense of Belonging and Success

Education-relevant synopsis: A key factor predicting student success is sense of belonging. Greater sense of belonging is associated with the development of a students' sense of an academic home. There needs to be a greater emphasis on developing a students' home range through deliberately creating opportunities for positive and productive interactions and creating safe places that span courses within a discipline and across disciplines.

Animals that are mobile with well-developed brains—think terrestrial vertebrates, especially birds and mammals—typically exist within a defined area described as a home range. The home range encompasses spatially distributed resources, including shelter and food, and predation risks that influence an individual's growth, survival, and reproductive success. An individual's home range is determined by tracking an individual, ideally throughout its life, and defining the limits of the geography it inhabits. In general, an individual that lives within its home range has a higher growth rate and a higher probability of survival, and is, as a consequence, more successful than individuals that leave their home range. Additionally, when mobile animals leave their home range, they experience elevated stress detectable by monitoring circulating hormone levels (Wingfield et al., 1997). And increased stress is never a good sign. One consequence of elevated stress is reduced capacity for immunity (Herbert & Cohen, 1993) and diminished cognitive function (McEwen & Sapolsky, 1995). And perhaps more viscerally, the probability of mortality increases. In deer, for instance, the probability of survival is about 40% greater if they remain in their home range than if they leave familiar areas, mainly due to predation by mountain lions (Forrester et al., 2015). There is evidence of decreased survival of humans when forcibly moved[11] away from their ancestrally defined home range (Becker & Ferrara, 2019). Even in plants, the effect of leaving home is negative; as a gardener, I know that not all plants survive being transplanted from the nursery or moved from one place to another in the garden.

Home ranges may also exist for individuals on college campuses. If students develop a home range, it is likely accompanied by a greater sense of belonging. A student's sense of belonging, of being within their "home range," is positively related to social and psychological well-being, a sense of safety through actions demonstrating support and caring, the development of self-efficacy and confidence in academic settings, and the development of a learning and friendship-based community through repeated interactions. All of these emergent behaviors are dependent on an underlying physiological state modulated by the abundance of circulating hormones. The inference, based on analogy with ecology, is that students—like other mobile and intelligent mammals—establish a home range and, once established, develop a greater sense of belonging, and this translates into greater success, including greater academic achievement, retention, and persistence (Pittman & Richmond, 2007; Hausmann et al., 2007; Thomas, 2012; Knekta et al., 2020).

There is considerable variation among students in their sense of belonging. There are likely many reasons for the variation. The first depends on the amount of time an individual has spent in the new environment. It is important to remember that students were voluntary migrants into the higher education environment from a place where they had established a home range. Mann (2001) argued most students entering the new world of "the academy" are in an equivalent position to travelers crossing the border into a new country and discovering barriers to entry and establishment. Moreover, students entering college face a plethora of new demands that act as stressors, including, but not limited to, learning how to cook, grocery shopping and other pedestrian activities associated with maintaining individual health and well-being, dealing with legal and financial issues, living with unrelated individuals, and engaging in time management. Sladek et al. (2016, p. 8) wrote that "daily stressors have been linked to poor physical and psychological health among college students, who report notably poor sleep, increased alcohol use, and concerning rates of suicidal ideation. . . . Adolescents' psychological responses to stress (e.g., coping skills) influence physiological stress reactivity and also predict well-being."

Based on the ecological home range literature, we might expect that the longer a person persists at a particular institution, the greater their sense of belonging. While there is an abundance of data about sense of belonging from surveys of first-year students, there are few data for evaluating the expectation that students' sense of belonging changes with time. Moreover, the data that do exist suggest there is no change (Ruedas-Gracia et al., 2023) or that the sense of belonging declines over time (Hausmann et al., 2007). What is clearly evident, though, are large differences among students in their sense of belonging. In addition to student effects, Knekta and McCartney (2021) discovered that class size matters for developing a sense of belonging; smaller classes allowed students to develop better connections with each other and their instructor. Additionally, an experimental study revealed greater physiological and psychological stress reactions of educators in classes with larger enrollments (Huang et al., 2022). Again, there are parallels with ecology. Stress is a density-dependent phenomenon: higher density is associated with higher circulating stress hormones in animals (Creel et al., 2013).

Of all the variables that impinge on sense of belonging, "students' background characteristics and college experiences explained 57.7% of the variance in students' sense of belonging to their respective college campus" (Cole et al., 2017, p. 1). "Background characteristics and college experiences" are vague and multivariate categories, but are suggestive of the effects of variation in social capital among individuals, in addition to other factors. One obvious example is the effect of race. Students at

CU–Boulder are predominantly white, and the campus is situated in a predominantly white community. This means that a white student leaving home and settling in a mostly white community probably feels more at home than a Black student leaving home and settling in a mostly white community. This difference, in turn, may influence whether individuals show up to take high-stakes exams or not. Although there are many reasons for students to not show up and take exams, evidence for an effect of race suggests there may be less of a sense of belonging for Black than white students at CU–Boulder.[12]

There are other factors at play as well, some of which may reflect the challenges students face when living away from home, often in settings with unrelated people with very different habits and expectations, and in situations in which access to good nutrition, sufficient sleep and regular exercise, and other life attributes positively correlated with good mental and physical health are limited or difficult. The issue of mental health may be particularly relevant. The current state of college student mental health is frequently labeled a "crisis," as the demand for services and severity of symptoms have appeared to increase in recent decades. The nation-wide Healthy Minds Survey of 90,000 undergraduates revealed that

> 44 percent of students reported symptoms of depression; 37 percent said they experienced anxiety; and 15 percent said they were considering suicide—the highest rate in the 15-year history of the survey. . . . The depth of these mental-health issues has become so severe that it's affecting college students' ability to persevere in their studies. Four in 10 college students have recently considered withdrawing from college, a study released last week shows. And the number-one reason why? "Emotional stress." Emotional stress was cited by 69 percent of bachelor's degree students and 55 percent of community college students. . . . The second biggest reason was "personal mental health reasons" (59 and 44 percent of bachelor's- and associate's-degree seekers, respectively), followed by "the cost of the degree program" (36 and 25 percent). When asked what emotional stress means to them, many students told researchers that coursework can be overwhelming, especially in combination with jobs or caregiving duties. Some mentioned depression and anxiety, or concerns about paying for college. The report found that, on average, community college students were more

likely than bachelor's degree students to say they were thinking about withdrawing or taking a break from school because of those problems. (Xiao et al., 2017, p. 407)

Student-reported sense of belonging in academic environments suggests institutions of higher education do not invest sufficiently in creating the conditions that foster students' establishing a "home range" and the emergence of a sense of belonging in academic settings. The problem is multidimensional, emergent, and persistent, and despite recognition of the problem, little has changed in how we do what we do to foster a sense of belonging within the university. Paying attention, as our leadership does, to aggregate statistics as a measure of how well we are doing paves over the multitude of problems and the decline in academic achievement on campuses due to the inability for students to feel "at home." As a real example of the disconnect between aggregate and individual perspective, the provost of our university recently communicated the following perceived successes in an institution-wide email on April 25, 2023: a 6.1% increase in first-year retention; a 7.3 increase in enrollment; and a 4% increase in sponsored research funding, an "all-time record." These are all, not surprisingly, financial indicators. However, unreported aggregate statistics include an all-time record of inequity in pay among faculty, an all-time record for the average class size, an all-time record for the number of students unable to register for a class they needed for graduation, and an all-time record for the number of classes that could not be scheduled in a suitable room with adequate space. My point is that there are many axes of institutional function, and the choices of indices we make influences our perceptions of purpose and success. Our purpose, in turn, influences how we allocate valuable resources, like time, energy, money, and intellectual effort. I pay attention to indices of achievement, affective status, and health and well-being. If the indices are positive, it is likely the indices the provost pays attention to and advertises will also be positive. But from where I sit in the world I inhabit, an emphasis on increasing financial resources without adequately allocating these financial resources in support of education suggests the provost and I live in different worlds with different values. These numbers betray the purpose of higher education as a common good that elevates the social capital of students. In fact, there is good evidence that the increase in density accompanying the increase in enrollment will erode the students' sense of belonging and decrease their ability to feel at home. Both outcomes undermine the values inherent in higher education as a public good.

Variation in the Persistence of Ideas

Education-relevant synopsis: The persistence of ideas varies over time. The loss of ideas reflects perceptions that some ideas have little or no value. Knowledge is lost piece-by-piece and the loss of one idea can accelerate the loss of other connected ideas. Knowledge is easily destroyed, because it depends on the connection among many different ideas. Teaching needs to pay much more attention to maintaining knowledge structures through making connections. Connecting ideas improves their persistence and increases the resilience of knowledge.

Individuals in ecological contexts are born, live for a period of time, and then die. The expected longevity of an individual depends on its biological properties, especially its size and its ability to secure sufficient resources for growth and maturation (Calder, 1983). Longevity is an emergent outcome of age-dependent mortality. It also matters if mortality is random (meaning that all individuals have the same probability of mortality regardless of their condition) or if mortality depends on an individual's condition (Chen & Maklakov, 2012). Some environments favor greater longevity than others (Scharf et al., 2015), and condition is influenced by diet and genetics. There is also a causal dependence of longevity and the investment of individuals in self-maintenance: longer-lived individuals invest more in maintaining biological structures and the integrity of function. Interestingly, individuals of a given species that invest more in maintenance are less susceptible to the negative effects of stress (Kirkwood et al., 2000). In addition to the dependence of longevity on functional properties of individuals, individuals can thrive or perish depending on their ties to other individuals. When individuals are born, for many species, they exist in a world of alliances and enemies. Beneficial alliances can improve an individual's chance of success—of survival and reproduction—and the enduring effect is the presence of similar (or identical) individuals across time (generations) and space (habitat spaces). Enemies can cause dysfunction and disablement, reduce the quality of life, and increase the probability of death.

Like individuals in ecological contexts, ideas have lives. They are born in the mind, persist for some period of time and eventually perish from passive memory loss or some active process of deletion. Like individuals, there are boundaries and internal consistency. Ideas exist in a world of positive associations and competition. Good ideas improve an individual's understanding of the world, strengthen ties to existing ideas, and form the basis for developing a better operational model of the world that contributes to making better decisions. Bad ideas can compromise an individual's capacity for achievement, weaken ties to other ideas, and erode the ability to make good decisions. Ultimately, the persistence of ideas depends on their positive value measured by their contribution toward understanding and making accurate predictions about the world from incomplete data. And, like individuals, ideas have a lifespan, because maintaining ideas in the mind in a functional form requires energy and diligence, resources often in short supply.

There is, I suspect, more memory loss than educators realize. I regularly repeat assessments over the course of a semester to assess the gain and loss of key ideas over time. Every time I implement successive assessments over a period of time, I discover a general and consistent pattern in the gain and loss of ideas. One example comes from following the fate of ideas that form the basis of knowledge about uncertainty. My assessment question asks students to "construct a visualization showing error in the estimate of the mean of a population and use your visualization to explain why we can never know the truth (the true parameter value) from a sample of a population." Each idea evident in student thinking is evaluated as being present or not based on a simple rubric. Among the key ideas necessary for understanding uncertainty, I focused attention on five: (1) there is always random sampling error, (2) there can be systematic error (bias) if sampling is not random, (3) random sampling error is not biased because the average of multiple estimates of the mean is statistically indistinguishable from the true mean, (4) systematic error results in estimates of the mean that tend to be scattered on one side or the other of the true mean such that the average of the means is far from the true mean relative to random sampling error, and (5) students should know that uncertainty due to error will be larger for biased sampling because it includes both random and systematic error. The presence of these ideas in the minds of students was assessed prior to teaching and learning (assessment 0), immediately after students had worked on sampling and visualizing the results of sampling (assessment 1), the week after doing the work as part of a review (assessment 2), and at the end of class as part of the final exam (assessment 3). During the time students were engaged in investigating error and creating graphs, about half of the students were able to articulate the ideas above; however, there was a consistent decay of these ideas such that by the end of the course only about 15% of students could articulate these ideas, even though the two sources of error were emphasized throughout the course.

I failed in my task to effectively educate students about the role of sampling on uncertainty. These results were a wake-up call. First, despite students being asked to read about uncertainty and understand the effects of random and systematic sampling error, engage in the process of estimating means under three different sampling regimes, and construct visualizations of the data as part of making sense of error and uncertainty associated with estimating properties of populations, less than half of the students showed evidence that key ideas were present and secure in their minds. Second, while the ideas were present for a brief period of time for some of the students, the ideas were gone from most of the students by the end of the semester despite the fact that uncertainty was a main, overarching, and big idea and formed part of every week's discussion. I realized, too late, that students were not learning how to effectively think about uncertainty and did not understand the connection between error and uncertainty. The increase followed by a decrease in the presence of key ideas in the minds of students is something I see frequently across different disciplinary contexts. Conversations with students revealed they were trying to remember different ideas about error and uncertainty as isolated elements rather than as a connected set of ideas constituting knowledge of a topic. My favorite metaphor for learning described by Melanie Cooper is that we often provide students with a pile of bricks; each brick is an idea and each idea is piled up. And we expect that by providing the bricks, they can build a functional building. Melanie showed a picture of the Taj Mahal to emphasize we often expected amazing things from our students. Most of the time when we assess students, they are left looking for a specific brick in a pile of what appears to them as identical bricks.

This humped-shape trajectory of new ideas in the minds of students is common. Ideas in the mind are born, they stay alive for a while, and they eventually die from memory loss associated with a student-perceived lack of real-world relevance. Another way to think about ideas is that they have a half-life. In the science literature, a half-life is a measure of the amount of time it takes for the elimination of a substance by some process of decay. In physics, unstable elements have a half-life determined by the rate of radioactive decay. In medicine, the half-life of a drug is influenced by its chemical structure and an individual's metabolism. Knowledge is thought to have a half-life: the half-life of knowledge is proportional to its value (Knudsen & Lien, 2023). For undergraduates, it may be that most knowledge has a low half-life; knowledge decays quickly because of its low apparent value beyond the exam or course. What I may be detecting is the short half-life of knowledge because students assign little or no value to thinking like a scientist and a lack of coherency across a disciplinary curriculum favors decay rather than active persistence. We know from analysis of diet that different items decay at different rates (have different half-lives) because some things are more digestible than others and that differences among diet items influence individual function and condition (Greenstone et al., 2014). Does knowledge that is difficult to learn have a longer half-life than things that are simple to learn? Or is the half-life predictable based on students' sense of the value of an idea? If so, successful teaching and learning will only happen if students care about what they are learning. For a teacher, there may need to be more emphasis on establishing the value of knowing, and following up by paying attention to the persistence of ideas over time.

Chapter 3

The Niche

Defining the Niche

Education-relevant synopsis: The concept of the niche has broad relevance for educational environments, because each individual functions differently, and with different success, in the varied learning environments encountered in an institution of higher education. The niche of a student is an "n-dimensional hypervolume," a complicated way of saying that there are many dimensions of a student's educational niche. Some environments are inhospitable and some environments are optimal for maturation, depending on the particular traits of individuals. Although niches are often properties attributed to populations or species, the niche is an outcome of an individual's capacity to function within a particular combination of environment and interaction variables within a particular discipline or course.

The original definition of a *niche* was a specific place for the display of a decorative object; more generally, it refers to a place or position that is particularly appropriate for the existence of something or someone. Ecology co-opted the "place . . . that is particularly appropriate for . . . existence" definition. In particular, Hutchinson (1957, p. 195) was very explicit. He developed the idea that there is a large number of variables that influence whether an individual can persist and thrive in a particular environment, and he defined the niche as a "n-dimensional hypervolume . . . which would permit . . . 'a particular' . . . species S_1 to exist."

In this context, the term niche refers to the match between, on the one hand, the resources an individual needs for growth and maturation and, on the other hand, the prevailing environmental conditions and the spatial and temporal availability of the resources. Hutchinson (1957) emphasized the covariation between the needs of individuals of a species and the availability of necessary resources across many dimensions. Thus, the niche is an emergent outcome of the needs of individuals in a varied world of fluctuating and spatially heterogeneous resources. Notably, there are many variables that define Hutchinson's "n-dimensional hypervolume" of an individual's niche.

The idea of the niche has flourished in the education literature. Much of the discussion has focused on the business of education. Its use is similar to the Hutchinsonian perspective of delimiting entities in terms of their properties in relation to environmental variables. Thus, there is an e-learning graduate certificate program in the US that has a niche distinct from other training programs (Van Rooij & Lemp, 2010). Popielarz and McPherson (1995) described niche edge and niche overlap hypotheses as a basis for validating the existence of competition as an explanation for the emergence of distinct groups in educational contexts. In their article "Race and Reform: Educational "Niche Picking" in a Hostile Environment," Hubbard and Mehan (1999) described how racism is one of the environmental factors that defines where students exist—their niche—in academic settings. The educational niche as a genetically based trait has made its way into the scholarly record. For instance, Oda (2021) asserted that "even if there is a genetic cost to transmitting norms of reciprocity through education, active teaching of the norms can evolve if a niche of reciprocal relationships is constructed as a result." In the hundreds of thousands of scholarly articles espousing the value of recognizing niches in social contexts, by far the most common approach is to describe the educational niche in the competitive world in which education is a commodity. Niche differentiation is considered to be essential for the success of educational entities. I am not particularly interested in the niche space of educational organizations (see also Hannan & Freeman, 1977); this is an area of scholarly work that can use more grounding in ecological theory and empirical data. In this book, I am more interested in the individual and the inhabited educational environment.

From the perspective of students, the Hutchinsonian perspective works. To make this explicit, I use his language with judicious word replacement (in brackets):

Consider two independent environmental variables x_1 and x_2 that characterize an [educational] setting. Let the limiting values permitting a [student to intellectually mature and achieve educational goals] be, respectively, x'_1 and x'_1 for x_1 and x'_2 and x''_2 for x_2. A place thus defined, each point . . . corresponds to a possible environmental state permitting the [student to exist indefinitely]. . . . We may regard this area as a rectangle . . . [or] whatever the shape of its sides. . . . Now introduce another variable x_3 and obtain a volume, and then further variables $x_4, \ldots, x_n$ until all of the [educational] factors relative to S_1 have been considered. In this way an n-dimensional hypervolume is defined which would permit the [student S_1 to intellectually mature and achieve educational goals]. (Hutchinson, 1957, p. 416)[1]

In Hutchinson's words, the niche of a student is an n-dimensional hypervolume: there are many dimensions of a student's educational niche.

Ecologists have defined a concept called "niche width" (Roughgarden, 1972). Niche width refers to the amount of variation that exists for each of the multiple variables that define or delimit the niche. If we focus exclusively on temperature and diet as defining variables of a niche, an individual can have a low tolerance of variation in temperature and diet specialization (a narrow niche width), a high tolerance of variation in temperature and a diverse diet (a wide niche width), or some combination of a high tolerance of variation for one and a low tolerance of variation for the other, conditions that may end up in an emergent intermediate niche width. The niche dimensionality can be represented as a bell-shaped curve along a single, linearized axis. For each curve, there is a general central tendency identified as the resource type or niche axis value that corresponds with the highest frequency of occurrence. In this context, frequency of occurrence is measured by the amount of time an individual spends in, or utilizes, a particular niche axis resource. If, for instance, the niche axis was temperature, the peak of the bell-shaped curve would be expected to correspond with the average temperature measured in the environment in which individuals of a particular species live. The spread (or dispersion) of the curve is a measure of the variation in resource types (or niche width values) experienced by individuals during their lifespan.

Importantly, the ecological niche applies to individuals. Although niche modeling is based on data from many individuals distributed across a range of environmental variables, the estimate from the model is the probability of an individual occupying a particular unit of space on a landscape. The niche only makes sense with respect to the fate of individuals:

individuals either exist or do not exist in places or at times depending on specific combinations of environmental conditions. Yet, the application of the niche, and niche modeling, is often described in the context of species. For example, Smith et al. (2019, p. 260) wrote, "Although there are many ways to estimate niches, a common starting point is the correlative ecological niche model (ENM), which identifies environmental conditions suitable to a species by finding associations between locations where a species is known to be present and the environment at those sites." Indeed, we can infer or estimate the niche for populations, subspecies, genera, and higher taxa based on the presence or absence of individuals at points on the landscape (Peterson, 2001; Smith et al., 2019), yet these higher levels of organization—the hierarchical scaling of diversity—are emergent from the actions of individuals. Thus, it is important to begin with the reality that niches are most relevant for characterization of individuals when making inferences. An emergent property of niche width conceptualization and delimitation is that there are "specialist" and "generalist" individuals.

Alleyne (2017) advocated that information science (the discipline) should diversify, because more varied entities have a "greater . . . ability to spread to new niches." Alleyne wrote, "Ecological theory states that survival of a population depends on its fit with its environment, more specifically with its niche . . . the larger, more varied and more flexible a population, the greater its ability to spread to new niches" (p. 24). This perspective, that the niche is a property of populations, misses the fact that the niche is an emergent outcome and an aggregate property of individuals. Both ecological and educational niches are constructs emergent from the analysis of the aggregated data about the behavior, activities, and locations of individuals. Students are individuals. They occupy niches within the broader landscape of the institution in which they are enrolled. There are places where students reside, eat, pursue interests, and achieve learning gains that furthers intellectual maturation. Like animals and plants and other organisms in nature, there are a set of environmental variables that define, to varying degrees, the habitat of students. The most obvious place is the classroom. Each classroom is characterized by a particular set of abiotic and biotic conditions that influence the presence and absence of individuals—evident by attendance—and also whether individuals thrive or are merely present. Abiotic conditions include whether the room where education happens is large or small and is shaped like an auditorium or not, whether the seating is fixed or moveable, whether the air is hot or cool, how information is transmitted, and the list goes on. Additionally, the density of individuals can be low or high, interactions may happen or not, and, if they happen, they can be productive or not. In short, there is a heterogeneous landscape in which students "forage" for knowledge and experience in the presence of others.

The Fundamental and Realized Niche

Education-relevant synopsis: There are two types of niches: fundamental and realized. This difference is useful when thinking about education, because the fundamental niche is the range of environmental variables that an individual can tolerate and be successful, whereas the realize niche includes the range of environmental variables that an individual can tolerate and be success-ful and whether there are interactions that either increase or decrease the capacity and success of individuals. Thus, it is important to consider both the physical and social environmental variables that influence student success. It is often the case educators are unaware of the n-dimensional hypervolume they create, and they may inadvertently, or purposefully, restrict the size of individuals' realized niches with negative effects on persistence and success.

There are two conceptualizations of the ecological niche that recognize the differential effects of abiotic variables and biotic interactions for defining where individuals live and when they are expected to be active. The fundamental niche refers to the entire range of environmental conditions in which individuals of a species can potentially survive and reproduce in the absence of any biotic interactions defined broadly as interactions with individuals of other species. The fundamental niche is determined by factors such as temperature, precipitation, resource availability, the availability of shelter, soil type, the existence of particular structural features of the environment, and more. The realized niche, on the other hand, is the actual range of environmental conditions in which individuals of a species are found in the presence of biotic interactions. Biotic interactions can include predation, competition for resources, parasitism, facilitation, and mutualism. These interactions may restrict individuals from utilizing its entire fundamental niche; consequently, the realized niche is smaller in dimension and scope than the fundamental niche.

Competition is an important mechanism limiting the realized niche (Connell, 1961; Dungan, 1985). Studies in the rocky intertidal—along the margin of the sea and land—have revealed, for instance, that space is a limiting resource. There are often multiple individuals of different species with very similar fundamental niches such that if each exists separately from the other, the individuals of each species occupy more-or-less identical places on the shoreline. However, when the two species coexist, there is a separation of individuals along some axis of environmental variation due to competition. For Connell's (1961) study species, it was the amount of time individuals were out of the water during the 24-hour day across an intertidal elevation gradient.

The niche variation among individuals partly reflects the fact that many variables define an individual's niche and that all individuals differ in their abilities as a consequence of genetics plus environmental influences during development and maturation. It is possible, for instance, that all individuals have the same tendency to use a particular combination of resources such that the modal characteristics of all individuals' niches is the same, but they differ in the frequency that particular niche dimensions are used or occupied. It could also be true that variation in the niche dimension defined by multivariate resources (i.e., the niche width) is the same but that the particular resources used differ among individuals; this scenario yields a set of resource use distributions that are of similar shape but offset along the multivariate niche dimension axis. Alternatively, the mean and variation that characterizes the distributions of resources among individuals may vary, but there is considerable overlap such that all individuals have overlapping niches. Finally, individual niches may be extremely variable, and as greater niche dimensionality is considered, the variation among individuals increases; moreover, it becomes increasingly probable that the niche spaces of some individuals do not overlap. This perspective most closely resembles what is observed in nature.

If we look carefully at the niches of individuals that are part of the same population and live in the same environment, it is clear individuals differ; additionally, there is evidence of niche guilds. In this context, a guild exists when there are two or more groups of individuals that can be separated based on statistical evaluation of the niche similarity of individuals. This idea of niche guilds is important because it is possible to objectively distinguish groups based on niche characteristics. Walker et al. (2023) wrote:

> We observed significant individual-level partitioning of food plants by bushbuck both within and between two adjacent habitat types (floodplain and woodland). Individuals with home

ranges that were closer together and had similar vegetation structure . . . ate more similar diets, supporting the prediction that heterogeneous resource distribution promotes individual differentiation. Individuals in good nutritional condition had significantly narrower diets, searched their home ranges more intensively, and had higher-quality diets than those in poor condition, supporting the prediction that animals with greater endogenous reserves have narrower realized niches because they can invest more time in searching for nutritious foods. Our results support predictions from optimal foraging theory about the energetic basis of individual-level dietary variation and provide a potentially generalizable framework for understanding how individuals' realized niche width is governed by animal behavior and physiology in heterogeneous landscapes. (p. 12)

Another way to find the stories about individuals' niches is to construct rank order distribution of the food they eat. Shifts in the ranked order distribution reflect the extent that individuals are able to occupy their fundamental niches or are increasingly impacted by biotic interactions that restrict diet and push individuals into realized niches. One example comes from sea otters. When otter density is high, individuals tend to specialize on particular prey items, whereas when otter density is low, specialization is absent (Tinker et al., 2012). The take-home message from conceptualization and delimitation of ecological niches is that they exist as abstract emergent properties of functionally different individuals living in heterogeneous environments subject to incessant challenges from changes in the availability of critical resources and the myriad interactions with individuals of the same and other species that can influence growth, maturation, and persistence. This is also a description of an educational niche.

While the learning habitat is often ignored, the message from ecology is that the characteristics of an inhabited place matter. Recently, educators have been asking if the properties of learning spaces matter, if the furniture and its organization matter, and if space can be designed in ways that encourage learning rather than serving as an inanimate background or, worse, creating barriers to learning. Indeed, Peng et al. (2022, p. 1) discovered that "the spatial attributes of active learning classrooms significantly affected the learning experience, specifically instructional interaction, furniture perception, learning support, and physical environment." Perkins and Wieman (2005, p. 32) discovered, using an experimental approach, that "seat location in a large lecture hall has a significant effect on students' attendance, grades, and beliefs about physics." In a large study of the effects of where students inhabited a classroom, which, incidentally, was titled "Classroom Ecology . . . ," the authors discovered "students sitting in the more central parts of the class had higher percentage grades and attended classes more frequently than those students sitting in the less central parts of the class. However, other studies failed to find an association between the seating location and student performance (Meeks et al., 2013; Navarro Jover et al., 2018). Given the tremendous variation in classroom structure and the configuration of seating and other less mentioned aspects of learning environments, it seems inescapable that there is a realized niche for thriving and a broader fundamental niche for existing.

At institutions of higher education, teaching and learning mostly happen indoors in spaces designed to house people for periods of time in seats. The learning spaces have characteristics that can influence the health and well-being of individuals, including temperature, available personal space, air quality and odor, and the density of individuals. There are also interactions that influence an individual's performance and productivity, including positive interactions—facilitation, cooperation, friendship—and negative interactions—bullying, lack of respect, agonistic behaviors, cheating. These environmental features can have positive or negative effects on individuals depending on the particular personality and intellectual properties of individuals. We need better data for a more robust assessment about how interactions among individuals influence students' niches.

Fundamental and realized niches apply in educational contexts. The fundamental niche of students refers to the entire range of learning environment conditions in which an individual (the student) can achieve the greatest possible learning gains. The realized niche, on the other hand, is the actual range of learning environment conditions an individual (the student) experiences in the classroom (or whatever educational context exists). The realized niche may be smaller than the fundamental niche, and the student's potential may be limited, in some cases severely, by prevailing learning environment conditions. Figure 3.1 shows two representations of 10 different niches arrayed along some quantifiable axis of learning: one representation is a bell-shaped (normal) curve and the other is the mean and the variation. Note that most of the fundamental niches are skewed toward didactic learning environments, in part because most college science classes are taught using didactic practices (Stains et al.,

Figure 3.1a–b. Left: Hypothetical example of the variation of students' fundamental niches across a linearized pedagogical axis. Right: The same information but represented by a point for the average and a horizontal line representing variation for each student. Two different realized niches due to instructor teaching style (didactic and student-centered) are indicated on the graph. *Source:* Created by the author.

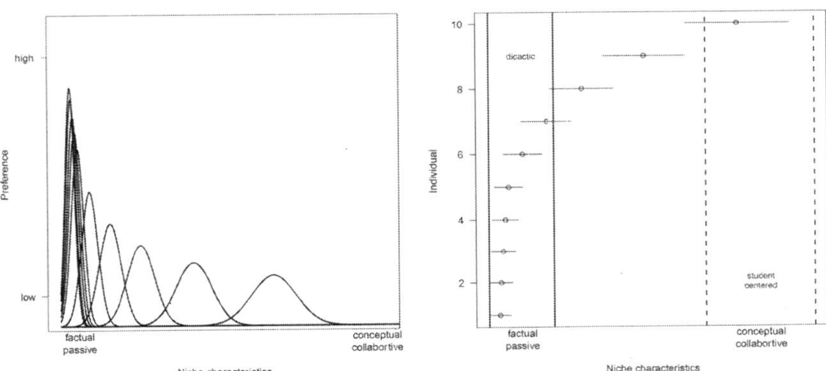

2018). The most common realized niche scenario evident for first- and second-year science classes created by the instructors is superimposed on students' inherent (natural) fundamental niches. Importantly, there are students who fall outside of the range of learning environment conditions defined by the realized niche. Ecological theory and empirical studies predict these individuals will fail to thrive; in the context of education, these individuals may receive low grades, drop courses, switch majors, or, depending on the constructed realized cognitive niches in other courses, leave college not because they are incapable of learning, but because the environment created for learning does not encompass the range of niche properties enabling intellectual maturation and learning successes.

The Cognitive Niche

Education-relevant synopsis: The cognitive niche is a specific type of niche that depends on an individual's ability to solve problems based on their knowledge and process skills; its existence recognizes that there are physical aspects of a student's niche (Can I function in a particular environment?)

and a cognitive aspect of a student's niche (Can I effectively solve problems, learn new ideas, and mature intellectually?). Recognizing that students' success depends on both the physical and cognitive properties of their learning environment should be a reminder to instructors that it is important to pay attention to, and create learning experiences with an awareness of, both dimensions of the realized educational niches manifest in classrooms.

In addition to the physical and interactive dimensions of niches, there are also aspects of the niche defined by cognition: specifically, there are cognitive niches:

> The cognitive niche is a loose extension of this concept [the niche], based on the idea that in any ecosystem, the possibility exists for an organism to overtake other organisms' fixed defenses by cause-and-effect reasoning and cooperative action—to deploy information and inference, rather than particular features of physics and chemistry, to extract resources from other organisms in opposition to their adaptations to protect those resources. These inferences are played out internally in mental models of the world, governed by intuitive conceptions of physics, biology, and psychology, including the psychology of animals. It allows humans to invent tools, traps, and weapons, to extract poisons and drugs from other animals and plants, and to engage in coordinated action, for example, fanning out over a landscape to drive and concentrate game, in effect functioning like a huge superorganism. These cognitive stratagems are devised on the fly in endless combinations suitable to the local ecology. They arise by mental design and are deployed, tested, and fine-tuned by feedback in the lifetimes of individuals, rather than arising by random mutation and being tuned over generations by the slow feedback of differential survival and reproduction. (Pinker, 2010, pp. 8993–8994)

The cognitive niche extends the dimensions of performance from the structure and function of physiology and morphology into the realms of behavior and cognition. One example is the choice by predators to specialize on particular prey types. Hunting different prey types constitutes a dimension of an individual's niche, and it has been suggested that through experience and learning, individuals hone this cognitive aspect of their niche; the emergent outcome is specialization on particular prey types. Specialization on one or a small subset of existing prey species confers an advantage, because it avoids the costs of maintaining diverse strategies and allows the improvement of singular strategies (Beecham, 2001). The details of the process of hunting specialization involve pattern recognition, memory, and learning (Beecham, 2001). For animals that rely on cognition and learning for survival, growth, maturation, and ultimately reproductive success, there is an ecological necessity for the emergence of an individual-specific cognitive dimension of their emergent niche. The fact that the cognitive niche develops as a consequence of inherent cognitive ability, the environment of potential resources, and learning makes it a useful construct for thinking about education.

Students in a particular class likely modify and revise their cognitive niche "on the fly in endless combinations suitable to the local ecology." Given that all students are different, there is a large range of possible cognitive niches, and it is likely the distribution of cognitive niche widths varies among students. Some may be able to perform at high levels across a range of environments and interactions; others may need very specific conditions for optimal performance. Additionally, some may be able to modify their cognitive niche in response to local conditions; others may be less adept at cognitive niche remodeling. Students occupy a cognitive niche defined by their abilities to make sense of information that depends, to varying degrees, on the environment created by an instructor, the covariation between the instructor and each student, and the interactions that happen among students. And like the ecological niche, there are fundamental and realized cognitive niches.

Niche Construction

Education-relevant synopsis: The idea that niches can be continuously constructed and remodeled is perhaps the most relevant aspect of thinking about niches in educational contexts. Education should happen in a way that allows students to modify their environment in ways that improve their performance and success; this is an important outcome of student-centered teaching and learning. It emphasizes agency and self-efficacy, and ultimately translates into academic success.

Niche construction is the idea that organisms modify their environment in ways that improve their performance and success. This contrasts with the view that the environment—including the biotic interactions—impinges on an individual and that success or failure depends on the outcome of the effects of the environment. Niche construction means that individuals have some agency and can modify structures and resources in ways that improve their success. Pocheville (2015, p. 558) wrote, "The research program on niche construction arose from an opposition to the externalist program in evolutionary biology, where the environment is conceived as a non-modifiable entity causing the evolutionary change in organisms. Proponents of the constructionist program point out, conversely, that by their activities . . . organisms modify their environment in such a way that the selection pressures they undergo can in turn be modified." Levins and Lewontin (1985, pp. 98–101) added that "organisms determine what is relevant," that they "alter the external world as they interact with it," that they "transduce the physical signals that reach them from the outside world," and so "transform the statistical pattern of environmental variation in the external world." In sum, "the organism–environment relationship defines the 'traits' selected because indeed the organism shapes to some extent the niche, hence its own selector."

Organisms that burrow are obvious examples of niche constructors, but there are many more, including organisms that build nests (the birds and the bees) (Laland & Sterelny, 2006), organisms that create chemical repositories that limit the negative effects of competitive neighbors (plant secondary compounds) (Wardle et al., 2011), and organisms that transmit viruses to neighboring individuals in ways that improve fitness (in bacteria) (Brown et al., 2009). Laland and Sterelny (2006) provide compelling examples and arguments about the pervasiveness and importance of niche construction in natural populations. It is also an important reason for the success of the human species (Laland et al., 2007).

We can transfer this ecological perspective into the realm of education. Using the framework of Levins and Lewontin (1985), we can claim, correctly I think, that students "determine what is relevant," that they "alter the external world" of information, and, "as they interact with it," that they "transduce the physical signals" about whatever content is being transmitted to them, and so "transform" the information in ways that align with their mental models and intuitions about the world. The interaction between the students and the environment determines, to some extent, the cognitive "traits" that survive, "because indeed the student shapes to some extent their cognitive niche, hence the student is its own source of selection." The cognitive niche is constructional, and its construction depends on the covariation between the cognitive properties of individuals and the environment in which the individual makes decisions and uses their intelligence to solve problems and, in the process, change their thinking. Finally, it is worth pointing out that part of niche construction in higher education is dropping courses and changing disciplinary focus, because some environments are hostile and other environments are more inviting.

At the core of the idea of cognitive niche construction is

> causal or instrumental intelligence: the ability to create and maintain cause–effect models of the world as guides for prejudging which courses of action will lead to which results. Because there are an infinitely large number of possible sequences of behavior (of which the overwhelming majority are maladaptive) "behavioral flexibility" is an insufficient characterization of our innovative adaptive pattern. Our cognitive system is knowledge or information driven, and its models filter potential responses so that newly generated behavioral sequences are appropriate to bring about the desired end. Of course, exploration, trial and error, and feedback are essential to the system, but, by themselves, they are inadequate to construct or maintain it. (Tooby & DeVore, 1987, p. 210)

Pinker (2003) expanded on Tooby and DeVores (1987) exploration of cognitive niche construction:

> Tooby and DeVore proposed that the human lifestyle is a consequence of a specialization for overcoming the evolutionary fixed defenses of plants and animals (poisons, coverings, stealth, speed, and so on) by cause-and-effect reasoning. Such reasoning enables humans to invent and use new technologies (such as weapons, traps, coordinated driving of game, and ways of detoxifying plants) that exploit other living things before they can develop defensive countermeasures in evolutionary time. This cause-and-effect reasoning depends on intuitive theories about various domains of the world, such as objects, forces, paths, places, manners, states, substances, hidden biochemical essences, and other people's beliefs and desires. (Pinker, 2003, p. 27)

Our ability to modify the world to increase survival also enhances cognition, because it is fundamentally a problem-solving act that depends on cognitive function. Furthermore, "We are surrounded by structures we interact with as cognitive agents. . . . We modify local environments . . . in order to make life easier" (Bertolotti & Magnani, 2017, p. 4763).

For humans, cognitive niche construction happens whenever we face challenges that require cognitive effort to achieve a desired outcome. This describes education. Thus, for every one of our students, we should imagine each one engaging in cognitive niche construction, and the particular emergent cognitive niches will depend on their niche construction efficacy and the characteristics of their local environment, including the people with whom they interact predictably and regularly in a classroom (or whatever) setting. As educators, we should be in the business of helping students construct cognitive niches and create productive scenarios through the emphasis on mutualistic interactions. Engaging and promoting cognitive niche construction is a core element of self-efficacy.

Studies of student interactions within educational contexts provide some indication of constructed cognitive niches. For instance, social network analysis revealed there is a variation among students in their ability to develop their membership in productive and collaborative groups. In large-enrollment courses, some students change interaction partners frequently and purposefully such that they maintain anonymity whereas others seek out the same individuals and develop strong ties with a small set of people (Buchenroth-Martin et al., 2017). The variation in student social connectivity can have important impacts on their sense of belonging, motivation, and attitude and affect persistence. Azmitia et al. (2013, p. 744) noted that students' capacity to develop their sense of identity in a discipline "is not an individual project. Rather, students' identities are constructed and negotiated within the context of [social] networks of family, peers, staff, and faculty who can instill a sense that they matter in the university community." Thus, a key aspect of emerging adults' successful transition to college is developing a clear sense of identity within a new academic environment by constructing the social dimensions of their cognitive niche.

Azmitia et al. (2013) repeatedly refer to the challenge and importance of students finding their "identity niche" within the university or college setting as a key determinant of success. Their inference is that students failing to find their identity niche explains failure. Although they referred to identity niche construction, their perspective is that the university or college setting contains a set of identity niches and the student's challenge is to find a compatible one. This emphasizes the view that niches are defined by the environment and individuals with certain characteristics (e.g., individual niche dimensions) do not persist because their niche does not exist. This implies there are many students for which their chosen college or university does not have a realizable niche that can support their success. The emphasis on how cognitive niche construction happens implies that universities and colleges, and mostly the faculty that interact with students regularly, need to have the ability for enabling students to engage in niche construction. This begins with the recognition that all individuals will have different realized niches, and that the construction of a niche depends on opportunities for repeated and safe testing of the alignment between individual identity and the social and cognitive dimensions that exist within a classroom. A key aspect of the process of cognitive niche construction is creating opportunities for social network development centered in academics.

One difficult aspect of cognitive niche construction is the socioemotional dimension of feeling content and "at home." Home is a constructed niche. The construction process depends on making connections with others who are also engaged in niche construction. The connections afford possibilities of strategy sharing, support revision of intrapersonal change, and allow comparison of successes and failures in ways that facilitate active niche remodeling. For educators, enabling and fostering the development of a supportive, safe, and productive learning community, in which students can make new connections through a semester, is a key aspect of enablement described by Bertolotti and Magnani (2017) as a key component of cognitive niche construction.

These considerations of the cognitive niche and its construction focus our attention on how students construct a niche for themselves within the structures defined by a particular course, including the nuances of the moves and language of the instructor, the complexity and scope of learning activities, the depth and perceived relevance of content, the developing social networks among individuals engaged in their own individualized cognitive niche construction activities, the performance expectations of both the individual student and the instructor, and the sense of identity and alignment with the discipline (e.g., science), among other things. These considerations underscore that the cognitive niche is, like the biological niche, a multidimensional construct within which individuals function, interact with others, and develop cognitive abilities. The idea that cognitive niche construction depends on enablement in much the same way that ecological niches depends on enablement (Bertolotti & Magnani, 2017) focuses attention on why and how teaching happens, and whether the structure and function of the teaching that happens in the classroom (or other contexts) enables individual cognitive niche construction or not. If teaching is unidimensional, and assumes all individuals inhabit the same niche, it is likely cognitive niche construction will be limited, or not happen at all. However, if part of the educational experience is the instructor and students working together in ways that increase the capacity of students to construct and remodel their cognitive niche, the picture of niche variation will be very different (fig. 3.2).

Figure 3.2. The same graph as in figure 3.1b except that each individuals niche has shifted to the right, toward a more conceptual and collaborative learning experience as a consequence of niche construction. The magnitude of niche construction is indicated by the thin horizontal dashed arrows. The dashed lines are meant to convey the idea that students can construct niches; that they are not fixed attributes of individuals but instead can be modified and can change. The dashed lines are different lengths; this is meant to convey that individuals differ in their capacity to change their educational niche. *Source:* Created by the author.

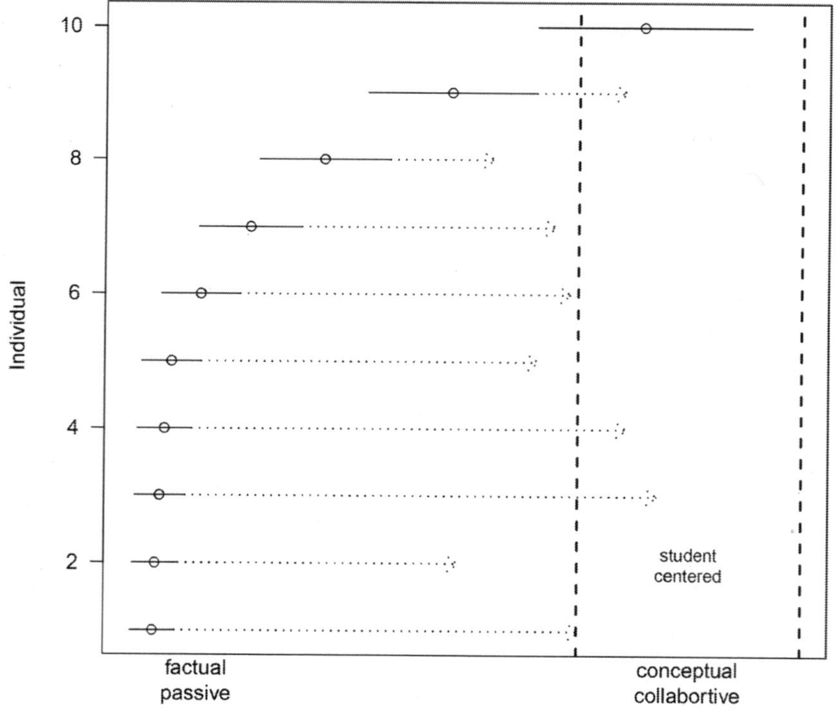

If we want to design, execute, and support learning experiences that allow all individuals to thrive regardless of their inherent cognitive niche, what should we do? I think the most important strategy is to move away from low-dimensional, high-stakes, rank-based assessments of performance that often assume uniformity of experience and identical innate ability among individuals; in other words, we need to move past a world in which there is a single "expert" cognitive niche. We need to create learning experiences that explore the complex landscape predicted from theories of intelligence—like the multiple intelligences theory (Gardner, 2011)—and embrace a world in which there are multiple cognitive states that conform to valuable cognitive function. Furthermore, we need to move toward students living in learning communities that allow them to construct their own cognitive niches instead of having them try to match the ones educators have in mind when they develop and execute teaching strategies and curriculum that may well all be outside the cognitive diet of students. To use an analogy from evolutionary biology, rather than assume there is a single cognitive phenotype that maps onto high fitness, we should assume that there are many, perhaps innumerable, cognitive phenotypes that map onto high ability; additionally, instead of one learning pathway from novice to expert, we should expect many pathways, and also expect some individuals to back-track and perhaps shift their tactics on how to summit a cognition function peak (see chapter 1 and fig. 1.1). Exploration of the multidimensional cognitive landscape should be rewarded. Sometimes exploration appears as if students are not understanding a topic or assimilating new information and ways of thinking and doing in expected ways. Rather than penalize these students with a low grade, we should interview them and encourage them to continue exploration, and perhaps provide some tips and strategies about how to navigate the difficult landscape from which they construct a comfortable and productive cognitive niche. The best way to do this is adopt a teaching framework that is student-centered and is used to construct learning experiences that reveal, support, and challenge student thinking and actions (see BSCS, 2018).

Chapter 4

Interactions

Defining and Describing Interactions

Education-relevant synopsis: Students can interact in education settings, and the interactions can be competitive or cooperative depending on the intentions of the educators. Education can also be individualistic and devoid of authentic interactions. Ecological theory clearly predicts the greatest gains from cooperative interactions; thus, educators should become expert in the ability to create productive, cooperative interactions in the classroom (or wherever education happens). Additionally, educators should avoid emphasizing competition.

People are different, and in social settings some may tend to participate and work with others in groups, while some individuals limit interactions to one-on-one or act alone. Szolnoki and Chen (2021, p. 1) wrote, "Some people like to be part of a larger group while other persons prefer to interact in a more personalized, individual way." The social tendencies of individuals influence whether they interact with others in meaningful ways—in ways that have discernible effects—or act individualistically. In other words, individuals can either be interdependent or independent. Furthermore, whether you are individualistic or have a group-oriented mindset, the existence of different types of interactions across space and time can have significant consequences.

There are various types of interactions between individuals that differ with respect to their effect. If we define an interaction in terms of whether there are positive or negative effects of one individual on another, there are four scenarios, described as competition, interference, assistance (or commensalism), and collaboration (or mutualism). A competitive interaction exists if there is a net negative effect on both interactors. A negative effect means that status or gains of an individual decreases as a consequence of the interaction. At the other extreme, a mutualistic or collaborative interaction has a net positive effect on both interactors. Commensalism describes a case in which one of the two or more individuals involved in an interaction benefits but there are no discernible effects on the other individual or individuals. Conversely, interference is competitive but there is a negative effect on only one individual; the other gains from the interaction. These four types of interactions are omnipresent and ubiquitous in nature and in education settings. Indeed, these four types of interactions constitute the social fabric of society. There is, of course, a scenario in which individuals do not interact with others—we can think of this as individualism. We can visualize the outcomes of no interaction (individualistic) competitive and collaborative (or cooperative) interactions using ecological theory known as the Lokta-Volterra equations. The predictions are clear: competition limits the gains of different types of individuals and collaboration expands the possible gains to different types of individuals relative to a scenario in which there is no interaction (fig. 4.1).

Figure 4.1. The outcomes from Lotka-Volterra interaction equations for multiple individuals. The dashed horizontal line denotes the carrying capacity indicative of the available resources. Left: The gains assume all individuals have equal access to resources and equal capacity for gain; the variation among individuals reflects stochasticity (randomness). Middle: The gain of individuals in a competitive environment. The different trajectories of gain reflect both stochasticity and different competitive ability. Right: The gain when there is collaboration; assumes individuals are equally capable collaborators. For ecological context, cumulative gain is measured by the production of offspring. For education, cumulative gain can be estimated by educational achievement or the increase in cognitive ability or social capital. *Source:* Created by the author.

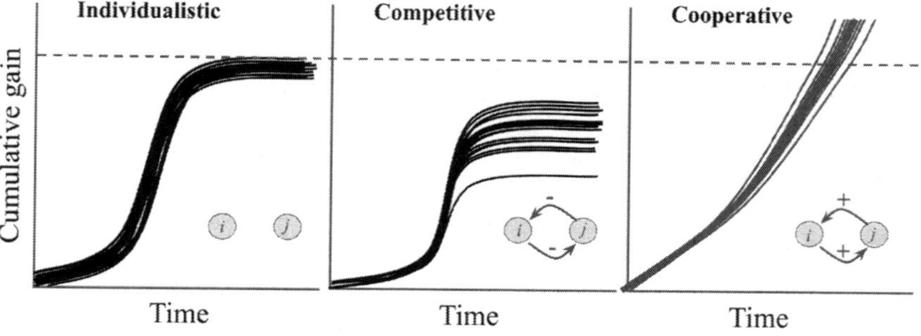

Competitive and Negative Interaction Effects

Education-relevant synopsis: The existence of competition in education is pervasive, normalized, and often expected, despite the reality that competition reduces the achievement of all individuals, even the winners, when compared with more cooperative interactions. Competitive environments limit the realized niches of individuals and fail to recognize and accommodate the variation in cognitive abilities and capacities of different students. Educational places are meant to be places where students can learn how to construct productive cognitive niches; competition erodes this capacity and instead emphasizes reaction rather than construction. Because grades are fundamentally an outcome of a rank-order competition, grades should be replaced by a more authentic measure of students' cognitive development in ways aligned with the goal of emphasizing cognitive niche construction.

There is a rich history of empirical and theoretical work on ecological interactions from which analogy from ecology to education can generate useful inferences. Competition models tend to be density-dependent; more individuals translates into more intense competition and larger negative effects. And different types of individuals have different abilities and efficiencies in how they use resources. Each type of individual is assigned a competition coefficient that describes its competitive effect on all other types of individuals; when there are more than two types of individuals, each type of individual can have a unique, and negative, effect on all other types of individuals (Hu et al., 2022).

Constructing a competition analogy between ecology and education posits that there is some degree of similarity between gains in ecological and education contexts. In ecology, the gains reflect the accumulation of resources for growth, survival, maturation, and reproduction of individuals with the net effect of an increase in numbers of individuals over time (i.e., ΔN). In education, the gains reflect the accumulation of knowledge and academic achievement with a net effect of an increase in intelligence and cultural capital. This view of intelligence aligns with theory and empirical work from cognitive science (Frith, 2007; Tenenbaum et al., 2011; Carter et al., 2012; Schaafsma et al., 2015). In addition, there is a variable in the models that is described as the intrinsic rate of gain (labeled r). In ecology, the intrinsic rate of gain represents the ability of individuals to transform resources into the production of offspring minus the loss of individuals due to death. In education, the intrinsic rate of gain might best be thought of as the inherent capacity of an individual to assimilate and represent new information (i.e., new cognitive constructs) in the brain coupled with the loss of existing information in the brain. In both ecology and education, the intrinsic rate of gain is influenced by both genes and environment. Examples of the effects of genes and the environment includes neural architecture of the brain, sensory capacity, the development and maturation of individuals, cognitive practice, diet, sleep, behavioral characteristics, and a variety of other variables known to influence cognitive capacity (e.g., Leeson et al., 2008; Kanai & Rees, 2011; Ullen et al., 2016) (see chapter 2).

There are other important inferences. For instance, the ecological models predict that as the number of different functional types of individuals increases, stable coexistence is maximized if competition is reduced or nonexistent (Hu et al., 2022). If there is competition, stable coexistence and persistence of individuals is possible only when the number of different types of individuals is small. Because all students differ, we can think of the number of different types of individuals as the number of students. When there are large numbers of students, competition will reduce the success of some individuals relative to others, resulting in winners and losers, large variation in the experience and academic achievement of individuals, and the emergence of social capital inequity. In effect, what competition models assume in an education context is that if one individual gains more ideas (or cognitive ability generally), another individual is negatively affected, gains less, and vice versa, relative to a case without interaction. Some will question the premise that competition has detrimental effects and may argue, instead, that it is a mechanism for increasing overall success and fuels the emergence of innovation. However, from the perspective of the average individual, the theory and empirical data from ecology clearly show that competition reduces average gains relative to environments without competition. In terms of numbers, if there is a winner, there are many more losers. If competition is reduced—for example by reducing class size—everyone does better.

There are competitive scenarios that play out in the classroom. For example, it is often the case that one or several students are more vocal, ask more questions, and engage more frequently with the instructor in ways that effectively monopolize time; other students are left waiting and may shift their focus from what is happening in class to other things. Time is a limiting resource. Furthermore, because time is limited, if a small number of students monopolize time, it means opportunities to learn about other things or ways of thinking may be compromised; with negative effects on all individuals. For this reason, instructional strategies should structure student-faculty interactions and create scenarios in which interactions are equitable and not limiting. In general, any aspect of education in which resources, especially the ability of the instructor to directly engage with students, are limited is subject to the negative effects of competition.

There are also commonly used educational tools that use competition as an incentive. Online apps (e.g., Kahoot) are used for creating, in a gamelike environment, competition with the purpose of motivating students to learn. In Kahoot students receive points for a correct answer to a question, and they are ranked based on how quickly they answered. At the end of each question, there is a top 10 leaderboard, and with each question, the relative rank of individuals is displayed, with highlights of individuals that shift upwards in the ranking. At the end of the Kahoot quiz, the top three ranked individuals are displayed and praised by the instructor for their knowledge and engagement. A number of publications have asserted that Kahoot improved "the quality of student learning in the classroom, with the highest influence reported on classroom dynamics, engagement, motivation and improved learning experience" (Licorish et al., 2018, p. 1). In a review of the effects of Kahoot, it was revealed that using the online game has a number of significant drawbacks stemming from its emphasis on getting to the correct answer quickly and its reliance on selecting a single correct answer (Wang & Tahir, 2020). Kahoot is an explicitly competitive educational environment in which there are few winners, mostly losers, and the specific competition coefficients depend more on affective characteristics of individuals than on direct interactions between students or the knowledge individuals have gained as a consequence of teaching. When explicitly competitive strategies are enacted in classrooms, the pedagogy assumes students are efficient and experienced in their competitive ability and, perhaps more importantly, that everyone is playing in ways that maximize their learning. It is likely both of these things are not true in most contexts. Moreover, for students who shy away from competition for myriad reasons, enacting explicitly competitive strategies that effectively take over the classroom can be exclusive and cause a decrease in motivation, increase anxiety, and reduce a students' cognitive capacity. Moreover, the explicit emphasis on speed devalues the considerable value of slow thinking strategies.

A more general effect of competition stems from the way students are evaluated. In most college classes, students are explicitly ranked based on the accumulation of numbers of points allocated to various assignments and assessments. It is often the case that anonymized rank order and score distributions are made public. Students can see themselves in the data with the implicit or explicit expectation that high-ranking students will get positive feedback and low-ranking students will become more motivated to learn: there is no objective evidence that these expectations are true. Moreover, the rank-order distribution is subject to categorization such that individuals receive a particular grade, and each grade is associated with a set of values, either explicitly by the instructor, university, and society at-large, or implicitly by the students. Rank-order grades instill a sense of competition among students even though there is no evidence of limiting resources, unless, of course, the instructor's pedagogy includes a requirement that there needs to be certain percentages of each categorical grade. Limiting the number of students who receive an A or a passing grade as part of a sorting strategy, a strategy that is well entrenched in higher education and described as "curving" grades, is inherently competitive. "Multivariate logistic regressions reveal that high levels of perceived competition in one's classes are associated with increased risks of depression and anxiety, especially among queer, first-generation, Black, and Latino/a students" (Posselt & Lipson, 2016, p. 973). While competition may be motivating for some students, for most, its effects are negative as predicted by ecological models and empirical studies.

For most classrooms, especially ones in which there are ranked grading systems, it seems inescapable that competition happens, and it is likely that in such an environment, competition is pervasive and may be intense. For example, Wilkins (2012, p. 771) wrote, "Teachers guide pupils' orientations to learning and personal development according to a certain logic or rationality, where pupils are encouraged to engage in pedagogic tasks as autonomous, competitive subjects. Through their participation in these educational practices, pupils in effect are incited to calibrate their behaviour on the basis of enterprising tendencies and formulate success in narrow utilitarian terms as the outcome of competitive behaviour." This form of teaching normalizes the idea that there are always "winners" and "losers" and this type of outcome is largely "motivated by market-driven prerogatives, values and incentives in which one person's 'success' necessitates another's relative failure." Wilkins (2012, p. 773) continues, "Competitive learning invokes a field of possibilities and sites for discursively and materially constituting subjects as 'self-governing,' but self-governing within a standard rationality that champions the economisation of the calculating self (as entrepreneur, as consumer, as active user, as co-producer, as prudential risk taker, etc.). This is precisely because such pedagogic techniques and strategies evoke and promote a formal rational view of subjects as somehow autonomous and self-maximizing." Wilkins's work (and that of many others) show that competition exists as a normal part of many instructors' pedagogy in ways that align with and reinforce social norms in which people are ranked, and the emergence of ranks reinforces the idea that competition is an effective pedagogical strategy. The institutionalized system of ranking by grading is a construct for promoting competition, rewarding winners, and punishing losers. The idea that competition makes "it possible for teachers to identify potential gaps in performance and to render the differences useful by aligning them to group-based measurements of effort and work levels" may happen, and may, as Wilkin's imagines, produce actionable data for identifying achievement gaps and working towards closing the gaps. However, it is also possible that by identifying the gaps, the pernicious negative effects of competition have eroded the ability to achieve greater learning gains through other more positive-interactive strategies. Moreover, the literature supports claims that competition exacerbates, rather than reduces, variation in learning gains among students based on gender, race and socioeconomics (Johnson & Johnson, 1974; Niederle & Vesterlund, 2010; Wilkins, 2012; Ors et al., 2013).

The pervasive negative effects of competition is clearly evident from ecological theory and empirical data on competition in populations. Nonetheless, there are also many documented cases in which competition is invoked as an effective pedagogical strategy. For instance, Slavin (1977, p. 647) claimed "competitive and individual reward structures are more effective than cooperative ones for increasing performance" while, at the same time suggesting "Mixtures of cooperative and competitive or cooperative and individual reward structures appear to be the most promising avenue for producing positive effects both on academic achievement and on social connectedness." A meta-analysis comparing real-time, in-class competition with no competition for learning showed an increase in test scores for competitive compared with non-competitive learning environments, and that the effect was most pronounced at the University level (Jurado-Castro et al., 2023). It is likely that the positive effects of competition on measured learning gains may reflect assessments that favor individualism rather than mutualism. Moreover, the results may simply be biased because of the pervasiveness of competitive education strategies coupled with the dearth of cooperative strategies.

If we use empirical data and well-developed theory stemming from ecology as guides, education is best accomplished by eliminating competition. This means discarding grading (Stommel, 2017) and resisting assignment of points to student work (see Zerwin, 2020). Instead, we should concentrate on developing learning activities that promote positive interactions in place of competitive interactions and foster and facilitate cognitive niche construction.

Individualism and Solitary Individuals

Education-relevant synopsis: Individualism is the idea that students should be evaluated based on their demonstrated competence in the absence of other individuals. As such, individualism devalues interaction and the social construction of meaning. Individualism fails to recognize that all individuals are dependent on others for their success. Humans (and many other organisms with and without brains) are social and depend on interactions with others; any attempts to emphasize individualism in education should be eliminated in favor of learning in an explicit and deliberate social context.

Individualism emphasizes the autonomy of the individual by prioritizing independence, self-reliance, and individual rights over the needs or interests of a group. Dewey (1916, p. 49) wrote that "there is always a danger that increased personal independence will decrease the social capacity of an individual. In making him more self-reliant, it may make him more self-sufficient; it may lead to aloofness and indifference. It often makes an individual so insensitive to his relations to others as to develop an illusion of being really able to stand and act alone—an unnamed form of insanity which is responsible for a large part of the remedial suffering of the world." Put differently, living a solitary life, a life of staunch and trenchant individualism is, in a complex world of limited resources, insane.

It is common to think of individuals in ecological contexts as being on their own and acting in ways that further their selfish interests. This idea can be extended down to the level of the gene. Dawkins's (1976) wrote a book, *The Selfish Gene*, in which he supported the contention that individuals

> are survival machines—robot vehicles blindly programmed to preserve the selfish molecules known as genes. . . . Individuals

are not stable things, they are fleeting. Chromosomes too are shuffled into oblivion, like hands of cards soon after they are dealt. But the cards themselves survive the shuffling. The cards are the genes. The genes are not destroyed by crossing-over, they merely change partners and march on. Of course they march on. That is their business. They are the replicators and we are their survival machines. When we have served our purpose we are cast aside. But genes are denizens of geological time: genes are forever. (pp. 19–20)

At the heart of this argument is that individuals will do anything to survive because they are machines attempting to propagate genes into the future. The will to live, to survive, that seems to embody all life is a survival strategy encoded into all life. Genes are the only bits and pieces of biology that truly self-transmit into the future, leaving behind biological carcasses. Our first instinct—encoded in our genes, according to Dawkins—is to grab as many resources as possible, for self-preservation and self-advancement, regardless of cost. Hardin (1968) introduced us to what he called "The Tragedy of the Commons." In this scenario, individuals seek to advance their self-interests at their peril. There are examples from other species besides humans that suffer from the tragedy of the commons. A study of a species of gerbil—a type of rodent—revealed individuals will harvest more food when they exist in the presence of others than they would normally, and this behavior ultimately reduces the success of all individuals (Berger-Tal et al., 2015). Another example comes from the world of bacteria (Rankin et al., 2007, p. 846): "Bacteriocin production in bacteria may likewise be seen as a tragedy of the commons. The production of bacteriocins kills other conspecifics. . . . Bacteriocin production creates a situation where group productivity is reduced: while the individuals which produce the antibiotics stand to benefit, the group would do better if everyone restrained from producing bacteriocins. In this case, the social good is living in a bacteriocin-free environment, and this good is destroyed when all individuals produce bacteriocins." While the tragedy of the commons is ultimately a story about the deleterious effects of competition, it is driven by individualism: the sense that what matters most are selfish interests. Thus, while it is important to think about the case in which individuals do not interact, in nature and in educational settings, individualism—actions without effects on others—is impossible except in the abstract. Indeed, as far as I can tell, there are no examples in nature that do not involve some degree of competition, even for solitary individuals like leopards and other large predators (Stander et al., 1997; Makuya & Schradin, 2024).

Yet, within educational contexts, individualism is pervasive. Johnson and Johnson (1974, p. 215) defined individualism as a scenario "in which individuals are rewarded on the basis of the quality of their work independent of the quality of work of other students." Individualistic approaches attempt to isolate the effects of the environment on the learning gains and achievements of individuals mainly for the purpose of attributing gains to individuals. In this sense, individualism is a meritocracy, yet it is easily corrupted in systems in which resources are limited and recognition is necessary; for example, when it comes time to grading individuals using rank-based systems typical of academic settings. It is also important to point out that academic cultures—at least at my university—are individualistic. Awards for accomplishments are bestowed on individuals, salary adjustments are considered for individuals, and career benchmark promotions are typically based on an individual's accomplishment, even though, in reality, all of us depend on others for our success. The African proverb, borrowed by Hillary Clinton, "It takes a village," emphasizes that the success of individuals depends on many people. In *The Rational Optimist*, Matt Ridley (2010) emphasizes that the ability of people today to engage in education and pursue scholarship depends on literally millions of people laboring over years in ways that generated capital so that academics and students can divert their energy away from securing shelter and food and instead focus on advancing knowledge and intellectual maturation. Individualism is an abstraction useful for gaining an understanding of the effects of interaction; yet, it is a myth and does not exist in the real world. It is, effectively, a null hypothesis: useful in the abstract, absent from reality.

One example of an individualistic education approach that illustrates the ridiculousness of individualism as a pedagogically important strategy is learning-by-teaching without an audience (Lachner et al., 2022). Normally, learning-by-teaching "involves situations in which students explain the previously learnt contents to another student to stimulate generative cognitive processes that may be conducive to learning. . . . Learning-by-teaching activity primarily [happens] in interactive settings, such as during peer tutoring or cooperative learning in classrooms or synchronous online learning environments" (pp. 583–584). These strategies typically show positive learning gains (Chi et al., 2001; Duran, 2017); however, learning-by-teaching without an audience—without interpersonal inter-action—has resulted, in some cases, in null-effects (reviewed in Lachner et al., 2022). This underscores the idea that interactions matter.

Importantly, the reason to emphasize that contradiction between the idea that individuals exist as solitary beings without effects on others and the reality that individuals consume resources in a world in which resources are finite provides an important context for reflecting on many pedagogical practices. My perspective is that if we, as educators, use educational frameworks that are individualistic, that if we focus on the gains of individuals in isolation from others and without explicitly acknowledging or accounting for interaction effects, we unknowingly create a competitive environment. This is true for the simple reasons, as Rachel Carson stated, that "in nature, nothing exists alone." At the very least, each individual consumes resources and even if we engineer the equalization of the distribution of resources to all individuals, there will be ways in which the negative effects of competition remain intact. It is true that continuing efforts to provide a highly structured and equitable distribution of resources for learning using online platforms and moving away from ranked-based grading and other pernicious and conventional education strategies improves education. But if we follow this strategy to its logical conclusion, education will be run by artificial intelligence, with eloquent avatars and curricular tracks created based on individual pro-files. And ultimately the effects of competition will emerge from the stark reality that being online, and leveraging the power of artificial intelligence consumes enormous amounts of energy. Call me a luddite, but there is a better way that leverages the fact we are hardwired to be social, exist within groups, and barter and share commodities, including knowledge.

Cooperative and Positive Interaction Effects

Education-relevant synopsis: The success of humans as a species has depended on collaborative or cooperative interactions among individuals. This out-come of human evolution in an ecological context can be predicted from simple models. It makes sense, therefore, that education leverages positive, cooperative interactions to advance the academic achievement of individ-uals. One challenge is recognizing and reducing or eliminating cheating. Another challenge is paying attention to intention and fairness such that the transactional events that define cooperative interactions are perceived by all participating individuals as yielding favorable outcomes. Cooperative inter-actions also lead to collective intelligence in which an outcome is a diverse assemblage of individuals with different knowledge and abilities that can more effectively solve difficult problems than assemblages of similar-minded individuals. Finally, there is abundant evidence, consistent with ecological theory, that the benefits of cooperative interactions exceed the gains from competitive and individualistic learning experiences.

Nature is populated by diverse organisms that benefit from mutualistic interactions, even when it seems the individual is a solitary actor:

> From the algae that power reef-building corals, to the diverse array of pollinators that mediate sexual reproduction in many plant species, to the myriad nutritional symbionts that fix nitrogen and aid digestion, and even down to the mitochon-dria found in nearly all eukaryotes, mutualisms are ubiquitous, often ecologically dominant, and profoundly influential at all levels of biological organization. Although mutualisms can be simply defined as reciprocally beneficial relationships between organisms, they range from diffuse and indirect interactions to highly integrated and coevolved associations between pairs of species. Such mutualisms usually involve the direct exchange of goods and services (e.g., food defense and transport) and typically result in the acquisition of novel capabilities by at least one partner. (Herre et al., 1999, p. 49)

Indeed, engaging in trade is a form of collaborative or cooperative inter-action that explains the success of most life forms on the planet, and certainly explains the incredible success of humans (Ridley, 2010).

Developing and maintaining mutualistic and cooperative associations depends on the rewards to each participating individual. If individuals have better success growing, maturing, and reproducing as individuals than as part of an association or consortium of multiple individuals, then mutualism and cooperation will likely fail relative to individualistic or competitive strategies. However, mutualisms are common in nature, underscoring that in many scenarios, organisms working together and leveraging the different capabilities of the interacting partners is the best recipe for success. This is certainly true in the evolutionary history of life on Earth. Thus, we should pay attention to the details of mutualisms in an effort to create productive, collaborative interactions among individuals in ways that can transform education from a competitive process with ranking of individuals as a deliverable to education as a mutualistic process with the emergence of highly collaborative individuals as a deliverable.

The challenge is that once mutualism emerges as a successful strategy, it is subject to cheating; that is, individuals can take advantage of the propensity for sharing resources without offering anything in return. As Yu (2001) noted, "Cooperation invites cheating, and nowhere is this more apparent than when different species cooperate, known as mutualism. In almost all mutualisms studied, specialist parasites have been identified that purloin [steal] the benefits that one mutualist provides another" (p. 529). The fact that individuals can become successful parasites of mutualisms suggests there are specific conditions for maintaining mutualisms. There are a variety of models described for understanding the conditions for the stable persistence of mutualisms in the context of opportunities for cheating (Yu, 2001). The prisoner's dilemma is a widely investigated model, and cooperation emerges from a tit-for-tat strategy. If two individuals repeatedly engage in interactions with some rewards, the stable strategy that emerges is that each partner mimics what the other partner does. If the first partner defects, the second partner defects. If the first partner cooperates, the second partner cooperates. Because the payoffs are greater when both partners cooperate, the best strategy is for both partners to cooperate. Yu (2001) notes that tit-for-tat is a retaliation strategy, and for "retaliation to work, each player must recognize other players individually and remember each player's action from the previous round of play together. . . . Also, retaliation strategies fail against highly mobile players, in large groups, in single rounds of play, and if the players are allowed to 'short-change' each other" (p. 530).

Another strategy is referred to as by-product mutualism. In this scenario, individuals do not care what their interacting partner does; they cooperate because they are "hardwired" to maximize their personal gains. Thus, there is no need to invoke reciprocity or tit-for-tat as a necessary route to cooperation. Because this model is simpler than models invoking retaliation (or decisions that depend on the actions of others), by-product mutualism is the most parsimonious explanation for the occurrence of cooperation. However, decision-making is rarely based on simple payoff maximization:

> Humans bargain. They anticipate and try to influence each other's behaviour. Strategies based on reputation building, trust, scorekeeping and punishment can flourish under conditions where the short-term costs of cooperation are outweighed by its long-term benefits. . . . Unconditional strategies such as "cooperate all the time" may arise if exploiting others imposes a net cost on the actor or, conversely, if resisting exploitation imposes a net cost . . . humans can be induced to cooperate at unexpectedly high frequencies under a wide variety of experimental conditions. (Palameta & Brown, 1999, pp. F3)

Thus, there is good evidence from behavioral ecology, especially of social animals, that cooperation is a valuable strategy that improves the condition of individuals that engage in cooperative behaviors. One visceral example from nature is the effect of hunting pack size and pride size on the predation success of wolves and lions, respectively. For these animals, cooperation is essential because success as individuals is so low. The challenge of securing difficult to subdue and dangerous prey is best solved by cooperation. For wolves, the short-term costs of expending energy and risking injury associated with taking down a large bison is more than compensated for by the longer-term gains of securing a place in the social hierarchy of a wolf pack that ensures access to sufficient food for growth, maturation, and reproduction (MacNulty et al., 2014). Performance-based hierarchy ranking is probably evident in lions, and other social animals. Importantly, for such a difficult task, more wolves are better, suggesting solving such a difficult problem benefits from cooperation. Similarly, for lions, securing food is much more successful if there are multiple individuals working together, and the gains afforded by cooperation are greater than the costs of food sharing. These are examples of tasks in ecological contexts that cannot be accomplished without cooperation. Studies of group size in humans show similar patterns, suggesting that for many species behaviors enabling living and working in groups may be "hardwired" adaptations.

Humans are social organisms. It is likely that our ancestors going back in time millions of years were social. Indeed, studies of hunter-gatherer human societies have revealed "mobile hunter-gatherers live in groups dominated by links between nonrelatives, where residential group membership is fluid and supports large-scale social networks of interaction" (Bird et al., 2019, p. 96). The success of groups depends on cooperation (Casari & Tagliapietra, 2019). How can the inherent tendency for cooperation be leveraged in educational settings? The models suggest the key factor promoting mutualisms is repeated interaction coupled with payoffs that encourage cooperative behavior. The payoffs may include penalties for defectors, but, as Yu (2001) noted, what really matters is there are payoffs for cooperation.

Is there evidence from education research that cooperation is more successful than competitive or individualistic strategies? If we import our understanding of the effects of interactions from ecology, the prediction is that the rate of gain and the total achievable cognitive ability is greater when students work cooperatively than if they work independently or interact in the context of competition-based pedagogy. This prediction is supported by empirical data from education research. For instance, Johnson et al. (2014) described large and positive effect sizes of mutualistic interactions on five measures of cognitive ability—including attitude, esteem, support, interpersonal interactions, and achievement—when compared with competitive and individualistic education strategies. The positive effects of cooperative learning were large and consistent across multiple dimensions of human cognitive function relevant for educational gain.

Additionally, a metaanalysis revealed "a positive effect of cooperative learning on achievement and attitudes" and that "the age level of the students and the culture in which the study took place are associated with variations in effect size" (Kyndt et al., 2013, p. 133). Additionally, the effect size was larger for tertiary (college) level students than for secondary students. Natasi and Clements (1991) noted "that there are no types of learning tasks on which cooperation is less effective than competition or individual work for enhancing learning. In fact, for most tasks, except those requiring the simplest rote skills, cooperative situations are superior. Findings are consistent across age groups (elementary through college), ability levels, variations in cultural and ethnic background, and subject areas, including mathematics, language arts, social studies, and science" (p. 112; see also Johnson et al., 2000).

Cooperative learning fosters collective intelligence. Collective intelligence is defined as the general ability of a group to perform a wide variety of tasks; it is a property of the group and the members of the group. Woolley et al. (2010, p. 686) noted that collective intelligence is "not strongly correlated with the average or maximum individual intelligence of group members but is correlated with the average social sensitivity of group members, the equality in distribution of conversational turn-taking, and the proportion of females in the group." Additionally, collective intelligence does not preclude advances in individual intelligence; it is additive and happens as a consequence of the benefits of working in groups. Part of the effect may be related to the fact that cognitive capacity for individuals is greater when working in groups than when working alone. Kirschner et al. (2009) found that

> learning by an individual becomes less effective and efficient than learning by a group of individuals as task complexity increases. Dividing the processing of information across individuals is useful when the cognitive load is high because it allows information to be divided across a larger reservoir of cognitive capacity. Although such division requires that information be recombined and that processing be coordinated, under high load conditions, these costs are minimal compared to the gain achieved by this division of labor. (p. 31)

The evidence aligns with the predictions of canonical ecological models in which interaction coefficients are positive instead of negative.

A key aspect of cooperation, and the emergence of a collective gain, is intention and fairness. In a transactional scenario, if two cooperating individuals have the perception of receiving more gain than the other, the net result, perhaps realized after multiple episodes of interaction, is that any short-term gains are lost because the interaction is eliminated as a consequence of obvious violation of fair trade and greed. If, for instance, I have a commodity that you think is essential, and you have a different commodity that I think is essential, there is an incentive to trade. If, however, one of us attempts to gain more than they exchange—there is a short-term gain for one individual, a loss for the other individual—it is likely the interaction will break down, because the core principle of fairness has been violated, and if this happens, both individuals suffer the consequences. Thus, as an educational strategy, setting up the conditions for productive cooperation requires paying attention to transactional properties of interactions. All group members must participate by actively and genuinely sharing their knowledge and ability, and all group members should bring something of value to the interaction. In classroom situations, a productive means of achieving these conditions is through the use of a jigsaw learning activity (Slish, 2005; Baken et al., 2022). A jigsaw learning activity involves providing each member of a group key information—either content or a process skill—and the product of group work should explicitly value all of the pieces of the jigsaw puzzle. The jigsaw is named because it is designed for individuals to bring their piece of the puzzle and fit it together with the other pieces for generating a coherent whole.

It's worth briefly describing how to create and implement jigsaw learning activities. The key to their success is that each individual in a group becomes an expert about their particular piece of the puzzle. If, for instance, the topic of study is coevolution, each student is provided with different information about the interaction between the species suspected of coevolving (see Hoskinson et al., 2021). The Hoskinson et al. (2021) example focuses on crossbills (a type of finch), pines, and squirrels. Once students become familiar with their skill or information, students with the same information are encouraged to explore, discuss, and make an evidence-based claim about the information. Ideally, each student is assessed on their knowledge prior to beginning their interactions with members of their group that have different pieces of the jigsaw puzzle. Once students have become experts, students share their information and develop a collective claim based on the evidence from all members of the group. In the case of the coevolution case study, students construct a claim about whether coevolution is happening between all possible pairs of the three species (crossbill, pine tree, and squirrel) and summarize the evidence for the claim. Students have access to the rubric for evaluating a claim. In a typical class of 60 students, there are 15 groups that generate 15 different claims and summaries of the evidence. These products can then form the basis for feedback and also serve as a means of making student work public for the purpose of supporting and challenging student thinking. The activity also provides a means for engaging in self-reflection about the actions and value of cooperative work, and can form the basis for describing how science happens. This latter aspect can be explored by using one of the sources of information for the jigsaw activity and describing the different contributions of the coauthors of the published work. The clear message is that science—and many endeavors—benefits from collaborative work and the emergence of collective intelligence.

Interaction Varies over Time

Education-relevant synopsis: It is clear that cooperative interactions yield greater academic and learning gains than other strategies; however, the value, productivity, and types of interactions that happen in groups of students can vary over time and among groups. The variation is largely due to differences in personality and demographically defined identities of individuals. Additionally, there is immense complexity introduced into learning experiences when individuals interact, and the complexity can lead to unexpected outcomes. Educators need to anticipate complexity, allow for intrapersonal variation and promote collaborative outcomes. Educators need to learn how different students interact and engage with students in ways that emphasize the suite of behaviors categorized as being cooperative.

Personalities are defined as consistent individual differences in the performance of specific behaviors. In animals, the propensity for interaction depends on personality; there are different personalities and correspondingly different propensities for interaction (Hasenjager & Dugatkin, 2015). Dimensions of personality include aggressiveness, boldness, sociability, activity level, and explorative tendencies. Even though there is recognition that individuals have different personalities (and propensities for interactions), personality often varies more within individuals over time and in different contexts than between individuals (Biro & Adriaenssens, 2013). Differences in personality contribute to differences in the frequency, duration, and characteristics of interactions. For instance, Pike et al. (2008) discovered that

> bold individuals had fewer overall interactions than shy fish, but tended to distribute their interactions more evenly across all group members. Shy fish, on the other hand, tended to associate preferentially with a small number of other group members, leading to a highly skewed distribution of interactions. This was mediated by the reduced tendency of shy fish to move to a new location within the tank when they were interacting with another individual; bold fish showed no such tendency and were equally likely to move irrespective of whether they were interacting or not. The results show that animal social network structure can be affected by the behavioural composition of group members and have important implications for understanding the spread of information and disease in social groups. (p. 2515)

In addition, Trompf and Brown (2014) discovered that "boldness and sociality affected decisions to use conflicting social and private information.

Bolder females used social information to avoid competition and/or potential patch depletion, whereas highly social individuals preferred the presence of conspecifics over rich foraging opportunities. There was no evidence of a speed–accuracy trade-off in a spatial associative learning task; rather, bold female guppies learned both more quickly and more accurately than shy females" (p. 99). In birds there are so called slow and fast explorers. Slow explorers tended to stay with the same individuals and flock, whereas fast explorers had more numerous interactions for shorter periods of time and were more likely to move between flocks (Aplin et al., 2013). These and other results show that individuals with different personalities interact differently with other individuals, and there is expected to be variation of interactions between individuals and within individuals over time depending on personality and context.

Moreover, each individual has a unique chronotype (see chapter 2). Solomon and Zeitzer (2019) discovered an association between an individual's chronotype and personality traits. Refinetti et al. (2016) discovered that there is variation in the chronotype—and correlated behaviors—within individuals on consecutive days, but that the within-individual variation was less than the variation among individuals. In addition to chronotype, prior experience and immediate conditions modulate behavior and influence interaction propensity and duration (this is often referred to as sociability) (Stamps et al., 2012). These and other factors increase the variation of interaction of individuals over time. Overall, heritability (the genetic effects) of personality traits associated with sociability is low (Dochtermann et al., 2015), and we should expect variation both within and among individuals in the classroom for behavior linked to learning and collaboration.

Bold and shy describe fish and individuals in classrooms. In fact, if I engage in word replacement, the paragraph above (from Pike et al., 2008, p. 2515) provides a remarkably accurate description of what happens in classrooms.

> [Student] social networks can be extremely complex and are characterized by highly non-random interactions between group members . . . bold individuals had fewer overall interactions than shy [students], but tended to distribute their interactions more evenly across all group members. Shy [students], on the other hand, tended to associate preferentially with a small number of other group members, leading to a highly skewed

distribution of interactions. This was mediated by the reduced tendency of shy [students] to move to a new location within the [classroom] when they were interacting with another individual; bold [students] showed no such tendency and were equally likely to move irrespective of whether they were interacting or not. The results show that animal social network structure can be affected by the behavioural composition of group members and have important implications for understanding the spread of information and [learning] in social groups.

Evidence for these claims about students comes from Buchenroth-Martin et al. (2016), who found, using social network analysis, what they termed "wanderers" and "settlers." Wanderers correspond with bold individuals or fast explorers and settlers are most similar to shy individuals or slow explorers.

In addition to behavior, aspects of individual identity (e.g., sex and age) predict interaction frequency. For instance, ungulates (e.g., deer and their kin) form sexually segregated groups and interactions happen mostly between individuals of the same sex (except during reproduction). Main (2008, p. 693) concluded that sexual segregation is an "evolutionary response to differences in reproductive strategies: males choose habitats to maximize energy gains in preparation for rut, and females select habitats with combinations of resources that contribute to offspring survival." In groups comprised of both sexes, like in mongoose, the ratio of males to females varies in response to environmental conditions, and, importantly, cooperative interactions are more evident when ecological condition are variable and can be predicted by probability of reproductive success: individuals that engage in more cooperative behaviors have higher reproductive success when ecological conditions are harsh (Marshall et al., 2016). In a study of spider monkeys, there is strong sex segregation. Group sizes are larger for males than females; additionally, females develop associations with other females in ways that are dependent on the presence of dependent offspring, and females with offspring actively avoid areas with males because males are dangerous (Chapman, 1990). There are other species and ecological contexts in which group composition and opportunities for interaction vary by sex and age. Overall, the demographic structure of groups is variable, depending on species and ecological context, and the structure influences the types and frequencies of social interactions in ways that regulate conflicts, create affiliations and alliances, facilitate cooperation, and facilitate information transmission (Sosa et al., 2021).

Interactions among individuals of the same species in ecological contexts are context and individual dependent and, as a result, extremely variable.

What does behavioral variation for interactivity in the classroom look like? In this context, interactivity is the propensity or frequency of an individual's interaction with others. I often ask students to engage in student-centered learning that involves interaction among students in small groups culminating in some evidence-based claim. When I collect interaction data, I calculate the mean number of interaction events and the standard deviation. The coefficient of variation (CV)—the standard deviation divided by the mean—provides a useful metric for estimating interaction inequality. Interaction data from two different activities for a set of five groups in two sections[1] of the course show that there is tremendous interaction variation among individuals, and among groups (fig. 4.2). The

Figure 4.2. The summary of interactions among students working in small groups on two different cognitive challenges (top and bottom) in two separate sections of the same course (left and right). For each of the four sets of observations, the circles are individuals and the black lines show undirected interactions based on records of conversation and student orientation. Each line connects two circles (students) that interacted. The thickness of the lines is proportional to the number and duration of interactions during an activity. Dashed lines are students who were part of a group but were not discernibly social and did not interact; their connections to another individual is arbitrary. The mean and sd (standard deviation) values are for the numbers of separate episodes of interaction across all groups within each of the four separate learning events. *Source:* Created by the author.

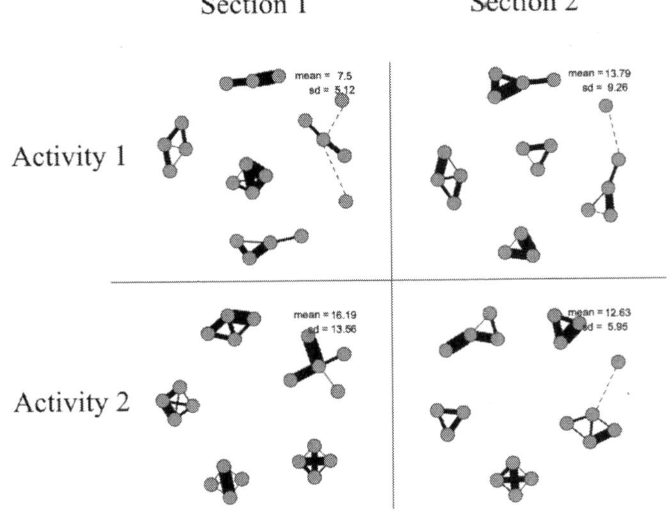

activities were not jigsaws but did offer opportunities to become engaged in solving a problem. One value of these data is we can estimate inequality and attempt to intervene in ways that reduce the CV while maintaining a high average interactivity. The CV scores for jigsaw lessons typically have higher average interactivity and low CV scores.

A visualization of individual interactivity over time revealed higher variation within individuals than among individuals over time (see chapter 2). The most general result was that interactivity varied over time for most individuals, sometimes a lot. Likely causes of the variation might include the effects of diet and metabolic state (Han & Dingemanse, 2017), context defined by the particular cognitive challenge (Sih & Del Giudice, 2012), group membership (Koski & Burkart, 2015), and various other factors (including chronotype). In education settings, I think it is safe to say that, with a few exceptions, individual interactivity varies more within individuals over time than among individuals, recognizing that there is tremendous variation among individuals. A plot of the average and variation of individual interactivity revealed a positive correlation; the more individuals interact, on average, the more variable they were over time. In fact, the results of an observational study of a student-centered, interactive learning experience underscores one of the compelling claims in the individual chapter: individuals differ from each other for phenotypes—namely, their propensity for engaging in interactions—with effects on learning. This inference may have profound implications for enacting student-centered, interactive learning pedagogies. It depends whether the intraindividual variation is due to the effects of what happens in the classroom or is a manifestation of the state of individuals engaged in interaction.

There is clear evidence that student identity and behavior influence the frequency and productivity of interactions in small groups (Springer et al., 1999). Eddy et al. (2015, p. 1) discovered that "self-reported preferred roles in peer discussions can be predicted by student gender, race/ethnicity, and nationality" and that these roles and whether students were able to interact productively depended on whether they were able to engage in their preferred role. In another study (Theobald et al., 2017), researchers discovered, not surprisingly, that friendship had an important influence on interaction, and that the presence of a "dominator" personality decreased interaction frequency and productivity; it was often the case that dominators were males. It is clear based on many years of experiences working with small groups in educational contexts that an important component of an individual's interactivity is group composition, namely, the combination of personalities and demographic identities. Some people work better together than others. Ideally, students are able to overcome interpersonal obstacles and achieve productive interactions regardless of membership. This requires trust, an emphasis on dignity and shared values, and a cognitive challenge that fully engages everyone. It is worth mentioning that jigsaw challenges impose structure that can increase interaction frequency and productivity and limit negative effects of personality (Theobald et al., 2017). An additional critical variable is the number of individuals in a group.

Learning in Small Groups

Education-relevant synopsis: A key aspect of a cooperative learning environment is that students work in groups. There are costs and benefits of working in groups; moreover, the costs and benefits are dependent on group size. Ideally, group size is optimized such that the collective gains are greater than can be achieved by individuals working alone and greater than the gains for larger groups. One challenge is that optimal group size is dependent on the traits of individuals comprising a group—including personalities, demographic and social identities, and academic abilities—and the particular cognitive challenge. Educational challenges that combine individualistic and cooperative strategies provide a useful means of investigating optimal group size and group-dependent gains, and provide the basis for showing students the value of engaging in cooperative-based education in an explicit social environment. Two important outcomes of monitoring cooperative learning are that optimal group size and permanence are context-specific and dependent on the types of group work; moreover, the benefits of working in groups may depend on how long a particular set of individuals have been working together and students' sense of permanence of group compositions. Cooperative learning requires significant investment into developing authentic opportunities for collaboration and cooperation: problems must be complex, difficult, authentic, and relatable. Useful strategies include two-stage exams, jigsaw challenges, and independent research that requires specialization of students on different tasks directed toward an integrated and connected product.

A group is a subset of a population. Individuals in a group often include family members but there may also be unrelated individuals. Many animals—including humans—live and work in groups. Within the group, both competitive and cooperative interactions may happen. Similarly, there are costs and benefits of living in groups. The fact that individuals of so many divergent species live and work together in groups suggests the benefits outweigh the costs, on average, and that individuals who "go it alone" are less successful than if they joined and participated in groups. Markham et al. (2015) noted, "Animals form groups when the benefits of aggregation—including decreased predation risk, facilitation of cooperative infant care, increased probability of winning intergroup competition, and information sharing—exceed the costs of maintaining close proximity with conspecifics. Conversely, costs are primarily derived from intragroup competition for limited resources, such as food and reproductive opportunities, and increased probability of disease transmission" (p. 14882).

Another cost of living and working in groups is conflict among members of a group due to hierarchy and differences in strength and ability to secure resources. In some groups, there is a dynamic at play in which some members of a group try to secure more benefits for themselves at the expense of subordinates; in turn, subordinates leave or stay in the group depending on the relative costs of staying or leaving (Vehrencamp, 1983). The inequity of realizing the costs and benefits among members of a group has been described as skew: "Ecological factors affect both the net benefit of grouping and the options for leaving, and thus establish the limits of skewing. . . . The degree of skew increases when the benefit of group breeding relative to solitary breeding increases, and when the degree of relatedness among group members increases" (Vehrencamp, 1983, p. 327). Thus, social manipulation exists in groups, and it is likely within a group of different types of individuals, there is social manipulation resulting in some degree of skew; the intensity of skew will likely reflect a variety of factors.

Higashi and Yamamura (1993) developed a general model for the existence and persistence of groups (fig. 4.3). Groups will exist if the benefits to individual members exceed the benefits that can be accrued by single individuals in the same environment. Furthermore, there is an optimal group size and a stable group size. The optimal group size is the number of individuals in a group in which the success of individuals is maximized. The stable group size is the number of individuals for which the benefits to individuals acting alone and individuals functioning in a group are equal. The stable group size can be much larger than the optimal group size. Importantly, the fact that the model is parabolic and bends down reflects the reality that in all populations in which functional groups exist both competition and cooperation coexist. The curve in

Figure 4.3. Model showing the dependence of individual success (described as fitness) as a function of group size. The horizontal dash line is the success of a single individual living and working in the absence of interactions with others. The vertical dashed lines show the optimal group size (the line to the greatest success value) and the group size in which the average success of individuals in a group is equal to the average fitness of an individual living alone. *Source:* Created by the author. Modified from Higashi and Yamamura (1993).

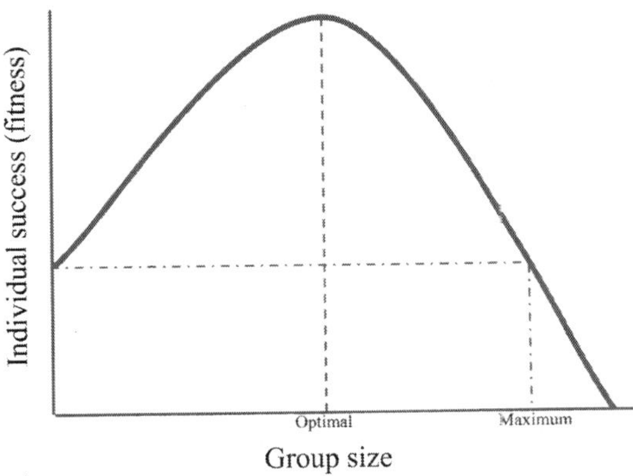

figure 4.3 bends down because there are finite resources being allocated to an increasing number of individuals. If group size is greater than the stable group size, the negative effects of competition are greater than the positive effects of cooperation.

The benefits of living and working in groups vary depending on the difficulty of problem-solving and the payoffs to individuals. In social predators (like wolves and lions), the benefit of working in groups varies depending on the type of prey. The payoff—measured as the metabolic gain—differs depending on the challenge. Small prey items have less metabolic gain but also involve less metabolic expenditure than large prey. In lions, for instance, the net gain of resources is positive across a large range of group sizes when the prey is wildebeest, whereas smaller prey (gazelle) provide net gains only for small group sizes (in this case, two individuals). Thus, the benefits of working in groups for solving problems or securing resources for growth and reproduction are context-dependent.

Estimating the effects of group size on the metabolic gain of individuals is a decidedly benefits-oriented outlook on the cost and benefits of living in a group. Other behavioral ecology studies have focused on the costs. Pride (2005) focused on a model that minimizes the costs imposed by stress from intergroup conflict (mainly predation) and intragroup conflict (mainly competition). Small groups are vulnerable to predation and conflict with other groups; with increasing group sizes, these negative stresses decline; however, the costs of intragroup conflict increase with increasing group size. Thus, in this model, optimal group size exists when the sum of these two costs is minimized (fig. 4.4). Pride (2005) used the concentration of stress hormones in the blood of individuals as an indicator of metabolic cost of being in a group. He found that circulating levels of stress hormones were lowest at intermediate groups sizes and that optimization is evident only as an abstract long-term average effect, because short term variation in prevailing conditions causes shifts in levels of stress. Thus, at any given time, the balance between intergroup conflict and intragroup competition alters the costs incurred by individuals.

In humans there is clear evidence that living, working, and solving problems happens in groups. There is an abundance of information and inferences about competition and cooperation. Lamba and Mace (2011) engaged in a large-scale experiment designed to study the conditions promoting cooperation or resulting in defection (i.e., competition). In their study, cooperation was defined as willingly distributing the benefits of working in a group to all members of the group. They discovered two important results. First, cooperation is negatively associated with village population size. This is similar to the predictions of Higashi and

Figure 4.4. A model of optimal group size based on minimizing predation and minimizing conflict among individuals. *Source:* Created by the author. Modified from Pride (2005).

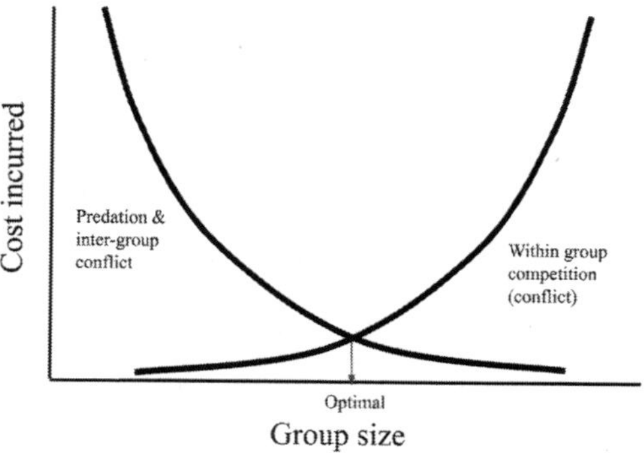

Yamamura's (1993) model in the sense that as population size gets larger, there is greater incentive for individuals to defect and act individually and competitively than altruistically and cooperatively. Second, Lamba and Mace (2011) discovered that cooperation is negatively associated with relatedness, especially relatedness among females. Lamba and Mace (2011) concluded, "Behavioral variation [in the extent individuals are cooperative] currently attributed to cultural norms may . . . be driven by ecological and demographic differences between populations" (p. 14429). Thus, while individuals may be hardwired to be social, whether they are cooperative or competitive in social contexts depends on the intersection of the prevailing environmental conditions, relatedness to others, and the behavioral tendencies of individuals.

There are other organisms that participate in cooperative behavior for reasons that differ from gaining resources or limiting stress. For prey species, surveillance and avoidance of predation may be more efficient and less costly in a group than for individuals. Perhaps the most relevant model stems from the "many-eyes" hypothesis; that group size is positively related to predator surveillance. The basic idea is that "an individual forager can devote less time to vigilance (and more time to feeding) as group size increases without any lessening of the group's ability to detect an attack. Basic to this hypothesis is the assumption of collective detection: that all members of the group are alerted to an attack as long as it is detected by at least one individual" (Lima, 1995, p. 11).

One of the main factors supporting the formation and persistence of groups in social organisms subject to predation is the role of predator surveillance. Surveillance has a cost, because it takes time away from foraging. Archetti (2000) imagined the following scenario: "Two individuals observe a predator approaching and must decide, separately and without coordination, whether to give the alarm, which would spoil the predator's ambush. An alarm call would be beneficial for both individuals because it would deter the predator from this and future attacks; each player, however, prefers that it is the other player to report the presence of the predator" (p. 475). In this context, there is a benefit for sounding the alarm if few or one individual bears the cost, and the individual that acts on behalf of others changes with each successive predator challenge. However, if many individuals volunteer and bear the cost of surveillance and predator alarm, then the benefits of living in a group decay because the collective good of an individual's action is not realized. Archetti (2000) wrote:

> If one or few individuals are enough to perform an action that produces a collective good and if this action has a cost, living in a group can be beneficial because the cost can be shared with other individuals. Without coordination, however, the production of a collective good by the contribution of one or few individuals is inefficient and can be modeled as a volunteer's dilemma. In the volunteer's dilemma the individuals that pay the cost for the production of the collective good benefit from their action if nobody else volunteers, but the cost is wasted if too many individuals volunteer. Increasing group size reduces the need of volunteering for each member of the group; the overall benefit for the group, however, decreases too because the larger the group is, the less likely it is that the collective good is produced. This problem persists even with a high degree of relatedness between group members; an optimal, intermediate group size exists that maximizes the probability to produce the collective good. (p. 475)

Studies of optimal group size for social animals in ecological contexts suggest observed group size is an emergent outcome of myriad processes, including, but not limited to, competition, interference, cooperation, vigilance, and predation. Some of the factors contributing to the emergent optimal group size include the gain in metabolic resources and the limitations of stress relative to the costs of maintaining group integrity and cohesion. Some of these factors are likely to play roles in educational settings when students work in groups. One key difference between ecological and educational contexts is that group size in educational settings is usually not an emergent property of the system, but is more often a fixed feature determined by pedagogy and other aspects of the educational environment. It is often the case, for instance, I limit group size to three or four students. Competition, individualism, and cooperation exist in ecological settings, and the success of individuals under each scenario depends on the properties of individuals, the environmental context, and availability of resources. The same is true for educational settings. Thus, we should imagine that many of the same principles governing the emergence and functional property of groups in ecological settings also happen in education contexts.

The clear benefits of group work are evident by the fact that many educators create learning experiences with group work as a central pedagogical factor. However, even though students are asked to work in groups, they often have the expectation that their actions will be evaluated as individuals rather than as members of a group. Yet, we know from ecology that individuals may have better success functioning within groups than if they worked alone. If we paraphrase Markham et al. (2015, p. 14882) and replace ecological factors with things that happen in classrooms, we can say that, if allowed (and encouraged), students form groups when the benefits of aggregation and collaboration—including reciprocal facilitation of learning, increased probability of producing high quality solutions to problems, forming mutually productive social ties, and enhanced information sharing—exceed the costs of maintaining close proximity and sharing knowledge with peers. Costs are primarily derived from competition for resources and an increased probability of cheating, free-loading, and social manipulation causing inequity. Thus, even though the intended pedagogical structure may be cooperative, expectations may exist that erode the integrity of the cooperative intent.

We can look to ecology for strategies that may improve the formation and function of groups in educational settings. This is important because the group enables increasing collective and individual intelligence. Advancing collective and individual intelligence are two main educational goals. There are three important axes of variation in cooperative structures: group size, whether all group members are invested in collaboration, and the inherent complexity or difficulty of the activity proposed as an educational (and collaborative) opportunity.

The model developed by Higashi and Yamamura (1993) for interrogating the effects of group size for the success of individuals applies to educational contexts. I have investigated the effects of group size on student learning gains in many contexts. A general strategy for estimating gains is pre- and post-activity assessment. The summary graphs have the parabolic shape of Higashi and Yamamura's (1993) model (see fig. 4.5). Groups should exist if the benefits to group members exceed the benefits that can be accrued by single individuals in the same environment. I have abundant evidence that this is true across a wide range of contexts. Furthermore, there is an optimal group size. In general, for most contexts and challenges, group sizes of three or four are usually optimal, and the described stable group size (the group size where the two dashed lines intersect in fig. 4.5) is larger than the optimal size. The curve bends down, in part, because there are finite resources being allocated to an increasing number of individuals, and if group size is greater than the stable group size, the negative effects of competition exceed the positive effects of cooperation.

Figure 4.5. Estimate of the dependence on student learning gains relative to group size. Each point is the average learning gain and the error bars are 95% confidence intervals. The horizontal and vertical dashed lines identify the maximum group size for which gains are larger for the group compared to the individual. The graph is constructed to mirror Higashi and Yamamura's (1993) model. *Source:* Created by the author.

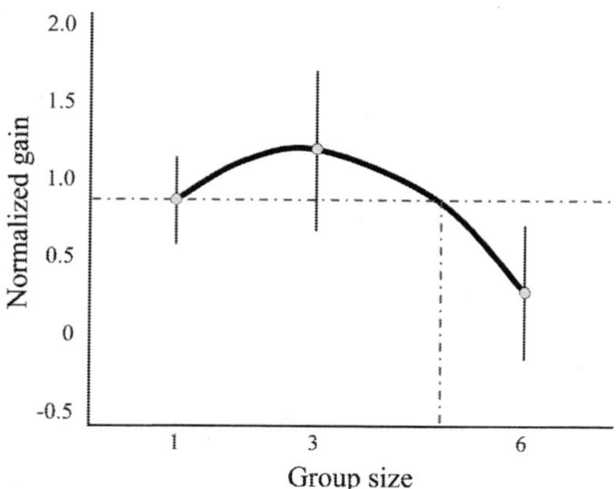

Two-stage exams provide a promising way of estimating the gains of individuals learning individually and as a part of a collective (in a group) (Martin, 2018). In two-stage exams, students complete an assessment individually and then are asked to complete the same assessment in groups. Thus, there are two scores resulting from administering two-stage exams: the individual scores for all members of a group and a single group score based on the combined efforts of the group. These two scores define three performance types that reflect the outcomes of individualistic and cooperative actions. If the group score is greater than the average individual score, there is evidence of cooperation. If the group score is less than the average individual score, there is evidence of interference and competition. If the group score is equal to the average individual score, there is evidence of individualism. Importantly, this particular framework is similar to the Higashi and Yamamura (1993) model (fig. 4.6). In this case, he positive effect is the area of the graph above the horizontal dashed line, the negative effect is the area below the horizontal dashed line, and the additive effect is the horizontal dashed line.

Figure 4.7 shows two examples of two-stage exam scores. Each point is a student. These data underscore that student success increases,

Figure 4.6. Comparison of the Higashi and Yamamura (1993) ecological model describing the dependence of individual success on group size and a two-stage assessment model in education in which group productivity depends on individual scores. The rectangular boxes in the Higashi and Yamamura model correspond with the areas defined as positive interaction effect, additive effect, and negative interaction effect for the two-stage model. *Source:* Created by the author.

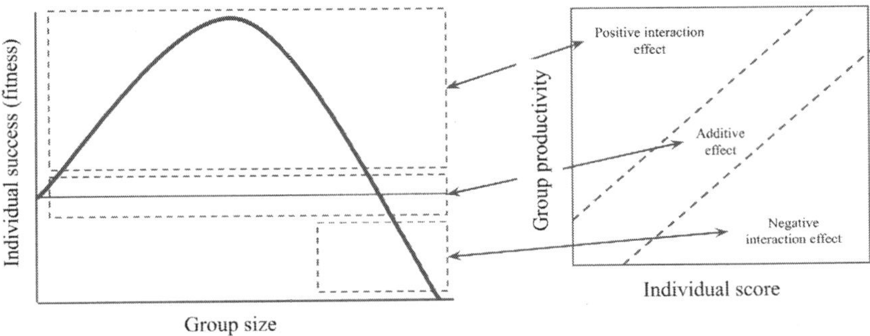

Figure 4.7. An example of the results from a two-stage exam. Each point represents the score for an individual in two contexts: as individuals and as members of a group. The average individual score is the proportion of individuals in the group that answered a question correctly as individuals. The group score is a measure of the success of the group. The model categorizes individuals in the upper-left corner as engaging in positive interactions, individuals in the lower-right corner as engaging in negative interaction, and individuals that fall out along the diagonal as individuals for which interaction effects are not evident. The abundance of points in the upper left corner indicates students mostly engage in positive and productive interactions. *Source:* Created by the author.

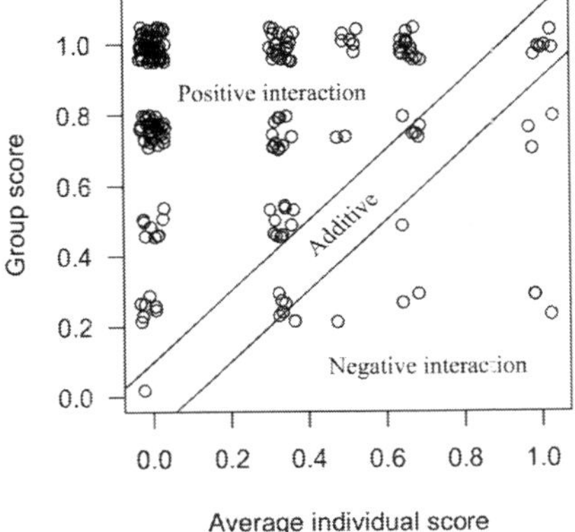

on average, when they are in groups. However, there are many cases in which individual success is unaffected by being in a group (the points that fall in the diagonal space) and cases in which individual success is lower than expected based on their individual score, suggesting the negative effects of competition exist. This simple structure for quantifying success of individuals in two contexts provides a useful tool for investigating the interplay of cooperation, competition, and individualism in educational settings.

The data from figure 4.7 can be organized such that individual success is dependent on group size following the Higashi and Yamamura model; and the data matches the expectations of the model (see fig. 4.6). Without a dedicated investigation of the effects of group size on individual success, it is not possible to reliably estimate the optimal group size and the "stable" maximum group size defined by Higashi and Yamamura (1993). Nonetheless, there are claims about optimal group size in the literature. One is that eight students is too large, and that four is ideal when students are assigned the roles of assigner-reporter, recorder, spokesperson, and monitor (Michaelsen et al., 2023); the claim that four is ideal stems from the fact that only four assigned and described roles exist. Using the framework for understanding group size in ecological settings provides a useful framework for investigating optimal group size in educational settings, and how we might figure out the dependence of optimal group size on the complexity of cognitive challenges. "Optimal group size and permanence are likely context-specific and dependent on the types of group work used in class" (Connell et al., 2023, p. 8). Moreover, the benefits of working in groups may depend on how long a particular set of individuals have been working together, and students' sense of permanence of group compositions (Connell et al., 2023).

Investment in group learning involves putting effort—mental and physical—into working together in ways that enable all individuals to participate in the construction of individual and collective intelligence. Educators have to create authentic opportunities for collaboration toward a common goal, and students have to be present, supportive, and committed to the success of the group. How do we create authentic opportunities for collaboration and recognize and reward productive group work? What lessons can we take from ecology for improving the structure and function of groups in ways that best advance students' learning gains?

Before describing my favored strategies for promoting cooperation, it is worth emphasizing a few perspectives from ecology that contribute to the success of group work. The first is taken from the "many eyes" hypothesis. Instead of surveillance for predators, the "many eyes" can be directed toward making sure the product of group work is complete and satisfies the sense of what is necessary and complete based on more than one individual. Thus, the "many eyes" is similar to surveillance, but with a specific focus on ensuring quality and completion. The second stems from the observation that engaging in a significant cognitive challenge, like a wolf taking on the short-term costs of expending energy and the risk of injury associated with taking down a large bison, is compensated by the gain of securing a place in a social group with the expectation that others will do the same. The willingness of others to work on behalf of the group depends on evidence that all members of the group share the same interest in the success of the group. Finally, it is worth noting that being in a group can increase or decrease stress associated with interpersonal interactions. A factor that can decrease stress may include working together with the same set of individuals in ways that create shared expectations and greater predictability of interactions. Thus, implementing group work should (1) emphasize motivation for individuals to fully participate, (2) reward individuals that work on behalf of the group, and (3) limit anxiety and stress associated with interacting closely with other individuals.

There are a variety of strategies for promoting cooperation and collaboration in the classroom. I routinely use two approaches. The first is the use of two-stage exams (described earlier) followed by a discussion of how the group uses the information from the individual portion of the exam, how they engage in discussion, what happens when there are differences in perspective, and how consensus happens, especially for questions in which most of the students in the group answered incorrectly during the individual portion of the exam. Another approach for providing an opportunity for group learning and the advancement of collective intelligence is the use of jigsaw challenges. A jigsaw is a cognitive challenge in which team members need to assemble multiple, different sources and types of evidence to make a claim. The purpose of a jigsaw challenge is that each person is responsible for constructing a piece of the puzzle and working with others to fit the pieces together into a coherent whole that tells the story in the data. I have developed several jigsaw challenges with the ultimate goal of demonstrating that coherent claims about how the world works often depend on the integration of independent investigations aimed at understanding a multivariate, complex phenomenon in nature. For both of these strategies, it is important that rewards favor evidence of positive interactions and the collective contributions of individuals more than the individual actions of individuals.

Complexity and Difficulty of Cognitive Challenges

Education-relevant synopsis: There are three important axes of variation in cooperative pedagogical structures, including group size, whether all group members are invested in collaboration, and the inherent complexity or difficulty of the activity proposed as an educational (and collaborative) opportunity. Complexity depends on the degree of abstraction required by a cognitive challenge, its orderliness (i.e., whether there is a single pathway to a solution or multiple pathways and many different possible outcomes), the continuity of a problem that depends on whether the problem changes as more details are discovered or it stays more or less the same, the organization of the problem solution (Is it a network of connections or a single line of connections?), and whether the process being investigated is direct or emergent. Thus, enacting cooperative teaching involves managing complexity: of the problem and of the students engaged in interactions.

As we learned from lions and wolves, the payoffs from group work depend on the complexity and difficulty of the problem. If you are a lion, it is more difficult and complicated (and dangerous) to take down a zebra than a gazelle; if you are a wolf, bison present a more difficult and dangerous challenge than deer. Similarly, cognitive challenges vary in complexity and difficulty, depending on the breadth of knowledge required, the intricacy of the procedural elements, the connectedness among parts of the problem, whether the challenge is hierarchically structured or interdisciplinary, and other properties (Jonasssen & Hung, 2015). There are several important attributes or dimensions of challenging problems. Abstraction refers to the representation of the content and context of a problem that either facilitates or impedes analogical transfer of one problem to another (Jonasssen & Hung, 2015). Orderliness refers to the ability to enact a particular directed sequence of behaviors. Continuity of a problem is the degree to which attributes of problems remain the same or change over time or with change in context or details; high continuity problems are more easily solved and transferred than low continuity problems (Jonasssen & Hung 2015). Organization is the idea that the structure of a problem can range from simple, with few and ordered connections among the parts—a linear network—to complex, with many parts that are connected in multiple ways—a complex network. Finally, complexity varies depending on whether the process of solving the problem is directed with a specific achievable objective or emergent with an unknown outcome.

In many ways, all good teaching involves problem-based learning that involves one or more cognitive challenges. The problems are typically introduced as a means of achieving specific learning gains with the intent of increasing students' knowledge and intellectual sophistication. Cognitive challenges may be very simple: making a connection between two ideas, or between an idea and data. The challenges can also be more complex and more difficult, like constructing a new and more predictive mental model of the world that correctly predicts outcomes or the properties of phenomena for scenarios that are new to the student. Jonassen (2000) described a taxonomy of problems ordered by the inherent structural properties, from algorithms (highly structured) to resolving dilemmas or policy problems (loosely structured).

My view of cognitive challenges that are relevant for promoting productive and collaborative group work is that they consist of definable parts (ideas), connections between ideas, and a directionality of the process of assembling the connections among ideas. So, for instance, let's say the cognitive challenge—the problem to be solved—is to describe the association between precipitation and temperature from weather data. The data consists of a table of observations of temperature and whether or not there was precipitation for a large number of days. The ideas consist of (1) establishing an association between variables, (2) visualizing the data, in this case using an x-y scatter plot, (3) conducting a statistical analysis and overlaying the results of the analysis onto the graph, and then (4) using the data for constructing a story. Thus, there are four steps that move in a direct path from data to claim. This type of challenge might be best accomplished by having two students work together to reach consensus on developing a directed algorithm from data to visualization, analysis, and claim. In this particular simple and direct cognitive challenge, students will likely have discovered that precipitation is more probable when it is cooler than warmer. This would be a valid and straightforward simple claim from the data.

A more complex problem involves having students become stakeholders with different interests related to enacting a plan for the conservation of an endangered species. Imagine, for instance, the endangered species lives in a freshwater spring in a desert in which there are municipal and agricultural interests in groundwater extraction. Depending on the scope of the problem, the stakeholders could be a person representing the interests of a federal agency (e.g., the US Fish and Wildlife Service) responsible for the oversight and protection of endangered species, a scientist interested in conservation biology, a farmer with an interest in maximizing agricultural yield, a civil servant representing the interests of a growing municipality, and perhaps a member of the general public with strong interests in natural and cultural histories associated with desert springs. Typically, in situations involving multiple stakeholders, there will also be a mediator and someone with the responsibility of taking notes and recording deliberations and constructing a document that reflects the contributions of individuals. I have been involved in these sorts of community-based evaluations of endangered species plans and there are typically many more individuals involved, but these six or seven key roles are typical stakeholders. The process of developing a coherent plan from diverse stakeholders will be more emergent than direct, and may result in multiple possible outcomes as a consequence of interactions between individuals. The number of different stakeholder perspectives and the associated arguments increase the complexity; in addition, the stakeholder perspectives interact in unpredictable ways with key information that makes the process emergent.

I mentioned earlier that there are three important axes of variation in cooperative pedagogical structures, including group size, whether all group members are invested in collaboration, and the inherent complexity or difficulty of the activity proposed as an educational (and collaborative) opportunity. Of course, there are other axes of variation. One that is particularly troubling is the ability of individuals (students) to productively engage with each other given the seemingly increasing proportion of students who report being depressed or have high levels of anxiety. It could be that having students work in groups fosters a sense of belonging and self-efficacy and provides opportunities for friend-making and education about mental health, with indirect effects that increase students' sense of well-being (see Priestley et al., 2022; Mali et al., 2023). Alternatively, forming small groups can create scenarios that exacerbate mental health issues, including the emergence of unconscious bias and microaggressions among members (Levchak, 2013; Miles et al., 2021). Thus, deciding to emphasize cooperation and use small group activities as a way to practice being cooperative and learn how to behave in ways that are productive in the context of others can come with a cost. As educators, we are not often trained how to manage interactions and scaffold and support individuals who have mental health challenges that intersect with education. It is in our best interest to seek professional training in ways that improve our abilities to foster productive, collaborative, safe, and effective interpersonal interactions in small groups. It also means we have to pay attention to what happens in groups, and make sure the environments we create in classrooms are safe, and feel safe, for students.

Interaction Effects Depend on Context

Education-relevant synopsis: There are interaction effects in education; performance of individuals in a particular environment depends on the environment in which the individuals developed and matured. Students with interpersonally oriented learning styles benefit more from interactive learning environments, whereas students with other learning styles may benefit more from didactic teaching or impersonal sources (e.g., textbooks). We know, though, that interactive learning and student-centered learning have the largest average effects on student gains. Thus, a goal of education is to limit negative interaction effects such that all students can be maximally successful in environments in which knowledge and intelligence is socially constructed through interpersonal interaction. This requires recognizing students' abilities and supporting them through the process of socialization necessary for success in interactive learning environments.

There is often differential success within ecological populations. Differential success describes cases in which some individuals grow, mature, and are more successful than other individuals. Success can be measured by growth rate, maturation, survival, and reproductive success. Differential success happens because individuals differ in form and function and there are environmental effects that influence individuals differently. The success of individuals is determined by two main factors: the phenotype—form and function—of individuals and the environment in which they live. For individuals with different phenotypes that have measurably different performance properties, the effect of the environment can vary (fig. 4.8). These graphical portraits of the effects of phenotype and environment are referred to as norms of reaction. "Norms" refers to measured (or measurable) performance and "reaction" is how performance of two or more phenotypes depends on the environment. P × E describes a scenario in

Figure 4.8. Four different performance outcomes for two individuals with different form and function (phenotype, denoted P) in two different environments (sites 1 and 2). See text for explanation. *Source:* Created by the author.

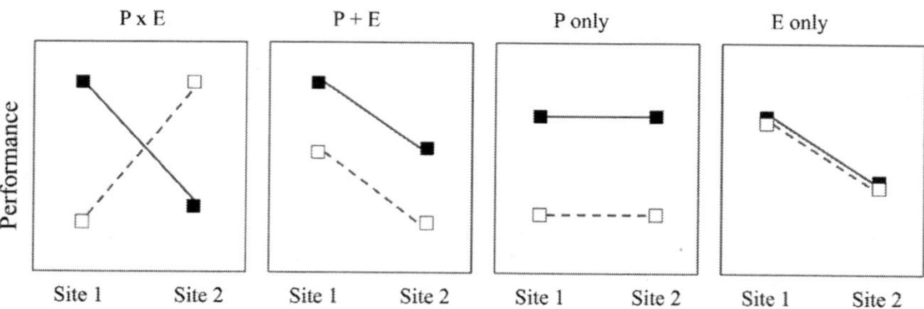

which there is an interaction between phenotype (P) and environment (E). P × E is evident when the lines describing the average performance of different individuals cross. P + E describes a scenario in which the phenotype indicated by the filled square has higher performance scores than the open circle in both environments and one environment results in higher performance than the other environment. P refers to a case in which there is a difference in performance between phenotypes without an effect of the environment. And finally, E describes a scenario in which there is no effect of phenotype but the two phenotypes have different performance scores in the two environments.

There are good examples of studies investigating the effect of phenotype and environment on an individual's success. Piola and Johnson (2006) focused on the growth and survival of individuals of the same species in different environments. The species is an organism called a bryozoan. A bryozoan is a marine invertebrate that forms small colonies on rocks. They sampled individuals from two localities in nature: one from a site with metal toxins and one from a site without the toxins. They studied the effects of living in a site with and without toxins by growing individuals from the two different environments in experimental environments in which the amount of metal was controlled by the investigators. When individuals from the two different environments—with and without toxins—were grown in sites without heavy metals, the individuals from the population that lived in the location without heavy metals did the best; when the two types of individuals were grown in sites with heavy metals, the individuals from the population that lived in the location with heavy metals did the best. More importantly, though, if we summarized the four growth rates, there was evidence of P × E. The growth rate of individuals that lived in the presence of environmental toxins in nature had growth rates that were similar whether or not there were toxins in the experimental conditions. By contrast, for individuals from environments without environmental toxins, the growth rates were very different depending on whether toxins were present or not. In the absence of toxins, these individuals grew relatively fast; when the toxins were present, the individuals actually had a negative growth rate.

The study by Piola and Johnson (2006), and many other similar studies, shows that the performance of individuals in a particular environment depends on the environment in which the individuals developed and matured. This study emphasizes that individuals have differential success because there are different challenges in different places: success is dependent on the environment context. Much of the effect of whether an individual is living in a "native" or "foreign" environment reflects local adaptation. Additionally, there are other axes of variation in performance. Ecological studies of dioecious plants—individual plants are either male or female—have revealed there are different outcomes depending on whether individuals are male or female in response to variation in soil moisture. Males tend to be more abundant in more extreme sites (higher soil salinity and lower soil moisture) and females tend to be more abundant in more benign conditions (lower salinity and higher moisture) (Freeman et al., 1976). Additionally, in social mammals, variation in growth, survival, maturation, and success is dependent on the social rank of parents (Johnson, 2003).

Another way to reveal local adaptation is by using a common garden experiment. In this case, individuals who may be locally adapted to different environments are transferred into a single, common environment—most often a study done with plants, hence the name "common garden"—and the successes of individuals, across a variety of variables, are measured. What we often see is that the two different individuals vary in their performance. If they do, there is evidence of adaptation. If we compare the growth in the common garden with their growth in their native environment, it is possible to reveal P × E. In study after study, ecologists have discovered that individual performance depends on the covariance of individual characteristics with the prevailing environment conditions (Fokkema et al., 2021).

Is there evidence of P × E in educational contexts? The relevance of focusing on the interaction between phenotype and environment from ecological studies is that it may be important, and indeed common, in educational contexts. Individuals who grow up in an environment where they face constant challenges develop strategies that enable them to deal with any environment: challenge breeds resilience. As part of their resilience, they may have rates of academic achievement and intellectual maturation that are independent of environment. By contrast, individuals who grow up in a less challenging environment may have less capacity for dealing with adversity and perform poorly when the environment is challenging, but perform exceptionally well when the environment is benign. The existence of P × E should be an expectation for all educators.

There is evidence of P × E in academic settings. For instance, decades ago, Domino (1971) performed an experiment with 100 college freshmen and showed evidence of a P × E interaction effect; the interaction was described based on students' achievement orientation and an instructors' teaching style. Much of the literature on learning styles of students stems from the discovery or assumption of P × E effects in education. For instance, Andrews (1981) found evidence of P × E interactions effects referred to as Aptitude-Treatment Interaction: "Students with interpersonally oriented learning styles benefited more from interactive learning opportunities, while those with other learning styles gained more from impersonal media (such as textbooks)" (p. 161). Walker et al. (2017) compared student learning gains and affective traits between two sections of a large, introductory biology course: the only difference was that one section was lecture-based (didactic) and the other was interactive (Stains et al. 2018). Walker et al. (2017) discovered lecture courses generated greater gains in confidence than the interactive course, but, importantly, there was variation among students in their gains in confidence within each of the two sections. Additionally, information from focus group interviews revealed some students preferred being told the correct answers to questions, a strategy that was more common in lecture, than engaging in more constructivist learning with a focus on general principles rather than answers, a strategy more common in the interactive section (Walker et al., 2017). There are likely other differences in outcomes among students within each "treatment." These differences may be best explained by whether the environment of a lecture-based or interactive-based pedagogy is more similar to the students native (familiar) educational environment. In this case, the native environment is either fact-based with an emphasis on the correct answer or focuses more on principles and critical thinking. The substantial fraction of students who appeared to prefer the didactic education experiences suggest that the environment in their high school prior to attending college was characterized by teaching built around standardized testing and correct-answer-emphasis teaching. Another way interaction effects have been inferred is by comparing instructional strategies with students' perceptions of the teaching effectiveness, although the inferences generated using this type of correlational study are likely to be frail (e.g., Erdle Murray, 1986).

To my knowledge we do not know the extent of P × E in educational settings. However, we do know that P × E is a product of adaptation, and adaptation is common in nature and is likely common in the lives of people. Rather than operate as if P × E does not exist, we should assume P × E as a default and try to better understand the effect of the environment—including teaching modality—on individual students using pedagogical frameworks that reveal, support and challenge student thinking (BSCS, 2018). We need to know more about each student. This means we need to reduce class sizes and increase the frequency and quality of interactions between educators and students. Additionally, rather than measuring success based on the distance to a particular educational objective, we should focus more on measuring gains from where students begin their academic journey. What I am advocating for, especially in higher education, is more direct interaction between educators who are fully committed to achieving the greatest possible student gains and their students. Furthemore, we know P × E generates complexity and complexity is best addressed by first understanding it; thus, educators need to reveal the P x E evident in their population of students. Learning about each student and the effects of academics on them is a first step for unraveling some of the complexity.

There are multiple modalities of teaching, and different instructors often use one type or the other. What this means is that students may develop strategies that yield positive results in one environment and are then challenged to learn in another environment in the next semester, or even in a different class in the same semester. The range of possible P × E interactions depends on the number of categorically different teaching modalities. Stains et al. (2018) described three: didactic, interactive lecture, and student centered. I can imagine a number of possible outcomes of P × E interactions. Perusal of the literature with an eye toward evaluating the success of different pedagogical structures manifested as teaching modes (see Stains et al., 2018) suggests there are effects of nativeness (or familiarity) and foreignness (or unfamiliarity) on learning and affective behavioral gains. We expect gains for students will be highest in new pedagogical environments that best match their native environment (Fig. 4.9, left). If students are familiar with didactic teaching modes, they are likely to do better in a didactic environment than in an interactive or student-centered environment. Similarly, if a student is familiar with and comfortable in a student-centered environment, they are likely to perform better in this environment than in the other two. The expected P × E interactions for three environments are depicted in figure 4.9 (left). Ideally, educators are trained such that such interaction effects are limited; if this were to be done, it is likely that we would observe a rank-order of success that is the same regardless of what strategy students experienced prior to a new pedagogical environment (fig. 4.9, right).

There is good and increasing evidence that student-centered learning yields the best learning gains across multiple dimensions of cognitive gains. The existence of the effects of past experiences—so called native environments—on success suggests that educators need to spend time allowing

Figure 4.9. The comparison of teaching in which there is a large P × E interaction effect and a small environment effect and vice versa. In the graph on the left, the box color (black, grey, white) reflects the "native" environment of a student; native refers to the environment in which a student's academic abilities developed. Each student is subject to a common garden experiment and their performance measured. The expectation (left) is that there is P × E interaction (see text). However, if education is effective and students learn how to be productive in a student-centered learning environment, the effect of P × E interactions can be diminished or eliminated as is evident in the graph on the right. *Source:* Created by the author.

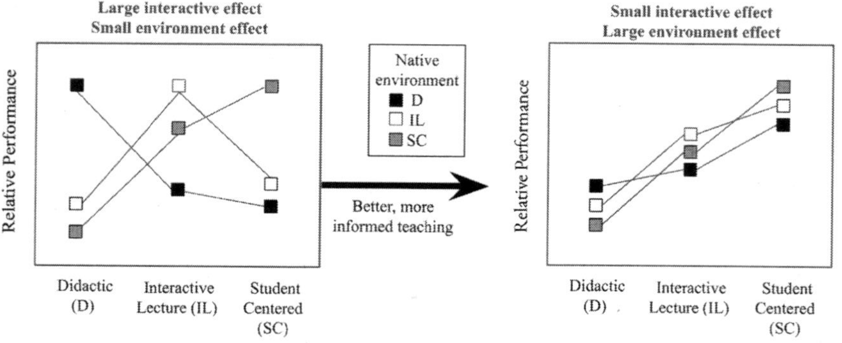

students to become accustomed to a particular pedagogical structure. In other words, students need time to adjust, to feel comfortable in and familiar with a new environment, before their recorded performance achieves its inherent potential. I utilize a highly structured, student-centered and active environment in which students are repeatedly asked to solve problems in groups using knowledge gained from homework done prior to class. Repeated surveys aimed at getting students to reflect on their learning experience in class repeatedly revealed that becoming comfortable can take from 5 to 8 weeks of a 15-week semester; roughly one third to one half of the time. As educators, we need to be patient. Gaining a sense of belonging and accompanying affective characteristics, including self-efficacy and an improved sense of value for particular education experiences, is key for achieving sustained learning gains. In addition, it is important to explain to students the purpose of student-centered teaching and an emphasis on gaining competence for critical thinking instead of recognizing correct answers. Animals and plants change when introduced into new environments, a phenomenon referred to as phenotypic plasticity. As educators, we can assist in advancing the cognitive flexibility and resilience of students by challenging them with new and productive learning environments provided we support the change necessary for success.

At the end of the day, because students have probably experienced competition in sports and other forms of human activities in which there are winners and losers, there is little reason to construct competitive learning environments; we get enough experience and training in how to be a winner and loser. Instead, students need opportunities for practicing cooperative behaviors and experiencing an individual's role in developing collective intelligence. Moreover, we are surrounded by messaging about the value of individualism and the right of individuals to pursue self-interests as a core aspect of a democracy. Yet there is an abundance of evidence that individualism promotes the tragedy of the commons and ultimately unravels the social fabric that maintains the integrity of society. What we need is clear recognition of the tremendous positive effects of cooperation that begins by emphasizing cooperation, collaboration, and mutual interests early on and throughout our education systems, with the ultimate, longer-term goal of advancing prosperity and the quality of life of all people. It takes a village to produce productive individuals, and it takes productive individuals to collaborate to make a village.

Chapter 5

Populations

Population Thinking

Education-relevant synopsis: Populations are comprised of many individuals; the properties of populations emerge from the myriad choices and actions of individuals. Aggregated properties of populations, such as means, variances, and proportions, are abstract representations useful for monitoring change. Population thinking is essential for understanding the emergent process of education because it happens as a consequence of the aggregated effects of many ideas.

Populations are aggregations of individuals. I use general models and ways of thinking stemming from ecological theory and empirical data for gaining an appreciation for the dynamics of educational populations, including the population of ideas that reside in the minds of individuals, the population of students that make up an academic discipline, and the populations of academic communities that make up an institution. Ultimately, all of the measurable and aggregate properties of populations revealed by statistical summaries are due to the choices and actions of individuals pursuing intellectual maturity and academic achievement. That the population is an aggregation of individuals does not take away from the fact that the analysis of populations, especially in a comparative framework, provides important information about change. If there is a desire to make change in education aligned with the perspective of the National Academies of Sciences, Engineering, and Medicine laid out in the introduction, monitoring the properties of populations is necessary, but it is important to remember population-level characteristics are emergent properties from the aggregations of the myriad lives of individuals. James Pearson (n.d.)

captured this idea in a poem: "All a leaf knows / About building a tree / Is to turn towards the light."

Population thinking is essential for understanding change. The change of ecological populations happens mostly as a consequence of the birth and death of the individuals that differ from each other. Population thinking stems from the realization, emphasized by Ernst Mayr (1959, p. 2), that "only the individuals of which the populations are composed have reality" and that "the larger group, the population, is an abstraction" (Hey, 2011, p. 255). The change of educational populations happens mostly as a consequence of the recruitment and retention of individuals that differ from each other. For knowledge, change happens as a consequence of the gain and loss of ideas in the minds of students.

The population in an ecological context was emphasized by Charles Darwin in the *Origin of Species* and is essential for understanding emergent processes like ecology and education, because function and change happens as a consequence of the aggregate effects of many individuals. Each individual can be thought of as an agent with a specific range of actions and function, and all individuals within a population differ to varying degrees. It is the variation among individuals that is important. And, most importantly, aggregates of individuals are best described by the central tendency—the average—and the variation among individuals—usually characterized by the standard deviation. Additionally, population thinking is essential for understanding the emergent process of learning, because learning happens as a consequence of the aggregated effects of many ideas.

What Is a Population?

Education-relevant synopsis: Populations are conceptualized as a coherent group of individuals coexisting in the same place and time. This naturally leads to delimitation criteria useful for describing and comparing populations. In educational settings, populations are most evident based on disciplines: students affiliated with different academic disciplines can be delimited and categorized as being part of different populations. And, importantly, each population is subject to unique opportunities, incentives, and barriers. Currently, institutionalized structure causes increasing divergence among discipline-delimited populations resulting in silos of understanding and limited opportunities for inter- and cross-disciplinary interaction. Delimiting populations and quantifying differences among population can aid efforts toward developing more integrated, coherent, and liberal outcomes in ways that can promote mutual understanding that transcends disciplinary boundaries.

In ecology, populations are aggregations due, in part, to discontinuities in the spatial and temporal availability of resources supporting the reproduction, birth, and maturation of individuals. The conceptualization of a population as a group of individuals of the same species that co-occur in space and time such that they have opportunities to interact and mate with each other establishes ways of delimiting whether some group of individuals consists of one, or more than one, population. The delimitation criteria for natural (ecological) populations fall into several categories (table 5.1). It is not necessary for all criteria to be evident when defining populations.

Table 5.1. Delimitation criteria for populations

Type	Ecological criteria	Educational criteria
Temporal coincidence	Individuals are alive at the same time.*	Individuals are present at the same time.
Spatial proximity	Individuals are in sufficiently close proximity to potentially interact.	Individuals are in sufficiently close proximity to potentially interact.†
Genealogical cohesion	Individuals in the same population have more similar genotypes through shared ancestry than they do with individuals from other populations.	Individuals in the same population have more similar disciplinary interests through shared experiences than they do with individuals from other populations.
Phenotypic similarity	Individuals are part of a single underlying distribution of trait values.	Individuals are part of a single underlying distribution of trait values.
Reproductive compatibility	Individuals can potentially reproduce with any individual of the opposite biological sex.	Not especially relevant for educational populations, although we entertain the idea that collaboration depends on productive compatibility of individuals.

*In a cultural context, if an individual dies, they still exist as a historical entity; however, they no longer participate in actions and interactions with real and measurable ecological and societal footprints.

†Remote learning is included, because technology creates "proximity" such that two people can interact in the same digital space.

My past research focused on many different species and has involved delimiting populations mostly for the purposes of estimating the abundance and distribution of individuals and identifying populations that may be at risk of extirpation. Separation of individuals in time is straightforward, because individuals that do not exist at the same time do not have opportunities for interactions and cannot mate with each other. Separation of individuals by location is more uncertain, because it is not always evident if individuals observed in different places interact or have opportunities to interact. We can determine proximity, but not always interaction. Plants may interact through the actions of pollinators. And animals may interact because they can move. Additionally, individuals that live in different places and appear to be separated from each other may have brief opportunities to interact or move between localities as a consequence of exceptional and episodic environmental change. For example, in the desert southwest of North America there are many springs that form discrete freshwater habitats on the landscape. Fish inhabiting different spring pools are isolated from each other such that each spring pool comprises a separate population; however, during flooding associated with episodes of exceptional precipitation, normally isolated populations may be mixed together (Paulson & Martin, 2019). Thus, the limits of populations may be ephemeral. Similar things may be happening across the complex landscape of a college or university.

There are a variety of ways for evaluating whether a sample of individuals comprise one or more than one population. Figure 5.1 provides one example of data supporting the existence of one population and more than one population using genetic transmission lines visualizations. A transmission lines visualization shows ancestor-descendent connections relative to measurable properties (trait values) of individuals. When there is one population, there are many lines that cross without apparent gaps in the association of ancestor-descendant relationships and the trait values of individuals (fig. 5.1a). By contrast, if there are gaps in the association of ancestor-descendant relationships and the trait values of individuals (fig. 5.1b), we can assign individuals to different groups. Gaps in the association between genealogy and trait values suggests not all individuals interact, or have the capacity to interact, in ways predicted by differences in one or more traits. In this particular visualization, one population splits into two discernible populations.

Another way of conceptualizing and delimiting populations is to measure multiple features of individuals suspected of being part of two

Figure 5.1a–b. Genetic transmission lines visualizations showing the association between trait values and ancestor-descendent relatedness for individuals. Each line connects an ancestor and its average descendant. When there is only one population, there are no apparent gaps (A) whereas the existence of gaps (B) supports the claim that the set of sampled individuals comprises two separate populations. *Source:* Created by the author.

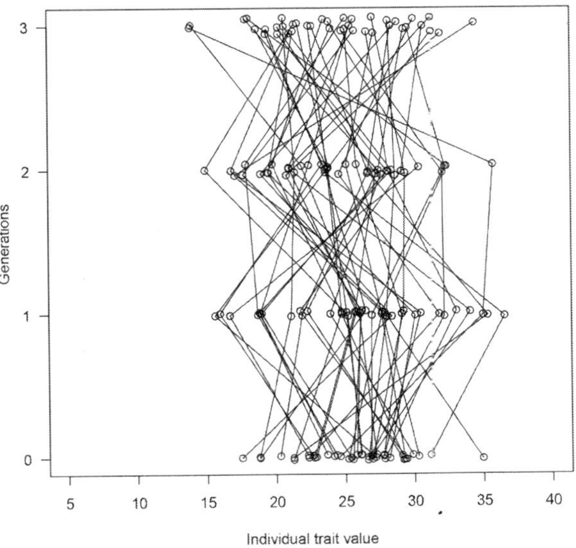

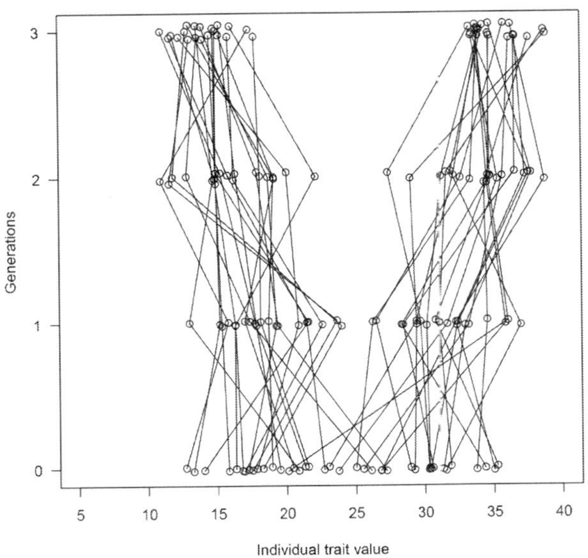

different populations and visualizing or statistically testing whether the hypothesis of two populations is evident in the data. If there is clear separation of individuals into two or more statistically delimited groups, there is evidence of distinct populations. The ability to delimit populations based on criteria that stem from the conceptualization of populations as unique, real entities is important because it provides the basis for proposing and evaluating hypotheses explaining why individuals differ.

At institutions of higher education, students sort themselves into groups identifiable as populations depending on their choice of disciplinary emphasis for their studies. The choice reflects the combined effects of students' interests and an institution mandate that students have a disciplinary emphasis. The disciplinary emphasis is an explicit institutional requirement for gaining some perceived threshold level of disciplinary competence and experience. In my department, students are required to have completed specific courses and a certain number of elective upper-division courses. Ideally, the upper-division courses engage students at high cognitive levels with a particular set of core concepts, content, and process skills. For example, students can choose to study genomics, ecosystem ecology, or evolutionary ecology, and other specific domains within the broad disciplines of ecology and evolutionary biology. Thus, educational populations consist of individuals with shared interests, motivations, and experiences on a journey toward graduation with a diploma that certifies completion of a higher education experience and an indication of disciplinary emphasis. An important consequence of their disciplinary interests is that students tend to separate into groups such that they are more likely to see the same, or similar-minded students, in different classes over the duration of their training at the institution. This happens because there are discipline-specific course requirements, and the courses tend to be increasingly focused on some aspect unique to a discipline. If we were to construct a cultural (or informational) transmission lines visualization for students that depends on the courses they take over time, it would resemble the ancestor—descendent genetic transmission lines visualization from ecology whereby individuals appear to separate into different populations (fig. 5.2).

If the hypothetical transmission lines visualization is real, we should expect evidence of two populations of students based on course enrollment data. The data consists of a matrix with the course and semester as a column and each student as a row. Each element of the matrix is a zero if a student did not complete a course and a one if they did. Using a

Figure 5.2. A hypothetical flow-through-time-and-space visualization based on the observation that students become increasingly specialized within two different academic disciplines (labeled MCDB and EBIO). Each point is a student. The x-axis is a scale of interest and experience. Each line connects the same student over time. Students' interests and experiences change over time as a consequence of their classes over a duration of four years. The points at the bottom of the lines (y-axis = 0) show student interests and experiences at the beginning of their studies. *Source:* Created by the author.

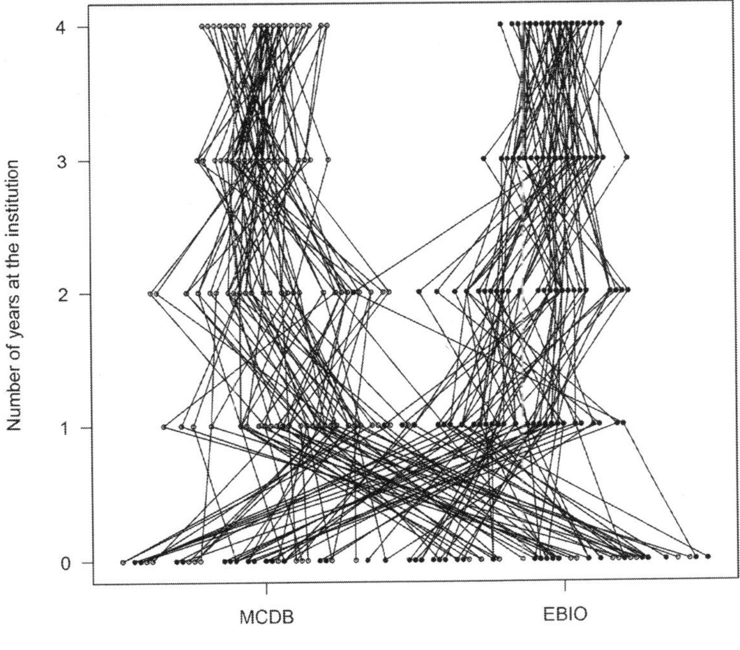

technique called nonmetric dimensional analysis (NMDS), the differences among all students can be estimated and plotted in two dimensions: it is clear from the NMDS analysis that individuals separate into two groups (fig. 5.3). Importantly, if we were to include all of the discipline-defined populations in the College of Arts and Sciences (or across campus), there would likely be many clearly distinguishable clusters: each cluster is delimited as a separate population in much the same way ecologists delimit populations. We should ask ourselves if differentiation and specialization are appropriate or desirable emergent outcomes of education, or if we should construct pedagogical structures that favor different emergent outcomes.

Figure 5.3. A nonmetric dimensional scaling plot for students in EBIO and MCDB. The data were generated based on whether a student was enrolled or not in a combined set of 1,230 courses for 300 students for the 2017 cohort. All 300 students graduated with a degree in either EBIO (162 EBIO students) or MCDB (138 students). The distance between points reflects the degree of differentiation in the courses completed. *Source:* Created by the author.

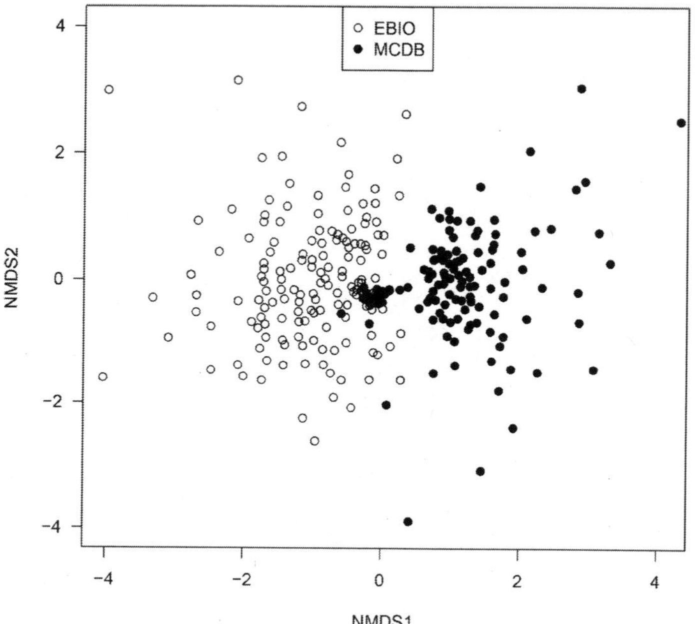

One important aspect of the differentiation between the two discipline-similar populations is that the apparent overlap mostly reflects the effect of shared experiences in courses that are not part of either discipline and are lower-level (mostly freshman-targeted) courses. For example, of the 300 individuals sampled from the disciplines of EBIO and MCDB, 270 (90%) enrolled in a large first-year chemistry course (almost a complete overlap between the disciplinary populations). Additionally, a large fraction of individuals from both majors (140 students out of 300) enrolled in a first-year psychology course. There were few examples in which students from both departments were in the same course taught at a higher cognitive level such that the similarities and differences between the two disciplines might become apparent. For instance, of the 150 students who completed an important "core" disciplinary experience for EBIO students (a course on evolutionary biology) only 2 (1.3%) were from the MCDB disciplinary population, and of the 152 students who completed a second important "core" disciplinary experience for EBIO students (a course on ecology) only 1 (< 1%) was from the MCDB disciplinary population. The core fundamental ideas of ecology and evolutionary biology were not included in the experience for students in the MCDB disciplinary population despite the fact that *all biology evolves and happens in ecological contexts*. Ideally, students of biology have similar trajectories through the big ideas, core concepts, and science process approaches; yet, at CU–Boulder and many other large research universities, students become disciplinarily siloed. The effect is that the expectation higher education students are adequately educated about the true scope of biology based on current pedagogical frameworks (e.g., the NGSS framework; see Laverty et al., 2016) is unlikely to be true. In my mind, this is a failure of the highly structured, discipline-focused neoliberal model of higher education.

Another emergent property from the presence and absence matrix for a cohort of students is that students have very diverse interests. The data from my department—Ecology and Evolutionary Biology (EBIO)—provides a good example. When I looked at one cohort of students who first enrolled at CU–Boulder in 2017 and graduated with a major in EBIO, the 162 students completed 970 different classes. Furthermore, of the students who self-identified as a member of the EBIO disciplinary population and who graduated with an EBIO degree, 115 (71%) were immigrants into EBIO from one of 19 other disciplinary populations. Looking at the same data for MCDB, the 138 students who graduated with a degree in MCDB had enrolled in 754 different classes. Of the students who self-identified as a member of the MCDB disciplinary population and who graduated with a MCDB degree, 24 (17%) were immigrants into MCDB from one of 12 other disciplinary populations. Remarkably, only 1 student migrated from MCDB into EBIO. The difference in immigration into the two departments reflects differences in curriculum-based barriers. Whether the borders between disciplines are open—like EBIO—or have walls—like MCDB—requires explanation. Stout barriers—walls of exclusion—likely characterize many disciplines.

The siloization of education is an outcome dependent on directing students based on policies favoring specialization at the expense of a more holistic experience. While there are general curricular requirements aimed at gaining experiences across disciplines, students complete most of these courses at lower academic levels (they are typically first or second year courses) and many have large enrollments. For instance, if students from the many different departments across campus want an experience in thinking like an ecologist, they typically enroll in one of three large-enrollment, first-year courses in our department. These courses cannot provide sufficient training for students to be able to think like an ecologist because the pedagogy does not sufficiently emphasize revealing, supporting, and challenging student thinking: there are simply too many students to make this happen in a way all students feel like they belong. College is meant to be a public good and a foundation for democracy and civic engagement. Both of these important cultural properties depend on citizens capable of grappling with complexity, thinking critically and creatively, and engaging in informed and reasoned discourse with an appreciation for the different ways people think. If we train our young adults as specialists, and this is accompanied by specific ways of thinking, will they be capable of making rational and empathetic decisions, or will they retreat to what they know best and fortify their perspective rather than cooperate and reach consensus? This is an open question.

What would a flow-through-time-and-space visualization look like for students if we emphasized developing more holistic ways of thinking, appreciation of the scope and complexity of life, and becoming more expert with strategies for cooperation between individuals with different perspectives instead of emphasizing disciplinary specialization. At face value, it would be one in which teaching happened in multi- or interdisciplinary ways with students from different disciplines coming together in classes at higher levels (as juniors and seniors). Movement of students between disciplines would be different and the emergent outcome of enforced specialization would not be evident (fig. 5.4).

Populations can be conceptualized and delimited based on ideas (rather than individuals). The idea that ideas can form discrete and different populations is evident from the diversity of different disciplinary units (departments or majors). Ideas, like people, have lives. They are born, they mature and they can persist, sometimes indefinitely, or they can die. The population of ideas can be conceptualized and delimited in much the same way as for populations of students. There are common ideas that transcend disciplines just as there are common student experiences across divergent disciplines. There are also ideas unique to specific disciplines. In my discipline, there are a number of core or big ideas that serve as a foundation for building a coherent and mature discipline-specific paradigm. In ecology and evolutionary biology, concepts such as evolution

Figure 5.4. Transmission lines graph for an hourglass model of disciplinary emphasis. See text for more explanation. *Source:* Created by the author.

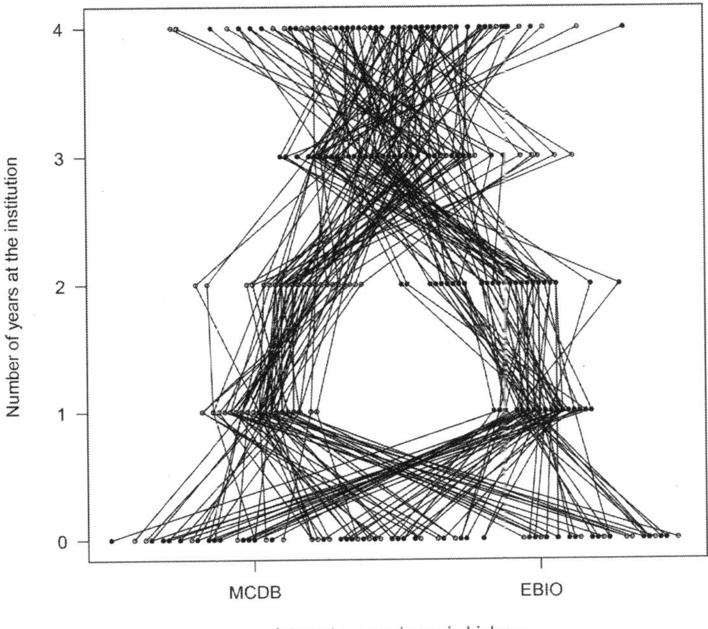

and trophic webs are emergent knowledge constructs composed of many aggregated ideas. Evolution includes the ideas of spontaneous mutation, drift, differential survival, differential reproductive success, heritability, reproductive capacity in excess of available resources, interaction effects between individuals, interaction effects between genes, and the list goes on. Furthermore, each one of these listed ideas is, itself, an aggregate of smaller ideas. For instance, mutation includes the idea of a double helix composed of four biochemically distinct molecules that differ in their inherent stability. It also includes the idea of stochasticity and a uniform probability distribution across nucleotide pairs in the genome. And there are other smaller-scale ideas within the aggregated idea of spontaneous mutation.

At CU–Boulder, there are 100-plus different majors. The different majors focus on different sets of ideas. If I was able to describe the universe of ideas that span the 100-plus different majors, there would be some that would be present in all majors and many that are restricted to specific disciplines. Rozumko (2017) described an approach for delimitation of disciplines based on the frequency and types of adverbs used. Adverbs provide information about the value and use of particular ideas associated with expressions of uncertainty. Rozumko focused mostly on the words *indeed, perhaps, clearly, certainly, of course, arguably, possibly,* and *reportedly*. All of these reflect different prevailing ideas about uncertainty. What Rozumko found was that there were differences in the use of specific adverbs by discipline. The point of introducing this particular discovery is that for the critical, core idea of uncertainty, there are different ways of characterizing and valuing uncertainty among disciplines. This suggests that individuals from different disciplines will vary in their uncertainty about the world. There may be one objective truth about uncertainty, but disciplinary norms may mean that different people think differently about uncertainty depending on their experiences. This example highlights an outcome of discipline-divergent educational experiences: students of different disciplines will have different ideas about the world. While this can be a good thing, the discovery that the meaning of uncertainty varies across disciplines makes the task of coming to consensus difficult.

There are other scholarly investigations of what makes a discipline based largely on the ideas that form the core elements of a discipline. Stocking (1995) engaged in a study of the disciplinary boundaries within anthropology; it is a discipline that appears to have experienced continuous evolution over more than a hundred years as a consequence of the birth and death of ideas (in much the same way as populations of individuals evolve by births and deaths). There is mention of the ideas of de-biologification and socio-biologification of anthropology. Additionally, ideas that have driven the diversification of the discipline of anthropology including, but not limited to, the ideas of ethnological, humanistic, linguistic, medical, psychological, and urban anthropology have varied in use and importance over time. Stocking's (1995) historical monograph underscores the dynamic, emergent outcome of the evolution of knowledge and ways of thinking. There are similar interrogations of other disciplines, including linguistics. For instance, Gal and Irvine (1995) discussed the ideas of iconicity, recursiveness, and erasure in relation to disciplinary boundaries. An interesting twist about the reality of different disciplines is, from the perspective of an information scientist, individual disciplines may not exist, because knowledge and ideas are increasingly multidisciplinary (Beghtol, 1998). Thus, there is a tension between the differentiation and divergence of academic disciplines and their coalescence as a consequence of ideological convergence. Nonetheless, academic institutions appear to be evolving in ways resembling adaptive diversification in which the rate of emergence of new disciplines exceeds the loss of disciplines through fusion or extirpation. At the core of differentiation or coalescence is the set of ideas that constitute the basis for disciplinary delimitation.

It would be useful, in the context of better understanding discipline differences, to rigorously assemble a presence-absence matrix of core and essential ideas across disciplines. While there are various frameworks that have been developed specifically for science education purposes, including Vision and Change from the American Association for the Advancement of Sciences and the Next Generation Science Standards, in practice most science classes in the two most closely related biology departments at CU–Boulder—MCDB and EBIO—operate in ways that emphasize and teach different sets of ideas. Assembling these data is difficult, because getting a coherent description of the core ideas within one of these disciplines requires the collaboration of many faculty who are all busy managing and supporting research programs and engaging in teaching and service. The fact that this information is not readily available, beyond simple access to syllabi, remains a symptom of a systemic problem.

Recruitment and Persistence

Education-relevant synopsis: Disciplinary populations form, develop, and persist over time as an emergent outcome of recruitment, persistence, and migration. Fluctuations in numbers of individuals and productivity from year to year and trends evident over multiple years suggest many of the processes happening in the ecological context happen in educational contexts, including density-dependent and density-independent environmental and interaction effects. In addition, there are likely unexplainable effects best attributable to stochasticity.

Newly formed islands or empty patches of habitat provide a useful context for understanding the origin, establishment, and persistence of populations. If an individual encounters a new island, or an open patch of habitat, they settle and begin to establish themselves. Once established, individuals persist for a period of time with a time-dependent survival probability and limited longevity. This scenario matches the dynamics of a variety of marine invertebrates. Hughes (1990) investigated the change in the number of individuals in a population over time (a phenomenon known as population dynamics) for a bryozoan. The biology of a bryzoan's life cycle includes beginning life as a small larva that floats around in the water column as a member of the plankton community. Individuals settle on hard surfaces (usually rocks) and change—referred to as metamorphosis—in ways that allow them to live and grow attached to a hard surface instead of floating free in the water. The sequential process of settlement, metamorphosis, and establishment is defined as recruitment. Once established, individuals grow and mature into an adult individual. Each individual in the new environment occupies space and consumes resources in ways that limit the recruitment of other individuals. Recruitment is episodic, often seasonal, and the set of recruits define a cohort. Persistence depends on survival (the opposite of mortality). Hughes discovered that the mortality rate of individuals was density independent and the equilibrium population size was determined by the ratio of recruitment to mortality rate.

Hughes's findings can be represented by a simple model: the number of individuals at time T is equal to the recruitment at time T (i.e., R_T) plus the number of individuals that survive during the period T − 1 (i.e., $s \times N_{T-1}$), where s is the probability of survival and N_{T-1} is the number of individuals at time T − 1. Thus, the model predicting population size is $N_T = R_T + s \times N_{T-1}$. This simple model can produce dynamic results depending on the values of R and s. It is also useful for modeling populations across a diversity of taxa, including plants and animals; it is also useful for modeling the dynamics of individuals—students and ideas—in educational contexts (e.g., Ahn et al., 2007; Chandler et al., 2018). Figure 5.5a is an example of the composition of a population if it began as a blank slate (no individuals present) and recruitment and survival happened over a period of time. In this particular example, the new recruits that colonize the site for each time period are indicated by different shades of gray (from white to black). The total number of individuals declines over time because the size of individuals increases over time in ways that limit recruitment (fig. 5.5b). This particular example shows that a population at some point in time reflects the history of recruitment and whether past recruits survived.

The model in which survival is density independent and recruitment plays a large role for determining abundance is a general feature of populations across diverse taxa (see Sutherland, 1990). Recruitment is a process that depends on the existence of specific signals or information from the environment that trigger individuals to settle in a particular location. Importantly, recruitment is usually density-independent and variable over time (Sutherland, 1990); as a consequence, the total number

Figure 5.5a–b. 5.5a: Population age structure for individual bryozoans over time. The bars show the number of individuals over time for five different cohorts established by recruitment (labeled R1–R5); each shade of gray is a different cohort. Modified from Hughes (1990). 5.5b: A cartoon of the growth of an individual bryozoan over time. *Source:* Created by the author.

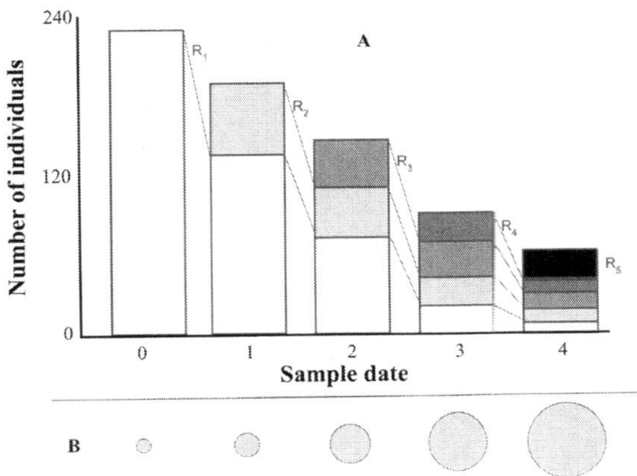

of individuals in each cohort may differ. Once individuals settle, they are subject to a variety of biotic and abiotic stresses that influence persistence. These factors might include competitive interactions with other individuals, being preyed on and the loss of biological integrity as a consequence of exposure to extreme environments, among other factors.

An extension of this model recognizes that some animals are not sessile and individuals can move between habitats as a means of escaping competition, predation or environmental extremes (Hiddink, 2003). If we add migration to the model, population size will be a function of two additional factors, $m_i \times N_{T-1}$ and $m_e \times N_{T-1}$, where m_i and m_e are the probabilities of immigration and emigration, respectively, and the difference ($m_i \times N$) minus ($m_e \times N$) is the net migration. If immigration is greater than emigration, the number of individuals in the population increases all else being equal. If immigration is less than emigration, the number of individuals in the population decreases, all else being equal.

Age-structured recruitment and survival models are useful for describing the abundance of students. In words, the number of students inhabiting a particular discipline in year T—denoted as N_T—is equal to the recruitment in the current year plus the number of individuals that persisted from the previous year plus the net number of migrants minus the number of students that graduate. The only new term is graduation. Graduation removes individuals from the population. In an ecological population, graduation might be considered a scenario in which individuals have a particular longevity. For college students, longevity is typically 4–7 years. In the population of the bryozoan described by Hughes, recruitment was negatively density dependent because increasing population size decreases the available space for new recruits. Interestingly, at CU-Boulder, recruitment appears to be density independent. In addition, different disciplinary populations show evidence of statistically-detectable declining recruitment rates (e.g., English), constant recruitment rates (e.g., MCDB and EBIO) and increasing recruitment rates (e.g., psychology) (fig. 5.6).

Persistence is counted in ways that recognize the hierarchical structure of the university. There is persistence in the University, persistence within the college, and persistence within a specific discipline (fig. 5.7). Persistence in the University is determined by the number of individuals

Figure 5.6. The number of recruits into four disciplinary populations from 2013 to 2023. For the psychology population, the recruitment increased (slope = 37, p < 0.001), for English, recruitment declined (slope = –3.5, p < 0.01), and for the other two—MCDB and EBIO—there was no evidence of sustained change. *Source:* Created by the author.

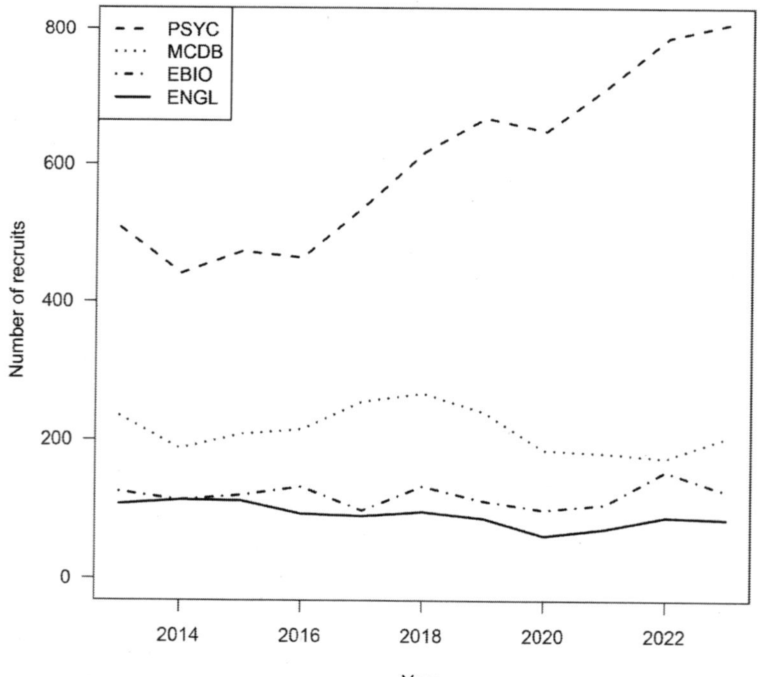

Figure 5.7. Model showing the net movement of students into and out of particular disciplinary populations (labeled 1–3). The lowercase letters identify colleges (e.g., College of Arts and Sciences, College of Engineering). The large oval is the university. Arrows indicate pathways of the movement of individuals that influence persistence following recruitment. Note that arrows exiting the large oval are individuals the leave the University; these arrows are not bidirectional. *Source:* Created by the author.

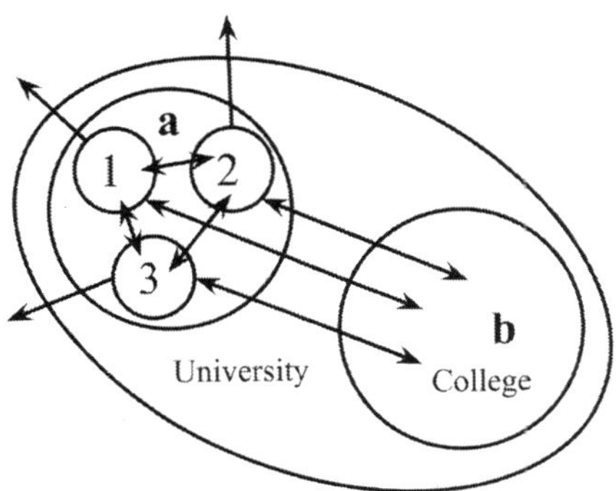

that leave the University. This is the aggregate statistic University leaders pay most attention to because of its strong effect on tuition revenue. Persistence at this level is similar across disciplinary populations, suggesting that it is density independent (fig. 5.8). Persistence within a disciplinary population is also determined by net migration that can happen between colleges—like the College of Arts and Sciences and the Leeds School of Business. For the four disciplinary populations (PYSC, ENGL, EBIO, and MCDB), there are differences in persistence due to emigration into a different college: emigration rates are higher for PSYC and ENGL than for EBIO and MCDB (fig. 5.9).

When we focus on the net migration for each of the four disciplinary departments (ENGL, PSYC, MCDB, and EBIO) across a decade, there are fluctuations over time. Some, like EBIO and ENGL, experienced a net positive migration (more immigrants than emigrants), whereas PYSC and MCDB experienced net negative migration (more emigrants than immigrants) (fig. 5.10). The best explanation for the net migration numbers appears to be density. Regression of the net migration on the number of students revealed a negative slope for all four (ENGL, PSYC, MCDB, and EBIO) departments. When the number of individuals was lower, immigration > emigration; when the number of individuals was higher, immigration < emigration. The density dependence of population size,

Figure 5.8. Persistence of students at the university in four disciplinary populations (departments). In these data, students that do not persist leave the university. The lines come from linear model predictions based on multiple cohorts of students. *Source:* Created by the author.

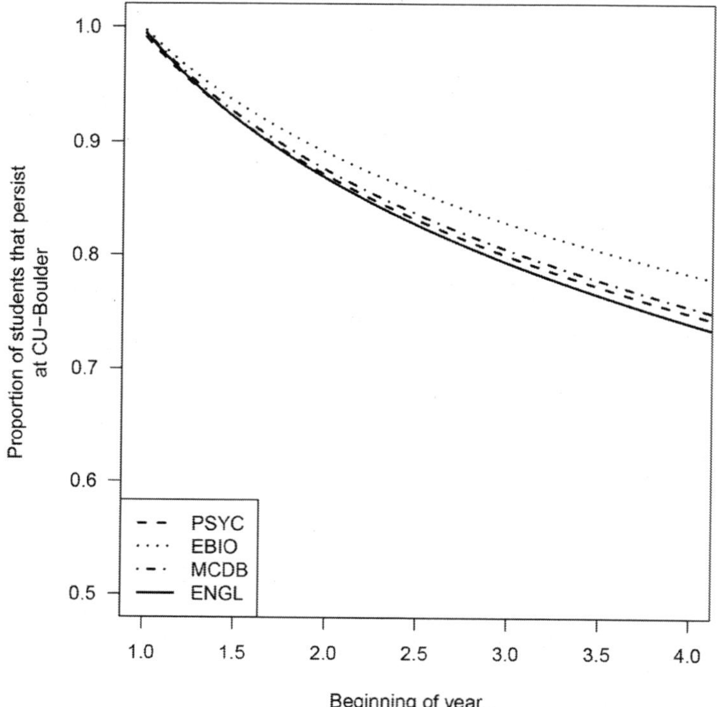

regulated by net migration, is characteristic of populations in ecological contexts, suggesting population dynamics is regulated, to some extent, by students changing their major and making decisions to leave one group and join another one based on some set of criteria that appears to be density dependent.

Recruitment and net migration combined to generate population age structure. Age structure is the numbers of freshman, sophomore, juniors, and seniors. A look at the age structure for two biology populations—MCDB and EBIO—shows the outcomes when recruitment and net migration differ (fig. 5.11). The model was broken into five age categories: new recruits ($R = N_0$), and individuals that have completed 1, 2, 3, and 4 years ($N_1 \ldots N_4$) of school, respectively. The data were based on a single cohort. The population size is divided into residents and immigrants.

Figure 5.9. The proportion of students who persist in the university but emigrate from the College of Arts and Sciences into a different college (e.g., Business, Engineering, etc.). The lines come from linear model predictions based on multiple cohorts of students. *Source:* Created by the author.

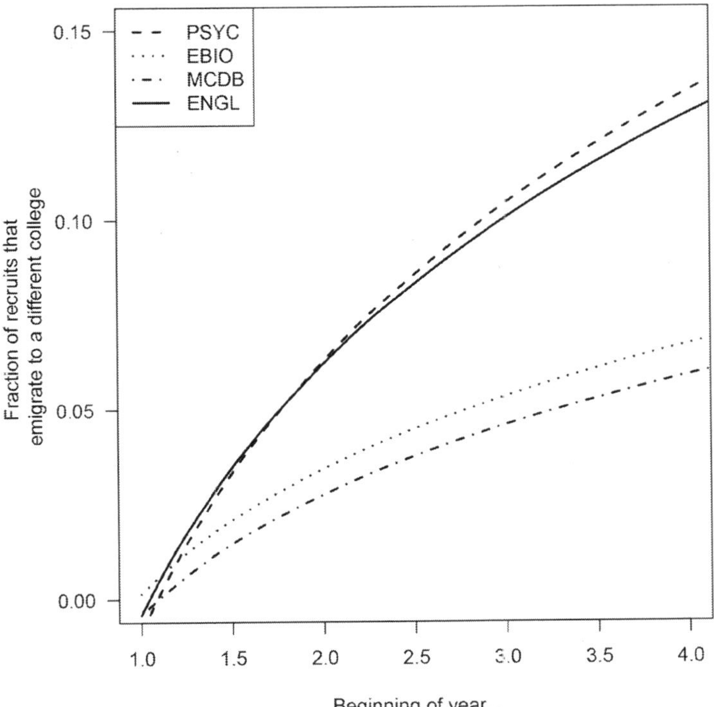

Residents are defined as the initial recruits. Immigrants are defined as individuals who migrated from another discipline into the population. The difference between the populations reflects an approximately twofold difference in recruitment (MCDB > EBIO) and a substantial difference in the flow of individuals from immigration (EBIO > MCDB).[1] As a consequence, the age structure of the two populations differs (fig. 5.12), because the processes influencing the numbers of individuals in the two populations—namely, recruitment and net migration—differ between them.

Published persistence and migration data suggest students who persist often change their major. Astorne-Figari and Speer (2019, p. 75) noted that "over a third of students switch majors during their time in college, suggesting that major choice is best understood as a process." They also suggested that grades signaled to students that there interests and chosen academic

Figure 5.10. Estimates of net migration for the year following recruitment. Zero net migration is indicated by the solid horizontal line. *Source:* Created by the author.

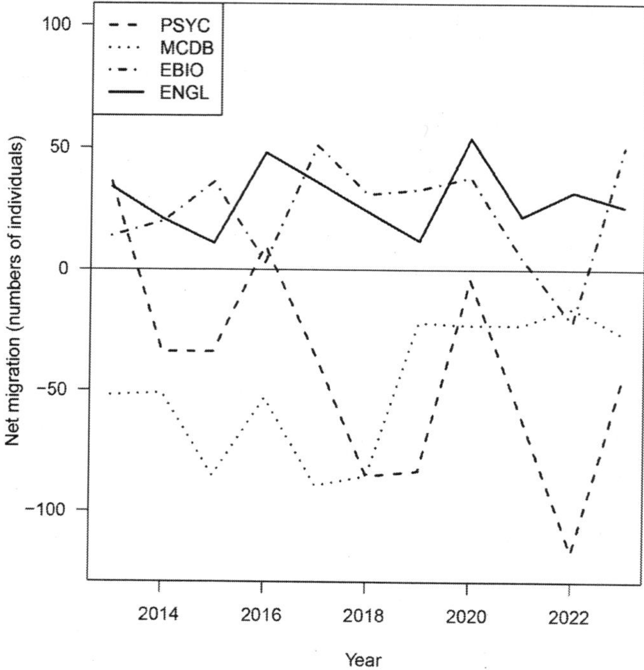

Figure 5.11. Comparison of the number of residents and immigrants for two different biological disciplines (labeled A and B) at CU based on cohort data. *Source:* Created by the author.

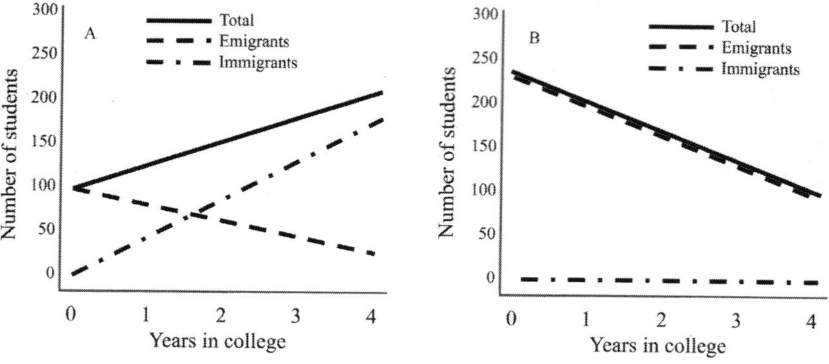

discipline were not matched, and that this dissonance caused or predicted switching majors: "The lower the grades, the larger the switch in terms of course content. When students switch majors, they switch to majors that

Figure 5.12. The age structure of two different departments for the 2016 cohort of students. The same general pattern evident in the data for 2016 is evident for other years. *Source:* Created by the author.

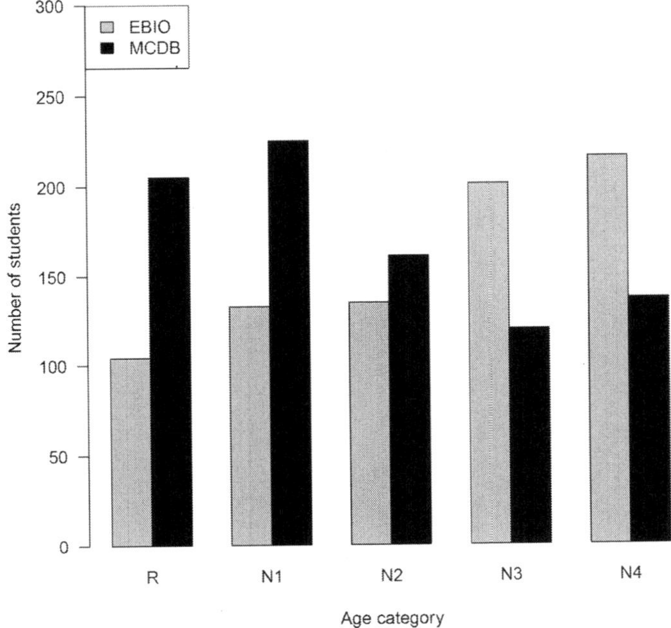

'look like them': females to female-heavy majors, and so on. . . . Women flee competitive majors at high rates. . . . Women are far more likely to leave STEM fields for majors that are less competitive—but still somewhat science-intensive—suggesting that leaving STEM may be more about fleeing the 'culture' of STEM majors than fleeing science and math."

The results from Astorne-Figari and Speer were based on a longitudinal study that began when the students were between 12 and 16 in 1997; thus the data provide an indication of what was happening in the early 2000s. At the time, there were very few studies addressing the questions about why students change majors, how prevalent it is, and what disciplines experience the greatest exodus and influx. Astorne-Figari and Speer showed that the largest net migration losses came from, in order of rank, biology, computer science, engineering, and earth and physical sciences; the largest net gains were into business, social sciences, economics, and philosophy. Analysis of data from a decade after Astorne-Figari and Speer's study revealed many of the same results; about 40% of students changed their major at least once, females changed majors more frequently than males, and females left STEM disciplines at higher rates than males (Denice, 2021). Overall, the rate of switching majors as a function of number of accumulated courses was more or less constant except for transient "bursts" in the first year at the end of the first and second semesters. These data indicate a large flux of students moving among disciplinary departments, suggesting net migration plays a large role in governing population size over time.

The clear applicability of recruitment, persistence, and migration as key parameters influencing the growth of academic populations means that understanding change in population size—the number of students in a major—and its productivity—the number of graduates per year—reflects these processes that all happen more or less continuously. Thus, when we look at trends in population size (numbers of students) (fig. 5.13), the number of individuals that are successful in a given population (fig. 5.14),

Figure 5.13. The number of individuals in four different populations from 2002 to 2024. *Source:* Created by the author.

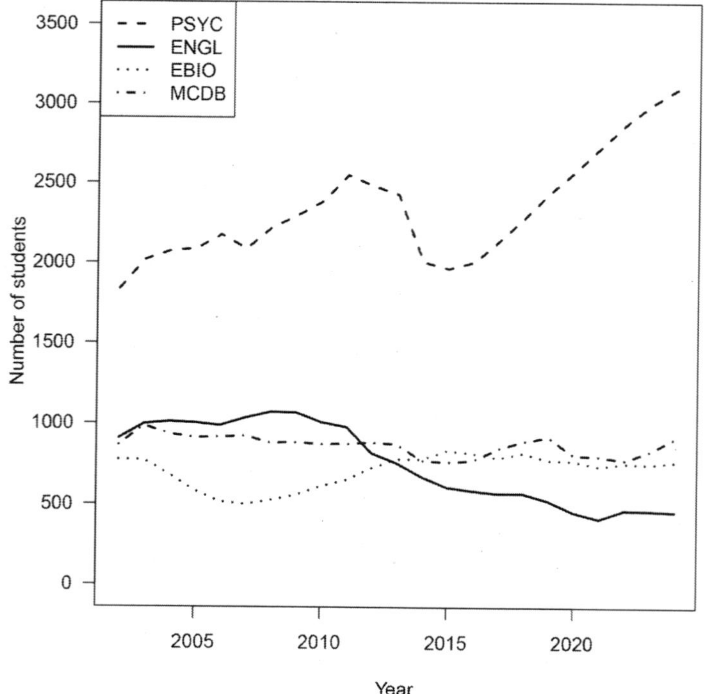

Figure 5.14. The number of individuals that were successful (graduated with a degree) in four different populations from 2002 to 2024. *Source:* Created by the author.

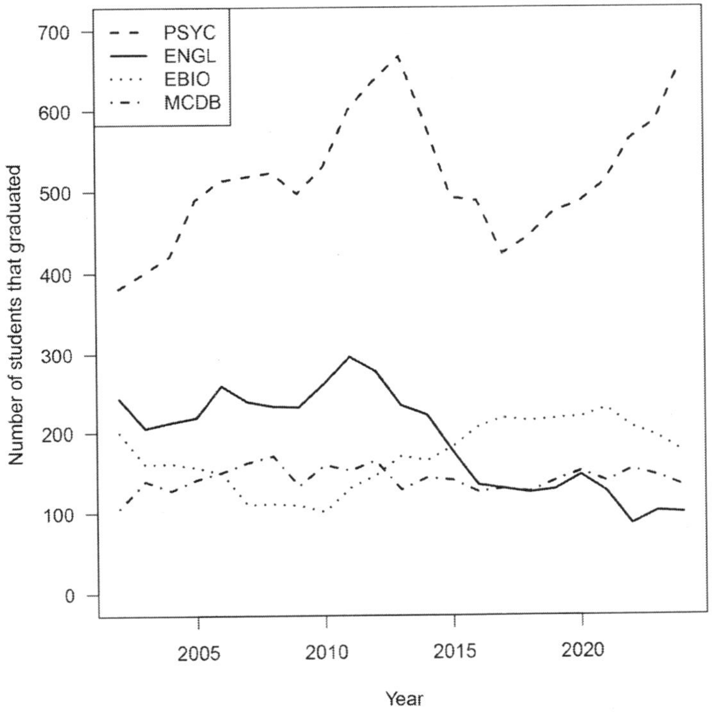

and the productivity of populations estimated as the number of graduates per enrolled student per year (fig. 5.15), we should ask about the effects of recruitment, persistence, and migration. There are probably multiple cultural factors at play that affect students' choices that in turn determine aggregate properties of populations.

That there are population dynamics of disciplinary populations of students is evident in the data. Fluctuations from year to year and trends evident over multiple years suggests that many of the processes happening in ecological contexts happen in educational contexts, including density-dependent and density-independent environmental and interaction effects. In addition, there are likely unexplainable effects best attributable to sto-chasticity. The trends and oscillations in the data are emergent outcomes of recruitment, migration, and graduation happening over time in constantly changing environments.

Figure 5.15. A graph of the productivity of four disciplinary departments estimates by the number of graduates per year divided by the total number of enrolled students. Note that the productivity varies over time and that three of the four are statistically indistinguishable; the productivity of the MDCB disciplinary population is lower, on average, than the other three. *Source:* Created by the author.

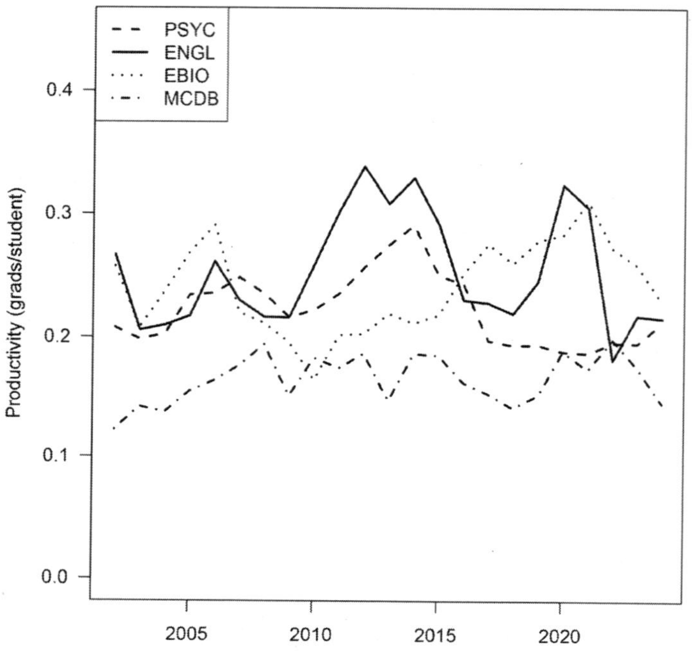

Populations Vary Depending on Context

Education-relevant synopsis: Different populations decline or increase dependent on prevailing environmental conditions determined by large-scale cultural factors. One important factor is the increasing perception that higher education is a commodity for advancing the status of individuals rather than serving as a public good. The shift in number of students across large-scale disciplinary populations (e.g., STEM disciplines versus social sciences and humanities) is causally associated with global culture change and the increasing neoliberalization of higher education.

Populations in nature are embedded in landscapes and ecosystems, which, in turn, are influenced by global climate change. Different populations of species may be responsive to these changes depending on the interaction between biological characteristics and climate change. Some populations may increase in both size and distribution, while others may decline and shrink. For some species, change in population dynamics can be explained by latitude (Helmuth et al., 2002; Perry et al., 2005; Burrow et al., 2011) and elevation (Rasmann et al., 2014; Chan et al., 2016). Perhaps the best data come from studies of birds. In Europe, some species, like the Middle Spotted Woodpecker, have undergone population range expansion, whereas populations have been extirpated and the geographic distribution has contracted for other species, like the Crested Lark (Howard et al., 2023). Over many species, approximately 40% of the variation in population trends—whether populations increase or decrease in size or do not change—can be explained by an interaction between the biological properties of species with change in climate and land use (Howard et al., 2020). When biologists asked what features of birds and butterflies best explained their response to climate change, the most evident predictor was the degree of habitat specialization: greater specialization was associated with greater risk from climate change (Julliard et al., 2004).

It is likely that the divergence in growth rates among disciplinary units in the landscape of an institution of higher education reflects the effects of cultural climate change. The different trajectories of change evident for ENGL and PSYC exist for all disciplinary populations in the College of Arts and Sciences to varying degrees. ENGL and other arts and humanities disciplinary departments began their decline at about the same time, beginning in 2009–2010. By contrast, the populations inhabiting the landscape of the natural sciences have experienced sustained increases (with notable exceptions of Geography and Geosciences). If we sum up the changes at the scale of three disciplinary divisions—Arts and Humanities (AH), Natural Sciences (NS), and the Social Sciences (SS)—the divergent trajectories are clearly evident: NS is on the rise and AH and SS are in descent. Such large-scale changes in the academic landscape suggest the effects of large-scale cultural climate change. One trigger for initiating a large-scale cultural climate change was the financial crash of 2008. Mintz (2023) provides a sociological critique of English as a viable disciplinary population that highlights multiple interacting factors contributing to its decline. The problems are deeper than the general sentiment that students turned away from disciplines perceived to be associated with poor job prospects to STEM disciplines at this time (Goulas & Megalokonomou, 2019). While there is no clear way to discern a causal effect of the 2008 financial crisis, the outcome reflects changes in recruitment and net migration. It is as if the AH populations exist at high latitudes and elevations, two environments experiencing greater negative effects of global warming. Population declines in ecological contexts can also happen because of the effects of pathogens (e.g., McCallum, 2012) or the accumulation of deleterious alleles as a consequence of inbreeding and small population size (Lynch et al., 1995). One example of a cultural infection by a deleterious meme is the decay of reading books (Jones, 2022). Thus, the reduced recruitment into the ENGL disciplinary population may reflect the decline of reading as an elective activity of young adults. Thus, there is variation in response to cultural climate change registering in different disciplinary populations with similarity to the variation in response of different species to global climate change. While it is possible that the patterns are simply noise, the fact that there are discernible trends suggests otherwise. The rise of science and the apparent fall of the arts and humanities is especially troubling because solutions to some of the world's most vexing problems stem from issues of cultural values, interpersonal interactions, and human nature that fall mostly within the domains of the humanities and social sciences; ideally, higher education evolves in a way that emphasizes the value of interdisciplinary training, because the most vexing problems straddle multiple disciplinary divides. One challenge for the future is better articulation of the values and perhaps greater integration of the arts and humanities with other disciplines through efforts designed to limit siloization and abolish the ideology that disciplinary departments are professions. In other words, there is a need to break down the neoliberalization of higher education and return to its core value as a public good (Newfield, 2016).

The aggregated landscape changes evident from patterns of the dynamics of the 45 disciplinary populations within Arts and Sciences are also evidence at the larger, college-level hierarchical scale within CU–Boulder. We might consider the various large-enrollment colleges as academic biomes. Examples of biomes include deserts, tropical forests, boreal forests, and tundra. The characteristics of biomes are primarily defined by prevailing temperature and precipitation determined by global differences in the flow of atmospheric moisture and incident solar radiation. These are emergent features of the planet Earth in orbit around the sun. While the College of Arts and Sciences (ARSC)—including the named divisions of Arts and Humanities, Social Sciences, and Natural Sciences—has more or less stayed the same over time, the Leeds School of Business (BUSN) and College of Engineering and Applied Sciences

(ENGR) have increased over time. The increase in numbers of students is mostly due to increases in recruitment. It seems inescapable that the changes reflect large-scale cultural climate change and also more localized investment from private-sector interests. Particularly noteworthy is the increase in the Aerospace Engineering population due, in part, to significant financial support from private industry (e.g., Ball Aerospace) and federal agencies (NASA). Additionally, the Computer Science disciplinary population grew by 154% from 2013 to 2023. The increasing enrollment likely reflects student interests in securing higher-paying jobs in the science and technology sector. The increases in enrollment for these two disciplines began in 2008–2009 on the heels of the global financial crisis.

A key reason for the shifting landscape of disciplinary success also reflects directed actions of leadership to subsidize particular disciplines at the expense of other disciplines through the enactment of a pernicious zero-sum game. At CU–Boulder, the College of Engineering and Applied Sciences (ENGR) and the Law School (LAWS) have been financially supported by a tax on the College of Arts and Sciences students. The campus leaderships' goal appears to be buttressing the reputation of CU–Boulder as a destination for training in engineering and law at the expense of the liberal arts, and the strategy appears to be working. What is troubling is the subsidies are not evident to the students and families who recruit into the College of Arts and Sciences.

The Environment Imposes Limits

Education-relevant synopsis: There are two important factors that limit the growth of populations: the resources available for supporting the maturation and success of individuals (the carrying capacity concept from ecology) and the space necessary to function normally in the absence of negative stress (referred to as saturation effects from ecology). Saturation is a biological phenomenon, and it is best defined as the maximum number of individuals that can achieve their maximum productivity in a particular space. "Carrying capacity" is the available resources for sustaining the maximum learning gains. The negative density-dependent effects of carrying capacity and saturation play out in the context of enrollments in courses. In many courses, population sizes exceed both saturation threshold and carrying capacity, suggesting that learning gains and academic achievement are less than what we hope to achieve; yet, institutional structure and large-scale enrollment strategies limit the ability to reduce class sizes.

There is a concept in population ecology called the carrying capacity (denoted K). The first definition of carrying capacity was the number of individuals that a particular environment can support without injury or deterioration of the environment (Hadwen & Palmer, 1922). This definition recognizes that individuals influence the environment in which they live as a consequence of consuming resources. Injury or deterioration are ideas meant to describe the negative density-dependent effects of a population: the larger the population, the more the environment is "under pressure" and experiences "deterioration." There is also the idea of saturation. Aldo Leopold (1987) compared the concept of saturation and carrying capacity. Leopold pointed out that a particular species of bird "has a saturation density of approximately one bird per acre (0.4 ha). He reasoned that an 'internal force,' such as intraspecific interactions among the quail, 'sets an upper limit beyond which wild populations do not increase.' . . . The saturation density is a species-specific characteristic that does not vary from place to place. The carrying capacity, on the other hand, is a characteristic of the habitat" (Pulliam & Haddad, 1994, p. 141).

Pulliam and Haddad (1994) constructed a simple model describing how saturation (denoted S) and carrying capacity (K) can influence population size (or the density of animals) (fig. 5.16). The example stems from their work on sparrows. For sparrows, grass seed is a main food resource. Increases in grass seed availability cause an increase in the density of animals to a point, and then there is evidence of saturation. Saturation is an indication that there are other resources necessary for life besides food and shelter. Leopold's "internal force" may simply reflect that individuals need space. Many species are territorial and actively engage in agonistic interactions with other individuals to maintain space. If there is crowding, individuals suffer stress, can lose weight, and have lower reproductive success and higher mortality rates. These are features of the biology of individuals as a consequence of exceeding saturation. On the other hand, as long as grass seed production increases, the carrying capacity of the environment increases. Carrying capacity is a measure of the productivity of the environment for providing food and other essential resources for supporting populations. Of course, grass seed production—or any other measure of biological productivity—cannot increase indefinitely, and if there is a carrying capacity of the environment in which a population lives, increased numbers will lead to a reduction in resources—a deterioration of productivity—with consequences that will play out in the future.

Figure 5.16. Left: Comparison of saturation and carrying capacity based on data from Chipping Sparrows (from Pulliam & Dunning, 1987; Pulliam & Haddad, 1994). Right: Visual model showing the various factors that influence population size. E = establishment of a population, k is the population size maintained by predation and disease, S is the saturation point, and K is the carrying capacity. For population sizes larger than the carrying capacity, the population crashes because of environmental damage due to unsustained resource use. Disease is expected to happen when density approaches or exceeds saturation and this is a factor that can also precipitate a crash. *Source:* Created by the author.

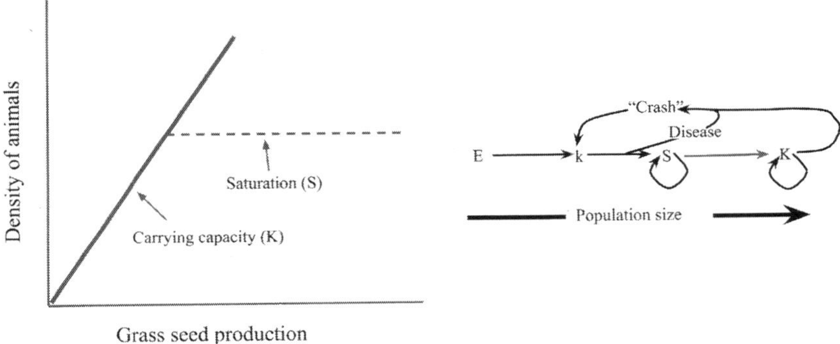

Pulliam and Haddad (1994) noted that Leopold's idea of saturation is rarely mentioned separate from K, and if we consider the saturation effect due to an individual's need for some amount of space, it is simply another essential resource for the birth, growth, and maturation of individuals that comprise a population and that contributes to environmental deterioration. The carrying capacity—encompassing saturation—is a key parameter in the logistic model of population growth, namely, $dN/dt = rN(1 - K/N)$, where dN/dt is the rate of change of population size, r the combined effects of recruitment and survival, N is the number of individuals, and K is the carrying capacity. The units of K are numbers of individuals.

In most real-world scenarios, r and K are likely to change over time both as a consequence of the characteristics of the individuals that make up the population and because the abundance and availability of resources changes due to the combined effects of consumption of resources and the variation in the environment in ways that influence the production of resources. Examples of environmental factors are the amount of rainfall and temperature. Most populations are assumed to be near the hypothetical carrying capacity (or saturation) and it is assumed that fluctuations in population size reflect changes in the availability of resources or stochasticity. Stochasticity is simply the fact that the population size at any given time cannot be fully predicted. Critically, r and K are both influenced by inherent properties of individuals and the effects of factors external to the individuals determined by biotic and abiotic factors. Also important is the fact that r is determined by two different processes—recruitment and survival—whereas K is an abstract outcome of the emergent process of population growth. In most populations, the two factors interact in complex ways that result in what ecologists refer to as population dynamics. While saturation and carrying capacity may be real phenomena, they may be difficult to observe or infer except for under controlled conditions. If we look at natural populations and assume population size is an emergent outcome of both saturation and carrying capacity, the seemingly chaotic fluctuations in numbers of individuals makes it seem that these two abstract phenomena do not exist, or that the world is wildly variable (e.g., Krebs et al., 2017). The latter is closer to the truth.

The definitions of saturation and carrying capacity are relevant in education settings. Saturation is a biological phenomenon, and it is best defined as the maximum number of individuals that can achieve their maximum productivity in a particular space. Carrying capacity is the available resources for sustaining the maximum learning gains. These two concepts—whether they exist or not—prove useful for interrogating student gains. If a disciplinary population does not change in numbers, we can infer that it is limited by density or resources, or both, and that it is at carrying capacity or saturation, or both. The measurable outcome is that the population does not trend higher or lower over time: it stays more-or-less the same, with fluctuations best explained by stochasticity.

The populations inhabiting the EBIO and MCDB disciplinary population at CU–Boulder havbe been at or near capacity for the last 10 years or so (see fig. 5.13). In both populations, there is variation in the population over time that likely reflects stochasticity associated with recruitment, persistence, and migration. In addition, the amount of variation in the number of students over time in each disciplinary population differs; the number of students in MCDB varies more over time than in EBIO. In both populations, however, there are reasons to suspect that student populations exceed both the saturation and carrying capacity. The apparent cap on population size for two educational populations inhabiting divergent biological disciplines suggests there are factors that limit population size in academic settings. In nature, limiting factors include shelter (space), access to resources for fueling growth and maturation, and density-dependent antagonistic interactions among individuals. In education, it may be that the same factors are at play. There are limitations due to the space available in classrooms (set by enrollment limits), the capacity of educators to teach (a resource), and density-dependent effects (the effects of class size and density on cognitive function). The very real limitations on space are evident every semester at CU–Boulder. There are waiting lists for classes, enrollments frequently exceed room sizes, and courses are often taught in rooms that are inadequate for certain pedagogical approaches. This is an emergent outcome of an economically motivated strategy to increase recruitment every year. Here is a message from the director (chair) of my department describing an all-too-familiar situation when we need to schedule the times and rooms for courses for each semester.

> There are widespread issues with respect to classroom space for F24 [Fall 2024]. . . . I suspect there is not an immediate solution to this. I can say that there are . . . EBIO courses for which there were absolutely no classrooms available at a time [and] at the capacity that we needed, so we needed to reduce the enrollment cap to meet the size of the available room. There was also one additional class that needed to move to non-traditional meeting times to find a classroom. This is obviously a bad thing to not be able to meet student demand because of space limitations.

It is important to realize that the statement "the capacity that we needed" is not one based on pedagogy and a knowledge of the dependence of learning gains on density of students. It is a need driven by demand. It is often the case that the demand for a class—and the classroom spaces—exceeds supply.

The issue of supply and demand plays out every semester, and its existence provides information about the apparent ceiling on population size in EBIO and MDCB. In one year, there were two sections of the same first-year course that had reached maximum enrollment; the excess students spilled out onto waiting lists. Because there were so many students on the waiting list, we opened a new section of the course. The course enrollment of 50 students was quickly met, and, remarkably, the list did not include any of the students on the existing waiting lists. This taught me that the apparent carrying capacity of disciplinary populations—like my own department of EBIO—are set, in part, by the number of available seats listed during the student registration period. If students fail to get into a class, they may elect to enroll in other classes and even pursue graduation through other disciplines that may have greater availability of seats. In fact, there are many cases at my institution in which admitted students are forced to enroll in disciplinary training programs that are not their primary interest because of limitations on capacity. This is one of the factors contributing to migration of students among disciplines. This brings me to the issue of class size and whether education effectiveness is density-dependent.

Does it matter if the density is low or high? We know the number of students matters: it matters for how teaching happens and it matters for learning gains. For instance, class size is an important component of an academic carrying capacity described by Ebuara et al. (2020) in their exploration of public universities in Nigeria. They wrote:

> Carrying capacity remains one of the major challenges to access to universities in Nigeria. The universities need to be expanded according to the demand to avoid being over-populated and facilities being overstretched. The term carrying or absorption capacity refers to the maximum number of students that the institution can conveniently sustain for quality education available based on human and material resources. Carrying capacity is indicated by how well enrollment of the university matches available human and material resources. The carrying capacity means that students are admitted based on the facilities available. These facilities include adequate lecture rooms, well-stocked libraries, good staff/student ratio, accommodation, etc. (p. 179)

Their work focused on the optimal faculty-to-student ratio, values that are, apparently, discipline dependent. They noted that the "optimal" ratio is 10 for the sciences: that is 10 students for each faculty member. Perusal of the average student-to-faculty ratio for 21 institutions of higher education in Nigeria revealed a modal value of about 30:1, with a very large range (Ebuara et al., 2020). At CU–Boulder there are three ratios that are easily obtainable. One is the published (and advertised) ratio of number of students per faculty member for the campus: 18 to 1. Another is the number of students that have identified a particular discipline as their home population relative to the number of tenure-track (TT) faculty members;[2] in EBIO this number is 24 to 1. And, finally, there is the number of students taught in a particular disciplinary course relative to all rostered faculty in the department; for EBIO that number is 63 to 1. The difference between the two ratios for EBIO reflects the fact that teaching professors have very much larger numbers of students than TT professors. Additionally, I calculated the average class size for four disciplinary populations (EBIO, MCDB, PYSC, and ENGL) that were regular 3 or 4 credit-hour classes taught by a single faculty member. The average values ranged from 27 to 81 (table 5.2). Clearly, student-to-faculty ratios are high, much higher than advertised, and certainly much higher than the 10:1 ratio claimed to be optimal for learning to think and communicate like a scientist (Ebuara et al., 2020). Table 5.2 also includes a slope value based on the dependence of the proportion of students that received a low grade (C- or worse) and class size. Student outcomes relative to class size are indicated by the magnitude of the slope: increasing large values indicates decreasing success relative to class size. For all disciplinary populations examined except ENGL, larger classes result in poorer student outcomes. Clearly class size is a component of the disciplinary saturation and carrying capacity in an education context. These data and a broader survey of class sizes and student-to-faculty ratios indicate there is heterogeneity across disciplinary populations, there is enormous variation across classes within a discipline, the real-life class sizes experienced by most students

Table 5.2. Statistics about class size (90th percentile and average) and the proportion of students with a bad or failing grade relative to class size*

Pop	90th percentile for class size	Average class size	Slope (x 10^{-4})†	p
EBIO	117	53	2.1	< 0.001
MCDB	112	45	5.8	< 0.001
PSYC	160	81	3.0	< 0.001
ENGL	35	27	0.6	0.44

*All classes less than 17 students were omitted (these are often lab-based or recitations).

†The slope is from a linear model with class size as predictor and year and term as covariates. The slope provides an indication of the strength of effect of class size on student success.

are much larger than the advertised value, and there is clear evidence that increasingly large classes have detrimental effects on student success.

But what about density? The limiting effects of space may be particularly important. Many classes have too many people. Saturation is based on the reality that there are limits to density and that crowding has measurably negative effects on biological function. Bush and Lotz (2000) wrote that crowding is "very common in managed systems where the intent is to get the 'biggest bang for the buck.' For example, gardeners know that too many plants in a prescribed area will result in a poor crop; so too do aquaculturists raising fishes, crustaceans, or shellfish" (p. 212). In animals, the negative effects of crowding appear to be mediated by circulating hormones that cause physiological and psychological stress responses. Additionally, the effects of crowding may vary by sex. Brown and Grunberg (1995) studied the effects of density on the level of circulating stress hormones in rats and discovered that crowding causes more stress in males than in females; by contrast, females were more uncomfortable (more stressed) when isolated than males. Pride (2005) also discovered differences in the effect of density (group size) on circulating stress hormones in a natural population of lemurs. In this case, female stress hormones were lowest at intermediate group sizes and higher when there were fewer individuals and also when there were many individuals; males, by contrast, were unaffected by group size. Similarly, studies of mice maintained at low and high densities revealed there are detectable and predictable changes in gene expression in the hypothalamus and white adipose tissues (Lin et al., 2015). In short, there is abundance of evidence for the idea, described by Pulliam and Haddad (1994), that density may be regulated in natural populations by behavior—referred to as saturation—prior to the population achieving carrying capacity.

There is evidence that the effects of crowding observed for animals in artificial and natural settings are also evident for students in educational contexts. Tucker and Friedman (1972) noted that crowding has been associated with abnormal behaviors, changes in body chemistry, and decreases in immune function. In addition, they also pointed out that individuals of many species have a specific interindividual distance that triggers fight or flight responses, and that the effects of crowding depend on whether interactions are competitive or cooperative. One of their conclusions, based on studies of students at three universities, is that as density increases, the interaction between individuals decreases, and they explained that this observation is an outcome of behavior linked to physiological and psychological stress reduction. Furthermore, Knowles et al. (1976, p. 647) discovered that social groups "create a social space boundary that deflects others away from the group and that the extension of this boundary increases with the size of the social unit." Thus, the high density of people on college campuses, both inside and outside the classroom, may be triggering stress responses, and it is likely that the magnitudes of the responses vary among individuals. It may be that the maximum capacity limits of classrooms, especially large classrooms, are higher than the saturation value of students for the space, and as a consequence teaching is happening in ways that create stress independent of, and in addition to, the stress associated with cognitive challenges introduced to promote learning. Indeed, Nagar and Pandey (1987, p. 147) discovered that "crowding and noise lead to deterioration of . . . performance on cognitively complex tasks" and that "density and noise generated a negative feeling in the subjects" and a decrease in students' satisfaction with their performance in the class compared to noncrowded conditions. It is likely many of our classrooms are operating past saturation. In ecology, systems beyond saturation are prone to population crashes. In education contexts, we can infer from analogy that crowding leads to cognitive limitations (Hellmann & Jucks, 2017) and perhaps cognition crashes in which hard-won learning gains are lost.

As members of the profession of higher education, we appear to be engaged in a giant experiment on the density-dependent effects of class size on academic success without explicitly realizing what we are doing. The most profound outcome may be an increase in the ability of individuals to tolerate crowding instead of producing demonstrable increases in critical and creative thinking abilities. There is a simple solution: make class sizes and student-to-faculty ratios smaller. This, of course, runs counter to entrenched financial models in higher education that emphasize *increasing* class sizes. This is an inevitable outcome of an institution model that prioritizes population growth through the combined actions of increasing recruitment and increasing persistence. More than 100 years of positive student population growth at CU–Boulder (University of Colorado Boulder IR, 2025) is the emergent outcome of these policies.

The fact that students' perceptions about the value of tuition is negatively associated with crowding (Hellman & Jucks, 2017) suggests we need to pay attention to the spaces—and densities—in which education happens (Beckers et al., 2016). Is there an optimal student-to-faculty ratio? I imagine the shape of the curve relating student gains across a variety of different measures of performance and intellectual maturation to class size looks like a parabola. The left side is pulled down by the fact that smaller classes offer students less opportunity for engaging, collaborating, and interacting with their peers and developing, with the support of their peers, a sense of belonging, among other things. The right side of the curve is pushed down by negative density-dependent effects (e.g., the negative effects of crowding and limitations on access to the professor and other educational resources) manifest as a reduction in grades and the probability of successfully completing a class. The high point of the parabola is an optimum, and this optimum likely varies, to some extent, with the discipline, teaching style, instructor capacity, students, and other aspects of educational experiences. There are reams of data that can be mined for getting some sense of whether there is an optimum and what it might be.

Perusal of survey data from students across many disciplinary populations shows evidence of the existence of an optimum. Figure 5.17 are

Figure 5.17. The dependence of student perceptions of the opportunities for interaction depending on class sizes for 1321 classes offered in the EBIO disciplinary population over a period of three years. Grey points are average survey scores for a specific class. The solid line connects the geometric mean score along a sliding window of class sizes (window size is five) and shows the trend in the data. The vertical dash line is the class size corresponding with the peak interaction score. *Source:* Created by the author.

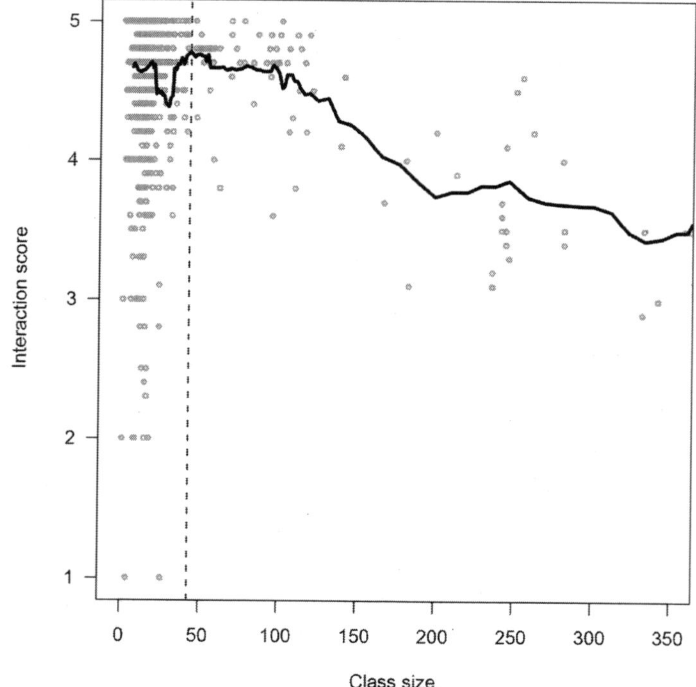

data from one measure of students' self-assessed opportunities for engaging in activities predictive of education gains: the ability to interact with their peers. For peer interaction the optimal class size is 48. Similar results were evident for a number of different dimensions of teaching, including collaboration, feedback, opportunities for creativity, and aspects associated with grading. The graph of student success, estimated as the percentage of students with a grade of C or better, decreases with class size (fig. 5.18). These data provide a sound argument for advocating class sizes should be in the neighborhood of 40–50 individuals. These estimates apply to the EBIO population, but are likely similar across divergent disciplines.

As alluded to earlier, the student-faculty ratio varies among courses, among professors, and over time. In my disciplinary population, we routinely offer what we refer to as "core" disciplinary courses with enrollments that exceed 100 students per semester (fig. 5.19). This number of students

Figure 5.18. The average proportion of students who received a score of C or better relative to class size for all EBIO courses taught from 2008 to 2018 (n = 2,817). The solid line shows the predictions from a linear model. *Source:* Created by the author.

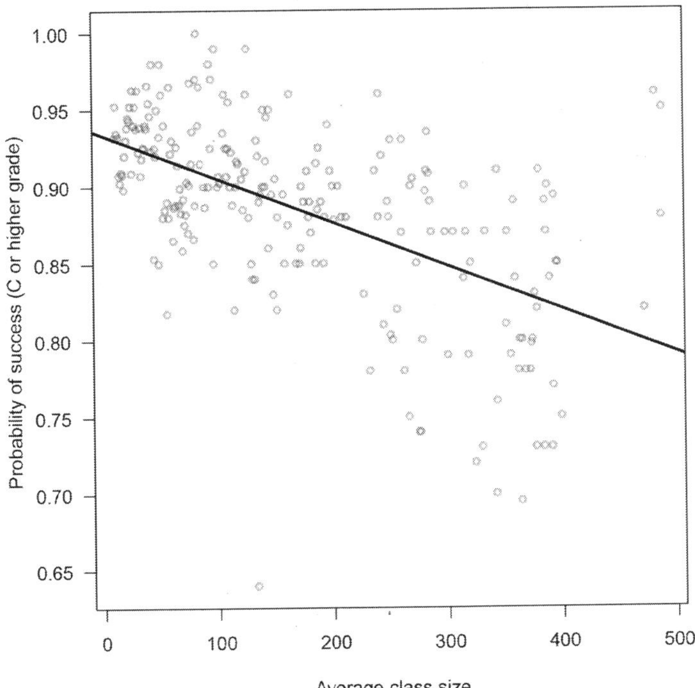

Figure 5.19. The class sizes for the five disciplinary core courses in EBIO from 2006 to 2022 that are offered with the expectations students enroll in these classes during their first, second, and third years. The estimated optimal class size is indicated by the vertical dashed line. *Source:* Created by the author.

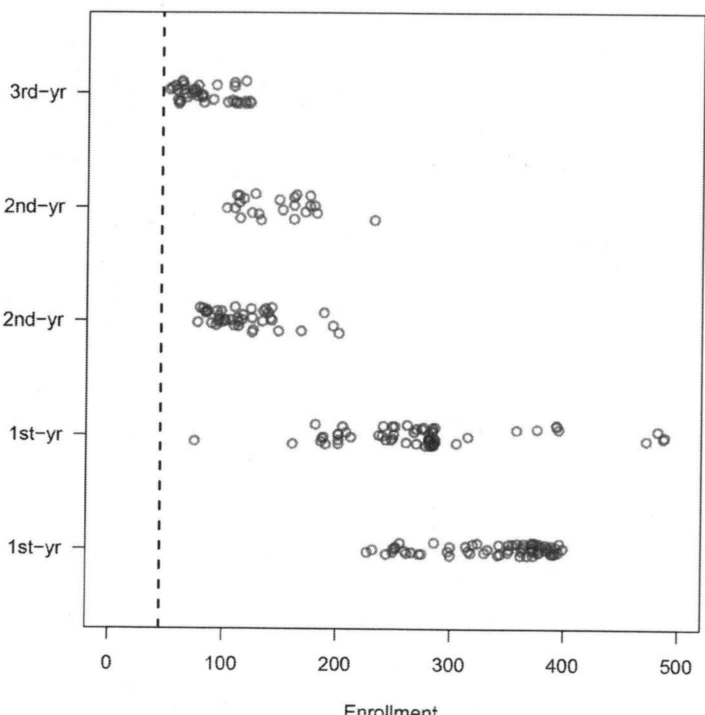

is categorized as large (Stains et al., 2018) and it is often the case that the number of students is at or near the maximum room occupancy. There is clear evidence that such large classes increase students' anxiety and "negatively affect student cognitive and affective outcomes" (Cooper et al., 2018, p. 6); moreover, a large fraction of the students may be experiencing physiological and psychological stress triggered by crowding. The population size of large classes is, in my opinion, past saturation and carrying capacity and vastly exceeds an optimal size. Additionally, these courses are taught by disciplinary experts; they are not education experts; cognitive challenges and assessments tend to be low dimensional (see Matz et al., 2018) and students are provided few, if any, opportunities for authentic interactions, collaboration, and creativity. Finally, such large class sizes provide few, if any, authentic opportunities for developing students' sense of belonging in science.

The Movement of Individuals between Populations

Education-relevant synopsis: Students may be engaged in a "win-stay, lose-move" strategy that determines whether they persist in a particular disciplinary population or migrate to a different population. The fact that students may be engaged in an evaluation of the merits of staying or moving suggests student dispersal among discipline populations should be supported and barriers that exist removed in ways that increase productivity. A comparative analysis of two similar disciplinary populations shows barriers influence the propensity and direction of movement of students among disciplines.

Populations change in numbers and characteristics as a consequence of the movement of individuals, referred to as migration. There are two different types of migration. One scale of migration involves the independent movement of *individuals* between populations; the other involves the coordinated movement of whole populations in response to seasonal variation in the abundance of resources. While the fantastic seasonal migration of animals is a remarkable and amazing ecological phenomenon, there is not, to my knowledge, a similar phenomenon that happens in an educational context. Thus, the discussion of migration is focused on the movement of individuals acting independently or in concert with a very limited number of peers. In ecological contexts, individual migration is also described as dispersal. Dispersal is defined as the movement of an individual or their propagules (such as seeds, spores, larvae, etc.) from their natal location to other places where they become established and reside through the remainder of their life. Dispersal can vary over time and can be categorized into three stages: individuals leave a specific population, individuals move to a new location, and individuals establish in a new location (Peniston et al., 2024). There are so-called endogenous and exogenous factors that influence all three of the stages of dispersal. Endogenous factors are restricted to the population, and include density, resource abundance, and the presence or absence of mates or social opportunities. Exogenous factors are environmental and impinge on the populations from outside. In ecological settings, this can be many different things: temperature, wind, storms, extreme disturbance, water flow, and so on.

The spatial movement of individuals can be modeled as density-dependent habitat selection. Habitat is described as localized and heterogeneous, with patches of resources separated by uninhabitable or low value places. Individuals are imagined to move among patches in which the amount of time an individual spends in a particular patch is determined by the density-dependent resource level. High levels of resources will keep individuals for longer periods of time; low levels of resources promote shorter residence times. Thus, individuals are assumed to move in ways that maximize their access to resources across a heterogeneous environment. There are, however, other factors at play. Individuals may express some degree of site fidelity in which they inhabit only a small range of the population's collective home range. Whether animals stay put and exploit a single or small number of resources or animals move across the heterogeneous landscape and forage on many different spatially-separated resources may depend on whether they use a "win-stay" and "lose-shift" strategy. Interestingly, individuals often stay in particular patches (habitats) longer than expected based on resource abundance, suggesting the threshold for winning and losing may change the longer an individual stays in a particular site or focused on obtaining a particular resource. Additionally, enacting a "win-stay" and "lose-shift" strategy depends on an individual's tendency to specialize on particular resources (Wakefield et al., 2015). Barack et al. (2022) wrote:

> Patch foraging is the iterated accept-or-reject decision to stick with a known but potentially depleting option or disengage and search for something that might be better. This description characterizes a wide array of decision contexts, including when to search for resources like food, water, minerals or sexual encounters; internal searches through concepts, memory or strategies; or searches for abstract resources such as for information or reputation. These decisions can be solved using simple algorithms derived from optimal foraging theory, such as the Marginal Value Theorem (MVT). These algorithms dictate that individuals should leave a depleting resource patch when local intake rates fall below the average for the environment. Hundreds of species tested—from bees to birds to monkeys to humans—either quantitatively or qualitatively behave in accordance with the predictions of such models, suggesting that evolution long ago settled on a near-optimal solution to the challenge of determining when to abandon a depleting resource and search for a new one. (pp. 1–2)

Finally, studies of ecological systems have revealed generalities. For instance, the distance between population—both in units of geographic distance and habitat difference—influences dispersal (Terborgh, 1973). There are often differences in dispersal probability and distance between the two sexes; across many taxa, males disperse more often and disperse further than females (Lawson Handley & Perrin, 2007). Additionally, there are differences in dispersal depending on age (Bowler & Benton, 2009). The effects of resources, disciplinary distance, sex, and age may all be evident in educational settings.

As described earlier in the section on "recruitment, establishment and persistence," students disperse across the disciplinary landscape of higher education. The students may be engaging in some type of optimal foraging for resources toward achieving the goal of intellectual maturation and graduation. Ideally, the structure of the curriculum includes providing students opportunities to sample different disciplinary habitats that are, in the context of foraging theory, "patches" of resources. Students may adopt a "win-stay" and "lose-shift" strategy. A win might be determined by a good grade or a positive experience. Alternatively, students might also specialize in a particular habitat patch (disciplinary environment) early on and stay put even if moving may be beneficial. In this case, students may lack sufficient information for making informed decisions necessary for optimizing the "lose-shift" aspect of the "win-stay" and "lose-shift" strategy. They might come into a discipline, or migrate from one discipline to another, because of parental or external effects independent of resources (Leppel et al., 2001).[3] Given the ubiquity of evidence from comparative studies of many different species, it makes sense to assume students may conform to the predictions of optimal foraging theory from ecological studies.

There will also be variation among students' inherent tendencies to stay or leave a particular patch of cognitive resources. In an experimental study, Barack et al. (2022, p. 1) found that human foraging conforms to the expectations from optimal foraging theory, but more importantly discovered that individuals "whose scores on the ADHD scale crossed the threshold for a positive screen departed patches significantly sooner than participants who did not meet this criterion . . . [and] also achieved higher reward rates than individuals who did not." They concluded that individuals with attributes of ADHD may have foraging advantages in some environments, and suggest that ADHD may be an adaptation for exploration. Evidence of a genetic basis of ADHD, and also that there is heritable genetic variation for exploratory behavior in other species suggests that we should expect variation in how students cognitively forage.

Moreover, how long students stay with a particular topic or work on a particular learning activity reflects variation in their inherent tendency to act in ways consistent with the "win-stay" and "lose-shift" strategy, a tendency modified by their history of engaging in selective cognitive foraging throughout their life as a student.

One factor that limits students' abilities to move among disciplinary habitats are required courses for success within a particular disciplinary habitat. Some disciplinary populations have larger numbers of required courses, or more restrictive options, than other disciplinary populations. For example, in MCDB, there are about twice as many specific required classes than in EBIO. Moreover, many of the specified required classes in MCDB can be used for achieving success in EBIO whereas the converse is not true. The enforced specialization of students who may begin their cognitive foraging in MCDB may allow them to adopt a "win-stay" and "lose-shift," because if they shift from MDCB into EBIO they can still be successful; however, the "win-stay" and "lose-shift" strategy is less likely to be successful for EBIO students immigrating into MCDB, because the disciplinary specialization required by MCDB makes it an untenable choice. Students cannot effectively use the "lose-shift" option, because a shift from EBIO to MCDB requires having to take more required classes that may delay graduation, a decision that may be prohibitively costly. There are likely many cases in which there are barriers that interfere with adopting "win-stay" and "lose-shift" strategies for success in higher education. Thus, unlike ecological models in which individuals can move freely among patches and their success depends on the relative abundance of resources, movement of individuals in higher education is more restrictive and depends, to a varying degree, on where individuals first become established.

Migration of students between disciplinary populations is at the heart of contrasting pedagogical philosophies. On the one hand, many disciplinary populations emphasize the depth of student experience within a single discipline; on the other hand, knowledge of different ways of thinking often requires being part of multiple disciplinary populations. It is not clear whether one strategy is better than the other, because the answer is dependent on the individual students and their goals. What is clear, though, is that the ability of students to cognitively forage across a diverse landscape is limited, sometimes severely, to the extent that they cannot adopt a "win-stay" and "lose-shift" strategy in ways that allow them to find a disciplinary population in which they feel at home and productive. If, however, we returned to a liberal model of education, in which the purpose of higher education is for the common good rather than designed in ways aligned with developing students as experts in an increasing specialized economy, the structure of higher education would more closely resemble a heterogeneous landscape with individuals sorting themselves out into particular patches (disciplinary populations) depending on their ability to engage in a "win-stay" and "lose-shift" strategy. To make this work, the structure of curricular requirements should be more fluid and less siloed such that dispersal is encouraged rather than penalized. Ultimately, the ideal strategy results in an emergent outcome in which individuals are distributed across disciplinary habitats according to their sense of belonging and perceived value of a particular discipline.

The Effects of Environment

Education-relevant synopsis: Different disciplinary populations have different academic cultures that cause differentiation in ways of thinking, knowledge, and skills. The different academic cultures effectively cause local adaptation that reinforces the institution-driven siloization of disciplines. This, in turn, limits interdisciplinary interaction and the ability of students in different disciplines to effectively engage with individuals from other such disciplines. Specialization is driven by the perception that higher education exists as a tool for professional development rather than as a public good. Ideally, there should be an increasing emphasis on interdisciplinary interactions and the gain of the ability to work with individuals with varied skills, knowledge, and perspective toward common goals.

There are three key parameters—recruitment, persistence, and migration—that combine in myriad ways that cause population size to change over time. These same processes influence the characteristics of populations. By making the analogy between ecological and educational populations, we can leverage some of the reasons why ecological populations differ for making inferences about why educational populations differ. Ecological populations are different mostly because aspects of the environments differ. For example, the morphological characteristics of individuals sampled from different populations of sticklebacks (a small fish related to seahorses) differ, an observation that suggests different populations are subject to different environmental or biotic effects, which influence survival in ways that cause two or more populations to diverge in characteristics (DeFaveri & Merilä, 2013). Because differentiation of ecological populations is an outcome of evolution, the key features underlying the emergence of differentiation is that there is variation among individuals and the biotic and abiotic aspects of the environments cause certain types of individuals to be more or less successful. This aligns with a general property of evolution that all adaptation is local.

The average properties of individuals in different populations may also differ as a consequence of the influence of environmental differences during the growth and maturation of individuals independent of inherent genetic effects. This type of variation is often referred to as phenotypic plasticity. The idea is that individuals vary—are plastic and moldable—in response to changes in the environment. It is common in the literature to find studies of individuals that are genetically similar but have different characteristics when they live and mature in different environments. These types of experiments are referred to as common garden experiments, and generally consist of bringing individuals from different populations to the same place to grow and mature. There are also reciprocal transplant experiments in which individuals from one population are moved into another population, and vice versa, to see how they will grow and mature relative to their "home" environment. For example, Williams et al. (2008, p. 239) wrote that they "found substantial population-level plasticity for size, fecundity and date of first flowering, with plants performing better in a garden in Germany than in Montana." In another study, scientists found that "ninety-nine percent of variability in traits and their plasticity co-varied" with the place of origin (Singh & Roy, 2017, p. 39). The upshot of many studies is that individuals vary in their abilities depending on where they live due to the effects of genes and the environment.

The ubiquity of structural and functional differences between individuals from different populations in nature suggests we should expect similar differentiation between students inhabiting different disciplinary populations. This is true if the environments of disciplinary populations differ such that there are differences in the characteristics of newly recruited individuals, individuals that migrate, and individuals that persist. Studies attempting to estimate differentiation of cognitive function between individuals that inhabited different disciplinary environments suggest the results evident for ecological settings are likely evident in educational settings. There is a theory of academic disciplines built on the idea that the success of individuals with different personality types covaries with the disciplinary properties (Holland, 1966; Stuart et al., 2000). At its core is the idea that both students and faculty have perspectives and ways of thinking that can be categorized into six personality types: realistic, conventional, enterprising, investigative, artistic, and social. These properties, in turn, influence students' self-selection into specific academic disciplines. I think the basic thesis that there is positive covariance between students' interests and the academic disciplinary properties is true, especially during the process of recruitment. However, my experience is that the more individual students are characterized using some dimension of personality, knowledge, affect, and skills, the more it is evident that there may not be convenient categories; instead, the variation among individuals is best modeled as a normal, bell-shaped distribution with a clear central tendency toward some emergent factor accompanied by an abundance of variation. Furthermore, the high rate of migration among disciplines, especially among disciplines without substantial barriers to the flow of students, argues that the theory of academic disciplines and student success supported by Holland and Stuart and colleagues may be insufficient. Instead, I argue that theories about population differentiation stemming from ecology and evolution provide a more coherent and predictive framework for gaining an increased understanding of the process and outcomes of higher education.

There are, nonetheless, some statistics that popped out of Stuart et al. (2000, p. 62) with profound implications for why the structure and function of higher education is the way it is today. Survey data from faculty about their perceptions of undergraduate teaching, the students, and the preferences for teaching revealed some insightful stories. For example, faculty perceive that the increasing specialization of undergraduate teaching—and the proliferation of ever more specific academic disciplines—is a good thing (a correlation [r] of greater than 0.87). A corollary is that faculty think that there should be more specialized training of undergraduates (r > 0.7). Finally, faculty also prefer teaching students who have a clear idea of their career future (r = 0.83). Not surprisingly, faculty prefer to teach their particular specialization (r = 0.7). All of these features of faculty perspectives may be useful and aligned with the goals of higher education, but, at face value, conform to a more neoliberal model than they do with the liberal model of higher education. In my experience, many of my colleagues teach as if they are training students to follow in their footsteps rather than pursuing the general goals of becoming critical and creative thinkers and self-assured and self-efficacious citizens, among other relevant dimensions of intellectual development and academic achievement. A liberal arts education does not exist for the purpose of professional training; instead, it exists as a means of raising the critical and creative thinking skills of individuals in ways that allow them to pursue any number of diverse professions.

Neumann (2001) asserted that different disciplines emphasized different modes and contexts for teaching. Neumann wrote that among disciplines "different values and emphases have also been found in relation to curriculum and assessment issues, as well as different conceptual structures and knowledge validation methods." Some disciplines "had tightly structured courses with highly related concepts and principles," while others had more "open course structures and were loosely organized." Some disciplines put "greater importance on student career preparation and emphasize cognitive goals such as learning facts, principles and concepts," whereas others placed greater importance on broad general knowledge, on student character development and on effective thinking skills such as critical thinking" (p. 138). It's not surprising to find evidence, as did Berkowitz and Stern (2018), that there are differences in cognitive ability for four main axes of function for students in engineering compared with those in a math-physics program. It is generally true that for academic environments defined by pedagogy, the personalities and perspectives differ across all disciplinary populations on a particular campus, and the general tendency is for increasing diversification and disciplinary specialization as the world becomes more diverse and complex.[4] Kolb (1981) summarized some of the processes underlying observed differences among disciplinary populations: "For students, education in an academic field is a continuing process of selection and socialization to the pivotal norms of the field governing criteria for truth and how it is to be achieved, communicated and used, and secondarily, to peripheral norms governing personal styles, attitudes and social relationships. Over time, these selection and socialization pressures combine to produce an increasingly impermeable and homogeneous disciplinary culture and correspondingly specialized student orientations to learning" (as quoted in Neumann, 2001, p. 141). The extent of differentiation between groups inhabiting different scholarly disciplines does not only reflect the topics emphasized, but also reflects, to varying degrees, strategies that result in differential success depending on student characteristics imposed by instructors and course structures. While my goal is not to engage in a deep analysis of instructor and course structure effects on students' membership within a particular population, there is clear evidence for differential persistence by discipline with concomitant effects on the characteristics of students.

The processes giving rise to statistically describable differences among individuals inhabiting different disciplinary populations begins with recruitment and continues as a consequence of actions and student experiences that influence persistence and migration. Students may decide, based on experiences in one or more courses, that they really don't belong in a particular discipline and change majors or leave college altogether. Seymour and Hewitt (1997) wrote about individuals who stayed in a particular discipline (major) or switched at some point into a different major: "What distinguished the survivors from those who left was the development of particular attitudes or coping strategies. . . . Switchers invariably distinguished experiences they perceived as bearing directly on their decisions to leave S.M.E. [science, math, engineering] majors and problems of less significance which they need to accommodate, tolerate, or resolve, in order to stay" (p. 30). The interaction between educators, the physical conditions in educational settings, and the students sort individuals into different disciplinary populations, and the process of sorting results in the emergence of different cultures, ways of thinking, and perceptions of how the world works among academic disciplines. Whether the emergence of cultural diversity among disciplines is more beneficial than diversity within disciplines is not something that has been validly assessed. My perspective is that among-discipline diversity is inevitable, but that it is important to retain and encourage practices that promote diversity, including diversity in ways of thinking and knowing and communicating, within disciplines. I have focused on the difference between two biology departments: one focused on the very small and mostly direct processes in biology (MCDB) and one focused on properties and processes that span all scales of biology, from molecules to ecosystems with a tendency to grapple with emergent processes (like ecology and evolution). The fact that MCDB students do not receive much training in how to think like an ecologist or evolutionary biologists suggests that the differentiation between the two academic populations may have real consequences, especially given that all cellular and molecular processes are influenced by ecology and exist because of evolution.

There are many reasons that the differences among disciplinary populations may be beneficial. However, when the differences have negative effects on student success attributable to instructors and learning environments, we should strive to intervene, diagnose the problems, and propose and implement solutions. Large variation in student success due to instructor effects may indicate the existence of educational malpractice. Malpractice is limited in science because of the peer review process; a similarly strict quality control mechanism is generally lacking in higher education, at least at my institution. We do implement regular student surveys as a check on the student perceptions of educational outcomes, but it is unclear how these data are used to intervene in ways that improve student experiences. One way the data can be used is to demonstrate, as I have done, that class sizes are often too large. What we do about it remains the rub. More generally, there is an overarching broader issue about the effects of sorting students as a consequence of events during their lives as students. If higher education is a public good, one outcome should be a population with a good understanding of the world we live in that leverages different ways of thinking and includes historical contexts. The apparent siloization of students by discipline may contribute to a greater societal discourse of mutual misunderstanding and a general failure of empathy. If I do not understand the premise of where people are coming from, it makes collaboration difficult and limits trust.

Changes in Interacting Populations

Education-relevant synopsis: A general outcome of ecological interactions— especially consumptive ones—is the emergence of a stoichiometry of numbers of individuals. An increase in enrollment and numbers of students is expected to result in an increase in number of faculty that directly interact with students. This is evident only for non-tenure-track teaching faculty and not for research-dedicated faculty. The differential response of the two groups of faculty underscores the increasing divide between the two missions of the university. Additionally, the increasing numbers of students is also accompanied by an increase in the number of large-enrollment classes, another sign of a rift between the synergy between teaching and research.

Recognizably different populations interact through the interactions of individuals. A simple example is that an increase in abundance of individuals categorized as primary producers results in more resources for individuals of other populations that depend on the primary producers: more grass seed translates into a larger sparrow population, all else being equal. Similarly, an increase in the numbers of snowshoe hares—a type of rabbit—typically results in a greater number of coyotes or lynx, or both (O'Donoghue et al., 1997). Pielou (1974, p. 1) remarked that populations are always changing in size, and that the changes in size "may occur quickly or slowly, and the effects on other populations may be marked or slight." The effects on other populations can be indirect through a common large-scale change, or direct because more of one type of individual affects the numbers in another population.

Is the interdependence of interacting ecological populations evident in higher education? The short answer is yes. Students are, in some ways, like plants in ecological contexts. An increase in numbers of students is accompanied by an apparent increase in resources, because each student comes with tuition dollars: more students = more money. And money is like carbon generated by photosynthesis: just as more available carbon translates into more animals, more money translates into hiring more people. At CU–Boulder, the number of students in classrooms has been increasing more-or-less continuously for as long as the institution has existed. Over the last 15 years, the total number of students enrolled in classes increased by approximately 2% per year. This increase in "primary productivity" is matched by an increase in the number of faculty educators in classrooms;[5] however, the two different populations of faculty—those with tenure and those without tenure—have changed in dramatically different ways.

To answer the question of interdependence, it's important to categorize faculty into those that teach and are directly connected to the students and faculty whose jobs are mostly focused on research and scholarly activity and rarely interact with undergraduate students. Counts of students and faculty in the classroom show sustained and apparently correlated increases (fig. 5.20). The net result is that the ratio of student enrollment to the number of faculty has remained more-or-less constant. This is expected in the same way numbers of sparrows increase when the abundance of seeds on which they depend for food increases. However, if we count the number of tenure-track (TT) and non-tenure-track (NTT) faculty individuals as comprising two different populations, there is clear evidence that Pielou's "effects on other populations" differs for the two populations dependent on the student population. While increasing tuition dollars are paying for more faculty, most of the gain in faculty involved in teaching is due to increases in the NTT population of individuals. The trend of hiring more NTT faculty to meet the increasing demand for teaching in response to increases in number of students is a financial decision because NTT faculty salaries are less, and often much less, than TT faculty salaries. And this strategy is evident across many institutions of higher education nationally. The disparity of the interdependence of the populations of NTT and TT faculty with the population of students reveals a divide in the culture and function of a university. These data argue in favor of a zero-sum model in which investment in teaching comes with a decline in research and vice versa; resolution of this model involved creating and sustaining two classes of people: those with tenure and privilege and those without tenure or privilege. Privilege refers to the status and professional capital afforded to individuals by the institution.

In contrast to the constant ratio of students-to-faculty, there has been a bumpy increase in the ratio of executives to faculty over time. There are three stories in these data. First, prior to 2008 there was roughly a constant ratio of executives-to-faculty of about 1:100. Second, both the numbers of

Figure 5.20. The total student enrollment in courses (solid line × 100), the total number of different TT professors in the classroom (dashed line), and the total number of NTT professors in the classroom (dashed-dotted line) from 2007 to 2023. *Source:* Created by the author. Data from Institutional Research.

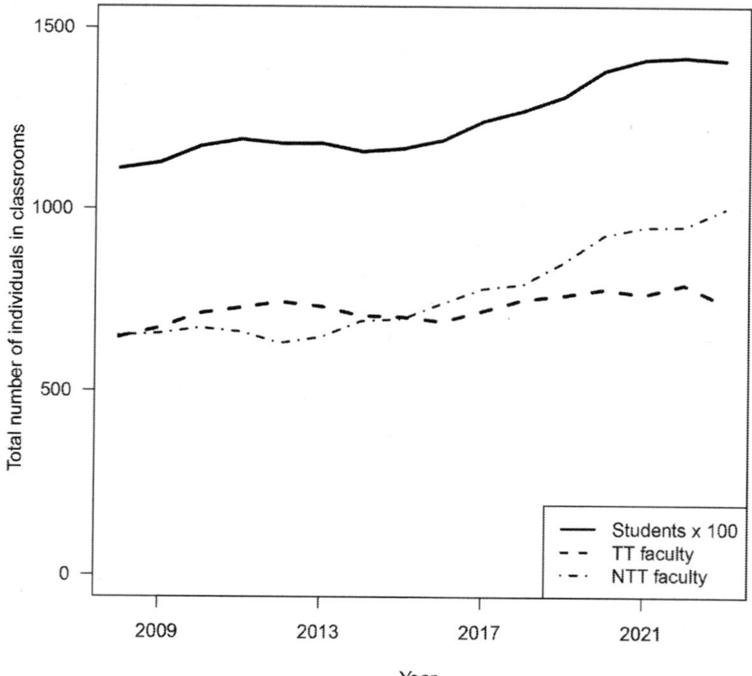

faculty and numbers of executives decreased markedly during the most recent financial crisis that began in 2008. Finally, the numbers of faculty increased at about the same constant rate since the financial recovery beginning around 2010, whereas the number of executives increased at a faster rate. This pattern is evident nationally.

The combination of increasing numbers of students and faculty over time translated into an increase in numbers of courses. More alarmingly, there was also an increase in the number of large courses (fig. 5.21). (A large course is defined as course with an enrollment that exceeds 100 students [Stains et al., 2018].). The increasing numbers of large courses was accompanied by a campus-wide initiative administered through the Center for Teaching and Learning that promoted large courses. All participants were NTT faculty.

Ideally, the interdependence of the faculty and student populations happens in ways that reduces class sizes and the numbers of high-enrollment, dense, and stressful learning environments in favor of places

Figure 5.21. The number of large-enrollment courses from 2007 to 2020 at CU–Boulder. *Source:* Created by the author.

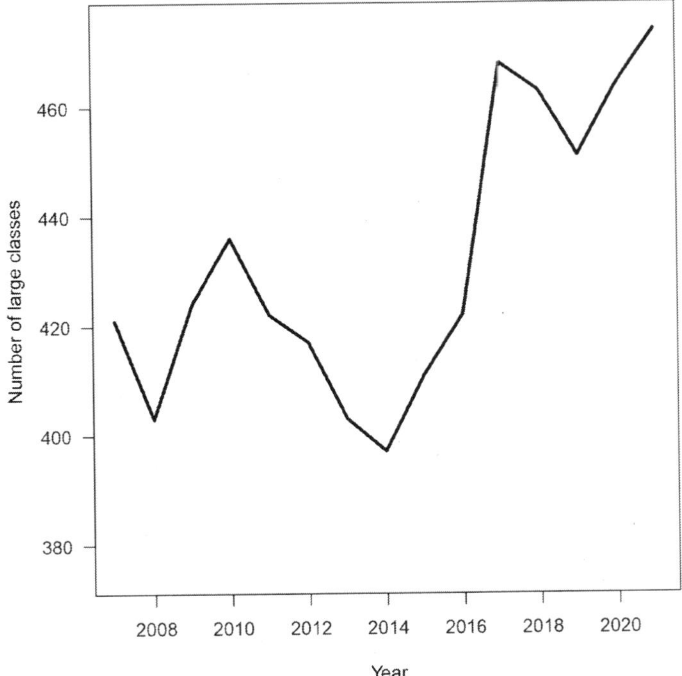

that cultivate self-efficacy and a sense of belonging. What is counter to the goals of higher education is that we, as educators, know that small class sizes are better for students and that pedagogy matters, and yet the number of large courses taught using strategies that depart from research-supported best practices appears to be on an unstoppable increasing trajectory. What appears to limit the growth of large-enrollment classes is large rooms.

Population Dynamics of Ideas

Education-relevant synopsis: Ideas are the units of knowledge and, like individuals in populations, the number of ideas in the mind changes as a consequence of recruitment and persistence: there is a population dynamics of ideas. A common outcome of education is an increase in ideas in the minds of students due to recruitment of new ideas associated with teaching and learning followed by the loss of ideas due to failure of establishment and lack of persistence. This recurrent outcome implies we need to emphasize the establishment and persistence of ideas perhaps by paying more attention and time on forging connections among new and existing ideas in students' minds.

The ecology of populations of individuals is also relevant for thinking about populations of ideas. Ideas are the individual units of knowledge and there are two scales of population-level aggregation. One is the population of ideas in the minds of individual students. The other is the population of ideas in the minds of all students within a particular course or disciplinary unit. The simplest model borrowed from ecology is one that includes recruitment and survival. In words, the number of ideas at time T, labeled N_T, is equal to the recruitment (or assimilation [Ausubel 2012]) of new ideas plus the survival of ideas that were already established. This is the same core model used for describing the population growth of students and animals in ecological contexts. And like the model described by Hughes (1990), survival may be density independent. This means that established ideas survive with the same probability regardless of the number of ideas in the mind of a student. Additionally, recruitment of new ideas may be density-dependent, an assertion that stems from the discovery of cognitive load. Cognitive load is the idea that only a small number of new ideas can become established in the mind in some defined period of time. A greater number (or density of ideas) means the next new idea is less likely to establish (recruit) into the mind of a student.

Analysis of mental constructs evident in the minds of students supports the applicability of recruitment and survival models as a framework for conceptualizing and analyzing the gain and maturation of intelligence. For instance, in a course focused on quantitative and critical thinking, students were taught about uncertainty as a consequence of random and systematic sampling error. Uncertainty as a dynamic mental construct was conceptualized as consisting of separate rubric items (nodes or ideas). The items were (1) we cannot know the truth because of sampling error; (2) there is always error from sampling unless all individuals are sampled; (3) there are two sources of sampling error, random and systematic; (4) the two types of error are additive; (5) random sampling error is not biased; (6) the average of estimates from random sampling error is indistinguishable from the true parameter value; (7) systematic error is biased; (8) systematic error causes consistently smaller or larger estimates of the true parameter value; (9) uncertainty due to sampling error can be investigating by repeatedly estimating a parameter value using the computer or repeatedly enacting a sampling scheme independently multiple times; (10) the uncertainty due to random sampling can be reliably estimated based on sample standard deviation (s) and the sample size (n) using the equation sd/sqrt(n); and (11) the uncertainty due to systematic sampling error cannot be reliably estimated, because bias is revealed only when the truth is known (see rubric 1). These ideas are abstract for most people with poorly developed abilities for quantitative and scientific thinking, and despite repeated reference to these ideas and engaging in activities designed to make the ideas apparent and understandable, student gains are modest and the mental construct of uncertainty gradually erodes over time (fig. 5.22). It is clear from these data that if knowledge of uncertainty is an essential mental construct for achieving mature and competent scientific thinking, then the emphasis on this key concept should be carried through multiple subsequent courses after this introduction to the topic in a first-year (1000-level) course.

The example about the dynamics of ideas in the minds of students is evident across many different contexts; the expectation is that the number of ideas increases by recruitment and the number of ideas decrease because they fail to persist. You can see the recruitment and loss of ideas if you repeatedly assess student knowledge and understanding. In the context of the example described above about bryozoans, each student essentially began the unit on uncertainty as a bare rock primed for the settlement of ideas from the population of ideas floating like plankton outside of

Figure 5.22. The gain and loss of understanding as an emergent of outcome of learning a set of ideas about uncertainty. The same free-response assessment was implemented at more-or-less regular intervals beginning at the beginning of class (0) and ending with the final exam (3). The solid line is the average proportion of students with a coherent, multi-idea conception of uncertainty. Each dashed line is one of nine distinct ideas. *Source:* Created by the author.

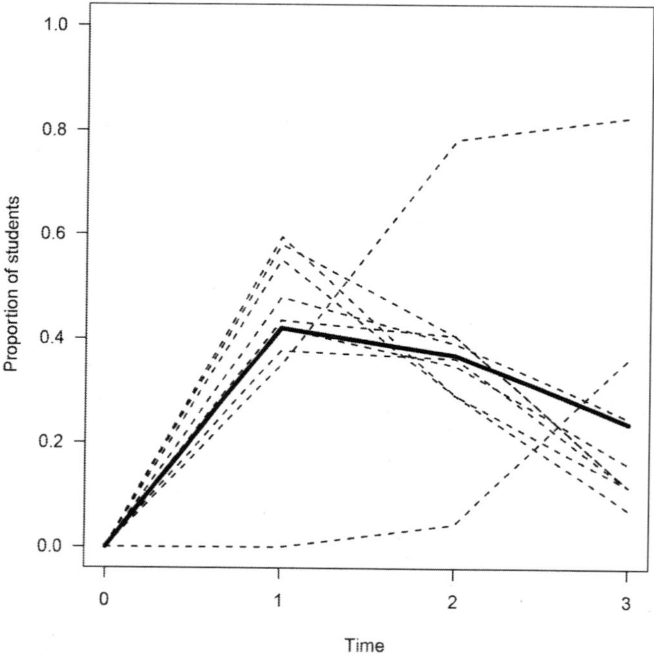

students' minds. The rise of the abundance of an idea reflects recruitment. Following recruitment, an idea survives or is lost. Some ideas have high survival and their abundance in the populations (represented by all the students' minds) increases due to recruitment and survival. Other ideas persist for a time but have low survival and, after time, perish. Thus, the population of ideas within the mind of a single student, and collectively in the minds of an aggregation of individuals, changes over time. The job of educators is to enact learning that enhances the outcomes of idea recruitment and survival. It is likely there are effective strategies for recruitment (and settlement) that differ from strategies aimed at increasing the probability of idea survival. Ecology and education data clearly show recruitment and survival are separate processes necessary for the emergence of ecological communities and intelligence. What this means is that, depending on context and the particular ideas educators think are important, it may be necessary to craft strategies that increase recruitment, followed by strategies that increase persistence. Most of education emphasizes recruitment. We need more attention on strategies promoting persistence. Persistence is best accomplished by curriculum alignment across multiple courses students encounter at different times and stages of intellectual maturation. Too often, though, course curricula exists as an archipelago without explicit connections and pedagogical coherency. In my disciplinary population we attempted establishing curricular alignment but too many of the TT faculty operate as independent agents, partly because of a lack of effective academic leadership.

Are There Limits to Knowledge?

Education-relevant synopsis: There is an enormous universe of ideas, and there is evidence that increases in knowledge accelerates the birth of new ideas. Yet, the pliable and immature minds of most students imposes limits on their capacity to integrate new ideas. Education needs more focus on the hierarchical structure of knowledge, to reveal differences in the value and importance of different ideas, to emphasize the dependencies of ideas instead of forging ahead with the objective of conveying all ideas as equally valid, equally relevant and equally worthy of learning. The connections among ideas mean the inevitable loss of ideas may cause an avalanche, leaving students as novice as they were when their education in a particular discipline began. There needs to be more emphasis on the explanatory power of associations of ideas rather exposure and strategies for memorization and remembering.

Unlike the budget models that drive increasing enrollment at the institution level, there are limits on the educational resources necessary for the advance of individual and collective intelligence. This might suggest there are limits to the number of ideas that can be effectively taught. Are there limits on the population of ideas in the minds of students? In *The Rational Optimist*, Matt Ridley (2010, p. 248) writes that "the more knowledge you generate, the more you can generate." Or the corollary, the more ideas you have, the more ideas you can generate. This implies that knowledge is without limits. Chamberlain (2020) described aspects of the growth of the population of ideas that constitute knowledge:

> Different types of knowledge have different rates of growth but it is generally acknowledged that human knowledge is increasing at an extraordinary rate. Arguably we may have reached a point where relevant knowledge is increasing faster and in greater quantities than we can absorb. However, while knowledge is increasing, the useful lifespan of knowledge is decreasing. Consequently, we need to be constantly replacing out-of-date knowledge with new knowledge in a continuous process of unlearning and learning. Knowledge alone however is not sufficient and as important is the ability to apply good judgment based on knowledge . . . what we know as wisdom. It is knowledge and wisdom put into action that gives us insight. (p. 1)

Thus, like populations of individuals in ecology and the population of students in education, ideas have a dynamic existence as a consequence of the birth (origin) of new ideas, the maintenance of useful ideas, and the death (loss) of ideas that turn out not to have relevance beyond their abstracted existence in the minds of individuals. Nonetheless, within populations of individuals, rates of birth and immigration of ideas exceed the loss of ideas, suggesting there is no apparent limit to the number of ideas.

While knowledge is without limits for populations, there are limits on the population of ideas in the mind of a single student. There are likely saturation effects happening that influence the population size of ideas in the mind of a student. The same model used for thinking about optimization of class size applies to ideas. The optimum is determined by the number of ideas, the importance of each idea, and the inherent complexity of each idea. If there are too few ideas, knowledge is reduced in part because knowledge is both an additive and multiplicative outcome of the number of ideas. Knowledge in pieces means that an essential building block of knowledge is the idea, so having more ideas may correspond with greater knowledge: this is the additive effect. But ideas exist in relation to other ideas, and knowledge is built by making connections between ideas, and incorporating new ideas into an evolving, interconnected network of interacting ideas. This latter part is multiplicative because an increasingly well-connected knowledge network lends itself to incorporation, or resistance, of new ideas, and the sum of the interaction of two or more ideas is greater than their effects on their own. At the same time, the right side of the parabola is being pushed down because too many ideas can exceed the cognitive capacity of individuals, resulting in a cascading failure of learning (Russell et al., 1984; Achike & Ogle, 2000). This is known as cognitive overload.

Thus, education faces a dilemma. Regardless of discipline, the amount of available and arguably important information increases by the day. Perusal of the list of facts and ideas that constitute the content of a disciplinary population continues to increase as research pushes out on the expanding universe of the world's collective knowledge. For example, Ansari and Landin (2022) studied the change in content focused on climate change in biology textbooks published between 1970 and 2019. There was a more than a tenfold increase in the number of sentences coupled with shifts in content emphasis related to climate change. Ansari and Landin noted that, while "coverage of the effects of climate change, in text passages and figures, has increased and diversified over time . . . the amount of content, placement within the book, and communication of solutions have not kept pace with the severity or scope of the problem" (p. 10). The expanding universe of ideas is happening across an increasing diversity of disciplines at the same time students have a finite capacity for learning new ideas and developing a well-connected set of ideas into a coherent structure of knowledge. Are there insights or inferences we can gain from ecology to help resolve this conflict?

Studies of ecological communities have revealed the existence of core and peripheral species. Identification of core and peripheral species in ecological settings focused attention on interactions between functionally different individuals. Core species tend to be generalists that use a variety of different resources and tend to interact in ways that form the central players of a highly interactive network. Peripheral species, by contrast, tend to be specialists that use few different resources and have limited interactions with generalist species (Chacoff et al., 2018; Zografou et al., 2020). These two types of species can be delimited by their connectedness to other species and their persistence in a community over time. Are there core and peripheral ideas, and if so, how do we, as educators, focus more attention on the core ideas as ways for directing the organization and coherence of learning? Following ecology, ideas can be categorized as core or peripheral depending on their frequency of occurrence and their connectivity to other ideas within a discipline or across multiple disciplines. Students are often unaware of whether ideas are core or peripheral; they often treat all ideas as similarly valuable and worthy of trying to memorize. Additionally, students often collect ideas but fail to make connections between different ideas in ways that create knowledge and understanding. One of our jobs as educators is to help students understand the network structure of knowledge—that there are core and peripheral ideas—and build a core of generalist and strongly connected ideas that provide a scaffold for adding peripheral and specialized but nonetheless important ideas. Ideally, each individual adds their own peripheral and specialized ideas to a similar core structure in ways that promote both coherency and diversity. The difference between generalist and strongly connected core ideas and more specialist peripheral ideas was evident in Roche Allred et al. (2022):

> The goal of any science educator is to prepare students with sufficient meaningful and robust knowledge to support their growth as science learners, consumers, and even scientists. While it would not be expected that students become disciplinary experts after one or two semesters of introductory courses, ideally, they should start gaining a foundation that supports their development of scientific knowledge. These early science courses are often designed to cover a wide range of topics with the intent of offering beginning students exposure to the given discipline as either preparation to further their study in said discipline or related disciplines. [However] . . . introductory science curricula structured to consider a discipline's breadth instead of depth does not lead to the development of a coherent framework on which students can build their knowledge. Furthermore, the overwhelming amount of information covered in these courses leaves little room to support students' formation of a usable coherent network of knowledge in which they can build connections between topics, much less across disciplinary concepts. As a result, students tend to leave their introductory courses with limited usable and transferable knowledge; thus, these courses are failing to prepare them for advanced courses or future careers or to be scientifically literate consumers. (p. 1)

There are explicit pedagogical frameworks—like the Next Generation Science Standards (NGSS) and associated assessments—that emphasize disciplinary core ideas, the application of these ideas, and crosscutting concepts that form intellectual bridges among disciplines (Cooper, 2020).

The framework is well-developed and promotes the creation of links and interaction between ideas. Importantly, students were able to identify core and peripheral ideas based on their frequency of occurrence and their explanatory power (Roche Allred et al., 2022). Explanatory power is an emergent outcome connecting, organizing, and contextualizing ideas. Although the NGSS framework was based on educational research, the emergent outcome that there are core and peripheral ideas mirrors the core and peripheral species evident in ecological communities. To understand ecology, it makes sense to pay most attention to core species; to learn about ecology—or any other subject—it makes sense to pay attention to the core ideas. More importantly, it is not sufficient to tell students about the core ideas; if I tell students the core ideas and ask them to list them, they can do so but do not understand why they are core ideas (Roche Allred et al., 2022). Instead, students need to identify and know core ideas as a consequence of the processes of connecting, organizing, and contextualizing ideas.

Roche Allred et al. (2022) described differences between teaching introductory chemistry and biology in ways that emphasized core ideas either through actions or words. They noted that "core ideas can connect students' knowledge, and make it accessible, if they are developed over time throughout the curriculum. On the other hand, if a particular core idea is treated as a topic, it will not serve this purpose, and it will be more difficult for students to make connections across ideas and phenomena." Thus, as educators, we need to imagine core ideas as core species and create opportunities for students to experience the connectedness of core ideas as the basis for knowledge and coherency of understanding. Core ideas are integral to all ideas in a discipline rather than simple topics that serve as chapter headings (Roche Allred et al., 2022). Our job is to repeatedly emphasize educational experiences in which the core ideas appear in different contexts in ways that form connections to other ideas and serve as a foundation of explanatory power. Once students have a robust well-connected set of core ideas, they are ready to grapple with the expanding universe of ideas and can add, at an appropriate time and context, more specialized and peripheral ideas that will become important parts of their evolving mental models of how the world works.

Chapter 6

Communities

Community Thinking

Education-relevant synopsis: Education happens in a community and, as a process, results in the emergence of community. Education and community exist in a synergistic, positively reinforcing cycle that powers the emergence of individual and collective intelligence.

Communities consist of populations of species inhabiting and interacting in a particular ecological context. The difference in scale between populations and communities is that populations consist of a single type of individual—a single species in ecology or discipline-specific student in education—whereas communities include multiple species and multiple disciplinary types, respectively. No matter where you are, the first thing you notice about a place in nature is that there are often many species, and for every species you observe there are probably hundreds or thousands more that you cannot see. There is a web of interdependency among individuals of different species that manifests in a variety of different ways. Perhaps, as Capra (1994) noted, "the most important way in which they depend on one another is a very existential way: they eat one another. That's the most existential interdependence you can imagine" (p. 2). A core aspect of the science of ecology is discerning the network of consumptive interactions: who eats who and how much eating happens. Thus, to understand communities, to engage in community thinking, is to think about interactions among a set of diverse individuals. And, as Capra emphasized, one of the reasons we study ecological communities is so we can build more resilient, more productive and sustainable communities of humans living with other species.

At the heart of communities is diversity. Cesar Chavez said (quoted in Obama, 2012), "We cannot seek achievement for ourselves and forget about progress and prosperity for our community. . . . Our ambitions must be broad enough to include the aspirations and needs of others, for their sakes and for our own." Community thinking includes, as Cesar Chavez emphasized, the "aspirations and needs" of all individuals that share a common dependence on resources and others for their livelihood, happiness, and well-being. Community is a state of mind and a place where events and interactions happen.

What Is a Community?

Education-relevant synopsis: Many of the approaches for describing ecological communities apply similarly for elucidating the properties and characteristics of educational communities, including the community of ideas in the minds of students; particularly relevant are multidimensional scaling and network analyses. These approaches yield rich data about the diversity, connectivity, and change in intelligence and social interactions.

An ecological community refers to an assemblage of populations of different species that live and interact with each other within a particular area over some period of time. The composition and organization of an ecological community depends on a range of factors, including the physical and abiotic characteristics of the habitat and the ability of individuals of different species to become established in a particular locality. While the focus of community ecology is often the species, the relevant unit remains the individual, because it is individuals that determine whether a particular species is present or absent in a community and it is individuals that interact in myriad ways. Community ecology attempts to describe and explain the diversity and abundance of individuals of different species as emergent outcomes of recruitment, survival, movement, productivity, interaction, and reproduction. The compelling questions of community ecology are why and how the aggregate properties of communities change over time.

There are a variety of different approaches for thinking about, analyzing, and visualizing communities. Many of the approaches can provide useful perspectives and actionable data in educational contexts. I will focus attention on two methods for describing the properties of ecological and educational communities: nonmetric dimensional scaling (NMDS) and networks. NMDS begins by describing a community based on the presence and absence of individuals of different species. The presence and absence of species can be binary in which presence equals 1 and absence equals 0, or the data can include information about the abundance of individuals. I will focus on binary data. It is often the case that ecologists seek to compare different communities for making inferences. The composition of multiple communities is best described by a matrix: each row is a community, each column is a different species and each cell of the matrix is a 1 or 0. These data can be transformed into a distance matrix summarizing the number of different species between all pairs of communities. From the summary of differences among communities, we can use a variety of techniques for visualizing and making sense of the differences among communities. NMDS collapses the differences among communities into two dimensions and the values can be visualized on an x-y coordinate graph. Each point is a community; points that are closer to each other have a greater similarity of species composition than pairs of points that are more distant in the 2D graphical space. Figure 6.1 illustrates the connection between presence-absence matrices and the visualization of the similarity of communities in x-y graphical space.

Figure 6.1. A cartoon showing the visualization of the presence and absence of species data for communities in different lakes mapped onto an x-y bivariate space from an NMDS analysis. Points closer to each other have more similar composition of species than points that are further away. The irregular shapes are meant to be lakes. *Source:* Created by the author.

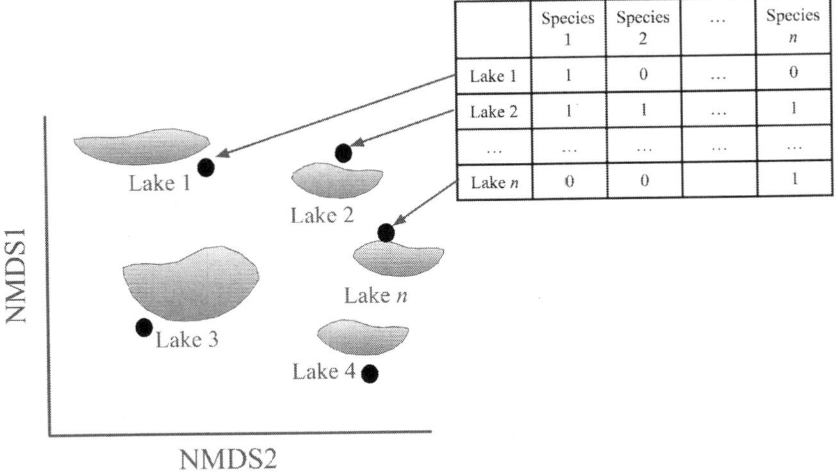

	Species 1	Species 2	...	Species n
Lake 1	1	0	...	0
Lake 2	1	1	...	1
...	...	...	...	...
Lake n	0	0		1

Each point is a different community defined by the presence or absence of different species. This approach has been used for evaluating a wide variety of hypotheses aimed at explaining why communities differ from each other, including the effects of environment (e.g., Paulson et al., 2021) and interactions (e.g., Sabo et al., 2017).

The same approach ecologists use to compare communities that exist, for example, in different lakes (fig. 6.1) can be used to compare the presence and absence of ideas—referred to as the community of ideas—in the minds of students (fig. 6.2). The analytical approach aligns with the knowledge-in-pieces framework for understanding intellectual maturation. Knowledge-in-pieces (KiP) predicts that learning is an emergent process of assembling pieces of information into coherent cognitive constructs containing multiple, interacting ideas (DiSessa, 1993). DiSessa (2017) stressed that KiP is not a coherent theory, but rather a description of a process. A core feature of KiP is that an individual's naive knowledge is rich, complex, and diverse. In addition, the collection of pieces of knowledge may have "many elements—hundreds or more" (DiSessa, 2017, p. 10). And each of the elements (which I am calling ideas) "have independent developmental histories" in much the same way individuals of different species in an ecological community have independent ecological histories. Each idea is like a species in an ecological community.

Figure 6.2. A cartoon showing the visualization of the presence and absence of ideas in the minds of different students mapped onto a x-y bivariate space from an NMDS analysis. Students closer to each other have more similar knowledge than students that are further apart. *Source:* Created by the author.

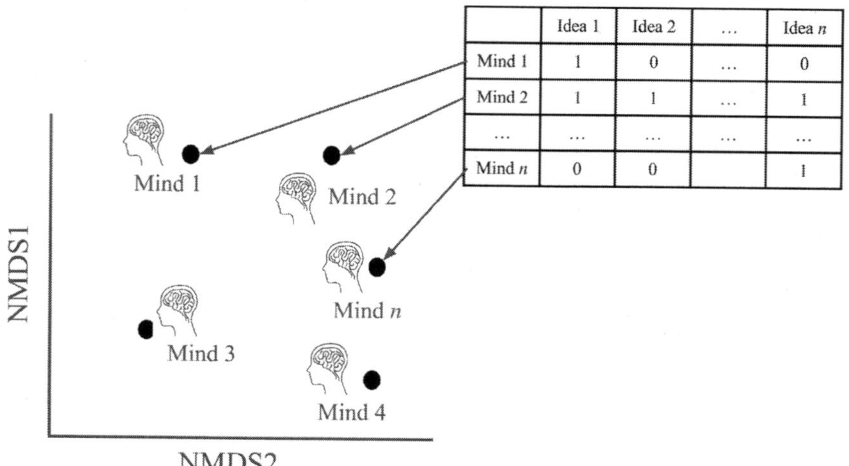

	Idea 1	Idea 2	...	Idea n
Mind 1	1	0	...	0
Mind 2	1	1	...	1
...	...	...	...	...
Mind n	0	0		1

The NMDS analysis aligns well with the metaphor of a lake with stepping stones (see chapter 1). Stanley and Lehman's (2015) analogy can be visualized as combinations of ideas—knowledge-in-pieces—in the minds of students. Student assessments can be scored for the presence or absence of ideas and the set of possible presences or absences of ideas can be interpreted as a set of "stepping stones in a lake." Individuals entering the lake as novices will find a myriad of ways of crossing the lake toward a mature understanding of ecology or some other topic. The number of possible stepping stones is determined by the number of ideas. Figure 6.3 shows an example of what the lake with stepping stones might resemble for 10 key ideas. Each stepping stone is a single combination of presences or absences of the 10 ideas in the mind of a student. At the left where the

Figure 6.3. A picture of the lake with stepping stones. The locations of the stones in the x and y space of the "lake" have been shifted by a small and random amount such that all points are visible. Each stepping stone is defined by the presence or absence of ideas in the mind of a student for 10 different ideas. In this example, there is 1 stone corresponding to a mind without any of the 10 ideas and similarly 1 stone for the mind with all 10 ideas; these stones are located at opposite sides of the lake. There are 10, 45, 120, 210, 252, 210, 120, 45, and 10 stones for 1, 2, 3, 4, 5, 6, 7, 8, and 9 ideas in the mind, respectively. Using Stanley and Lehman's analogy, individuals flow into the lake as novices and ideally flow out of the far side of the lake as a consequence of reaching an expert-like state of knowledge. *Source:* Created by the author.

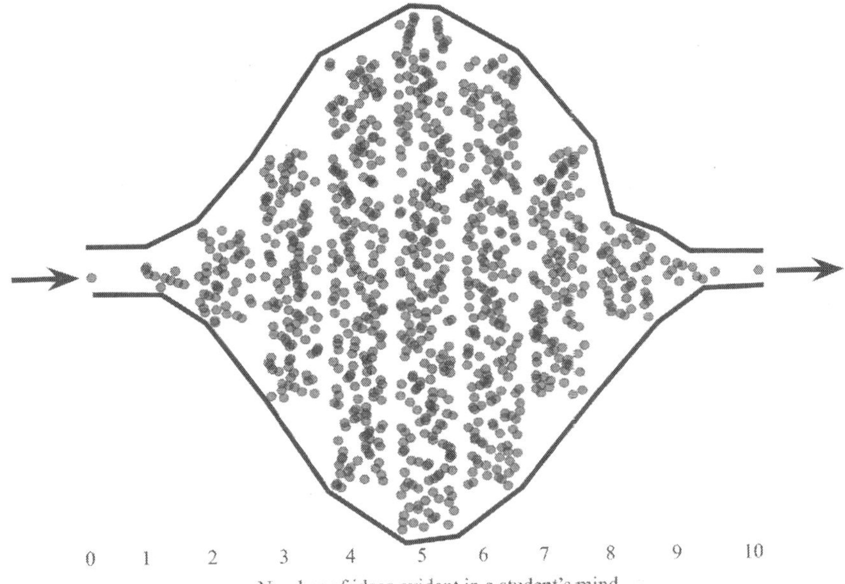

arrow enters the lake, there is no evidence of any of the ideas in the mind of a student: there are 0 ideas in the mind. At the other side of the lake, all 10 ideas are evident. The number of stepping stones is proportional to the number of different combinations of 0s and 1s. For this case of 10 ideas, there are 1,024 possible combinations of presences sand absences of ideas in the minds of students. In general, there are 2^n, possible combinations, where n is the number of ideas. The presence or absence of ideas assumes the idea is a fundamental unit of intelligence. Understanding the gain of understanding in the context of the KiP framework requires following the fate of ideas in the minds of students over time in the same way ecologists monitor the fates of individuals in ecological communities. The number of possible trajectories across the lake is, for all practical purposes, infinite, because students can backtrack and revisit stepping stones. It is worth noting that for a particular course, there may be hundreds or thousands of ideas. In our introductory biology course, for instance, there are at least 120 ideas because each of four summative assessments typically has 30 multiple-choice questions that cover the scope of the content; $2^{120} = 13,000,000,000,000,000$,000,000,000,000,000,000 possible cognitive states of understanding.

These pictures of communities based on the presence and absence of individuals of different species—for ecological communities—and the presence or absence of different types of ideas—for educational communities—are based on the presence-or-absence data without information about whether individuals or ideas interact. If we include the number of different ways ideas can be connected, the number of possible states of knowledge is much larger by multiple orders of magnitude.

A key aspect of ecological communities is the connectivity through interactions of its members. Interactions between individuals are often represented using networks. Capra (1994) noted that "the pattern of life is a network pattern. Wherever you see the phenomenon of life, you observe networks. . . . This was brought into science with ecology in the 1920s when people studied food webs. . . . The network pattern is not only characteristic of ecological communities as a whole, but of every member of that community. Every organism is a network of organs, of cells . . . and every cell is a network. . . . So what you have is networks within networks. Whenever you look at life you look at networks" (pp. 4–5). As Olesen et al. (2011) note, "Nature is organized into complex, dynamical networks of species and their interactions, which may influence diversity and stability" (p. 1). Networks form and become more complex over time as a consequence of cumulative interactions: first by the emergence of modules and then by the gradual fusion of modules into a larger-scale pattern (fig. 6.4). The

Figure 6.4. Different scales of networks: isolated individuals (no network), modules (middle two pictures), and a completely connected network that integrates interactions among diverse individuals over relatively long periods of time and across space. *Source:* Created by the author. Modified from Bascompte and Stouffer (2009, p. 1782).

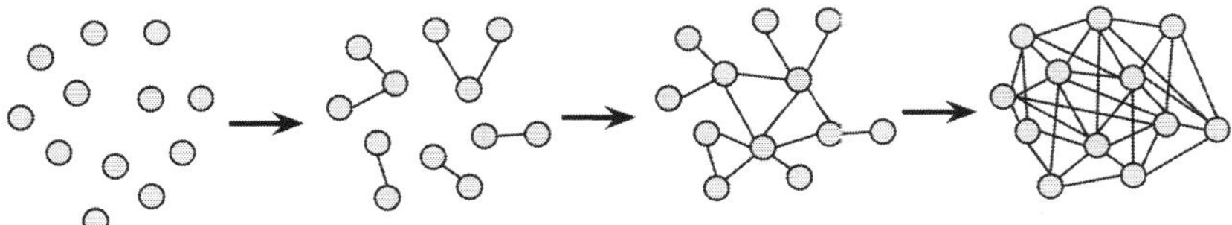

purpose of using a network summarizing interactions among individuals in a population is that it emphasizes the emergence of a higher order structure from the actions of individuals; interactions are at the core of ecology and education. Darwin wrote that "nothing exists for itself alone, but only in relation to other forms of life." He, of course, reiterates what the Buddha espoused before him: "Nothing ever exists entirely alone; everything is in relation to everything else." Interactions are at the core of "everything is in relation to everything else."

We can combine NMDS with networks to reveal the complexity of ecological and educational communities. NMDS places individuals in a context of similarities and differences among entities, and networks link the entities as a consequence of interaction. I use these tools as part of using scientific teaching for data-driven revision of curricula and teaching strategies. It is a journey that, at its core, emphasizes community. With these analytical techniques for revealing stories in data, it is worthwhile to explore how communities emerge and become established.

The Assembly of Communities

Education-relevant synopsis: Education can be described and analyzed in the same way ecologists have described the assembly and establishment of communities. The process of community assembly involves individuals and ideas in a propagule pool that settle in a location (for individuals) or in the minds of students, the loss or persistence of individuals or ideas following settlement, and ultimately the establishment of individuals or ideas. The outcomes of these processes contributing to the existence of a community of individuals in nature, of students in an institution of higher education, and of ideas in the minds of students are influenced by multiple environmental variables and various properties of the individuals, students, and ideas.

In the last chapter, I introduced a simple model in which recruitment and persistence determine the existence of a population and the changes in numbers of individuals that happen over time. Communities are like populations in the sense that they are born by recruitment of individuals, the community can grow in numbers of individuals and the diversity of individuals increases over time. The difference from populations is that a community consist of many different types (species) of individuals. Rather than the simple idea of recruitment, ecologists think about community assembly. Assembly is a continuous emergent outcome of recruitment and establishment of many different types of individuals in a particular habitat over time.

Imagine there is a new area inhabitable by organisms. Perhaps the new area resulted from a lava flow or was recently sterilized by a wildfire. Assembly is the process by which the new habitat becomes a place of community. It is useful to order the process of recruitment into several stages that constitute assembly. Figure 6.5 provides an illustration of the process for communities of species, students, or ideas; the same illustrative model applies to all three things. The first stage is settlement: an individual from a large regional pool of different types of individuals or ideas settles in the new habitat. Once an individual settles, it is subject to the vagaries of the environment. If the environment is too extreme, if an individual's fundamental niche does not encompass the range of variation in physical conditions (e.g., temperature, precipitation, food sources, shelter), then the newly settled individual does not persist and recruitment does not happen. Even if the environmental conditions allow for persistence, there may be biotic interactions—predation or some form of competition—that precludes persistence. If the settler survives the many abiotic and biotic factors that influence persistence, the individual becomes established, and it lives its life in the new habitat subject to the many challenges nature poses. This set of processes happens for many different types of individuals; eventually there is the emergence of a recognizable community of varying numbers of individuals for some set of species.

Importantly, all of the pre- and post-settlement processes are happening continuously and simultaneously as part of an emergent process even though they are organized in the illustration in a way suggestive of a direct process. Additionally, theory and empirical studies have revealed

Figure 6.5. An illustration of the process of community assembling from a regional pool of individuals of different species in an ecological context and for ideas and students in an educational context. The process begins with a large pool of propagules: individuals without a home that can settle into a particular locality. The environment and biotic interactions impose a filter that excludes some individuals. Some individuals that successfully settle may not survive long because of extreme environmental conditions, predation, or other factors that cause mortality. Individuals that do survive undergo some degree of adaption and reproduce; reproduction is an indication of the establishment of a species in a particular locality. *Source:* Created by the author.

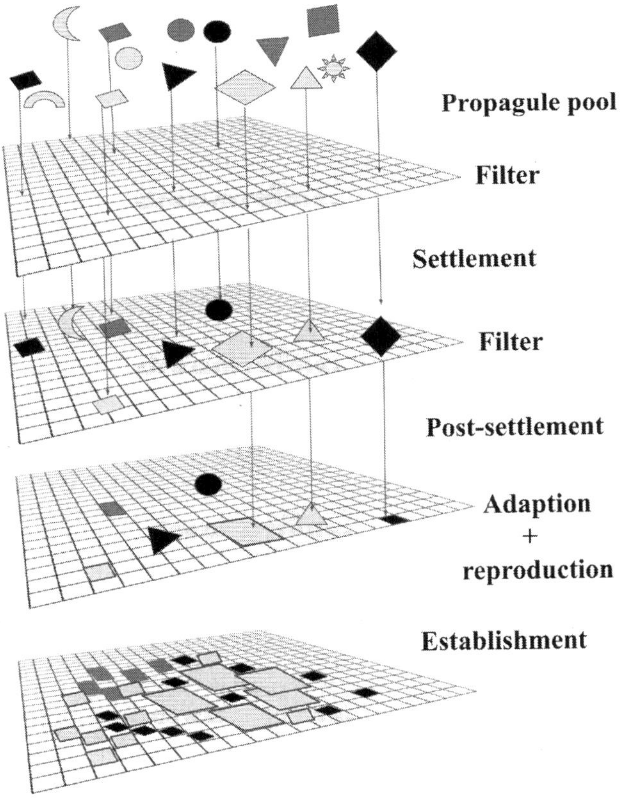

each stage is governed by stochastic and deterministic processes; as a consequence, if the process of community assembly happened multiple times from the same set of individuals and environmental conditions, the outcomes would be different (Chase, 2007). This is one of the hallmarks of an emergent process. I discuss each of the stages for all three contexts:

ecological communities, student communities, and the community of ideas in the minds of students. In doing so, I highlight the aspects of ecological community assembly that have relevance for education. As I go through settlement and post-settlement persistence, keep in mind that the same processes are happening for individuals in ecological settings, for students in educational settings, and for ideas in the minds of students.

The regional pool of individuals capable of settlement into a new ecological habitat are described as propagules. For plants, the propagules are most often seeds and the regional pool includes seeds from many different species. For a seed to settle in a new habitat, it must move from its birthplace where the mother plant lives; this generally happens passively by dispersal aided by wind or water, or settlement can happen actively as a consequence of being carried by an animal. Whether or not a seed of a particular species is present depends on the distance between the new habitat and the mother plant's location and its fecundity. Nearby and highly fecund trees are better represented in a new environment than distant and rare species with low fecundity. Settlement also depends on seed size, whether seeds have any features that increase average dispersal distance, and the particular type of animal that may move seeds across landscapes. These differences among species are playing out continuously in ways that most ecologists describe as a stochastic process of settlement influenced by various biological features that determine the average and variation in dispersal distances (Carlquist, 1967; Nathan, 2006; Vittoz & Engler, 2007). Similar stochastic and deterministic processes play out for other taxonomic groups, including microbes of various types (Ptacnik et al., 2010; Richter-Heitmann et al., 2020), fungi (Peay & Bruns, 2014) and animals (Paine & Levin, 1981). I can confidently insert students and ideas in place of seeds and the process of settlement is the same.

The regional pool of propagules often consists of many different species. Various studies have estimated propagule diversity. In marine reef fishes the propagules are fish larvae that live as plankton until they discover, with the aid of currents, a suitable place to settle. Kimmerling et al. (2018) documented 278 different species in the propagule pool associated with a habitat in the Red Sea. The abundance of different species of larvae is often positively correlated with the abundance of the different species of adult fish on the reefs. Kimmerling et al. also showed that for some species, there are no adults present in the community even though there are larvae in the propagule pool. These data suggest that certain species are incapable of settlement or establishment in a particular habitat, or that, just by chance, in a given year, some individuals do not successfully settle and become part of the community. Settlement also depends on specific combinations of environmental signals dependent on habitat type and the ability of individuals in the propagule pool to adequately decode available information and settle in a suitable location. For instance, in many marine fishes, a variety of chemical and physical variables influence settlement; Rittschof et al. (1998) noted that "chemical cues include inorganic and organic compounds, including stimulatory peptides and odors. Physical cues include surface energy, vibration and light" (p. 31). There are a couple of aspects of settlement in ecological contexts that are relevant for education. First, the abundance of a particular type of propagule positively predicts its settlement and eventual establishment; replace propagule with the words *student* or *idea*. And second, there are some types of individuals individuals and ideas, no matter how abundant they are in the propagule pool, that do not settle and have no chance of being part of a community because the appropriate conditions for settlement do not exist. This is also relevant for students in a particular discipline and for ideas in the minds of students.

There are different scales in the context of higher education in which propagule pools of students exist. There is a national scale. It includes all of the students planning on attending college. In the US there were more than 1,300,000 applicants that collectively submitted in excess of seven million applications in 2023 (Kim et al., 2024) There is an enormous propagule pool of individuals seeking to settle in more than eight thousand habitats of higher education. At CU–Boulder, in 2023, there were a record 57,539 applications for admission. Remarkably, the number of applicants has increased by slightly more than 14% every year since 2013. In 2023, about 80% of the applicants were admitted and 16% enrolled. Enrollment is analogous with settlement. Interestingly, the percentage of students enrolled (i.e., settlement) has declined from 30% in 2013 to 16% in 2023. Even so, the number of individuals who "settle" into the CU–Boulder habitat has increased steadily by about 2.5% per year, with a slight downturn during the Covid pandemic. The increase in settlement (also called recruitment) of students into CU–Boulder largely explains the consistent increase in the numbers of students enrolled over time.

The enrolled students can choose to settle in more than 50 different academic habitats. Table 6.1 provides some data for four habitats—ENGL, PSYC, EBIO, and MDCB—in the College of Arts and Sciences (University of Colorado Boulder IR., 2024). While the numbers of individuals differ among the four communities, the percentage of the applicants admitted and enrolled are similar. It is worth remembering that EBIO and MCDB are disciplinarily similar and graduate about the same number of students each year, yet the number of applicants, the number of students admitted, and the number of students that settle are very different. A key aspect of these data is that students are making choices about their propensity to settle in different habitats prior to their arrival. They have preferences and aspirations that influence settlement. Similar things are evident in ecological settings, especially in marine systems in which an enormous number of propagules do not settle in part because specific biochemical cues that guide individuals toward a suitable habitat are missing. An important story in the enrollment data is that only about 1 in 8 of the viable propagules—the students who were admitted—settle out from the plankton of students seeking higher education.

Every semester, students become propagules again when registration opens and students select courses toward achieving intellectual maturation and academic achievement. Each course can be considered a new habitat subject to the processes of settlement, post-settlement persistence, and establishment that describes community assembly. And, every semester, there are thousands of open habitats where students settle from an enormous propagule pool. Students can be categorized by their disciplinary emphasis, and they tend to settle in courses in their discipline: specialization begins with settlement. Diversity can be estimated by the number of students with different disciplinary affiliations. In my first-year (1000-level) quantitative thinking and statistics course, the propagule pool size is large and diverse. And while the students that settle out into this course are

Table 6.1. Applications, admissions, and enrollments in the Fall 2023 for four disciplinary habitats in the College of Arts and Sciences

Habitat (discipline)	Number of applicants	Number admitted (%)	Number enrolled (%)
ENGL	597	513 (86)	65 (13)
PSYC	4,174	3,356 (80)	580 (17)
EBIO	836	720 (86)	90 (13)
MCDB	1,854	1,670 (90)	219 (13)

Source: University of Colorado Boulder IR. (2024).

mostly EBIO students, the last time I taught the course, there were individuals representing 22 different disciplines. In one of our large-enrollment introductory biology courses, there were individuals representing 60 different disciplines. It is also notable that many discipline-defined identities are represented by single individuals, something that is also evident for ecological communities (Magurran & Henderson, 2003).

There are also limitations on settlement due to the particular characteristics of individuals other than disciplinary identity. Gender bias is an example of a factor that restricts settlement in ways that differ among disciplinary habitats. In physics, 80% of students are male, whereas the reverse is true for psychology: 75% female, 25% male. In general, the two genders "pursue science and mathematics courses in primary and secondary school in roughly equal proportion, but by the time they are freshmen in college, men are more likely to choose a science or mathematics major" (Matz et al., 2017, p. 2). Thus, gender is a deterministic factor influencing the assembly of communities by restricting settlement of individuals into different disciplinary habitats due to students' experiences prior to becoming eligible for college. Another factor is socioeconomic status (SES). On average, higher SES is associated with greater representation in science, technology, engineering, and math (STEM) disciplines. Niu (2017, p. 298) claimed "low-SES students may not possess the information and/or skills necessary to make well-informed decisions of STEM enrollment so as to maximize their opportunity to succeed in college." And gender and socioeconomics interact in ways that predict students' settlement into particular disciplines. "Having a father in a professional or executive occupation has a larger effect on female students than does having a mother in a similar occupation. The opposite holds for males. Women from families with high socioeconomic status are less likely to major in business; the opposite holds for males" (Leppel et al., 2001, p. 373). In general, as in ecological settings, there are a variety of factors that conspire to limit the diversity of individuals that settle into various academic disciplines.

Similar processes and patterns are happening at the scale of ideas. The regional pool of ideas is based on the contributions and consensus of what is important for students to know in a particular discipline. These ideas can be obtained from textbooks or efforts to compile key ideas from a community of scholars and educators in the discipline. One example comes from a large-scale assembly of key ideas for a first-year college biology course (Hennessey and Freeman 2023). The regional pool of ideas is vast;

it consists of 352 endorsed learning objectives. Endorsed means that the learning objectives were accepted by consensus from a large number of experts. Importantly, each learning objective includes multiple ideas. For example, the learning objective "Compare which bonds are responsible for producing a protein's (1) primary structure, (2) secondary structure (alpha-helices and beta-pleated sheets), and (3) tertiary structure" can be associated with multiple, embedded ideas, including, but not limited to (1) there are bonds between elements (e.g., carbon, nitrogen, hydrogen) that have different physicochemical properties, (2) there are different types of protein structures, (3) different protein structures are dependent on how biochemical elements and units of a protein interact with each other, (4) proteins are composed of amino acids and each amino acid has unique physicochemical properties, and (5) different amino acids interact in ways that cause the different types of structure. Furthermore, this latter embedded idea, namely that *proteins are composed of amino acids and each amino acid has different physicochemical properties* can be associated with the idea that different amino acids can be grouped into different physicochemical types depending on their chemical structure, that each element that forms part of an amino acid has its own physico-chemical properties dependent on atomic structure (numbers of element particles, including protons, neutrons and electrons) and that proteins are produced by a process called translation that adds amino acids together into a polypeptide chain. And so on. Thus, if we conservatively assume there are between 5 and 10 different ideas embedded in each of the 352 endorsed specific learning objectives, then the propagule pool of ideas is in the thousands for a single, first-year biology course. Remember, there are 2^n possible cognitive states, where n is the number of different ideas. If n is in the thousands, there are more possible cognitive states than atoms in the known universe. Thus, there are a large number of potential ideas that can settle in the minds of students during the phase of a student's life when the students themselves are settling and trying to become established in an academic community.

Of course, the list of endorsed key ideas for first-year biology education is distilled by the instructors that teach the course. Faculty vary in their choices of which of the many possible ideas they consider important and focus on in specific disciplinary courses. Thus, only a fraction of the ideas become part of the active pool of ideas that can settle in the minds of students. Over the years, I have been focusing on fewer and fewer ideas and making sure the ideas I do introduce connect to each other; thus my actions restrict the size of the pool of ideas that can settle into the minds of students. This is because of I have discovered that there is an inverse correlation between the number of ideas that settle and the number of ideas that become established.

Post-settlement refers to the events that happen after individuals or ideas settle in a habitat (natural or academic) or in the mind, respectively. It is mostly about persistence. Settlement coupled with persistence is defined as establishment in the sense of securing a place in the context of being counted as part of a community. For each of the three units of analysis—individuals in nature, students in academic settings, and ideas in the mind—there are two categories of processes that influence post-settlement persistence: environmental processes and interaction effects. Additionally, post-settlement persistence is often accompanied by some degree of conformity (adaption) to local conditions that increases persistence.

A variety of factors influence what happens after individuals settle into ecological habitats, including variation in environmental conditions (Nozawa & Harrison, 2007) and density-dependent biotic factors, mainly competition for food and space (Connell, 1985; Caselle, 1999; Osman et al., 1989). The processes are evident across divergent taxa and contexts. Of relevance for constructing analogies with education includes the discovery that post-settlement persistence depends on having adequate space and access to sufficient resources for supporting growth and maturation, particularly the reality that persistence is lower when densities are higher. Higher density of settlers makes it bad for everyone (Shaw & Antonovics, 1986). Enviromental and agonistic effects scale with density. Additionally, it is often the case that persistence and establishment varies among individuals depending on inherited differences: there are many examples from nature of density-dependent differences in survival associated with particular genotypes and heritable phenotypes.

Another important aspect of community assembly in ecological systems is priority effects. Priority effects refer to a scenario in which individuals of different species that arrive early in the assembly of a community can influence the number and types of individuals that become established later; in other words, the presences of particular individuals in a community can act as barriers or facilitators for the establishment of other species depending on interaction effects. Fukami (2015) noted that "the order and timing of species immigration during community assembly can affect species abundances at multiple spatial scales. Known as priority effects, these effects cause historical contingency in the structure and function of communities" (p. 1). Additionally, Garcia-Girón (2022) found "that historical contingency via priority effects can profoundly shape community assembly under the influence of environmental change. . . . [There are] both positive and negative species-to-species associations . . . suggesting that functional divergence can switch the inhibition–facilitation balance at the metacommunity level" (p. S38). An excellent example of priority effects comes from the work of James Drake. Drake (1991) designed and executed an experiment with three species of algae. He constructed six communities that differed depending on the order in which the species were introduced; there are six ways to introduce three species in order. Everything else across all experiments remained the same. There were some clear patterns in the data. One species increased in abundance at about the same rate in all experiments, indicating that it was insensitive to the presence of the other two species. The second pattern was that the abundance of the other two species depended on when they were established; in general, they did better when they were established earlier than the other two. Finally, one of the species only did well—density increased—when it was the first species of the three that became established. These results clearly demonstrated there are interactions between species during the assembly of communities and the effect of interspecies interaction varies depending on the species and the order in which species settle and become established. These results were striking even though the community was very simple. Imagine the complexity of real-world systems in which there are many different species and myriad interactions between individuals of the many species. Drake's experiment revealed variable community outcomes despite constant conditions across all experiments. The dynamics were due to the interactions among individuals of the different species, and these interactions depended on the abundance of different species. The existence of interaction effects, coupled with the fact that there are many possible interaction effects in communities, underscores that communities are emergent phenomena. I introduced this simple experiment because it is clear that one of the main drivers of emergent community-level structure stems from the interaction among different types of individuals, where types can refer to species in an ecological context or students and ideas in educational contexts. Moreover, the message that who is present in the community matters transcends ecology. Interactions between individuals—between students or between instructors and students—can either make or break persistence.

The different species portrayed by the shapes in figure 6.5 are themselves dynamic entities that change by adaptation. Additionally, individuals are often capable of changing during development, a phenomenon called phenotypic plasticity, in ways that increase the match between individual strategies for thriving and the characteristics of the environment in which an individual lives. This is evident in the illustration (fig. 6.5) as a change in shape that better "fits" the characteristics of the landscape (note the shape changes in ways that conform to the shape of the spatial grid).

Post-settlement persistence results in the establishment of a community. Once a community is established, a species may be part of the community for multiple generations through reproduction, or it can be extirpated in various ways. All the while individuals of new species settle and navigate or fail to navigate the various post-settlement processes that determine persistence. Once a community is established, the process of succession begins (see next section), and the community continues to change in ways that are both deterministic and stochastic.

It is likely that similar post-settlement phenomena in ecology are playing out in educational contexts following the settlement of students in particular disciplinary habitats (i.e., the various majors) and local academic communities associated with the enrollments in particular courses. In the previous chapter, I described that persistence varies by discipline. After we remove individuals who failed to persist anywhere within the habitat of higher education (they dropped out of college for various reasons), there are apparent differences among disciplinary habitats in post-settlement persistence: for the four disciplines interrogated earlier, there is roughly a twofold difference. The lower persistence of students who settled in ENGL and PSYC relative to EBIO and MCDB probably have different causes. Nonetheless, I can't help wondering if the enormous numbers of individuals that settle in PSYC have a strong negative density-dependent effect in the same way that crowding impacts post-settlement mortality in nature.

The role of filtering in higher education was reviewed by Matusov (1999). Matusov's interests were aligned with the process of community assembly. Matusov asked the question: How does a community of learners maintain its coherency through the process of community assembly? He described two different models: one was exclusionary and filtered individuals in the same way a sieve works, and the second was through a process of conformity. At the core of his questions and answers was the idea that disciplinary communities in higher education differentiate from each other as an emergent consequence of actions that happen within disciplines that either exclude diversity or change individuals toward a common way of being, belonging, and thinking. In some cases, he imagined individuals are gradually moved to the periphery of the community as if a "centrifugal process" is at work; this process eventually results in the loss of individuals and diversity.

Is there evidence of the exclusion and conversion models influencing the assembly of individual students into what is discernible as an educational community? In the exclusion model, individuals whose abilities or identities are not supported in particular disciplines or classes do not become part of the community: they fail to persist or become fully established because of their inherent properties. The lack of belonging will likely be evident from the lack of persistence of individuals at the university, the emigration of individuals from one disciplinary population to another, and statistics that reflect participation and engagement (e.g., grades, attendance, and withdrawals from a particular class). Perhaps the best evidence for the effect of an exclusion model comes from the work of Haak, Freeman, and colleagues at the University of Washington. They documented that an increase in course structure—involving pre-class preparation, use of formative assessment during class that involved active learning, and weekly low-risk assessments—resulted in a large decline in the achievement gap between individuals who historically would have established themselves in the course and disadvantaged individuals who were at risk of failure (Haak et al., 2011). Thus, it is possible to alter the environmental conditions and distribution of resources in ways that enable persistence rather than centrifugally eliminate students with diverse backgrounds.

Interactions among students in ways that resemble priority effects (Drake, 1991) or, more generally, competitive exclusion may also end in exclusion and lack of persistence (Zaret & Rand, 1971). One way this can happen is when students are asked to work in small groups and the composition of groups can lead to negative effects. Moreira et al. (2021) described three functional types of students using latent variables: emotional-unreliable (emotionally reactive, low self-control, and low creativity), organized-reliable (self-control but not creative), and creative-reliable (highly creative and prosocial). Assuming the three functional types described by Moreira et al. exist, different combinations of these three types can result in different group outcomes (Chang & Brickman, 2018). When thinking about education with an ecologically community-centered mindset, these three discernible functional types of individuals can be thought of as being distinct "species" level characteristics that increase community diversity and complexity. Moreover, each may perform differently depending on the composition of a group. Another functional dimension is whether students share interests. Gardiner and Smith (2018) found that individuals in groups with others that shared similar interests reported they engaged in more collaborative learning, experienced greater support, and were awarded better grades than students working in groups without individuals that shared interests. Students with shared interests may also factor into the finding that students' sense of safety and satisfaction vary within a group; both of these factors contribute to a sense of belonging (Hammar Chiriac, 2014). What is clear from studies of students working in small groups within the larger academic community of a classroom full of students is that, as described by Theobald et al. (2017, p. 1), "group dynamics vary, ranging from equitable collaboration to dysfunctional groups dominated by one individual." The variation is, in large part, due to different functional types of students and how they interact, and it may be the outcome of interaction depends on which functional type of individual establishes itself first. What is clear based on the work of Drake and others in the ecological literature and Theobald and others in the education literature is that some individuals will do well regardless of whether they are the first or last to establish themselves as part of the community. And some individuals will only do well if they work well with the other functional types in the group. Interaction effects, whether in ecology or education, play a huge role in the structure and function of communities. How well students interact influences whether they feel like they belong, and belonging is integral for becoming part of a community.

In my department, we are missing opportunities for developing a sense of belonging and self-efficacy, because our first-year, high enrollment, entry level courses focus exclusively on information transmission within a didactic, professor-centric modality in a large auditorium habitat.[1] Opportunities for making connections among students and between the instructor and students are not prioritized in favor of moving through content considered essential for understanding biology. When we stop and take a look at some of the data, there are two compelling stories about student success. The first is that there is significant attrition of students across the two first-year general biology courses. Even though a curricular structure exists that has students enrolling and completing the two courses in sequence—one after the other—the data suggest many students who successfully finish the first semester (between 70% and 80%

depending on aspects of student identity) do not complete the second course in the sequence in the same academic year. Many students depart from the sequence after one semester of biology and return to finish the second course later as sophomores, juniors, or seniors; some leave the discipline for another discipline and others leave the university. The lack of coherence between the two courses suggests our approach does not encourage students to stay in biology. When we asked students whether they would likely take more biology courses as a consequence of their experience in the first semester of general biology (n = 585), 3 out of 4 indicated they would not or were unlikely to enroll in additional biology courses. Estrada et al. (2017) wrote that "students who report utility value in courses are more likely to develop interest in advanced courses in those topics, including STEM courses." Utility value is the idea that students perceive educational courses as useful for their success. These data, interpreted in the light of utility value and expectancy value theory (Wigfield & Eccles, 2002; Cooper et al., 2017), suggest that students in the large enrollment courses did not "connect" to biology and failed to find utility value (or general value) in the discipline, and that both of these factors likely contributed to a lack of sense of belonging and a correspondingly lower probability of persistence.

A second story in the data is that there are detectable effects of race, first generation status, and an interaction between sex and race on student grades in the course. These data reflect, to some degree, the findings from a CU–Boulder campus climate survey that showed African-American and indigenous peoples failed to find a sense of community. Estrada et al. (2019) wrote, "Overall, research shows that European Americans most consistently are found to be more individualistic, with greater value placed on individual and independent accomplishment. In contrast, many HU [historically-underrepresented] students value community and cooperation more than individualism and competition, which can conflict with academic institutional values" (p. 3). My interpretation is that we failed to create community and a sense of belonging for all groups in our large-enrollment courses. Our go-to behavioral default is to favor individualistic and competitive pedagogies that run orthogonal to the proclivities and inherent personalities of some groups of students. Moreover, this default approach ignores theory and empirical work showing collaborative environments result in greater academic achievement than individualistic and competitive environments.

The data emerging from our two sequential general biology courses, and work from a number of scholars, suggests many students become alienated from biology, and from STEM in general, largely due to the structure, function, and curricular emphasis of low-level, prescriptive, first-year gateway courses (Seymour & Hewitt, 1997; Keup, 2006; Kuh et al., 2008; Estrada et al., 2016; Petersen et al., 2020). We impose filters that limit persistence rather than cultivating a sense of belonging and training students to become more self-efficacious. We fail to use the gathering of people together for a common purpose as an opportunity for developing social networks grounded in academics. We can turn to expectancy value theory, or other theories tied to motivation, as a guide for increasing post-settlement persistence and establishment of students within a disciplinary community. Or, more to the purpose of this book, we can try to create interactions that build a productive network that sustains communities.

To counter disinterest and noninclusivity, expectancy value theory indicates we need to recognize students as individuals with interests, ways of thinking, and perceptions of value stemming from personal and cultural histories (Estrada et al., 2016; Dewsbury & Brame, 2019; Le, 2019; Dewsbury, 2020). Expectancy value theory provides a psychological framework for constructing the pedagogical structures determining how teaching and learning happens (Wigfield & Eccles, 2002; Cooper et al., 2017). There are six factors that influence student success (fig. 6.6); as educators, we

Figure 6.6. Model framework stemming from value expectancy theory, useful for guiding curriculum development and teaching strategies. Solid lines indicate potential effects. In this model, all possible effects are shown; however, not all effects may be evident in the complex reality of a classroom or training program. There is also a line from outcomes to the student-based factors indicating feedback. *Source:* Created by the author. Modified from Cooper et al. (2017).

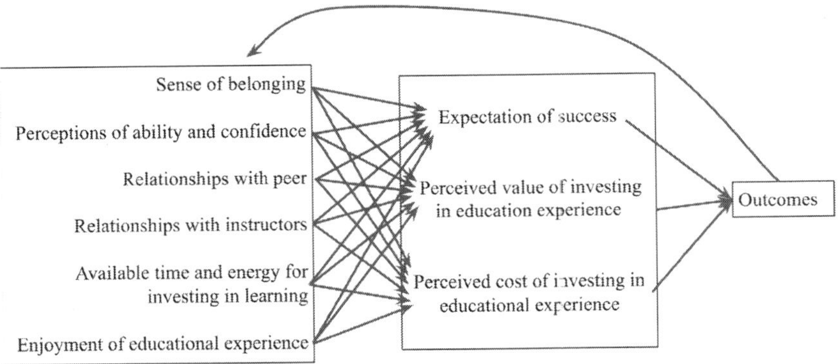

can directly influence four of the factors and maybe indirectly influence the other two. We can't directly influence the available time and energy students invest in learning and students' enjoyment of the educational experience; these are under the full control of students. We can influence students' sense of belonging by focusing on student-relevant content and giving students a voice in a safe environment. We can influence students' perceptions of ability and confidence with an emphasis on affirmation and a growth mindset. We can influence students' relationships with peers by creating opportunities for productive, engaging, and collaboration interactions in a safe environment that also encourages students to share stories of their lives. And we can influence students' relationships with us (the instructors) by engaging in conversations with students in small groups, using the students' names when we do so, and cultivating a community centered in academics and critical and creative thinking. Finally, if we implement the strategies for making gains in these four relevant student factors, we may indirectly influence how students invest their limited time and their enjoyment of participating in higher education. In short, educators play outsized roles in the assembly of productive and functional communities on positive trajectories toward personal enlightenment, empowerment, and aspiration.

Matusov also emphasized a post-settlement model of conformity that invokes some degree of adaption of individuals to the local conditions of a campus, discipline, or course. In this case, individuals need opportunities and strategies to learn how to belong and how to become a valued member of a community. Students should be encouraged to self-assemble into groups and learn strategies for effective collaboration, ideally in ways that intersect with student factors identified as important for positive expectancy value outcomes. The point is that the professor can enable adaption by providing opportunities for learning how to learn, developing a sense of belonging and greater self-efficacy, in addition to teaching core concepts, big ideas, and process skills characteristic of a discipline. We need to add one more dimension to the 3D education framework developed by the Next Generation Science Standards. The fourth dimension is all about affect with a sense of belonging and self-efficacy as core components. Ultimately, one of the overarching goals of education is developing students' sense of belonging and ability in one or more academic disciplines through a supported process of intellectual maturation and academic achievement for all students, not just those who pass through the post-settlement filter unscathed.

Once ideas are introduced and settle into the minds of students, what happens to them? Do they stay or do they go?[2] Bateson's "ecology of minds" is about how ideas assemble, become modified (or revised), and either persist or perish in the minds of students. We can use the same conceptual models developed for ecological communities and applied to students in educational contexts to make inferences about learning based on the state and fate of ideas in the minds of students. The same general concepts and issues are at play. Students come into a course with a large number of ideas that have previously become established in their minds. The course introduces a new set of ideas. Ideas settle into minds and the community of ideas in the mind of a student changes over time from the loss of ideas and the establishment of new ideas. Based on the topic, a set of ideas assembles into some sort of coherent structure—a mental model—that provides some degree of understanding and prediction utility. During teaching, there is an elaboration of the context and topic, and, in the process, ideas are filtered or funneled, resulting in the emergence of a core set of ideas that remain and become established as relevant. This process of winnowing is one model of learning: making choices about the validity of existing ideas for explaining new phenomena. This view of the assembly and establishment of ideas suggests ideas are static entities and that the presence or absence of particular ideas in the minds of students is mostly the consequence of a process of elimination. Ideas are more dynamic than static entities. Just like the properties of species established in a particular place and community can change by local adaptation and plasticity (Mittelbach & Schemske, 2015), ideas can change in the minds of students as a consequence of assimilating new information (new ideas) and revising existing ideas (Chi & Roscoe, 2002). The mind is constantly sifting, selecting, and structuring new input and making meaning of increasing complexity from the ideas and concepts it encounters. Moreover, the precise way our mind organizes the input it receives is unique for each of us. We process and integrate new input in an inherently personal and idiosyncratic way based on what we've experienced, what we know, what we value, how we learn, and what we are intending to accomplish at a given moment. Much (or all) of this takes place without us being aware of it.

Thus, the theory and empirical work in community ecology has established a rich model that describes how a functional and diverse community of individuals is an emergent property of several processes operating simultaneously and continuously. This model is remarkably similar to the process of education. Education involves the establishment of ideas in the mind from a shifting pool of ideas sampled as a consequence of through interactions with people that are part of an individual's immediate and extended social network, including individuals that may be remote and encountered through media (e.g., books, videos, lectures, and other modes of communicating information). The pool of ideas is continuously changing. When making sense of phenomenon, new ideas are assimilated; existing ideas persist, are purged, or are revised; and mental models that are tested and prove to be functional and predictive are retained and reinforced in ways that make them resilient. Recognizing that knowledge results from the assembly of ideas into coherent and functional cognitive constructs means that we can use theory and empirical results from community ecology to make grappling with the emergent process of education less uncertain, and to use strategies from case studies of ecological engineering as guides for how we might try to establish connected, coherent, and robust communities of ideas in the minds of students recognizable as knowledge.

The apparent close correspondence between ecological communities and the community of ideas in the minds of students suggests that a strategy of word replacement might be useful for making analogies between ecology and education explicit and poignant. Here is an excerpt from Kraft et al. (2015) about the role of environmental filtering:

> At its core, the environmental filtering concept focuses on the relationship between an organism and the environment, recognizing that not all organisms will be able to successfully establish and persist in all abiotic conditions. From this perspective, the environment is seen as a selective force, culling species unable to tolerate conditions at a particular location. If species that are able to survive at a location share common phenotypic traits conferring abiotic tolerance, certain phenotypic similarities reflecting this tolerance may be seen among community members. (p. 593)

Here is a stab at analogical word replacement for the purpose of transferring ecological inferences into the realm of education. In this case, the basic message is that environmental filtering will restrict the types of ideas that exist and persist in the minds of students, and there will be more similarities among the ideas that persist than with ideas that fail to establish in students' minds:

> At its core, the environmental filtering concept focuses on the relationship between an [idea] and [the context in which

it exists], recognizing that not all [ideas] will be able to successfully establish and persist in [the minds of] all [students].
From this perspective, the [student's mind] is seen as a selective
force, culling [ideas that are not perceived to be relevant]. If
[ideas] that are able to survive [in the mind of a student] share
common [features], conferring [an intellectual advantage in a
particular educational environment], certain similarities [will
be evident] among community [ideas].

Thus, we might hypothesize that the ideas that stick in the minds of students share particular properties, and it may be necessary to identify the
properties of the ideas that stick, and the ideas that fail to establish, as a
first step toward curricular and teaching strategy revision.

Succession and Change over Time

*Education-relevant synopsis: Education is a process of change, and like
change in ecological communities, it happens continuously, in predictable
ways, and results in predictable outcomes. In general, educational change
involves changes in the abundance of different ideas and types of students
over time, declines in the rate of production of coherent knowledge structures within the minds of students, increases in diversity (that is sometimes
followed by decreases in diversity) of thinking and knowledge, increases in
complexity of individuals in parallel with increases in the complexity of
their intelligence, a diminishing increase in productivity, and an increase
in the size and complexity of social networks. These are all outcomes from
an emergent educational process that happens in much the same way as
succession does in ecological contexts.*

Heraclitus's mantra that "change is the only constant in life" is an apt
description of the emergent processes of ecology and education. In ecological
contexts, succession is continuous change in a community over time. In this
section, the focus is on some general properties of succession that involve
the continuous settlement, establishment, and loss of species in a community.
Once a community becomes established, it changes continuously over time,
because there is turnover within the assemblage: new species become established, established species lose their "place," and there are shifts in relative
abundance and connectivity of species. Townsend (1989) wrote that the

> goals of community ecology are to recognize patterns that exist
> in composition, diversity, trophic organization, and stability of
> species assemblages in nature, and to understand the processes
> that determines these patterns. . . . Communities are, on the
> one hand, mere assemblages thrown together at random from
> a species pool or, on the other, tightly linked groups of inter-
> acting species. Moreover, we need to know whether community
> structure is controlled by deterministic interactions between
> species . . . , or by stochastic factors. (p. 36)

This idea that communities are "assemblages thrown together at random from a larger pool" and can become "tightly linked groups" describes, to varying degrees, what happens within the habitat of an institution of higher education.

There are multiple scales of community assembly in higher education: at the level of the institution, at the level of disciplinary units within the institution, and at the level of courses offered each semester. I will focus on the latter two. The community of students within a discipline changes in ways that resemble succession: established individuals leave, new individuals become established, and there are shifts in connectivity among individuals. Additionally, the communities of ideas within the minds of students also change in ways that resemble succession: established ideas are lost, new ideas become established, and there are shifts in connectivity among ideas that constitute the basis for intellectual maturation. Many of the same directional trends evident for ecological communities are evident in these educational communities.

There are several key properties of ecological succession. First, species increase or decrease in relative abundance over time as a consequence of births or recruitment and deaths or losses by other means (fig. 6.7, top left). Second, species persistence depends on their characteristics. Species capable of rapid growth typically have high relative abundance early in the process (e.g., forbes) but often do not persist for long periods of time, whereas species that grow more slowly but invest relatively large amounts of resources in structural properties (e.g., woody plants) have low rela-tive abundance early but tend to persist for longer periods of time and increase in abundance later in succession (fig. 6.7, top center). Third, the turnover of species slowly declines over time, reflecting the emergence of community stability (fig. 6.7, top right). Importantly, the fact that there is always turnover—that individuals persist and reproduce but also

Figure 6.7. Top left: Change in the abundance of different species over time due to changes in rates of gain and loss of individuals of the different species (indicated by different line types). Note that in real communities there are many species. Top center: Graph showing the change in abundance of different types of plants inhabiting a landscape in Kansas. Note the abundance of some types of plants increase over time (woody plants, dashed line), when other types of plants decrease over time (perennial forbs, solid line). Top right: The species turn over (gain and loss of species) over time. Bottom left: Diversity typically increases over time as a consequence of the settlement and establishment of new species over time. In some systems, diversity declines after reaching a peak. Bottom center: Complexity as measured using network statistics increases over time. Bottom right: Productivity increases over time. *Sources*: Created by the author based on Cook et al. (2005), Guo (2003), Losapio (2015), and Odum (1969).

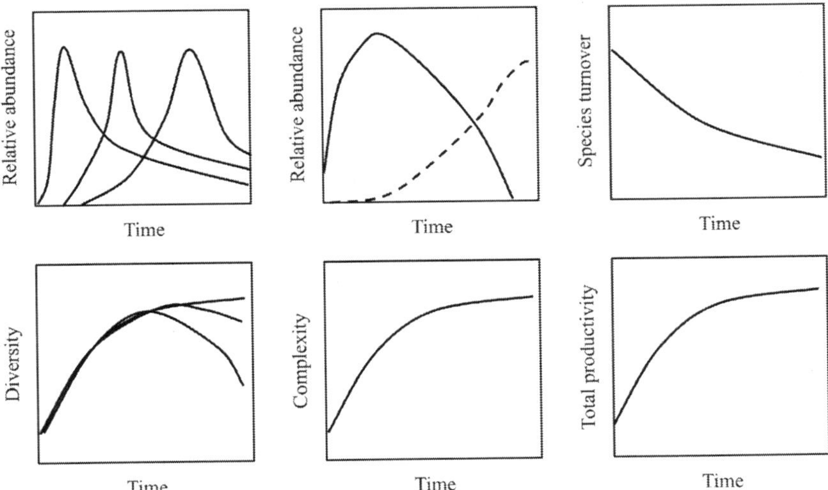

dwindle in numbers and disappear, depending on the species—indicates communities are dynamic entities; moreover, the amount of change over time declines asymptotically but never reaches zero. Fourth, the diversity of species changes during succession (fig. 6.7, bottom left). In most systems, diversity increases. In some cases, diversity increases and then decreases when the community achieves a state described as climax or mature. Fifth, communities become more complex, something that can be observed by monitoring the connectivity among species established through interactions (fig. 6.7, bottom center). Finally, succession is a process in which productivity increases over time (fig. 6.7, bottom right). What this means is resources are used more and more efficiently as the community matures. Importantly, all of these properties of communities that change over time are evident in communities of students in educational contexts and in the community of ideas in the minds of students. Making analogies that recognize succession applies to these two aspects of education means we can use ecological ways of thinking to help think about how teaching can influence succession in positive ways and what aspects of student productivity and thinking would be useful to monitor in ways that would enable data-driven revision of teaching and learning in real time.

A variety of mechanistic hypotheses have been proposed to explain the predictable turnover of species associated with succession. Conner and Slatyer (1977) got the ball rolling:

> Three models of such mechanisms have been proposed. . . . The first "facilitation" model suggests that the entry and growth of the later species is dependent upon the earlier species "preparing the ground"; only after this can later species colonize. . . . A second "tolerance" model suggests that a predictable sequence is produced by the existence of species that have evolved different strategies for exploiting resources. Later species will be those able to tolerate lower levels of resources than earlier ones. Thus they can invade and grow to maturity in the presence of those that preceded them. . . . A third "inhibition" model suggests that all species resist invasions of competitors. The first occupants preempt the space and will continue to exclude or inhibit later colonists until the former die or are damaged, thus releasing resources. Only then can later colonists reach maturity. (p. 1140)

Conner and Slatyer highlight multiple mechanisms to explain the patterns of succession observed in nature. For example, studies of succession in intertidal environments revealed that early successional species had variable effects on the establishment of later successional species, there are examples of species interactions in which there is a tolerance interaction and a facilitation effect, and there are both direct and indirect effects between species. One general result for trees is that the density quickly reaches a stable value and remains more-or-less constant as the diversity of trees increases. These features of succession describe aspects of the change in education communities over time, for both students and ideas.

One way to visualize succession uses the NMDS approach (see "What Is a Community?" above). Conceptually, an NMDS plot of succession—the change of a community as a consequence of the establishment and loss of species—looks like a snake moving through a graphical space until it arrives at a place where it circles within a particular domain of possible community states (fig. 6.8). Two different environments will have different successional "paths" through an apparent universe of possible community compositions defined by the presence and abundance of different species. In general, the amount of change is greater earlier in succession than later. Later succession change is continuous but the magnitude tends to be small and the direction of change more predictable than earlier stages. This picture of change describes the change in the community of ideas that forms the substance of knowledge in the minds of students over time.

The networks of interactions among species are also dynamic because individuals are born and die or come and go, species may be present or not in a particular year or season, and, correspondingly, the connections defined by interactions among species change over time. For example, analysis of rodent community succession revealed species richness

Figure 6.8. A NMDS graph showing the similarity of two communities in different environments over time. The earliest successional stage is the first point in a time series of communities linked together over time by arrows. Note that the length of the arrow decreases gradually over time, indicating that the amount of change of community composition slows over time. At some point the community will change in a predictable way that resembles a circle in x-y space. *Source:* Created by the author.

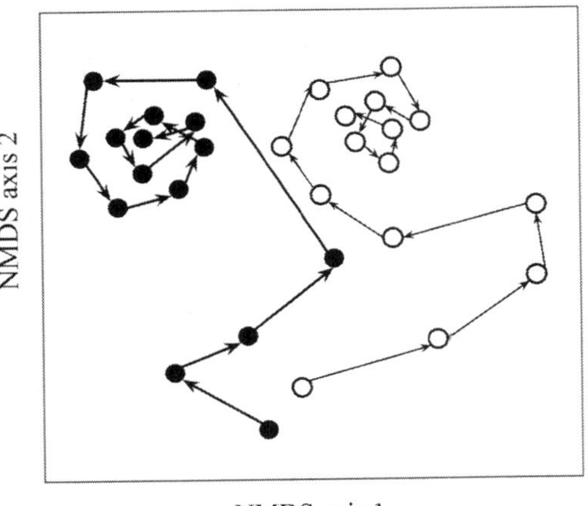

decreased, abundance decreased, and network connectedness decreased during succession, while network nestedness increased (Yang et al., 2018). (Connectedness is a measure of the average number of connections between individuals of different species and the plants on which they depend for food. Nestedness is an emergent property of having both generalist and specialist individuals, and describes a scenario in which specialists tend to feed on a subset of plants also exploited by a generalist instead of feeding on a plant that other species do not feed on.) In a study of plant succession, Ulrich et al. (2016) found that species turnover declined over time (e.g., see fig. 6.7, top right) and that neighborhoods within the larger community emerged as a consequence of interactions. Additionally, within identifiable emergent neighborhoods, competitive hierarchies emerged in which the same rankings were evident across neighborhoods. Based on these data, Ulrich et al. (2016) argued that filtering due to environmental features during community assembly and succession were weak, whereas competitive interactions explained most of the turnover of species over time. Finally, Losapio et al. (2015) studied the successional changes in ecological network connectivity and found link density among species increased over time, and, because link density is an indicator of complexity, there is a general increase in complexity during succession that confers stability and robustness against the potential effects of species loss.

Another aspect of succession, emphasized by Odum (1969, p. 262), is that it "results from modification of the . . . environment by the community; that is, succession is community-controlled even though the physical environment determines the pattern, the rate of change, and often sets limits as to how far development can go." In other words, community composition is an emergent process and involves, to some degree, niche construction. Odum (1969, p. 262) also emphasized that the culmination of succession is "a stabilized ecosystem in which maximum biomass (or high information content) and symbiotic function between organisms are maintained per unit of available energy flow." Climax communities have a low rate of gain and loss of species (Vance, 1988) or, in Odum's perspective, a low rate of change of biomass and information. Odum (1969) illustrated the process of succession and the characteristics of a climax community for both forest and microbial communities; the companion graphs showed evidence for the stabilization of the rate of accumulation of biomass and the convergence of respiration (loss of carbon) and production (gain of carbon) rates over time (fig. 6.9). Remarkably, relabeling the lines underscores the similarity between the outcomes of the emergence

Figure 6.9. Upper model: Odum's (1969) portrayal of the succession of a forest community. Lower model: An analogical model of learning. In this context, knowledge is analogous to biomass. The process of succession and learning is depicted as similar; in both graphs the solid line is a measure of net productivity: carbon production in an ecological community and net knowledge production in the minds of students. *Source:* Created by the author.

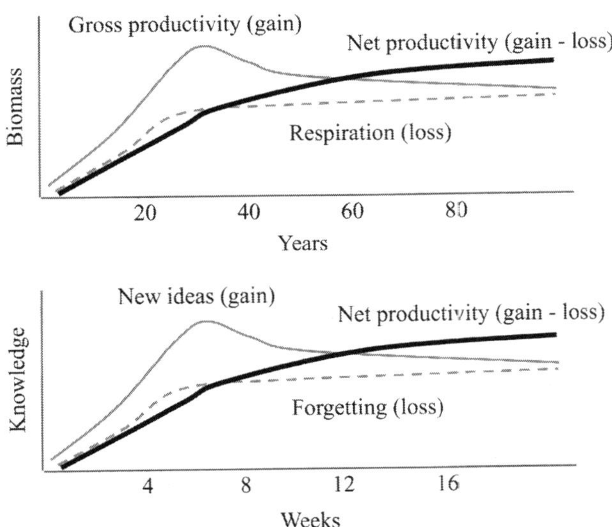

process of educational community succession and learning. There is also change that happens when the community reaches a steady state and the number of species (and the number of ideas) levels off.

Community succession is a mature science that forms the basis for work in restoration ecology and managing ecosystems. I describe some aspects of the succession in academic settings with the purpose of making explicit analogies for making inferences useful for directing and revising teaching and learning in ways aligned with allowing the emergent process of education to happen. The quote that education channelizes a free-flowing river has played a large role in why I emphasize that we often need to get out of the way, to stop trying to direct learning toward a particular objective and instead allow the emergent process of idea community succession to play itself out and flow like a river.

If educational succession is analogous with ecological succession, we should be able to detect change over time in important aggregate properties of communities. In particular, we should expect to see changes in community membership, shifts in the rank-order abundance of different types of individuals, increases in diversity and complexity, and an increase in total productivity. I'll begin with change in the membership of a community. Like many species in nature, there is an age-structure of an academic community within a particular discipline (like EBIO). This reflects the fact that individuals are "born" into the community when they settle as freshman. Once established these individuals move through the stages defined as sophomores, juniors, seniors, and fifth-year seniors as a cohort. At any given time, there are multiple cohorts that comprise a community. Each cohort changes in composition over time because some individuals leave and new individuals settle either by migration from a different disciplinary community on campus or by transferring from a different institution. The amount of turnover of individuals within a cohort declines in much the same way the turnover of species composition declines in ecological communities: the graph for academic communities looks like graphs constructed from data (see fig. 6.7).

There are also shifts in the rank-order abundance of different types of individuals. This shift is not due to the gain and loss of different types of individuals that explains the successional phenomena in ecological settings but instead reflects what I think of as the gain and loss of personality traits related to intellectual maturation and academic achievement. When most students settle and become members of a community, many use fast-thinking strategies (e.g., Kahneman, 2011): the functional properties of these individuals are analogous to pioneer, "weedy" species or forbs. There are differences between freshman and seniors for key traits, including the ability to integrate new information, the capacity for critical thinking and complex problem-solving strategies and being able to work collaboratively, and the ability to effectively communicate and engage in listening to learn strategies (Farrington, 2013). Some students do not change much and may leave, by graduation or for other reasons, without changing in discernible ways. However, most students change: fast, intuition-thinking strategies are replaced by slow thinking (e.g., Kahneman, 2011). This happens because students are dynamic entities that lose and gain characteristics. This is not succession per se, but there is a fundamental similarity at work.

There is also a change in the diversity of students. This happens because the membership of the community changes due to immigration from other disciplines and institutions. It also happens because the characteristics of students change as they integrate their sense of self with the disciplinary knowledge and ways of knowing. Because there are multiple subdisciplines within a particular academic discipline, and there are sub-disciplinary ways of thinking and sets of knowledge, the community of student thinking diversifies over time with the net result that community diversity increases. There are also aspects of diversity that may decline over time due to the gain and loss of individuals. We learned, for instance, that males are more likely to leave than females from the EBIO disciplinary community; in other communities (e.g., engineering), females are more likely to leave.

The connections between species in ecological communities increase over time as individuals interact. This increase in complexity happens in educational communities. Complexity is evident from interaction networks that emerge from repeated interactions. Zwolak et al. (2018) monitored the development of student interaction networks in a physics class and revealed the properties of networks stabilized after 8 weeks of instruction. At that point, various measures of the network properties differed markedly from ecological networks. In particular, when compared to ecological networks, the emergent education network was less dense, the distance between individuals was greater, and there were multiple large components and several disconnected "satellite" components (Zwolak et al, 2018). Nonetheless, you can see the emergence of complexity and the structural basis for collective intelligence through the construction and fusion of modules. Buchenroth-Martin et al. (2017) also monitored the development of a course-level, interaction-based community network in a biology class and revealed continuous change of the network over a span of 15 weeks; in this case, there was no evidence of an asymptote for any measures of network structure, and all individuals had coalesced into a single community. Various network statistics (e.g., density, distance, degree distribution) were similar to statistics estimated from real world networks, including ecological networks (Buchenroth-Martin et al., 2016). In addition, there were increases in the number of connections between individuals over time that pulled the network together, a phenomenon evident from measures of network diameter and from the increase in the density of interactions. Moreover, there was the emergence of neighborhoods (also called cliques). While these data were generated from a single class over the duration of a semester, similar phenomena were likely happening for the whole academic community within a discipline. Brouwer et al. (2018) found that academic networks, social networks, and academic achievement are correlated, resulting in the emergence of homophilous subgroups that, as the authors note, may be suboptimal for academic progress. Given the immense value of network data for understanding the structure and function of ecological communities, we, as educators and individuals interested in promoting academic success, should pay more attention to the emergence of academic networks and perhaps steer the emergent process of education in ways in which productive and cooperative ecological networks are built and maintained (Saavedra et al., 2009).

Finally, a hallmark of succession is a steady increase in productivity measured as the difference between learning gains and losses. The focus is on aggregated data for all students over the years spent in pursuit of academic achievement and intellectual maturation. There is no question that productivity measured by the gain in learning relative to the amount of resources used increases over time, in part because individual students get better, on average, at the challenging job of learning. However, I don't have access to data that would allow evaluating whether this claim is grounded in data or simply reflects hope. I strongly advocate that we engage in more free-response assessment strategies that can reveal gains in students thinking across multiple dimensions of intelligence centered in critical and creative thinking. Implementing pre- and post-instruction assessments at different times and in different courses for the duration students are enrolled in higher education can establish whether the analogical equivalence between ecology and education is true or not. Is Odum's portrayal of succession (fig. 6.9) evident for academic communities?

Ideally, education results in the continuous increase in the abundance and diversity of unambiguously valid ideas in the minds of students. This happens in the same way ecological succession happens as a consequence of the differential establishment and persistence of ideas. Ideas form the basis of knowledge; as a consequence, knowledge is dynamic and changes as a consequence of the continuous settlement, persistence, establishment, and loss of ideas in the mind. Ideas that are easily learned and that may exist as a consequence of rote memorization strategies are like the forbs. They quickly become established but may not be sufficiently robust to hold on when more substantial ideas become established. Ideas or strategies that are more difficult to learn, and that are successfully integrated with other ideas, are like the woody plants that increase slowly over time but persist. The distinction is important, depending on the extent that education focuses on nurturing and sustaining the ideas that have more substance (like woody plants) or focuses more on smaller, unconnected, and more fragile ideas (like the forbs). Perhaps, to make learning more effective, we should concentrate our efforts on growing the "woody plants" of knowledge instead of the pioneer "weedy" ideas that constitute the long list of facts we ask students to learn. It is also likely that there are positive associations between ideas that establish early and have facilitative effects on the capacity of individuals to foster the establishment of higher-level, more substantial "woody" ideas. In fact, the facilitation, tolerance, and inhibition models that explain the dynamics of ecological succession (see Conner & Slatyer, 1977) may apply to knowledge succession. Knowledge is an emergent outcome of the succession of communities of ideas in much the same way a mature ecological community is an emergent outcome of ecological succession.

Ecological methods can be used to watch succession happen in the mind of each student as they encounter new ideas and build knowledge. The approach begins as it does for species in a community. A presence and absence (1 and 0) matrix is constructed each time the mind is sampled (fig. 6.10). Typically, the minds of students are sampled by midterms or some intellectual challenge that reveals student thinking. These matrices

Figure 6.10. A presence-absence matrix for eight key ideas (the rows) evaluated over time using four separate iterations of the same assessment (the columns) for four different students (the different matrices). Open squares indicate absence, whereas filled squares represent presence of key ideas. The gains and losses of ideas differ among all four students. In the first case (left), there is a progressive increase in number of ideas and knowledge without loss. In the second case (middle, left), there is an abrupt increase in number of ideas and knowledge followed by loss. In the third case (middle, right), there is a complete gain of ideas followed by complete loss and a second round of wholesale gain. In the fourth case, there is a combination of gains and loss over time that is often evident for many students and that probably reflects a combination of random and deterministic effects on knowledge dynamics. *Source:* Created by the author.

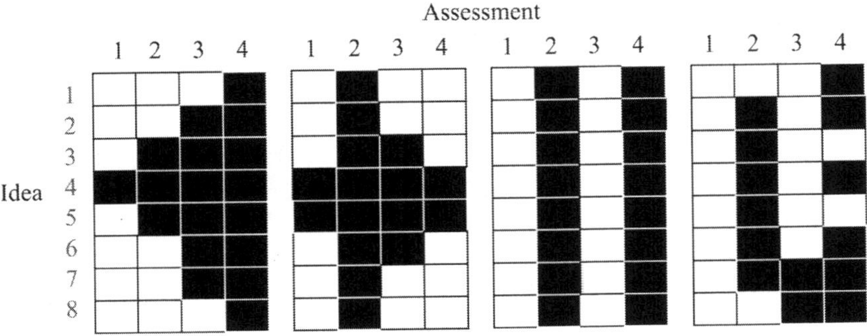

are indistinguishable from species' presence and absence matrices that describe ecological communities. The matrices underscore that ideas are gained and lost over time, and that the community of ideas in the minds of different students exhibit unique dynamics. One of the compelling results of repeated assessments over the course of a semester is that there is tremendous variation of the community of ideas in the minds of students over time and among students. This way of thinking and visualizing knowledge is closely aligned with DiSessa's conceptualization that learning happens through the collection and integration of knowledge-in-pieces. More importantly, succession has some general predictable outcomes. One of them is that because there are both stochastic and deterministic mechanisms explaining settlement and establishment, different communities of ideas in the minds of students will take different successional trajectories. Trajectories are defined by specific gains and losses of ideas over time for each student.

Early in the book (in chapter 1), I introduced the idea, from Stanley and Lehman (2015), that an emergent process is a lot like crossing a lake on stepping stones subject to the challenge that "the lake is covered in mist in which the stepping stones closest to the shore fade gradually as they wind into the fog. As you walk along the course of stepping stones over the water, the shore dissolves from sight behind you even as the other side remains cloaked behind the mist." Reaching the other side is the general objective, but there are many ways to cross the lake, with some dead ends and many forks in the road. The nonmetric dimensional scaling (NMDS) described earlier lends itself to constructing a "lake" and visualizing the set of "stepping stones" students take to go from novice to more expert. The data like those in the matrices of figure 6.10 generate the NMDS "stepping stones" on a mist-shrouded lake. In this context, the stepping stones are different combinations of the presence of different ideas in the minds of students. To keep the analogy with ecology of the mind in mind, each stepping stone represents a community of ideas, and there are multiple possible communities represented by the number of different stones. If we look at the lake and the existing stepping stones at different times during a curriculum designed to achieve an understanding of some set of ideas in biology—in this case key ideas necessary for understanding evolution—we can see that with each iteration there is some number of stepping stones that are visible (figs. 6.11a–6.11d). What is evident about the picture of stepping stones in the lake is that with each iteration of an assessment, new stones appear that reflect choices by students to take

Figure 6.11. The "stepping stones of a mist shrouded lake" of understanding based on the presence or absence of eight key ideas forming the basis of understanding about evolution. Each "lake" (labeled A, B, C, and D) shows the different communities of ideas in the minds of students (the "stepping stones" of understanding) estimated from the same assessment. The four assessments (A–D) were implemented at four different times during a course. Each "stone" is a different combination of ideas. *Source:* Created by the author. See Buck and Martin (2023).

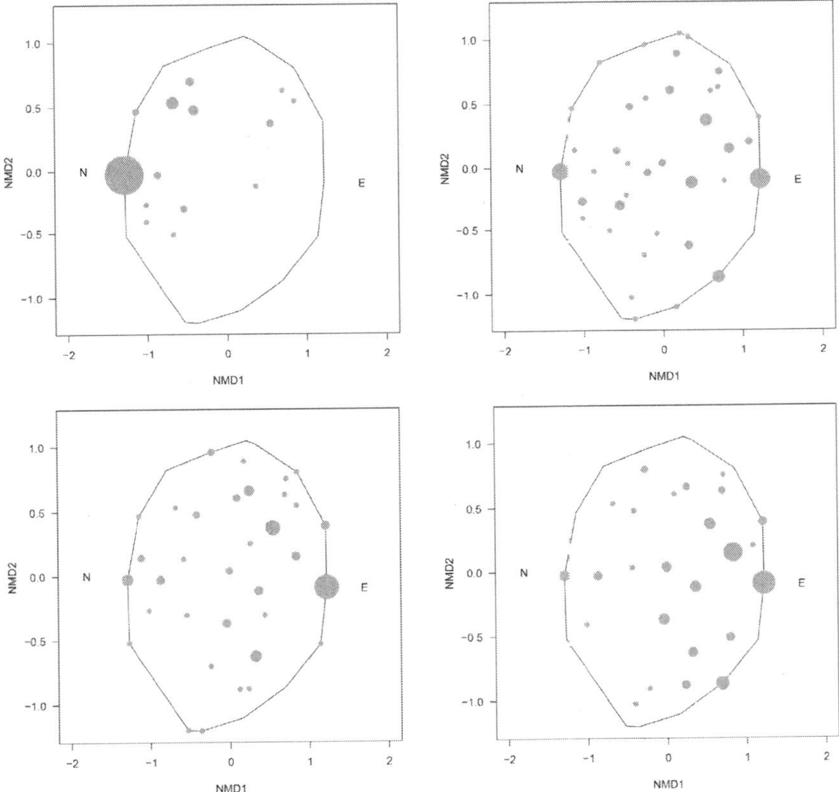

a "step" toward greater understanding. And some stepping stones disappear. As described by Stanley and Lehman, as students move across the lake, the "stepping stones closest to the shore fade gradually as they wind into the fog" while others appear. This is evident, to some degree, if you compare the first and last assessment iterations (fig. 6.11a and 6.11d). This picture is an emergent outcome of education and shows that there are multiple different assemblages of ideas in the minds of students that change over time. There is evidence of directionality. New stepping stones that represent new combinations of the presence and absence of elements of understanding emerge "from the fog" and are closer to the expert stones with each successive assessment. It is clear that there are many possible stones—many different communities of ideas—and many possible paths from one side of the lake to the other. Students can and do take many different paths from being novice to expert; our job is to allow them to pick a path and to pay attention more to how far they travel than whether they are correct or incorrect. If greatness is defined as intellectual maturation and academic achievement, there are many paths toward greatness.

We often imagine students take a direct path; that the objective is defined and the process is direct. Yet, if there are multiple key ideas, there are multiple paths across the lake, and how students cross the lake will depend on the particular steps they take, with each step being defined by the gain or loss of ideas and the formation or dissolution of connections between different ideas. The step-by-step contingency of learning is one description confirming education is an emergent process. Importantly, students may take paths across the lake that are direct, or they may backtrack as a consequence of inadequate assimilation of new information or simply as a consequence of changing their minds in ways consistent with experiential learning. When Buck and Martin (2023) looked closely at the combination of stepping stones students used to cross the lake from novice to expert, there was a remarkable diversity of paths; in fact, no two students out of 72 students chose the same set of stepping stones in the same order in their efforts to cross the lake. And some students moved toward being an expert at the same time others were backtracking because of the loss of ideas and taking the same or new paths toward becoming expert (fig. 6.12). One of the general take-home messages was that learning gains are often transient, knowledge is unstable, and ideas are frequently lost; nonetheless, it is important students continue to take the next step even if it is a combination of ideas already visited, because perspective will likely be different based on the experiences had since a particular stepping stone was first visited.

One of the things that becomes evident from looking at changes in the presence and absence of ideas in the minds of students over time is that the amount of change varies a lot among students. The change is evident if you sum the distance traveled across the NMDS bivariate space: the larger the distance traveled, the more students' minds change. The upshot is that students' who change their minds generally have greater knowledge than those whose minds appear resistant to change. There is nothing particularly remarkable about this discovery. This discovery

Figure 6.12. The "lake" of combinations of ideas constituting knowledge. In this case, the ideas are about the process of evolution. Each circle is a combination of the presence or absence of eight different ideas in the minds of students. Solid lines connecting points indicate learning gains toward the "expert" side of the lake whereas dashed lines indicate change marked by the loss of ideas. The darkness of each point and line is proportional to the number of individuals with the same set of ideas and learning trajectories, respectively. *Source:* Created by the author.

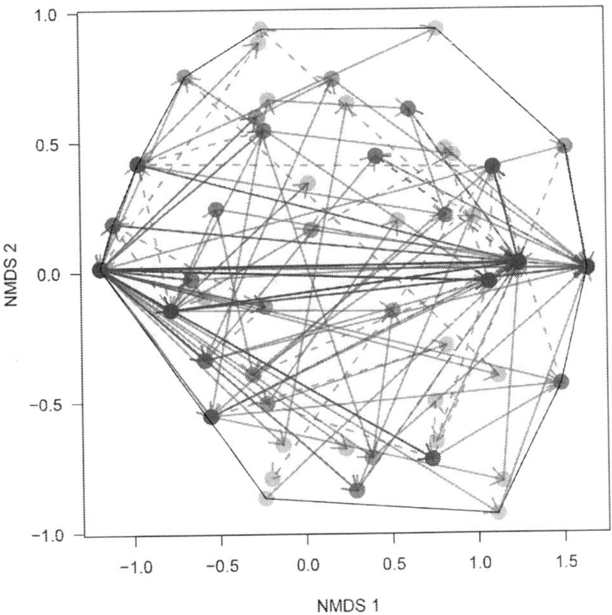

reminds us that we should be in the business of changing minds. It may be more important to monitor change and trajectory than to simply keep track of counts of correct ideas. It may be more important to encourage changing one's mind than to encourage correctness, and to encourage connections among ideas than to power through adding new ideas. And we should expect students take different paths with variable lengths toward their own conception of some evidence-based truth. What is clear from using these methods borrowed from ecology for monitoring change is that students' learning trajectories are different and underlying the differences is variation in motivation, ability, sense of value, prior knowledge, and a host of other variables. Applying ranked order grading to these data seems pointless; indeed, we should embrace the idea that education is more than an exercise in grading students based on points. In the context of the complexity of the process made evident by analogy with ecology, counting the points is pointless (Zerwin, 2020).

As highlighted in chapter 4, ideas within a disciplinary community interact, and I like to think idea succession as the increasing maturity of knowledge stemming from establishing connections among ideas. Knowledge can be considered to be an outcome of the succession of the community of ideas in which there is constant but diminishing turnover of ideas, and the gradual emergence of persistent ideas stabilized by connections to other ideas. This aligns with the knowledge-in-pieces (DiSessa, 2018) or knowledge-as-pieces (elements or ideas) framework. These frameworks suggest students build knowledge and understanding by making connections between quasi-independent elements (ideas). If knowledge consists of pieces, "if a learner's intuitive knowledge is elemental in nature, instruction should focus on how those elements are activated in appropriate contexts . . . focus more on refinement processes including addition, modification, elimination, and organization of the knowledge elements . . . [and] we should attempt to help students reorganize and reprioritize the elements and connections of their conceptual network" (Özdemir & Clark, 2007, p. 358). In ecological communities, there is an increase in connections between species over time. As a consequence, the complexity of communities increases, which contributes to increases in productivity and stability. A mature, highly connected, diverse community is more functional and productive than an assemblage of independent entities; the same is true for communities of ideas in the minds of students.

It is clear from the analysis of mature ecological communities that while the number of species remains more-or-less constant over time, the types of species changes over time. For the community of ideas in the mind, is there a similar pattern in which the total number of ideas does not change but the ideas that comprise the community change? There is some evidence that this may be true as a consequence of limitations on the capacity of the mind. One such limit is referred to as cognitive load. Cognitive load implies there is a limit on the capacity of working memory. Working memory is an amount of information (procedural, conceptual, informational, etc.) that is "available" or "held" in the mind and used during some cognitive task. The word "load" implies that there is a cost to holding information in the mind, and if a particular challenge requires holding too much information, some threshold load for efficient function is breached and the cognitive task fails. In an educational context, cognitive overload can inhibit or prohibit learning. Thus, learning ideally happens in a piecemeal manner in which bits of information are added to working memory but the total number of bits of information added in an episode of time is maintained below some overload threshold. Additionally, there may be a carrying capacity for ideas in the minds of students. As new ideas colonize and establish in the minds of students, other ideas may decay or be lost, and there could be some form of density-dependence in which the birth (or colonization and establishment) of a new idea in the mind of a student causes the loss of another idea. If students' minds are at saturation or carrying capacity, the rates of birth and death of ideas may be equal, and there is no net change in the number of ideas.

The connectivity of ideas may matter. Observations of the network structure of ecological communities often reveal two types of species categorized as core or peripheral. These two categories are delimited based on their abundance and connectedness with other species. Are there core and peripheral ideas, and if so, how do we, as educators, focus more attention on the core ideas as ways for directing the organization and coherence of learning? Identification of core and peripheral species in ecological settings focuses attention on interactions between functionally different individuals. Core species tend to be generalists that use a variety of different resources and tend to interact in ways that result in the existence of central players in a highly interactive network. Peripheral species, by contrast, tend to be specialists that use few different resources and have limited interactions with generalist species (Bascompte et al., 2003; Chacoff et al., 2018; Zografou et al., 2020). While the scale of core or peripheral categorization is continuous, the distribution of values for connectedness to other species and abundance clearly separate individuals as core and peripheral. If, for instance, we make a graph and plot the connectedness of a species to other species on the x-axis and the continuity of species' presence (measured by presence or absence over a sufficient duration) on the y-axis, the resulting data splits into two groups: a group of species that are always present year-after-year and are moderately or well connected to other species and a group that is weakly connected to other species regardless of the continuity of presence in the community. The former delimits core species and the latter peripheral species. Moreover, some species identified as core or peripheral can change over time depending on conditions and species present (Miele et al., 2020).

Not surprisingly, while all of the species comprise the community, the core species have larger effects on defining the functional characteristics of the community. The same is likely true for ideas. There are ideas that can be similarly categorized as core or peripheral depending on their frequency of occurrence and their connectivity to other ideas within a discipline or across multiple disciplines. However, students are often unaware of the different value of ideas—they often treat all ideas as similarly valuable and worthy of trying to memorize. Additionally, students often collect ideas but fail to make connections between different ideas in ways that create knowledge and understanding. One of our jobs as educators is to help students understand the network structure of knowledge—that there are core and peripheral ideas—and build a core of generalist and strongly connected ideas that provide connections for peripheral and specialized but nonetheless important ideas. The difference between generalist and connected core ideas and more specialist peripheral ideas was evident in Roche Allred et al. (2022).

> The goal of any science educator is to prepare students with sufficient meaningful and robust knowledge to support their growth as science learners, consumers, and even scientists. While it would not be expected that students become disciplinary experts after one or two semesters of introductory courses, ideally, they should start gaining a foundation that supports their development of scientific knowledge. These early science courses are often designed to cover a wide range of topics with the intent of offering beginning students exposure to the given discipline as either preparation to further their study in said discipline or related disciplines. [However] . . . introductory science curricula structured to consider a discipline's breadth instead of depth does not lead to the development of a coherent framework on which students can build their knowledge. Furthermore, the overwhelming amount of information covered in these courses leaves little room to support students' formation of a usable coherent network of knowledge in which they can build connections between topics, much less across disciplinary concepts. As a result, students tend to leave their introductory courses with limited usable and transferable knowledge; thus, these courses are failing to prepare them for advanced courses or future careers or to be scientifically literate consumers. (p. 1)

There are explicit pedagogical frameworks—like the Next Generation Science Standards (NGSS) and associated assessments—that emphasize disciplinary core ideas, the application of these ideas, and cross-cutting concepts that form intellectual bridges among disciplines (Cooper, 2020). The framework is well-developed and promotes the creation of links and interaction between ideas. Importantly, students were able to identify core and peripheral ideas based on their frequency of occurrence and their explanatory power (Roche Allred et al., 2022). Explanatory power is an emergent outcome of connecting, organizing, and contextualizing ideas. To understand ecology, it makes sense to pay most attention to core species; to learn about ecology (or any other disciplinary knowledge) it makes sense to pay attention to the core ideas. More importantly, it is not sufficient to tell students about the core ideas; if I tell students the core ideas and ask them to list them, they can do so but do not understand why they are core ideas (Roche Allred et al., 2022). Instead, students need to identify core ideas as a consequence of the processes of connecting, organizing, and contextualizing ideas.

Roche Allred et al. (2022) described differences between teaching introductory chemistry and biology in ways that emphasized core ideas either through actions or words. They noted that "core ideas can connect students' knowledge, and make it accessible, if they are developed over time throughout the curriculum. On the other hand, if a particular core idea is treated as a topic, it will not serve this purpose, and it will be more difficult for students to make connections across ideas and phenomena" (p. 11). Thus, as educators, we need to imagine core ideas as core species and create opportunities for students to experience the connectedness of core ideas as the basis for knowledge and coherency of understanding. Core ideas are integral to all ideas in a discipline rather than simple topics that serve as chapter headings (Roche Allred et al., 2022). Our job is to repeatedly emphasize educational experiences in which the core ideas appear in different contexts in ways that form connections to other ideas and serve as a foundation for developing a robust mental model of the world.

Education is an emergent process characterized by the existence of innumerable trajectories defined by the gain and loss of ideas. Imagine, for instance, two sections of the same course taught by different instructors using the same curriculum, the same lesson plans, the same assessments, and the same types of strategies when teaching. Despite the sameness, the trajectories of change in knowledge will likely be different, because there are so many ways different predictive variables interact in a world where all participating individuals interact in myriad ways and are engaged in niche construction. These differences are expected to exist, and instead of trying to emphasize conformity and a single dimension for rank-ordering of individuals based on perceptions of intelligence, we should embrace the diversity and uncertainty and center rewards on positive change—the trajectories of learning—rather than asking whether students have achieved a particular or specific objective. Rather than objectifying education and denying emergence, we should accept that the objective as the journey. It is better to have students focus on how far they have traveled instead of how close they are to a predetermined (and often student-irrelevant) objective.

Odum (1969, p. 262) wrote that "succession . . . has many parallels in the developmental biology of organisms, and also in the development of human society." To underscore his analogy with human society, I constructed a table (table 6.2a–d) following the criteria and format of Odum's table (1969, p. 265); I urge readers to consult the original table. I included a subset of categories with clear analogical connections between ecology and education. As educators, we should strive to pay attention to the various edusystem attributes as sources of information for gauging the change that happens to individuals as a consequence of constructed educational experiences. The changes can focus on aggregated data or individuals. For instance, the category of "community energetics" is replaced by "education energetics" and is meant to focus on the amount of energy invested in producing net learning gains. A net learning gain is the amount learned after allowing for the loss of knowledge. This is similar to the process of carbon gain from primary productivity minus the loss of carbon used by metabolism for sustaining life. Odum refers to "standing crop biomass." In education, this is the total amount of disciplinary knowledge in the mind of a student or the minds of students in a particular course or discipline. In the developmental stages (akin to first- and second-year classes), the total learning gains relative to existing knowledge is high, mostly because of the low amount of existing knowledge. This ratio declines over time and becomes low for intellectually mature students because the "biomass" of knowledge has increased over time. Similarly, the total knowledge supported per unit energy goes from low to high, because as students become increasingly intelligent, it takes less energy to hold more information: the energetic demands of learning are less about creating new and separate memories and more about making connections between existing knowledge with new ideas.

Table 6.2a. Educational energetics (replaces community energetics)

Attributes	Developmental stages	Mature stages
Total learning gains relative to existing knowledge	High	Low
Total knowledge supported per unit energy	Low	High
Net educational productivity (gains-losses)		
Structure of knowledge network	Linear	Weblike
Productivity emphasis	Quantity	Quality

Table 6.2b. Community structure

Attributes	Developmental stages	Mature stages
Available resources to individuals	External (professor-motivated)	Internal (self-motivation)
Diversity of knowledge	Low	High
Organization of knowledge	Loosely structured, flimsy, subject to decay	Well structured, stable, resilient, and adaptable

Table 6.2c. Individual characteristics (replaces "life history")

Attributes	Developmental stages	Mature stages
Magnitude of individual ability	Small	Large
Duration and complexity of sustained learning episodes	Short, simple	Long, complex
Cognitive niche	Poorly constructed	Well-constructed
Magnitude of individual ability	Small	Large
Duration and complexity of sustained learning episodes	Short, simple	Long, complex

Table 6.2d. Emergent outcomes

Attributes	Developmental stages	Mature stages
Entropy	High	Low
Information	Low	High
Conservation of resources	Poor	Good
Mutualistic associations (symbioses)	Undeveloped	Well-developed
Stability	Poor	Good

Odum included a category called "life history." Life history refers to aspects about the biology of individuals that function best during the early or late stages of succession. He used the attributes niche specialization (broad and narrow), organism size (small and large), and life cycle (short, simple and long, complex). I substituted niche specialization with cognitive niche (poorly or well constructed), changed organism size with magnitude of individual ability (small and large), and switched life cycle with duration and complexity of sustained learning episodes (short, simple and long, complex). Another important category is what Odum referred to as overall homeostasis. I changed this to emergent outcomes, because it included attributes such as symbiosis, stability, entropy, and information; these are outcomes of emergent processes. I changed the specific attributes without, in my assessment, changing the "parallels" between ecological succession and education.

The purpose of recreating Odum's summary table for thinking about education was, first and foremost, to honor a pioneer of ecosystem studies and to stand squarely on the shoulders of an ecologist with such a large impact and who clearly realized the value of analogical thinking. A second purpose was to describe various attributes of the process of education that can form the basis of assessment. We can, but rarely ever do, estimate the number and degree of mutualistic interactions between students. We can, but rarely ever do, estimate the entropy (disorder) of knowledge and how it changes over time. We can, and should, but rarely ever do, estimate the details of individuals' cognitive niches. In fact, we can, and should, but rarely ever do estimate all of the attributes listed in table 6.2a–d, and others that may have "parallels" between ecology—where the attributes are measured to gain insight into the emergent process of ecology—and education—where too few attributes are regularly measured, leaving us mostly in the dark about the emergent process of education.

The Diversity and Productivity of Communities

Education-relevant synopsis: Diversity and productivity are inextricably linked; yet the association resists easy description and prediction. Depending on context, diversity increases or decreases productivity and productivity increases or decreases diversity. An important inference is that diversity and productivity interact in myriad ways, and it is important to pay attention to both. For instance, diversity provides a way to measure the complexity of knowledge: more diverse knowledge is more complex. And more complexity depends on greater productivity. Thus, this short section is meant to remind educators that diversity and productivity are important components of the educational experience that applies to pedagogy, perspectives, and knowledge.

Diversity is the number or frequency of different things in a population or community. Diversity is important because of the general discovery that diversity increases productivity. Given this truth, it is important that communities are unified; namely, that the community shares common values, aspirations, and norms of behavior. As Mahatma Gandhi expressed, "Our ability to reach unity in diversity will be the beauty and the test of our civilization." The simplest way to measure (or estimate) diversity is to count the number of different things. In community ecology, the things are typically species. The count of the number of different species is known as species richness. Another informative measure of diversity includes information about the abundance of individuals of different species. These two measures of diversity can be very different. Imagine, for instance, two communities. In each community there are two different species; however, in one community, both species are equally frequent (i.e., they have the same abundance), and in the other community one of the species is rare (there is only one individual) and the other species is common. These two communities have the same species richness (i.e., 2) but have very different estimates of diversity if we take into account abundance. There are a variety of ways to account for variation in relative abundance; perhaps the simplest is to calculate the probability that two randomly sampled individuals are different. To calculate this number, we first need to calculate the probability that two randomly sampled individuals are the same. Using sampling theory, the probability of sampling an individual is its frequency in the population. In a community with equal abundance of two species, the probability of sampling one species is 0.50 (or 50%). Thus, the probability of randomly sampling from the community and sampling one of the two species twice is $0.5 \times 0.5 = 0.5^2 = 0.25$. Similarly, the probability of sampling the other species twice is $0.5 \times 0.5 = 0.5^2 = 0.25$. Because both of these are possible outcomes of sampling from a population twice, the probability of sampling the same species twice is $0.5^2 + 0.5^2 = 0.50$. The other remaining option is that the two sampled individuals are different; namely, $1 - (0.5^2 + 0.5^2) = 0.5$. This leads to a general equation for n species; namely, diversity $= 1 - \Sigma p_i^2$, where p_i is the frequency of the ith species. If there is only a single individual of one species and, for illustrative purposes, 99 individuals of the other species, $p_1 = 0.01$ and $p_2 = 0.99$. In this case, diversity $= 1 - (0.01^2 + 0.99^2) = 1 - (0.0001 + 0.9801) = 0.0198$. In the comparison between the two hypothetical communities of two species, the richness is the same but the diversity is $0.5/0.0198 = 25$ times higher in the case where abundance is equal. The message from these numbers is that the number of different things and their relative abundance matters.

There are three possible effects of diversity on productivity: diversity can have positive, negative, or no discernible effects. There is a rich body of theory and empirical data indicating diversity matters in ecological communities because diversity influences function. Perhaps the best demonstration of this comes from experimental studies in which plant communities were constructed across many different plots such that the number of species per plot varied from 1 to 32. In each case, the number of individuals in a particular plot was the same; plots differed in the number of different species. Importantly, the plants in the different communities had very different functional properties (i.e., there was functional diversity). Here is an excerpt from Tilman et al. (1997):

> Plants were classified into functional groups on the basis of intrinsic physiological and morphological differences, which influence differences in resource requirements, seasonality of growth, and life history. Legumes fix nitrogen. . . . Grasses with the three-carbon photosynthetic pathway (C3) grow best during the cool seasons and have higher tissue N than do grasses with the C4 pathway, which grow best during the warm season. Woody plants have high allocation to perennial stems and low growth rates, and forbs do not fix N and often have high allocation to seed. (p. 1300)

Whether the predictor variable was the number of different species or number of different functional types of individuals the results were similar: more diversity caused more productivity, up to a point. These results have been replicated in different contexts. It seems inescapable that diversity increases productivity. Increasing productivity is a measure of Gandhi's sense of beauty in the unity of diversity.

There are primarily two explanatory mechanisms for the dependence of productivity on diversity, and both may be at work. The first is that different types of individuals (i.e., species) have different niches and individuals of each species utilize different combinations of resources; when there are more species, a greater number of types and amounts of resources are used (Tilman et al., 1997; Kahmen et al., 2006). It is also possible some species can alter their uptake of resources in the presence of other species. Such "plasticity in resource use among the dominant species provides a mechanism that helps to explain the manner by which plant species with broadly overlapping resource use might coexist" (Ashton et al., 2010, p. 3252). In other words, individuals of different types of plants adjust their resource use in response to the presence of other individuals, and by doing so, both species coexist in ways that increase productivity.

The issue of the association between diversity and productivity in ecology is more complicated than portrayed by the graphs showing the dependence of productivity on diversity, however. In particular, diversity can be a predictor but also a response variable; when diversity is a predictor variable, the effects of diversity are modulated by the environment. When productivity is a predictor variable for diversity, it is directly influenced by the environmental conditions and availability of resources. Harsh environments with limited resources predict low species diversity (imagine precipitation-limited deserts); similarly, benign environments with abundant resources also predict low species diversity because of the capacity of a few species to monopolize the resources (imagine aquatic environments with an excess of nitrogen and phosphorus that become dominated by problematic algae). It is when resources are moderately abundant in an intermediately challenging environment that maximum diversity is predicted and often realized. The effects of different functional groups are more nuanced than suggested by the smooth graphs generated using mean values from large scale experiments in grasslands. Instead, different functional types of organisms can have very different individual effects that are modulated by the environment.

The idea that there are different functional types of species and that the overall function of a community (in terms of productivity) increases when distinct functional groups interact suggests that, if there is an analogical bridge between ecology and education in this context, we might expect similar patterns of the dependence of productivity on diversity and the dependence of diversity on productivity (or availability of resources and environment) in educational contexts. Can we expect the mechanisms underlying the positive effects of diversity on productivity in educational settings? Do some individuals "raise their game" in diverse social contexts? Do students become more narrowly focused on specific processes (i.e., express greater niche specialization) in diverse groups? Is there evidence that productivity (measured as the abundance of available resources for intellectual growth and maturation) influences diversity?

In this case, one relevant measure of diversity is the number of different pathways students take toward gaining academic achievement. For there to be a positive effect of diversity on intellectual maturation and academic achievement, we have to imagine students have different cognitive and behavioral niches and that the niches are complementary rather than competitive and exclusionary. Discovering complementarity and realizing its benefits takes time, requires repeated interactions, and stems from engaging in challenges that are multidimensional, complex and require collaboration.

Experiments like those carried out by Tilman and others are practically impossible in education settings, because there are no replicates of categorically distinct functional types of people. Nonetheless, Terenzini et al. (2001a) claimed that the

> evidence is almost uniformly consistent in indicating that students in a racial/ethnically or gender-diverse community . . . reap a wide array of positive educational benefits. Diversity in its various forms has been linked to such outcomes as higher minority student retention, greater cognitive development, and positive gains on a wide-range of measures of interpersonal and psychosocial developmental changes, including increased openness to diversity and challenge, greater racial/cultural knowledge and understanding and commitment to social justice, more positive academic and social self-concepts, more complex civic-related attitudes and values, and greater involvement in civic and community-service behaviors. (p. 511)

The claims by Terenzini et al. (2001b) and others suggest patterns evident in ecological systems are apparent in educational contexts; however, a closer look at the data suggests the inference of a positive effect of diversity on various aspects of student intellectual maturation and development remains elusive. I have yet to discover data showing a sustained increase in productivity with an increase in diversity or the number of functional groups stemming from research happening in educational settings. I think the problem is mainly the difficulty inherent in experimental design, conceptualizing and delimiting functional groups, and estimating effects. The data that do exist show small effects and are limited because most of the data stem from surveys or samples of convenience; Terenzeni et al.'s (2001b) evidence of a positive effect of diversity on students' self-reported gains in problem-solving and group interaction skills in engineering classes cannot be statistically differentiated from a model in which there is no effect of diversity: there were no statistically detectable effects of racial diversity on educational productivity. There are, however, demonstrable effects of gender (as a component of diversity) and age. Using an experimental design, Hansen et al. (2006) discovered "that male-dominant groups performed worse both in group work and in individually taken exams than female-dominant and equally-mixed gender groups after controlling for other group characteristics. Individual members from a group with more diversity in age and gender scored higher in exams" (p. 2).

Studies of the characteristics of group members—equivalent to functional types in the ecological literature—revealed assemblages of diverse individuals that exhibited interdependence may have the greatest productivity in educational settings (Channon et al., 2017). (Interdependence refers to the existence of "combinatorial strategies" such that each individual positively influences another person's experience; this is more or less equivalent to mutualistic interactions in ecology.) Channon et al.'s descriptions of diversity depended on whether groups included multiple functional types of people they identified as shapers, plants, team workers, monitor evaluators, completers, resource investigators, implementers, and international representatives (p. 20). These categories may more accurately represent personalities than abilities of individuals. Unfortunately, Channon et al. did not provide quantitative estimates of the effect of diversity. In another study, Wiggins et al. (2017) discovered that there were no detectable effects of including diversity variables (gender, socioeconomic class, and race) on education productively perhaps because it is likely these individual characteristics do not predict functional *cognitive* diversity. My perspective is that diversity should be estimated for cognitive and personality attributes—how people think, their experience, their motivation, whether they have a growth mindset, and other aspects stemming from their personality—without focusing on race, socioeconomics, or gender.

Despite the limited evidence for a positive effect of diversity on learning in educational settings, we should expect that the processes and patterns evident in ecological communities likely happen in the classroom. I think we should see evidence of the positive effects of diversity on productivity in the classroom if we create authentic incentives for realizing the benefits of interdependence and mutualism and pay attention to cognitive phenotypes and niche construction. Furthermore, I suspect the structural conditions required to achieve this type of learning experience may not conform to learning schedules that meet for relatively brief periods of time a couple of times per week. Education models like the one supported at Colorado College, in which students meet for extended periods of time every day of the week for three and a half weeks, may provide a better model for learning in ways that leverage the dependence of productivity on diversity evident in ecological settings. Moreover, there are also limitations on the spatial configuration of learning spaces that interfere with realizing the positive effects of diversity, simply because of difficulties in being able to move around and freely associate in ways that are natural for humans. To realize the expected benefits of diversity on students' intellectual maturation and academic achievement, we need to first create frequent, realizable, and authentic opportunities for interaction.

Is there an association between diversity and productivity for ideas and the emergence of knowledge? Another way of asking this question is: Does it matter if learning happens based on ideas that are similar to each other or ideas that are more different? Also, some ideas may have multiple parts—embedded ideas: Do ideas differ in their inherent diversity? The answer to this last question is yes, according to Ahmed and Fuge (2018): more diverse ideas "cover" or encompass a greater range of phenomena. Ahmed and Fuge studied students' solutions to an engineering design challenge focused on food production and consumption. If an idea is to compost the food in some manner, this has low diversity, because it only addresses the issue of what happens when food production exceeds consumption; it does not address aspects about production and consumption that might, for instance, make composting obsolete. The idea of idea diversity is useful and helps us focus on what Ahmed and Fuge refer to as coverage. Consider the following two ideas inspired by the learning objectives endorsed for teaching an introductory biology course (Hennessey & Freeman, 2023): (1) The genetic code is redundant because there are multiple codons that specify the same amino acid during translation. (2) Mutation of protein-coding DNA can have varied effects on the synthesis of a protein depending which codon position changes. These two ideas group together in the same disciplinary category but the latter one has higher diversity (greater coverage) than the former. If teaching was successful for both of these ideas, the productivity of teaching would be higher for the latter one. Furthermore, both ideas can be taught using a lesson that focuses on interpreting the genetic code; the difference would be how codons are introduced and investigated. It would be interesting to characterize the diversity of ideas and assess whether idea diversity, or, more accurately, idea coverage, influence the productivity of teaching and learning. Overall, there is an opportunity to investigate how idea diversity influences learning gains that begins with a quantitative estimate of idea coverage introduced by Ahmed and Fuge (see also Edwards et al., 2022).

Differences in Communities among Habitats

Education-relevant synopsis: Different environments produce different communities of students and of ideas. Differences due to the environment are expected outcomes of an emergent process. We should never expect that the same course taught by different instructors and designed in ways that make the experiences equivalent will, in fact, be equivalent: course equivalence is a myth. Being aware of the effects of the environment and cultivating productive environments remains important, nonetheless; we should strive to describe and embrace the differences rather than demand that students have the same experiences and learn the same knowledge.

There are discernible effects of habitat on community composition and function. For humans, the difference between rural and urban stands out. It also triggers a joke:

> If you stand naked on the front porch and the neighbors can't see you, it's rural.

> If you stand naked on the front porch and the neighbors call the cops, it's suburban.

> If you stand naked on the front porch and the neighbors ignore you, it's urban.

Underlying the joke there is a truth. Communities of people are different and the differences span multiple dimensions (Parker et al., 2018).

Much of community ecology focuses on explaining why different places harbor different communities. For plant communities, the numbers and abundances of different species is influenced by the availability of light for photosynthesis, the abundance of key nutrients (e.g., nitrogen and phosphorus, among others), space, temperature, precipitation, and the innumerable and varied interactions that happen between the various members of the community. Because there are so many variables with effects on the abundance and types of organisms that comprise a community, it is not surprising that no two communities are the same. There are also stochastic factors and myriad interaction effects that make each habitat and its inhabitants unique.

The uniqueness of communities was evident from the work of my colleagues and I that focused on estimating the degree of differentiation between two communities. One was a natural system and the other was constructed and engineered to emulate the natural system as a means of creating a new and identical environment for the protection of an endangered species of fish (Paulson et al., 2021). Despite attention to, and management of, the physical, biochemical, and biological details of the natural and constructed habitats, our work revealed the emergent communities in the two environments were discernibly and distinctly different. It proved impossible to emulate the natural ecosystem; the differences were evident for physical factors—sunlight, flooding, and temperature—and biological factors including the absence of a key species. Thus, despite a concerted effort to engineer and manage a habitat in ways that emulated the natural system inhabited by an endangered species, the two communities differed in myriad ways. In effect, engineering a habitat created conditions favoring the emergence of a new endangered species.

One axis of change in ecology is the abundance of resources supporting birth, growth, and maturation. Increasingly, global climate change and human activity have resulted in a steady and continuous background increase in the amount of carbon dioxide, nitrogen, phosphorus, and other resources fueling or limiting biological productivity (Smith et al., 2009). Continuous environmental change contributes to continuous change of communities, and in some cases communities become more divergent and others communities may converge, especially if environmental conditions become more and more extreme and favor a smaller and smaller set of species capable of existing in extreme environments.

Experimental studies that impose differences in the availability of resources can reveal dynamic and dramatic changes in the structure and function of communities. For example, in a large abandoned agriculture field, ecologists followed the fate of plant communities over a period of two decades for two treatments: one in which resources were added (by fertilization) and one that served as a control and did not receive nutrient supplements. The results clearly showed that the abundance of resources—in the form of fertilizer—altered the rank-order abundance of species. Additionally, fertilization also caused a decline in diversity. In this example, the addition of resources (fertilization with nitrogen and phosphorus) favored certain individuals relative to others. These results clearly demonstrated that the difference in availability of resources caused a difference in the ecological community that played out over time. It's not surprising that augmentation of resources causes shifts in relative abundance. It seems counterintuitive, though, that it also decreases diversity. The explanation is that different species have different functional properties and are "tuned" or adapted to specific niche characteristics. Moreover, the niche enabling growth, survival, maturation, and reproduction of individuals is multi-dimensional: there are many axes of environmental features and biotic interactions defining the boundaries of what is inhabitable. Increases or decreasing resources alters the niche dimensions of habitats in ways that favor some species and impose limitations on others. When resources are superabundant, eutrophication can happen, a process that decreases diversity and destroys the integrity and productivity of communities.

Is there evidence for differences in communities of students that are attributable to differences in resources? Are differences detectable between disciplines or between courses? To return to the pupfish story, when we followed the diversity and abundance of the two communities—the natural habitat and the engineered environment—over time, there were clear differences. Additionally, each community changed continuously over time. This particular example lends itself to thinking about what happens when we offer two different sections of the same course but try to engineer them so they use the same curriculum, use the same exams, and foster the same affective traits. This is often done as a way to ensure course equivalence; the assumption is that the learning experiences are equivalent between sections. The pupfish story tells us that for emergent processes—like ecology and education—we should not expect equivalence. We should expect the characteristics of the two communities to change over time in unique ways. Comparison of two sections of the same course using NMDS revealed a pattern of change based on aggregated data that resembled the portrait of change for the two habitats supporting pupfish. The idea that we can engineer equivalent education experiences for different groups of students being taught by different instructors goes against allowing education to be an emergent process.

The sensitivity of individuals of different species may have parallels with educational environments, because students vary in their functional properties and the ability to thrive depending on environment conditions. Variation in cognitive niche dimensions means that changes in available resources and environment will have differential effects on students. A change in environment may cause individuals who were performing at higher levels to slip a bit, and the rank order of individuals with respect to capability and academic achievement may shift. This was evident from studies of the effect of course structure and active learning on student achievement (Haak et al., 2011; Freeman at el., 2011; Eddy & Hogan, 2014; Dewsbury et al., 2022). There is also evidence, however, that active learning implemented with the expectation students engage in interaction generates anxiety, and a negative association between anxiety and academic performance suggests that there are shifts in rank order of individuals dependent on the intersection between anxiety, teaching mode, and achievement (Hood et al., 2021). Additionally, in some cases, depending on context and the intentions and abilities of educators, active learning environments may favor men more than women, in part because of self-reported lower self-efficacy of women than men (Aguillon et al., 2020). These specific effects can generate differences in communities.

One of the factors that has emerged as predictive for sustaining diverse communities of learners is a course structure in which there are many assessments of performance based on a variety of different cognitive challenges, including traditional exams but also active learning exercises including frequent multiple-choice "clicker questions" implemented in a peer instruction format, weekly practice exams comprising short-answer questions, and other challenges that represent continuous evidence of learning (Freeman et al., 2011; Haak et al., 2011). Courses with a variety and abundance of different types of assessments contrasts with courses in which assessments are infrequent, low-dimensional (see Matz et al., 2018) and high stakes (e.g., midterms and a final). Traditional courses with few high stakes (often selected response) assessments likely represent an environment at the top of a high mountain: cold, windy, and extreme. Importantly, Haak et al. (2011) discovered that the best model for the effect of pedagogical environment on student success included student diversity and course structure and the effect of these two variables was multiplicative (not just additive). The lesson imported from ecology is that we have to pay attention to whether we inadvertently impose "extreme" environments on students in ways that cause steep rank-order records of success.

Is it good that there are sometimes very different communities in the classroom? If the communities are emergent, if there is an increase in connectivity and complexity among individuals, and if students are able to pursue unique and varied trajectories of intellectual gain and achievement, then I think the answer is a definitive yes. In fact, we should actively encourage instructors to create opportunities for the emergence of communities that stem from the nuance and context of a particular discipline. If, however, the different communities exist because of decidedly different availability of educational resources, then the differences may be a symptom of poor instructor ability, constraints imposed by class sizes that exceed some critical threshold density, and inequities in the distribution of resources among students and among faculty rather than a positive outcome. We know the characteristics of the academic communities in courses taught using didactic and student-centered pedagogical practices will be different. In most cases, these differences are due to the effect of resources; our goal as educators is to allow differences to emerge as a consequence of education rather than as a consequence of inequities in access to resources or resource use that favors certain types of students.

The Role of Disturbance

Education-relevant synopsis: Disturbance is common in the world and it has the capacity to disrupt the structure and function of cognitive abilities. It is important to recognize disturbance and, because there can be both negative and positive effects, to engage in practices that limit the negative effects and recognize and act on the positive effects. Regular monitoring of students and the ideas in their minds is essential to identify whether disturbance has occurred and the magnitude of the disturbance, and for devising strategies for mitigating its negative effects and amplifying positive effects.

Disturbance is the disruption of the structure and function of communities usually in response to an episodic change in environmental conditions, including, but not limited to, fire, flood, high winds, and sustained extreme temperatures. The aggregated effects of disturbance can be positive or negative, depending on the outcome and the nature of disruption; however, the individual consequences that together define a disturbance event are negative, because individuals that comprise the affected community suffer injury or death. Sousa (1984, p. 356) defined disturbance as "a discrete, punctuated killing, displacement, or damaging of one or more individuals (or colonies) that directly or indirectly creates an opportunity for new individuals (or colonies) to become established." Sousa's description emphasizes that disturbance is an agent of change, because it causes the removal of established individuals that, with time, allows for someone or something new to become part of the community. Disaster is a particularly intense outcome from disturbance. There is the perspective that disaster triggers change, and change of this sort is often bad for most inhabitants (Klein, 2007). The other perspective is that disaster can be creative; "creativity enhances the ability to adapt to the demands imposed upon individuals and organizations during crises and bolsters capacities to improvise in new physical and social environments" (Kendra & Wachtendorf, 2003, p. 121). Disturbance is not always disastrous, though.

Three important factors of disturbance are its magnitude (the number of affected individuals), severity (the extent of damage or death), and frequency (the number of events per time). Chambers et al. (2013) compiled a history of disturbance events based on tree mortalities in forests and discovered that frequency is inversely related to magnitude (fig. 6.13). The distribution of the magnitude of disturbance events observed for trees in forests is probably general across many different environments

Figure 6.13. The frequency distribution of disturbance events of different magnitude. Magnitude is estimated by the area of forest affected. (2013). *Source:* Created by the author. Modified from Chambers et al. (2003).

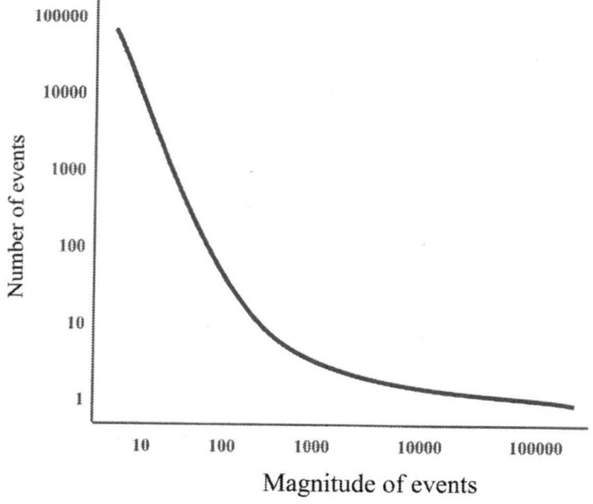

and sociocultural contexts. Large-scale and repeated disturbance can have the effect of permanently altering the species composition of communities. In general, communities are robust to the extinction of specialist, peripheral species but fragile if extinction happens to a core member of the ecological network (Dunne et al., 2002). Empirical studies show that the loss of a species can even lead to the collapse of an ecological community (Paine, 1966). Whether an extinction due to disturbance leads to secondary extinctions depends on the richness and connectivity properties of the community. In addition, repeated disturbance can destroy the capacity of habitat to support particular species and alter the normal successional processes due to the removal of key resources with each disturbance event. For example, in tropical landscapes, native forest is often repeatedly cleared to make the land suitable for cultivation of crops. The general practice involves clearing the land, growing a crop, allowing the land to be fallow for a period of time, clearing the land again, growing a crop, and repeating this process. An effect of this process is the loss of key nutrients. As a consequence of nutrient depletion of the soil, the community that can (and does) become established after agriculture is abandoned typically has low diversity and low productivity (Bauters et al., 2021). The hundreds or thousands of years of soil development and resource enrichment of natural places may be irreversibly destroyed by land use practices motivated by short-term profit.

In general, there are four outcomes following disturbance. These four outcomes are measured by the structure and composition of the emergent community (Seidl & Turner, 2022). The outcomes are most evident for forests because the spatial locations and sizes of trees define the structure, but structure can also be evident from the relative numbers and interactions of individuals of different species across a range of types of organisms (i.e., animals, plants, fungi, microbes, etc.). Resilience is when there is no change in structure and composition. Restructuring describes a scenario in which the structure changes but the composition stays the same. Reassembly changes the composition, but the structure remains the same. Finally, a regime shift is when both the structure and composition changes. The most remarkable and profound outcome is regime shift. One of the factors that makes regime shifts remarkable is that the changes in the community happen quickly and can have wide-ranging and often negative impacts (Bestelmeyer et al., 2011). Abrupt transitions between different community structures and composition happen when gradually changing environmental conditions pass some critical threshold value or when there is an abrupt, extreme disturbance. Bestelmeyer et al. wrote:

> State changes in biological responses are caused directly or indirectly by changes in environmental drivers. Drivers are usually abiotic and include changes in climate (e.g., temperature, precipitation), or land-use (e.g., resource extraction, nutrient input rates). Environmental drivers usually are considered "slow variables" because they typically change much more slowly than biological response variables. The textbook example of a slow environmental driver leading to a state change is long-term phosphorus input leading to an abrupt shift from oligotrophic (clear blue) to eutrophic (muddy green) lakes. Drivers can also change abruptly, however, with dramatic effects. Triggers (a.k.a. pulse disturbances) are either abrupt shifts in drivers or singular events, such as droughts, hurricanes, disease outbreaks, invasive species introductions, or fire, that directly affect biological responses. State changes often are caused by interactions among multiple drivers and triggers. (p. 3)

There is some evidence from ecology that some disturbance increases diversity and productivity of communities (Connell, 1978; Silva Pedro et al., 2016), although the effects on diversity and productivity will depend on the characteristics of the species in the community, the environmental context, and the magnitude and frequency of disturbance (Cardinale et al., 2005; Haddad et al., 2008).

It is likely resilience, restructuring, reassembly, regime shift, and increased or decreased productivity in response to disturbance can happen in educational contexts as well. Is there evidence of disturbance in educational communities? And if so, what are the effects? There are a few ways to characterize disturbance in education settings. Individual events that cause students to be absent from in-the-classroom learning activities represent a type of small-scale disturbance. In my own class, on any given day, there are students who decide, for myriad reasons, not to attend class. Documented reasons for absenteeism include course quality, students' motivation, topic, the sense of community in the course, workload, and time of day (Wolbring & Treischl, 2016); there are also factors that are student-specific, related to family, work, mental health, physical health, friends, and whether or not there was a recent snowstorm and there is fresh powder on nearby ski slopes. Lack of attendance in a didactic, content-delivery learning experience has little or no effect on socialization processes and experiences, but it does have a negative effect on the overall learning gains of the population of students. As expected, there is a negative effect on average gains with increasing absenteeism (Durden & Ellis, 1995). However, in student-centered educational experiences, when a student is absent, there is disruption: within-group dynamics are altered, there may be missing data or perspectives, interpersonal dynamics shift, and performance-based scores decline (Koppenhaver, 2006). These events are common and, with reference to the data from forests, they are similar to cases in which single or a few trees die and, as a consequence, alter the local conditions in the vicinity of the affected tree. The effect of absenteeism as a disturbance to productivity can be mitigated, however, by enacting student-centered pedagogy. For instance, Jakobsen et al. (2014) provided evidence that enacting student-centered pedagogy—in this case problem-based learning—increased attendance (decreased absenteeism). Thus, enacting student-centered pedagogy can limit the frequency of small-scale disturbance and its associated negative effects.

There are some cases when larger numbers of students are absent from class. Outbreaks of the flu or other viruses can cause relatively large numbers of students to stay away from school, and the effect is a transient reduction in the productivity of the population and a reduction of the gains possible for the affected individuals. For instance, Nichol et al. (2005) did a study based on ≈ 3,300 students enrolled at the University of Minnesota. The data were collected by survey, so it was a nonrandom sample of all students; however, the large number of volunteers suggests the results may be indicative of what happens at other large universities. Of the 3,300 students who completed the questionnaires, 91% had at least one cold or flu-like event between November and April. They reported that upper respiratory tract infections caused "6023 bed-days, 4263 missed school days, 3175 missed work days, and 45,219 days of illness" (p. 1263). Moreover, about 28% students reported they did poorly on a test and 46% did poorly on a class assignment as a consequence of the disturbance due to illness. These frequent and sometimes long-duration disturbance events reduce productivity; there are, as far as I can tell, no positive effects of this type of disturbance.

Another type of disturbance in educational systems manifests as changes in teaching modality as a student moves through a particular set of courses that constitute a training program. Teaching that is student centered and involves active participation and collaboration of students (see Chi & Wylie, 2014) stimulates intellectual growth and advancement towards a "climax" community of ideas in the increasingly expert minds of students. This is analogous to a productive ecological system. A disturbance happens when the productive learning environment changes to one that uses didactic, passive teaching strategies with the goal of having individuals (the students) memorize facts. Students are not provided opportunities to share their thinking with others and collaborate toward a common goal, and these experiences rarely result in the sustainable gain of core ideas. To make an analogy with ecology more tangible, we can classify individualistic, competitive, lecture-based classes as a slash-and-burn strategy. Bauters et al. (2021) wrote, "Repeated slash-and-burn cycles have substantially impacted soil total nutrient concentrations . . . increasing number of clearing cycles . . . [and]. resulted in an overall depletion of the total nutrient stock" (1429). We can substitute various resources for education, including but not limited to motivation, energy, interpersonal interaction, and sense of identity for the nutrients in an ecological setting. To make the analogy more compelling, we can do word substitution. Bauter et al's text in an education article might read . . . repeated didactic, low-cognitive level pedagogical strategies have substantially impacted the availability of resources . . . (and) resulted in an overall depletion of a student's capacity for intellectual development. There are similarities between slash-and-burn agriculture and the *status quo* of biology education in many institutions of higher education.

The effect of species extinction from disturbance may have parallels in education. To more fully articulate this hypothesis, here is a short passage from Christianou and Ebenman (2005): "The loss of a species from an ecological community can trigger a cascade of secondary extinctions. The probability of secondary extinction to take place and the number of secondary extinctions are likely to depend on the characteristics of the species that is lost—the strength of its interactions with other species—as well as on the distribution of interaction strengths in the whole community" (p. 95). By using word replacement—ideas for species—to make an explicit analogical bridge, the passage is provocative. The loss of an idea from the knowledge of an individual can trigger a cascade of secondary idea losses. The probability of secondary idea losses that take place and the number of secondary idea losses are likely to depend on the characteristics of the original idea that is lost—the strength of its interactions with other ideas—as well as on the distribution of interaction strengths among all ideas. Thinking about ideas as equivalent with species provides many analogical bridges between ecology and education suitable for honing in on the properties of ideas and how we can best manage ideas for constructing robust and connected networks underlying the emergence of disciplinary knowledge and the capacity to think like scientists and ecologists.

If we are interested in increasing productivity, whether in ecological or education settings, reliance on "slash-and-burn" (my perspective) lecture-based, didactic teaching approaches needs to be replaced by better and less destructive practices. Cultural change is imperative for the future of higher education. Additionally, we have to be willing to engage in data-driven revision of curricula, assessments, and teaching strategies as a regular part of our jobs as educators. Static curriculum and assessments accept and value complacency. In the absence of data-driven revision and change, we will continue to witness the destruction of a rain forest of cognitive diversity and productivity and its replacement by a monoculture of minds incapable of solving challenging and evolving problems through productive collaboration. The goal of education is not, as Thoreau warned, to make "a straight-cut ditch of a free, meandering brook." The goal is to allow the free, meandering brook to carve a path that traverses intellectual landscapes and eventually contributes to the ocean of ideas and solutions for solving pressing problems.

The disturbance caused by shifting educational environments and pedagogies also applies to the transition from high school to college. In addition to the change in developmental trajectories, the losses and gains of social ties, changing sociocultural contexts, and stratification systems (Benner, 2011), there are also shifts in class enrollment sizes and the correlated effects on teaching and assessment. The lack of coherence from high school to college represents a disturbance with potential lasting disruptive effects on students' intellectual maturation. Of particular importance is the shift from small class sizes and close, interpersonal proximity among students and between the teacher and student to large enrollment classes with few (if any) opportunities for authentic peer interaction and little or no direct access to the instructor. To underscore this difference, my colleague at a local high school teaches no more than 75 students across five different time periods of a day during a semester; the largest class size is less than 25 students. On average, the student-to-faculty ratio in a given course is $75/5 = 15$. By contrast, some of my colleagues teach more than 800 students across two or three different time periods of a day during a semester. The student to faculty ratio is in the hundreds.

It takes a very motivated student in such a high-density population to make a genuine interpersonal connection with the professor. Moreover, in such large classes, opportunities for interpersonal interaction and the development of social networks among students are limited or, more likely, do not happen.

If we (as educators) accept that each student occupies a different fundamental niche (see chapter 3) and that we, as individuals with limited time with students, are unlikely to significantly alter students' fundamental cognitive niches, then perhaps we should create learning environments that vary over time. This idea stems from my description of how coexistence and persistence is maximized in communities as a consequence of the variation of resources over time. Rather than offer the same educational experience every day over multiple days, educators might create different learning environments at different times by varying expectations and the resources provided to students. The disturbance in this context is varying the pedagogical framework that changes the set of fundamental cognitive niches that are favored over time. During some periods, the approach might emphasize content delivery using didactic approaches; at other times, the classroom might be flipped and students asked to know some content before they come together and make sense of information through collaboration and cooperation. Importantly, whatever teaching modality is implemented, it is important and necessary to remain committed to implementing well-established educational frameworks and teaching strategies that promote the organization, connection, and contextualization of big ideas and crosscutting concepts (Cooper, 2020; Roche Allred et al., 2022). It is also important to make sure students know why teaching modality changes and how they can be successful when confronted with different modes of teaching. This explicit and variable structuring of teaching style and mode can foster resilience.

It is important that educators subscribe to the idea that disturbance can be leveraged in ways that increase inclusion and diversity because it is implemented purposefully to enable greater alignment between students' cognitive niches and the provision of specific educational resources promoting learning. We need to work together to develop a coherent plan of intentional disturbance. Students should be "in the loop" about the purpose of changing teaching strategies and curricular resources, understand how regulated disturbance is a good thing, and that we pay attention to what happens to individuals and also analyze aggregated data and the stories of individuals for a more holistic perspective on the outcomes of teaching. The scale of managed disturbance is also important: do we implement managed disturbance within courses over the duration of a semester, do we implement it across courses within a disciplinary training program, or do we try to do both? If we do both, there will need to be greater emphasis on mutual understanding of different pedagogies among faculty, appreciation for differences in abilities and emphasis, and greater coherence of efforts and expectations. In other words, rather than offering an uncoordinated, individualized, and diverse set of student experiences across the large number of courses that form the basis for gaining a diploma, we should recognize that differences in pedagogy among courses is disturbing and we should more deliberately offer different pedagogical experiences stemming from an explicit set of core values about how intellectual advancement and the gain of academic and cultural capital is gained. Put differently, faculty need to shed the standard operating procedure of being a free agent when engaging in teaching and become part of a coordinated and collaborative team of educators implementing a similarly coordinated, connected, and coherent curriculum that constitutes an effective program of educational, intellectual, and social capital gains.

Invasive Species and Ideas

Education-relevant synopsis: There is a debate in the education literature about whether learning should build on misconceptions or learning depends on eradicating and replacing misconceptions. Ecology informs us eradication, if possible, is essential for developing mature and accurate knowledge about the world. Ecology also warns us that the invasion of ideas—especially demonstrably untrue and corrosive ideas—happens quickly and easily. Limiting invasion is possible if productive and well-connected communities exist.

Disturbance often creates a path into a community for invasive species. An invasive species also can be a biotic mechanism of disturbance. In this brief section, I introduce the idea that some ideas are like invasive species because of their effects on establishing a functional community of ideas in the minds of students. Many communities cannot resist the invasion of exotic species; the same is true for minds, as Victor Hugo (1877, concl., ch. 10) noted: "One can resist the invasion of an army but one cannot resist the invasion of ideas."

Species are described as invasive if they become established in ways that cause a significant change in the function, diversity, and taxonomy of a community. Most invasive species are categorized as exotic or non-native because they come from outside a particular community of interest, often from a different continent. Islands are particularly susceptible to invasive species. And most invasions happen as a consequence of human activity. Global trafficking of goods has resulted in many introductions of exotic species into communities, and although only a fraction of transported species are invasive, it only takes one to irreversibly change a community.

Once established, invasive species can have large effects on other species and typically cause declines in diversity. Eventually, invasive species become part of a community. Mooney and Cleland (2001) wrote:

> Since the Age of Exploration began, there has been a drastic breaching of biogeographic barriers that previously had isolated the continental biotas for millions of years. . . . The direct evidence of evolutionary consequences of the biotic rearrangements is of variable quality, but the results of trajectories are becoming clear as the number of studies increases. There are examples of invasive species altering the evolutionary pathway of native species by competitive exclusion, niche displacement, hybridization, introgression, predation, and ultimately extinction. Invaders themselves evolve in response to their interactions with natives, as well as in response to the new abiotic environment. Flexibility in behavior, and mutualistic interactions, can aid in the success of invaders in their new environment. (p. 5546)

I have worked on invasive species. One study investigated the effect of introductions of rainbow trout on the fate of native cutthroat trout (e.g., Metcalf et al., 2008). Rainbow trout are native to coastal streams of western North America; today the species has a worldwide distribution in temperate streams and lakes. The widespread distribution of the species stems from active reproduction and propagation in hatcheries coupled with widespread stocking of fish for recreation and food (Halverson, 2010). It is a textbook example of an invasive species made possible by human actions. The effects of trout introductions vary depending on context. In some places there have been little or no detectable effects on the native ecological community. For instance, the introduction of rainbow trout to high elevation streams in Hawaii did not appear to affect the stream insects (Englund & Polhemus, 2001). In most places, however, the introduction of trout caused discernible changes in communities; in particular, trout altered the niches of coexisting native species. Porcel et al. (2022, p. 2665) summarized comparative data that shows the introduction of rainbow trout is consistently associated with "changes in the planktonic communities . . . and shifts in the community macroinvertebrate structure . . . [Trout] exert a marked influence on the food web structure and nutrient cycles of . . . lakes." In Porcel et al.'s study, the change was most evident in the trophic structure, as indicated by the stable isotope analysis; the presence of trout "pushed" all members of the community to feed higher in the food web. Thus, the trout influenced community structure and function in part because they have strong effects on other species. In some cases, the introduction of trout caused decline in the number of individuals of native species. For instance, Knapp and Matthews (2000) discovered that

> negative effects of [introduced trout] on the distribution of frogs were evident at three spatial scales. At the landscape scale, comparisons between the two protected areas indicated that fish distribution was strongly negatively correlated with the distribution of frogs. At the watershed scale, the percentage of total water-body surface area occupied by fishes was a highly significant predictor of the percentage of total water-body surface area occupied by frogs. At the scale of individual water bodies, frogs were three times more likely to be found and six times more abundant in fishless than in fish-containing waterbodies, after habitat effects were accounted for. The strong effect of introduced fishes on mountain yellow-legged frogs appears to result from the unique life history of this amphibian which frequently restricts larvae to deeper water bodies, the same habitats into which fishes have most frequently been introduced. (p. 428)

The upshot is that invasive species can irreversibly change ecological communities.

Are there parallels between invasions into ecological communities by introduced species and the invasion and establishment of ideas in educational settings? Are there examples of invasive ideas with deleterious effects on the "ecology of the mind"? Can we use lessons from ecology to both limit the invasion and spread of ideas with deleterious effects and encourage the invasion of ideas with positive effects? Asking these questions prompts an important digression that gets at the issue of whether there are deleterious ideas or, to use a less provocative word, misconceptions. Put differently, there are true and false ideas about the world. True and false have objective truths in reality. However, things are not so simple. Maskiewicz and Lineback (2017) wrote a provocative paper entitled "Misconceptions Are So Yesterday":

> The title of this essay is excerpted from a broader set of statements one of the organizers of the 2012 Society for the Advancement of Biology Education Research (SABER) Summer conference posed at the closing discussion of the meeting. The attendees were charged with moving biology education research (BER) into its second generation, and one of the suggestions was to strengthen our research foundations by drawing from the learning sciences literature. While discussing the future of BER, the organizer stated: "Misconceptions are so yesterday." For some biology instructors, this may have seemed to be an odd statement. It certainly cannot be that students in the 21st century no longer have incorrect conceptions. The speaker's statement, however, may have stemmed from the fact that the word "misconceptions" is very rarely used in current science education and learning sciences literature (e.g., *Journal of Research in Science Teaching, Science Education, Journal of the Learning Sciences, Cognition and Instruction*), even though it is still common in practitioner-based BER. Why this discrepancy? The goal of this paper is to inform the growing BER community about the discussion within the learning sciences community surrounding misconceptions and to describe how the learning sciences community's thinking about students' conceptions has evolved over the past decade. We close by arguing that one's views on how people learn will necessarily inform pedagogy. If we view students' incorrect ideas as resources for refinement, rather than obstacles requiring replacement, then this model of student thinking may lead to more effective pedagogical strategies in the classroom. (p. 352)

What I like about this commentary on a process of collective under-standing of education is a recognition of how our understanding of the world—in this case education—changes as ideas are lost and new ideas gained. Maskiewicz and Lineback (2017, p. 352) continued: "The term misconception was widely used . . . to encapsulate the ideas that students' incorrect conceptions were often stable, widespread, resistant to change, and could interfere with learning. The natural consequence of this perspective of students' ideas is that incorrect ideas should be eradicated." In this context, misconceptions were perceived as invasive species in ecological contexts; they invaded the minds of students at some point in their development, changed the community of ideas and the structure of knowledge, and were resistant to control and eradication in ways that prohibited students' abilities to learn and understand biology. Maskiewicz and Lineback cited "Smith et al. (1994)" as the basis for making the case that "misconceptions are so yesterday." Smith et al. (1994) has been cited over 2,500 times and appears to be *the* seminal paper on misconceptions in education. Moreover, one of the coauthors is Andrea DiSessa, an architect of the knowledge-in-pieces framework. Smith et al. (1994) makes the claim that the constructivist theory of learning posits that students' prior conceptions—whether they are correct or incorrect—are "resources for growth within a complex systems view of knowledge. This theoretical perspective aims to characterize the interrelationships among diverse knowledge elements rather than identify particular flawed conceptions; it emphasizes knowledge refinement and reorganization, rather than replacement, as primary metaphors for learning; and it provides a framework for understanding misconceptions as both flawed and productive" (p. 115). Smith et al. (1994), Maskiewicz and Lineback (2017), and many others who followed the "misconceptions are resources" path assume prior knowledge is the foundation from which understanding is built, and therefore whatever prior knowledge students have is useful. In this context, "students learn by transforming and refining their prior knowledge into more sophisticated forms. Learning, from this perspective, is *not* the replacement of one concept or idea with another, but instead is a slow refinement of existing knowledge with relatively stable intermediate states of understanding preceding conceptual mastery" (Maskiewicz and Lineback, 2017, p. 353).

I appreciate this perspective, and that it is, in some ways, a statement that deficit thinking is not as productive as asset-based or strengths-based thinking. However, ideation theory, the knowledge-in-pieces perspective, and cognitive psychology[3] support a view that ideas are actual things in the same way individuals are things. Ideas are the fundamental units of knowledge and intelligence. My perspective is that education is similar to both ecology and evolution because it is an emergent process, and like ecology and evolution, change happens as a consequence of the birth and death of things: individuals in ecology and evolution, ideas in education. Assuming that education is an emergent process, ideas can die (they are lost from the mind) and new ideas can be born and establish themselves in the mind, and in this way, an individual's knowledge as a collection of connected ideas changes. There are correct and incorrect ideas, and a misconception is an incorrect idea that does not exist in nature in the same way as it does in the mind as an abstraction from nature. If we view misconceptions as resources and assume education is constructivist, then misconceptions as foundations persist indefinitely, but their effects are muted and minimized because they are effectively covered by whatever construction of more accurate ideas and knowledge happened as a consequence of education. It is possible education is both: an emergent process stemming from a birth and death process and a constructivist process in which everything is retained and undergoes transformation. I prefer to think of education as a process of births and deaths of ideas combined with the assembly of ideas into increasingly complex structures—models—that represent the world. Mine is a binary, zeros-and-ones perspective whereas the educators assuming misconceptions are foundational resources seem more like transformational. Transformationism was rejected as a coherent theory of evolution; the many similarities between evolution and education lead me to reject transformationalism as an operational description of education. My view is that misconceptions are more similar to invasive species with detrimental effects on ecological communities than they are resources. In fact, misconceptions compete for resources in ways that limit the success of correct conceptions. And as Dellantonio and Pastore (2021) affirm, "because misconceptions are embedded in a system, they cannot be rectified simply by replacing false beliefs with true ones" (p. 7473).

Misconceptions can be considered alien species that have invaded and become established in the minds of students. Smith et al. (1994, p. 120)[4] noted, in a section of their paper describing the central assertions of misconceptions research, that, "rather than being momentary conjectures that are quickly discarded, misconceptions consistently appear before and after instruction in substantial numbers of students and adults in a wide variety of subject-matter domains and are often actively defended" as being true and valid. Moreover, misconceptions can have profound, negative effects on learning and understanding and can become entrenched and limit or prohibit learning (Smith et al., 1994). Eradication of misconceptions is essential, in my view, if a mature, coherent, and accurate understanding of the world is a core educational goal. And as Smith et al. emphasize, idea eradication can be difficult, and for some ideas, impossible.

As someone who teaches evolution, there are established misconceptions that influence development of the community of ideas about biology in the minds of students. The ideas that evolution happens for "the good of the species" and that it is a directed process making species better are well-entrenched misconceptions. These ideas are invasive and influence the establishment and persistence of correct ideas. I have found that if students' understanding of evolution is built on these misconceptions, their ability to learn about the emergent process of evolution is compromised. I have found that it is best to confront misconceptions and try to help students replace them rather than use then as the foundation for constructing knowledge. Some ideas need to die before there can be new growth.

Interventions

Education-relevant synopsis: There is a strong incentive to engineer the human endeavor rather than allow outcomes from an emergent and complex process. Ecological restoration is an example of imposing a direct-process, engineering-outcomes mindset on an emergent process. The paradigm embodied by the myth of the objective is that we should abandon the direction-focused task of achieving specific goals and instead intervene in the educational paths of students in ways that promote the emergence of a functional knowledge structure rather than emphasize learning a specific content.

The history of ecology has been defined, in many ways, by a "man over nature" paradigm. Rossiter Raymond[5] wrote "What is Engineering? The control of nature by man. Its motto is the primal one—'Replenish the earth and subdue it.' . . . Is there a barren desert—irrigate it; is there a mountain barrier—pierce it; is there a rushing torrent—harness it. Bridge the rivers; sail the seas; apply the force by which all things fall, so that it shall lift things." We have been engaged in trying to engineer ecology since we have been subduing, irrigating, piercing, harnessing, and applying our collective force of extraction on nature. In response to the ecological damage wrought by wholesale subjugation of nature, ecologists have embarked on a crusade of restoration. Restoration ecology seeks to bring together population and community ecology in ways that direct how degraded communities can be engineered to increase diversity and productivity and save species from extinction. As a science, though, the fact that restoration defines the discipline suggests the intention stems from an impossible assumption that ecology is a direct process. It is not. We can't direct an ecological community to return to some idealized historical state. This is one reason why Palmer et al. (1997) wrote, "The problem of measuring restoration at the community level, particularly given the high amount of variability inherent in most natural communities, is not easy, and may require a focus on restoration of community function (e.g., trophic structure) rather than a focus on the restoration of particular species" (p. 291). Instead of thinking about restoration, it is best to imagine a process of engineering in ways that enable the emergence of a productive and diverse community. We may have to give up trying to "save" particular species or restore particular communities, and, instead, as Palmer et al. suggest, focus on other indicators of success. More importantly, we need to look forward, not backward. My view is that intervening in ways that influence ecological communities should be revised. Rather than looking backward in time and adopting historical states and conditions as objectives, we should look forward in time and engage in ecological intervention. Intervention is the idea that we identify ongoing issues and attempt to deflect the direction of change onto or into pathways that are more productive and resilient.

The subdiscipline of ecological intervention is where the rubber of theory and empirical work meets the road of community assembly and managed succession. It is ecology activated by the motivation and intelligence of humans interested in making the world a better place to live for all members of a functional community and fixing the degradation and damage wrought on an unsuspecting planet. In this sense, ecological intervention will have many similarities with education, because education is, ideally, data-driven intervention in ways that influence the evolution of students' cognitive niches. We need to ask if it is enough to establish a functional network of ideas—a knowledge network—even if the network is missing key ideas. My perspective as an educator and a common perspective among ecologists is that we need to distinguish between structural and functional outcomes and favor function over structure.

In general, the rank order of successful outcomes from ecological intervention by category is as follows: community structure > taxonomic diversity > functional diversity > taxonomic composition (Laughlin et al., 2017). Community structure refers to the network of interactions among individuals of different species. Taxonomic diversity is a measure of the abundances of different species or things. Functional diversity is a measure of the extent that different members of the community use varied resources in different ways. And taxonomic composition is the actual identity of species that comprise the engineered community. Laughlin et al. emphasized that the reason for this ordering of the success of ecological intervention is that these four aspects of communities are characterized by differences in variability as a consequence of the emergent process of ecology, and variability is inversely associated with predictability (fig. 6.14). Community structure is less variable and therefore more predictable and more amenable to intervention than the taxonomic composition. The variability and predictability of the other two properties of the community are somewhere in between community structure and taxonomic composition (Laughlin et al., 2017).

The findings by Laughlin et al. (2017) and others from studies of ecological interventions support using this framework for conceptualizing four key aspects of education across two dimensions: the variability of particular outcomes across communities or learners and disciplines (e.g., ecology, genetics, and evolution) and the predictability of outcomes (fig. 6.14). So, for instance, idea structure—the conceptualization of ideas as

Figure 6.14. Top: The order of different aspects of ecology resulting from ecological interventions with the goal of ecological restoration. The two scales for ranking—predictability and variability—are two sides of the same coin. Arrows indicate increasing predictability or variability. Modified from Laughlin et al. (2017). Bottom: The order of different aspects of educational gain resulting from educational intervention in ways that align with the ecological model. *Source:* Created by the author.

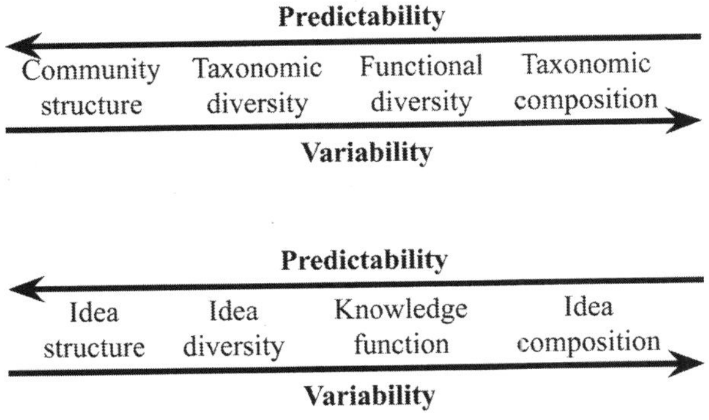

Predictability

Community structure	Taxonomic diversity	Functional diversity	Taxonomic composition

Variability

Predictability

Idea structure	Idea diversity	Knowledge function	Idea composition

Variability

being big or small and organized in such a way that small ideas contribute to big ideas—may be less variable, and, as a consequence, we might expect that all or most students in a class can hierarchically arrange ideas based on whether they are big or small. This would be an interesting prediction to test. At the other extreme, the specific composition of ideas in the minds of students may be highly variable both before and after learning happens and, as a consequence, the predictability of what specific ideas students gain and retain is low. I have good evidence that this aspect of Laughlin et al.'s prediction is evident. Thus, rather than beginning with a focus on content as a source of information for defining learning objectives, ecology suggests a more effective strategy—measured by predictability—is to emphasize connections between ideas—this is a measure of structure. Thus, perhaps the first lesson for educators from an analogy between ecological intervention and education is that developing a functional community of ideas in the minds of students may be easier and a more achievable outcome than establishing specific ideas in the minds of students.

One of my strategies when constructing and implementing lessons is to provide a structural diagram depicting the structure of knowledge (see fig. 2.9). The structure of knowledge is defined by the connections between ideas. Our current strategies when teaching biology often involve emphasis of a large number of different ideas. At the end of a semester, a thorough analysis of the curriculum might reveal hundreds or thousands of ideas introduced to students as important for disciplinary knowledge. The strategy emphasizes taxonomic composition—the most variability and least predictable outcome of ecological and educational intervention—over the structure of knowledge. It would be better to spend time on describing the interdependence of ideas—the interactions and connectivity of ideas—rather than ideas as distinct entities. Our current strategies are like giving students a pile of bricks without any way of knowing how to assemble the bricks into a house. A pile of bricks is useless, and yet the culmination of education at the end of a semester is often an assessment that asks whether there is a pile of bricks in the minds of students.

The main message from this brief foray into the similarities between ecological and educational intervention is to emphasize that there are multiple key outcome attributes that we can (and perhaps should) pay attention to and ideally measure. For ecology, the desired emergent outcome is a self-sustaining, dynamic, and productive community; for education, the ultimate outcome is the emergence of coherent and well-connected communities of ideas identifiable as knowledge. It is OK if species or ideas are missing as long as the community functions in ways that are productive.

Ecological intervention also takes on the challenge of controlling or eradicating invasive species because of their multiple deleterious effects on community structure and ecosystem function, and their financial costs (Colautti et al., 2014; Reeves et al., 2021). The first step necessary for controlling and potentially eradicating invasive species is identifying their existence in landscapes and documenting their abundance and effects (Colautti et al., 2014; Reeves et al., 2021). What we know, and what we have known since the emergence of invasive species in ecology, is that the success of invasive species happens as a consequence of inherent (genetic) factors that make some species good invaders and changes in the environment in which invaders live. This should sound familiar: it is about the inherent (genetic-influenced) characteristics of individuals and the environment in which they exist. I have been involved in projects with a focus on the control and eradication of invasive species. In one case study, crayfish invaded freshwater springs, an invasive that changed the structure, taxonomic diversity, functional diversity, and taxonomic composition of the communities (Paulson, 2012; Paulson & Martin, 2014). The eradication required the collection of key species and maintaining them outside of their native habitat while diverting the spring flow for a sufficient amount of time—more than a year—so that crayfish perished by desiccation. We followed the composition of the ecological community before and after removal of crayfish. The management actions resulted in the local eradication of crayfish and the emergence of a diverse ecological community (Paulson, 2016). Not all attempts at ecological rejuvenation by invasive species eradication are as successful; ours was successful because we could control the process. Importantly, though, our success was local; crayfish still exist within the broader watershed and reinvasion remains a possibility, because the movement of crayfish and its capacity for invading springs happens during episodic flooding. Nonetheless, what this work taught me was the value of targeted eradication and replacement as a means of managing the emergent process of ecology.

Because invasive species, and their detrimental effects, are often widespread, a continuing challenge is that managing ecological landscapes requires the coordination of efforts across land managers responsible for the ecological integrity and services provided by communities and ecosystems. Coordination among managers is difficult, and if there is defection, if one manager neglects to implement control or eradication strategies within their local jurisdiction as part of a collective effort, invasive species can persist and limit the effectiveness of control strategies (Epanchin-Niell et al., 2010). In other words, effective control requires all managers with oversight of landscapes with a particular invasive species to be on the same page. As I will emphasize shortly, effective control and eradication of misconceptions—and the fast thinking that allows misconceptions to flourish—requires dedicated, coordinated efforts across all educators who contribute to the intellectual maturation and academic achievement of students. If the efforts are local, there may be small successes, but the negative effects of invasive misconceptions will persist and ultimately undermine academic achievement.

Like ecology in which there are efforts to control the introduction and eradicate invasive species, educators attempt to control and eradicate misconceptions.[6] The first step is identifying and diagnosing misconceptions. Identifying misconceptions can be difficult, however (Coley & Tanner, 2015; Gouvea & Simon, 2018). Identifying misconceptions is subject to more uncertainty than we often imagine, in part because we are making inferences from incomplete information. Gouvea and Simon (2018) describe the problem: "To make the difference between observed data patterns and inference clear, we will distinguish between construal-based *formulations* and construal-based *cognition*. Construal-based formulations refer to spoken or written statements that communicate the logic of each construal; they are observable. Construal-based cognition refers to underlying patterns of thought; these patterns are inferred, not observed. This distinction is necessary, because . . . construal-based formulations often imply rather than explicitly articulate the logic that makes them problematic" (p. 2).[7] In biology education, the main frameworks for perceived misconceptions are teleological, anthropocentric, and essentialist thinking. It is difficult, however, to know whether an inferred misconception can be categorized into one of these types of misconception-laden thinking. For example, Gouvea and Simon (2018) argue that if cognition is modeled as a dynamic process of assembling pieces of information, expressions of an apparent teleological flavor are in-the-moment constructions rather than entrenched misconceptions. These limitations notwithstanding, there are persistent ideas in the minds of students with detrimental effects on the construction of coherent and predictive knowledge. For example, in evolutionary biology, there are many misconceptions; one of them is the idea that there is a selective "pressure" that acts like a "force" that causes evolution to happen (Nehm et al., 2010). This is an example of direct process thinking and it is pervasive when instructors teach about the process of evolution and in books used to convey an understanding of evolution (Nehm et al., 2010). In some ways, the implication that there is pressure and a force makes it easier for students to understand the outcomes of evolution. Yet, these terms, and how they are used, confounds a true understanding of the emergent process of evolution. It turns out that in both the field of ecology and evolutionary biology there are many examples of misconceptions—whether they are described in the context of teleological, anthropocentric, and essentialist thinking or as mistakes during the dynamic process of cognition construction of ideas in the minds of students. The question is: How do we train the cognitive process of idea assembly such that the outcome of student thinking is not compromised by misconceptions? How do we limit the invasiveness of misconceptions?

There are many general topics subject to misconception happening. In biology, the emergent process of evolution seems to be particularly rife with invasive misconceptions in part because "evolution often conflicts with our naïve theories, and intuitions about agency and purposiveness that developmentalists argue persist well into adulthood" (Heddy & Sinatra, 2013). Heddy and Sinatra, referencing others, also emphasize an emotional intersection with perceptions of evolution; that evolution means we are all, or should be, selfish, and that this perception may generate dissonance between personal beliefs and scientific perspectives resulting in disappointment and hopelessness. As a consequence, various groups have studied how we might teach about evolution that limits misconceptions. Heddy and Sinatra argue that misconceptions can be controlled, or limited, using teaching approaches described as transformative. Transformative teaching includes three core elements (Pugh, 2011). First, concepts (or ideas) have to be actively used by students in settings and contexts that are "in the wild," outside the classroom. For evolution or ecology, this might be in a park, a zoo or an accessible natural area (even a vacant lot if the setting is urban). Second, the teaching has to expand or change the perception of individuals. This means, effectively, that a student's perception of a thing is fundamentally altered such that when they look at it—say a mushroom growing on a dead tree—they think about it differently, and ideally more deeply and embedded in a richer context of interactions with other species or in terms of its existence as a representative of a deep lineage on the tree of life. Finally, transformative experiences must have personal experiential value. Experiential value is the idea that teaching changes the students' perception of themselves in the world. An ideal example might be the realization that students share a deep kinship and similarity with organisms in their environment, and that this realization changes how they think about and value nature. Of course, I'd guess all teachers teach with the hope of transformative emergent outcomes. What Pugh (2011), Heddy and Sinatra (2013), and others with a transformational teaching mindset articulate is that we, as educators, need to create opportunities for transformation, and these three aspects of transformation—active use, changed perception, experiential value—help us craft our approach. In effect, transformation is a product of student engagement, and student engagement depends on pedagogy. This type of teaching can be achieved using student-centered, active-learning pedagogy that involves making connections between what is being learned with the students' lived experiences, including connections to the world outside the classroom that is available to students (e.g., from newspapers, digital news feeds, and other sources), connections to students' individual biographies, and creating opportunities to put students into the frames of the stories being told when conveying the elements of understanding.

There are many good examples that accomplish core elements of transformative teaching. I often use drawing-to-learn strategies (Quillin & Thomas, 2015). For instance, I frequently ask students to draw pictures of the process of evolution. In one prompt, I ask students to draw a picture of the process of macroevolution—the gain and loss of species by speciation and extinction, respectively, over a long period of time—and have students include themselves and representative individuals of at least five other species in the picture. We do this more than once. When students first construct the picture, most draw a single lineage, or maybe a couple of lineages, and they—the students—are almost always at the end of the line and the other species are included as direct ancestors (or as stages leading toward the evolution of humans). A common progression begins with a single-celled microbe, passes through a dog or cat, a primate of some sort and ends in "me." By the end of the course, students draw a phylogenetic tree with many lineages emerging from many shared ancestors and all of the species are at the tips. We then use their trees for making biological predictions of the properties of species that depend on understanding shared ancestry. Importantly, students are constructing and revising their perceptions of the history of life, and they learn how to construct images that both accurately represent history and transform their view of life on Earth. Simple, fun, and sometimes the students' drawings are extraordinary. I often highlight students' work to the whole class and students are asked to vote on what they think is the best picture accompanied by the reason for their decision. This is not couched as a competition but rather as an opportunity for recognition of creativity and for students to see how others visualize their thinking.

I view this type of teaching as transformative and it seems to control misconception. However, misconception is not fully controlled, or eradicated, because transformative teaching requires engagement and all students do not fully engage. Moreover, one of the lessons learned about invasive species is that they are difficult to eradicate (Green & Grosholz, 2021), and, in some cases, eradication is impossible. What is true from ecology, though, is that the detrimental effects of invasive species in communities can be significantly limited by consistent and persistent actions aimed at removal. This can happen if educators collaborate and make it a goal to weed out misconceptions over multiple courses during the short academic life of most students. If the goal is an understanding of the emergent process of evolution, one of the core disciplinary content areas for biology education (see the Next Generation Science Standards or the American Association for the Advancement of Science science standards), evolution should be taught across all four years using transformative teaching practices and a mature and effective pedagogical framework (like the NGSS combined with the STeLLA [Lo et al., 2021] framework). And when we do this, we need to keep track of student understanding using free response questions scored by determining whether particular ideas are present or absent and if ideas are connected. If we do this, we can know how the community of ideas changes as a consequence of the gains and losses of ideas in the minds of students. We can watch succession and observe whether what we do as educators is effective and whether the invasive misconceptions persist in the community of ideas or are effectively eradicated. We can watch the emergent process of education happen. Unfortunately, in my disciplinary department, and in others, there is little curricular alignment and few opportunities to follow students' development across courses from the time they become established to the time they graduate. We have not achieved this type of collaboration because our culture is more individualistic and competitive than it is collaborative, and because many tenure-track faculty at a tier 1 research university are occupied with research and scholarly achievement at the expense of education.

In short, eradication of misconceptions requires the same diligence and effort that happens when eradicating weeds: identify, apply pressure to eliminate the invasive species, and replace it with another species so that the empty space is occupied and contributes resistance to future invasion. Importantly, because cognitive constructs are dynamic and subject to gain and loss, establishing correct conceptions will require repeatedly revisiting the key ideas and using formative assessments for monitoring the stability of cognitive constructs. Monitoring is an essential part of successful intervention.

The other side of the coin is intervention for the purpose of establishment of species that have been lost due to localized extirpations. And like the case of control and eradication of invasive species, it is oftentimes difficult for the focal species to become established, in part because the conditions that led to the extirpation of a species from a community often still exist. An important consideration is that the factors that improve the success of species establishment vary depending on context and the species. In grassland restoration projects, establishment success increases with the removal of existing organisms and their seeds in the soil seed bank combined with preparation of the soil (by tilling) (Kiehl et al., 2010); this may not be true for other environments (e.g., forests or deserts). Another factor is whether the introduced individuals begin as seeds, already germinated juveniles, or adults (for plants), as very young individuals or mature adults (for animals). For years, my colleagues and I were engaged in an intervention aimed at establishing an extirpated cutthroat trout into streams of Colorado's Front Range. It was clear that the introduction of more mature individuals had much greater success than when smaller, less mature and more vulnerable individuals were stocked. Additionally, Noël et al. (2011) showed that the establishment of plants in a wetland habitat was best predicted by the ecological similarity of locations between the source of plants being used for an introduction and the site of introduction: greater similarity was associated with greater establishment success. The number of separate introductions—introductions that happen at different times—increases the probability of successful establishment more than the number of individuals introduced (Hufbauer et al., 2013). Pywell et al. (2002) studied the effects of manipulating resources (nitrogen and phosphorus), soil preparation, and seed sources on the establishment of a functional grassland. The study revealed that "the most effective means of restoring diverse plant communities . . . was deep cultivation followed by the application of a diverse seed mixture comprising ecologically appropriate species. The most important constraint on achieving the assembly of these plant communities was seed limitation" (p. 307). Successful ecological intervention depends on identifying the limiting resources and eliminating the limitation. We can make the same claim for education: identify the limiting resources and eliminate the limitation.

There are several key dimensions that influence whether extirpated species can be established in communities. These features of establishment are listed in table 6.3 In addition, I included a parallel column describing an analogy with education. This list is by no means complete (e.g., see Godefroid et al., 2010; and others). What this list does, though, is underscore that establishment of ideas in the minds of students, like the establishment of individuals of extirpated or low abundance species in ecological settings, is difficult, and the challenge is distributed across multiple variables typical for emergent processes.

Table 6.3. List of factors in ecological and educational contexts that influence the success of establishing new individuals (ecological) or ideas (educational)

Category	Ecological strategy	Educational strategy
Presence of existing competitors	Remove existing individuals and their seeds (propagules).	Eliminate misconceptions.
Maturity and dependency	Introduce more mature individuals rather than seeds (plants) or immature stages (animals).	Introduce well-developed ideas with their connections to other ideas instead of isolated ideas.
Source of individuals	Choose individuals for introduction from similar environments.	Choose ideas that may be familiar to students.
Number of introductions	Repeatedly introduce individuals to increase probability of establishment success.	Repeatedly introduce ideas to increase probability of establishment success.
Preparation of the environment in ways that improve individual success.	Add resources to the environment that improve probability of establishment success.	Add resources that improve probability of establishment success.

The idea of introducing more mature ideas, or ideas connected to other ideas, makes good sense. Ideas do not become knowledge, do not become part of a coherent and useful model of the world, unless they are connected and integrated with other ideas. This is one of the main points of this chapter. Thus, rather than introduce one idea in isolation from other ideas, ideas need to be introduced as part of a system. Roth and Roychoudhury (1993) showed that concept maps—a picture of explicit links between ideas—contributed to the organization of ideas in ways that stabilized them in the minds of students; however, they also discovered that when advancing the establishment of an idea with the aid of including other ideas, there was a greater opportunity for, as explained by the authors, "unintended and scientifically incorrect notions [to] become ingrained and go unchallenged" (p. 503). One strategy that minimizes unintended outcomes is to build concept maps, or idea hierarchies, a few concepts at a time, continuously revise and add new ideas over time, and do so such that the emergent structure emerges over time rather than exists only as a consequence of a single activity. The best experience is to have students keep a digital notebook, and have them copy and paste existing concept maps prior to adding new ideas and making new connections. In this way, students and instructors can see the emergence of the structure of knowledge.

In ecology, the sources of individuals matter when trying to establish a species in an ecological community where it is absent; this is also true for ideas. The success of introducing new ideas in the minds of students depends on a somewhat intangible sense of the intellectual distance of the idea to existing ideas in the minds of students. This means that, as much as possible, we need to know what is in the minds of students, that we have revealed their thinking with elicit and probe questions, and we effectively use this information to choose ideas that are cognitively similar to existing ideas. If we do this effectively, each new idea, after being established, becomes a springboard for introducing the next new idea, and the next, and this process should be possible to sustain indefinitely. To make this more real, imagine we seek to introduce the idea that mutation is random. We would want to know what, in the minds of students, corresponds to something that is bona fide random. Perhaps it is the lottery, perhaps it is whether it will rain or where it will rain, or perhaps it is their sense that the world is chaotic. Each of these may be a starting point for cultivating an environment for establishing this new idea—that mutation is random. Additionally, increasing the number of times a new idea is introduced should increase its probability of establishment. However, like many things, context and approach matters. Simply saying the new idea over and over likely does nothing to improve establishment. Ideally, students are immersed in transformative teaching practices (described earlier) multiple times, ideally across their entire training program, in ways that make it clear to students that the idea is important and an integral piece of the structure of knowledge.

Finally, we should, as educators, pay attention to the environment in which students learn, and prepare the environment in ways that improve individual success. We often focus on what and how we teach, and fail to adequately consider whether the environment in which we teach has sufficient resources necessary for establishing new ideas. One of the key resources is engaging in pedagogical best practices and slow thinking strategies. Put differently, and more succinctly, the key resource is having time to effectively teach and for students to effectively learn. Time should be used based on what is accomplished rather than what has been planned. We have to be willing to give up the best laid plans to focus on successes that unfold in real time. Another important aspect is whether students have developed a strong sense of belonging and feel safe to explore, converse, interact, and test out their ideas publicly in ways that allow them to reveal their thinking as a first step toward revision and refinement by having teachers, mentors, and peers support and challenge their thinking.

Agriculture and Education

Education-relevant synopsis: Much of education happening today resembles agriculture: it is implemented as a direct process guided by objectives. Thinking of education as an emergent process challenges this perspective and provides an opportunity for comparing and contrasting education and agriculture. Education is like agriculture only if we continue objectifying the outcomes and imposing constraints on the natural tendency of education to be an emergent process.

Agriculture has been and mostly continues to be an exercise in making ecology a direct process. It is the ultimate control of nature in ways that increasingly divert resources toward fueling the population growth of a few species, mostly *Homo sapiens*. And it is done in ways—as Franklin Roosevelt pointed out when he said, "A nation that destroys its soils destroys itself"—that imperils the capacity of nature to supply the demands we make on it. I began the book with the story of the three sisters—beans, corn, and squash—and a contrast between ecology as a direct process (e.g., modern agriculture) and ecology as an emergent process (e.g., a hardwood forest). I also contrast education as a direct process and an emergent process. The allure of forcing emergent processes to be direct processes is attractive, because direct processes are more controlled, more predictable, and more amenable to generating profit than emergent processes. What we lose by prioritizing specific objectives is the ability to achieve greatness. Greatness depends on leaving open the possibility of achieving multiple, different outcomes that are unknown until they emerge. And some of the unknown but achievable outcomes represent innovation. Unknown and innovative outcomes often depend on the collective actions of a diverse community.

I came across the musings of a senior product marketing manager for artificial intelligence who wrote that "education is very much like fast food, and that it should really be more along the lines of agriculture." One of the stories from comparing agriculture and education in the context of whether they are direct or emergent processes is about how we nourish ourselves—both mind and body—and take care of the land and the ecological services on which all life depends. The protagonist of the story is diversity. In the context of agriculture, if we value diversity, it may mean abandoning the common practice of planting genetically identical plants (i.e., a monoculture) and instead using genotypically variable seeds (i.e., a polyculture). In the monoculture, insect pests and pathogens can easily move from plant to plant with large negative effects on productivity (Tooker & Frank, 2012). By contrast, polyculture means each plant presents pests and pathogens with a unique challenge due to the variation in genes associated with resistance to herbivory and infection. Table 6.4 summarizes some of the differences between monoculture and polyculture practices. Fundamentally, recognizing the value of individual differences and creating the conditions fostering a diverse community increases productivity. Similarly, manipulations of agricultural practices that increase the number of different individuals in the community can lead to "improved nutrition for farming communities, the creation of habitat for wildlife, and the enhancement of regulatory ecosystem services provided by insectivorous and snail-eating birds" (Horgan et al., 2017, p. 1355).

We can think about education similarly. If we value diversity, it may mean abandoning the common practice of large-enrollment, professor-centric, lecture-based pedagogy that ignores population-thinking and

Table 6.4. Differences between monoculture and polyculture agricultural practices

	Monoculture	Polyculture
Individual differences among plants	Absent	Present
Individual plants use resources differently	No	Yes
Variation in herbivore and pathogen resistance	Absent	Present
Herbivore or pathogen abundance	Higher	Lower
Sustainability of productivity	Low	High

Source: From Tooker and Frank (2012).

assumes all individuals function similarly and equally. A revision of Tooker and Frank's (2012) comparison between monoculture and polyculture agricultural practices in ways that apply to education provides a guide for enacting inclusive educational practices (table 6.5). The purpose is the same: we want to cultivate and promote productivity by leveraging the differences among individuals through the social construction of knowledge. Rather than compare and contrast mono- and polyculture, we can think of the educational equivalents of these agricultural conditions. Agricultural monoculture best corresponds with the didactic, professor-centric, content-based pedagogy, and polyculture best corresponds with a student-centered educational experience in which the purpose is to reveal the diversity of student thinking and support and challenge student thinking in ways that benefit all individuals and the overall productivity of the educational experience. Table 6.5 provides the basis of a coherent argument in favor of enacting student-centered, active-learning pedagogy. To do otherwise is malpractice. Yet, if we survey instructors and the courses in which they teach, we continue to find that professor-centric, didactic learning experiences, often in large-enrollment courses, is the most common teaching modality for STEM disciplines (Stains et al., 2018). This has become so accepted that my colleagues teaching in the arts and humanities often assume science classes are best taught using didactic practices with large enrollments. There is an entrenched misconception that science classes can be effective with large enrollments because science is about facts. This is a misconception that needs eradicating.

Table 6.5. Differences between didactic and student-centered educational practices

	Didactic	**Student-centered**
Individual differences among students	Ignored	Emphasized
Individual students use resources differently	No	Yes
Emphasis on sense of belonging and self-efficacy	Absent	Present
Frequency of cheating and social subversion	Higher	Lower
Course productivity and collective learning gains	Low	High

Source: Modified from Tooker and Frank (2012; see table 6.4).

I began this book in a place where ordered rows of corn meet hardwood forest. The ecotone where the two worlds contact and connect provide a stark contrast between two processes: one direct and predictable, the other emergent and infinitely dimensional. The ecotonal contact inspired the cover of this book and continues to provide contrast useful for guiding my educational journey toward embracing the challenge of teaching in ways that allow the emergence of surprising and inspiring outcomes that resist objectification.

Conclusion

In this book I emphasize the value of using language and knowledge from ecology as a basis for constructing inferences about education. The transfer of information and ways of thinking and doing from ecology into education stemming from analogy works and proves useful for making inferences that may fuel change in why and how teaching happens at the tertiary level. One way to make the transfer from ecology to education is to engage in word substitution. I have selected a few passages of text from a publication about community ecology and translated them into text relevant for education. The purpose of doing so, as I emphasized earlier, is to make the analogy explicit by transferring context and inference across disciplines. This exercise in word substitution can be done from a wide diversity of ecological research publications. Here I focus on a paper of broad scope and inference in community ecology. The paper spans scales of organization and time and in doing so provides a picture of how change happens.

Jackson and Blois (2015) wrote, "An ecological community can be viewed as a single point in a spatial framework of species distributions superimposed on environmental gradients and patchworks and in a temporal framework of population and biogeographic responses to environmental change and variability" (p. 4917). If we substitute constructs relevant for understanding education, with a focus on ideas instead of species, this quote might read: *A community of ideas can be viewed as a single point in a framework of idea distributions superimposed on instructional environment gradients and patchworks and in a temporal framework of individual responses to pedagogical change and variability of educational strategies.* Or, in plain English, the ideas evident in the mind of a student is one set of ideas among the many possible combinations of ideas that depend on teaching and the individual's response to educational experiences that vary over time.

Jackson and Blois continued, "Determinants of community structure and composition are a central focus of community ecology and tend to align with one of three modal concepts: interaction assembly, environment assembly, or neutral assembly. Interaction assembly . . . emphasizes [that] communities [are] structured primarily by strong interactions among species. Such interactions may include facilitation, mutualism, and trophic relationships (predation, parasitism, herbivory)" (pp. 4917–4918). For education, we can translate this to read: *Determinants of the structure and composition of knowledge are a central focus of education and tend to align with one of three modal concepts: interaction assembly, environment assembly, or neutral assembly. Interaction assembly . . . emphasizes the community of ideas in the minds of students is structured primarily by strong interactions among ideas. Such interactions may include facilitation (one idea makes it possible for another idea to exist), mutualism (ideas synergistically and positively reinforce each other), and hierarchical relationships (some ideas consume and replace other ideas).*

In addition, Jackson and Blois wrote, "Communities under environment assembly are structured primarily by species' physiological and demographic responses to the physical environment. The environment-assembly concept is . . . niche-based. . . . It is predicated on all species having finite environmental requirements or tolerances, which impose strong filters on community membership. Community composition is governed by whether potential members' fundamental niches overlap with the local environmental realization" (p. 4918).

In the world of education this might read: *The communities of ideas in the minds of students are structured by each individual's cognitive niche. Each individual's cognitive niche imposes some filter, depending on the learning environment, on which ideas take hold and which ideas remain elusive.*

Jackson and Blois continued, writing, "Neutral assembly considers communities to be structured entirely by random processes, particularly dispersal, recruitment, and mortality. Neutral communities have virtually unlimited membership, are nonequilibrium, and bear historical imprints; composition is influenced by legacies of past demographic and dispersal events, and hence community properties may drift as the result of singular events" (p. 4918). In the world of education this might read: *Neutral assembly of ideas in the minds of students is structured entirely by random events, particularly the flow of ideas from events and experiences outside of education and the random loss of ideas simply because the ideas do not take hold in the minds of students. Neutral communities have virtually unlimited membership (all ideas can potentially colonize a student's mind), the ideas are dynamic and ever-changing, and the community of ideas in the mind of a particular student is due to past events. In this model, the community of ideas in students' minds drift: ideas come and go without any apparent tethers to create stability.*

This strategy of engaging in analogy-making through word substitution and revision can be an excellent tool for making explicit bridges from one discipline to another: from the well-described and well-known ecological processes to the less understood world of how students learn and become self-efficacious and effective critical and creative thinkers. Just because it's insightful, here is another example. In this case, we adopt a longer-term perspective. Again, the quotes come from Jackson and Blois (2015). In this quote, Jackson and Blois tell a story about the community of trees over a long period of time based on pollen sampled from the sediments in Tower Lake: "All the major and most of the minor upland forest species in the surrounding region (central Upper Michigan) are represented in the Tower Lake record. Surrounding forests now are dominated by *Fagus grandifolia*, *Tsuga canadensis*, *Acer saccharum*, and *Betula alleghaniensis*, with scattered *Pinus strobus*. This combination of species has existed at the site for the past 1,400 y, starting with the colonization and expansion of *Fagus*, which expanded eastward in the region during the past 3,000 y. Thus, the forest community at Tower Lake has existed for no more than 1,400 y, and it arose from an interaction between local ecological processes (dispersal, demography, competition) and regional biogeographic processes (range expansion). Those regional processes depended in turn on local ecological processes at countless other individual sites, were driven by regional climatic changes spanning centuries or more, and may have been modulated by annual-to-centennial-scale climate variability."

If we revise the quote that stemmed from an investigation of the paleontology of ecological communities so that it applies to the evolving collective intelligence being conveyed and transmitted by education within a discipline (e.g., ecology or biology) through generations, it might read something like this: *If we collected evidence for all the major and most of the minor key ideas in a particular discipline over many generations, we would discover that the most common and well-accepted ideas evident today have existed for only a fraction of the history of the discipline. The current community of ideas arose from an interaction between local ideas generated from within the discipline and the incorporation of ideas from outside the discipline. The ideas emerging from outside the discipline depended on the processes in other disciplines that were driven by shifting intellectual and cultural climates spanning generations.*

We can apply this thinking to our understanding, through education, of a key idea in ecology. If we think about the concept of a niche, the community of ideas began with typological thinking: all individuals within a species are identical and the properties of species do not change over time. If we sampled the community of ideas now, the typological ideas that were dominant in the past are rare or absent. Instead of the idea that all individuals within a species have fixed and immutable traits, the most common idea may be that each species consists of a large number of individuals that all vary due to the effects of genes and environment. Similarly, the change of communities over time was thought to reflect deterministic processes. Now the idea that all change is due to deterministic processes with predictable outcomes is rare, because it was replaced by the idea that change is governed by a combination of deterministic and stochastic processes. Thinking about ecological process over time and evaluating how ideas about the world change underscore that what we think is important for students to know changes over time, and that the most persistent aspect is not so much what we know—the specific facts and ideas—but how ideas are structured and connected into knowledge that forms the basis for making sense of the world.

I have also revised another passage from Jackson and Blois (2015, p. 4917–4918): *Determinants of learning ideas and connecting ideas into knowledge happens as a consequence of three processes of learning: one emphasizing interactions, one emphasizing the effects of environment, and one that invokes random events. An emphasis on interactions is deeply rooted in a worldview in which knowledge emerges from strong interactions among ideas, especially competition between competing ideas and positive interactions that result in building a hierarchical structure of ideas into functional knowledge. Interaction-generated knowledge has limited membership of ideas and is largely governed by competition among ideas and the cognitive capacity of individuals. Knowledge developed based on the assembly of ideas due to the environment are structured primarily by ideas' resilience and stability within the developing minds of students challenged with navigating a complex landscape of information. The environmentally determined assembly of knowledge emphasizes a Grinnellian niche. It is predicated on all ideas having finite environmental requirements or tolerances, which impose strong filters on whether an idea is accepted and integrated in the cognitive development of an individual or rejected without enabling a robust competitive interaction between rival ideas. An example of filtering is the choice of topics or ideologies a student encounters during their education. In this model of cognitive development, different individual paradigms stem from different cultural contexts. Finally, knowledge may emerge from stochastic processes as a consequence of events that lead to the colonization or loss of ideas within the minds of students. This process is considered neutral in the sense that each idea is equally likely to be gained or lost in a student's mind, and an individual's knowledge is a more-or-less random assemblage of ideas. These three models of cognitive development are not mutually exclusive; each likely contributes to the community of ideas in students' minds.*

What is gained from the explicit, revisionist analogy between the description of a community of species and a community of ideas is that there are multiple models that explain the assembly and dynamics of ideas over time: an interaction-based model, a model in which the environment determines the outcome, and a stochastic model. Each of these provides a framework for generating and testing predictions, and evaluating the extent that learning is due to interpersonal interaction, the environment, and random events. The random model posits that ideas are likely to be present and absent over time and to lead to dynamics best explained by a stochastic process. By contrast, if the environment determines the outcome, some ideas will never be gained and the ideas that are gained are likely to remain and not be replaced by more accurate (competitive) ideas. Finally, the interaction model predicts a process of active and predictable change in ideas that increasingly resemble expert knowledge. Like real ecological systems, knowledge mostly exists as a consequence of an interaction model, but is also influenced by both random events and filtering by the environment. As educators, we need to work toward creating scaffolded opportunities for the interaction of ideas, connecting ideas, and rearranging the connections into natural hierarchical structures of knowledge.

There are other community-scale processes and outcomes that could enable useful inference from analogy for education. Nevertheless, I have provided a broad scope of topics and contexts. The purpose of this book, the reason why I wrote it, is that we can learn a lot about the process of change from paying close attention to ecology as a process. Ecology is an emergent process of change. Ecology provides myriad examples of change across many scales of time and space. Education is also a process of change; yet, it seems we remain stuck in a 20th-century view of the world as a direct, "control of nature," process. My hope is that the publication of this book provides a springboard for enacting an ecologically grounded pedagogy that enables the emergence of intellectual greatness in all students. Importantly, the greatness that emerges will be different among students; there will be a diversity of greatness that forms the necessary collective intelligences for confronting and solving many of the most pressing and confounding problems that emerged from an expanding civilization dependent on ecology.

In this book I have laid out a long argument that we can gain valuable insight and inferences about education by constructing analogies with ecology because both ecology and education are emergent processes. My purpose has been to think differently about education and come away with strategies for creating pathways of change inspired by nature. These pathways of change are only realized through thoughtful and purposeful construction of learning experiences. I began with the conceptualization of education as a process of hill climbing on a topologically complex landscape, with multiple peaks and valleys of knowledge. The fitness landscape imagined by Sewall Wright shows what an emergent process might look like, and leads to the inference that individuals and groups of individuals may traverse an expansive landscape of combinations of ideas that form the basis of knowledge. Pathways of enlightenment and knowledge gain should differ among students and, ideally, students arrive at different peaks of categorically "expert-like" knowledge. This inference naturally leads the question: How do students cross valleys and summit intellectual peaks? (See figs. 1.1 and 1.2.) Adopting an ecology-inspired pedagogy means enacting teaching as a science and collecting data on where and how students move across the effectively infinite landscape of knowledge and to use the information to both assist students in their quest and enable data-driven revision of teaching. Ecology is a science and its main tool for understanding why, how, and what change happens is to follow the interactions and fates of individuals of a population or community in the context of a continuously changing environment (Hughes et al., 2017). Thus, the actionable conclusion of this book is that we should consider emulating studies of change in ecological settings for better understanding and evolving education.

This book started with a glimpse at the data about students in an institution of higher education collected automatically from the two main streams: from the individual properties of students and from the enrollment and outcomes (e.g., grades and persistence) of individuals in particular courses. While these data are informative, they are also insufficient. In ecological settings, scientists often pay attention to the aspects of each individual's multivariate phenotype. Individuals in ecological settings are not simply characterized using categorical grades (A, B, C, etc.), but as a set of measurable features, and these features can be used in ways that can explain why some individuals are more successful—measured by survival and reproduction—than other individuals. In education settings, there are learning goals in each course a student takes. Whether students master a particular learning goal provides rich data for characterizing their multidimensional cognitive phenotype. Whether a student learns particular key ideas and builds a coherent and complex knowledge structure or whether ideas are fleeting and knowledge structures remain simple in the minds of students represents two categorically different outcomes that cannot be known using the current system of disconnected courses and categorical ranked outcomes. The archipelago of islands of instruction that form the basis of a students' higher educational experience can and should be better integrated by prioritizing collection of data that captures finer-scale dimensions of intellectual development. We have the capacity for characterizing aspects of the trajectory and complexity of intellectual development. Why settle for using grade point averages to capture the multidimensional cognitive phenotype of individuals?

Education would benefit from adopting a "big data" approach that has become central to studies in ecology. The National Ecological Observatory Network (NEON) emphasizes continuous collection of data across a large number of ecological variables over long periods of time as a core element of knowing why the world we live in changes, how it changes across many different variables, and what changes emerge as most important. Edmonds et al. (2022) noted that "the massive amounts and types of data NEON generates, in conjunction with other national-scale datasets, will allow the research community to better understand how . . . ecosystems function and respond to drivers of long-term change." Higher education can achieve similar goals, and ecologists have provided educators with realizable strategies for using data to better understand function and respond to drivers of long-term change. This realizable scientific teaching approach begins by developing a coherent monitoring framework. To take a page out of NEON's playbook, we need to shift our assessment strategies from a local, single-course perspective to one in which there is a large and evolving data matrix with date, geographical location (equivalent to the student), a set of abiotic variables (equivalent to course environments and pedagogical frameworks), and a set of biotic variables (equivalent to the presence or absence of pieces of knowledge in the minds of students) that spans the time and places where students work from matriculation to graduation. A critical component of the big data approach is development of assessment tools for measuring the presence and absence of student knowledge and abilities coupled with the measurement of environmental variables. Additionally, monitoring would require all faculty within a discipline—and ideally across disciplines—to participate and agree on a core set of knowledge and abilities and agree that in each course there are concerted efforts to collect relevant data from students and about the instruction strategies employed. I imagine that the number of pieces of knowledge and evidence of abilities would be large. Based on my own experience teaching both lower- and upper-level biology courses, the number of elements (label I_N in fig. C.1) of the collective intelligence matrix for a single student would be in the thousands. Moreover, each student should be assessed for each element multiple times over the duration of the higher educational experience.

Figure C.1. A small piece of a vast matrix of data estimating the emergent process of education based on monitoring individuals and the teaching environment over time within and across courses. The scale of the data depends on the number of students included, the courses included, the number of ideas included, whether the interactions of ideas is recorded, the type of teaching, and so on. *Source:* Created by the author.

Name	Date	Class	I_1	I_2	I_3	I_4	I_5	...	I_N
A	1/12/24	1210							
B	1/12/24	1210							
N	1/12/24	1210							
A	9/15/24	2040							
B	9/15/24	2040							
N	9/15/24	2040							
A	2/15/25	3080							
B	2/15/25	3080							
N	2/15/25	3080							

I will use a small part from one of my courses to illustrate the value of a data-based approach. I teach a course focused on understanding evolution. Most students entering the course, regardless of their prior educational experiences, occupy one of four different places on the Wrightian knowledge landscape (labeled 7, 8, 9, and 10 in fig. C.2). These places of knowledge are evident from asking students to illustrate the process of evolution (fig. C.3). These pictures of evolution differ markedly from expert-like visualizations of the process (fig. C.4). Importantly, this small example of the complexity and diversity of knowledge in the minds of students provides a glimpse of what the landscape might look like if knowledge across subdisciplines in biology and across disciplines were integrated into a single matrix and subjected to an analysis that revealed the topological complexity of novice plus expert-like ideas in the minds of students and the pathways students take to achieve knowledge and more accurate and complete understanding of the world. The provocative model of stepping stones across a lake of possibilities developed by Lehman and Stanley becomes the stepping stones up the endless slopes toward greater intelligence on a rough landscape with many peaks.

Figure C.2. A picture of a Wrightian landscape for knowledge of the process of evolution. There are 10 points, indicated by oval circles that describe different combinations of ideas that represent specific examples of knowledge about evolution. *Source:* Created by the author.

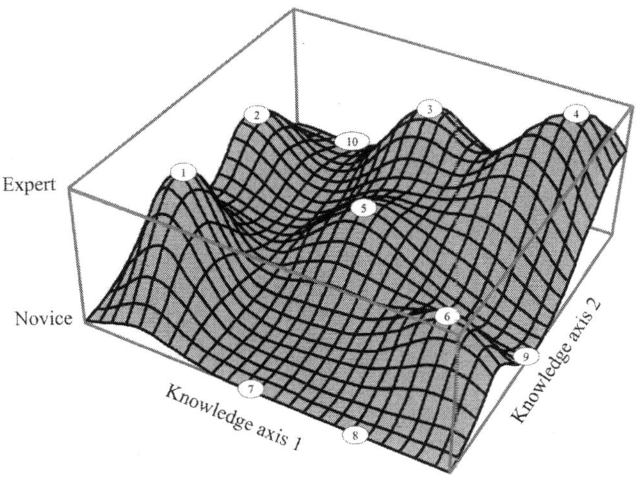

Figure C.3. Four examples of student visualizations of the process of evolution. Each of the four visualizations are insufficient to fully explain evolution and represent four different novice perspectives labeled 7–10 on a knowledge landscape (see fig. C.1). *Source:* Created by the author.

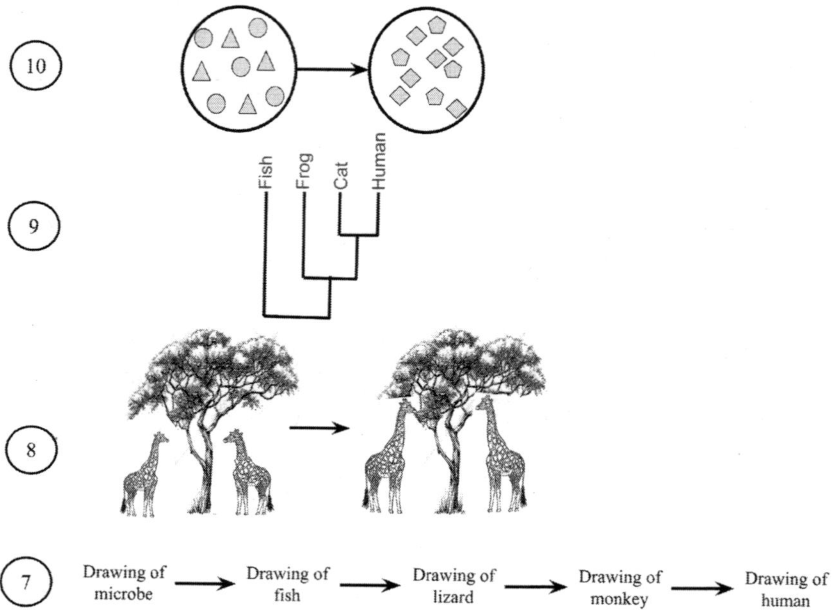

Figure C.4. An example of an illustration that has multiple ways of visualizing aspects of the process of evolution. Students may have different components of this visualization that correspond with various peaks (labeled 1–6) on the knowledge landscape (see fig. C.1). The details of this visualization are not particularly important, but this visualization departs in significant ways from novice visualizations (see fig. C.3). *Source:* Created by the author.

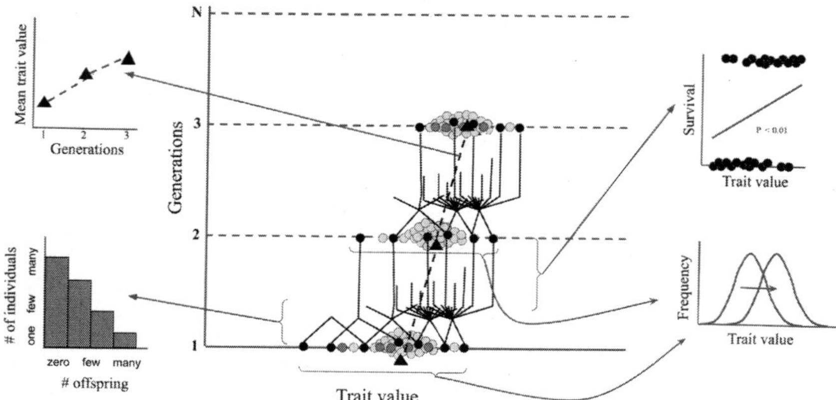

Achieving this NEON-like gold standard of educational data monitoring is beyond the capacity of the current structure of higher education because most faculty do not have time to engage in this type of data collection, curation, and analysis. However, we can emulate how the science of ecology is done. At NEON, there is a small army of technicians who specialize in data collection and management and work with problem-based ecological researchers in ways that use the data for interrogating ecological change and the processes driving change. Thus, if we remodel education following lessons from ecology, we would need to change the structure of most disciplinary departments. Each department would include one or more education experts well-versed in assessment and data collection and the management and analysis of big data. These individuals would work with faculty to implement assessments, and work with technicians in other disciplinary units to develop a coherent framework for integrating data across disciplines. Until this level of integration is established, and there is a commitment to constructing and managing big data in ways that are useful for engaging in data-driven revision and monitoring of student success, implementing an ecology-inspired pedagogy would conform to what is already happening: a few people doing things differently (see data from Matz et al., 2018). To quote the National Academy again (from the introduction), "While many instructors go to great lengths to serve their students, widespread equitable and effective teaching is dependent on changes to the larger system" (National Academies of Sciences, Engineering, and Medicine, 2025). Integration of education outcomes across disciplines through the tools and approaches of big data is dependent on changes to the larger system. My hope is that we can begin to enact changes by coming together with the goal of developing an inclusive, interdisciplinary data-based approach to monitoring student knowledge and enacting educational changes that leads to a greater number of students reaching peaks of excellence, many of which will be unique and previously unknown emergent outcomes. The science of ecology is mature and has much to offer the evolving science of education.

Notes

Introduction

1. And all of the data were publicly available.

Chapter 1

1. The use of standardized testing is an example of directed-process thinking in education. Restoration projects aimed at re-creating historical conditions is an example of direct-process thinking in ecology.

2. Assuming, of course, that everyone has equal internet access, which, we know, is not true.

3. In 2023, four firms (Bayer, Corteva, ChemChina's Syngenta Group, and BASF) control the majority of crop seed and agricultural chemical sales.

4. Cumulative archaeological evidence indicates *Homo sapiens* has actively manipulated tropical forest ecologies for at least 45,000 years (Roberts et al., 2017).

5. Ecology originates from the Greek word "oikos," meaning "house" or "dwelling place," and "logos," meaning "study" or "knowledge." The concept of ecology was first introduced by the biologist Ernst Haeckel introduced the word and some key concepts in 1866 in the book *Generelle Morphologie der Organismen* (General Morphology of Organisms).

6. Risch and Hansen (1982, p. 914) wrote that significantly lower numbers of both specialist and generalist beetles were found on their host plants (bean and squash) when grown in mixtures with corn than when grown in pure stands. The differences apparently resulted not from differences in rates of parasitism or predation of the beetles, nor from differences in beetle birth rates, but principally from differences in overall patterns of beetle movements. In mixtures with corn, beetles avoided feeding on host plants shaded by corn, and the cornstalks interfered in some way with flight movements of the insects. In addition, after beetles landed on nonhost plants, they remained on the plants significantly less

time than after landing on host plants; this result led to increased rates of emigration from mixtures.

7. Humans are composed of trillions of cells, about 10% can be categorized as belonging to the universe of human cells and 90% comprise what is known as the microbiome: a community of many different types of microbes that inhabit a typical human.

8. There are many examples of social species for which we could measure social capital and gain in social capital that ultimately influences reproductive success.

Chapter 2

1. In many ways, if education is successful, it may not be possible to cleanly separate individuals based on their knowledge and their thinking in the same way we can for their observable physical characteristics.

2. These birds are native to savannah habitats in Africa.

3. We have known for more than a thousand years that certain elements (like lead) in the diet of a developing human causes cognitive impairment; in 200 BC, the Greek physician Dioscorides observed that "lead makes the mind give way." In the United States today, a Natural Resource Defense Council analysis revealed that "186 million people in the United States—a staggering 56 percent of the country's population—drank water from drinking water systems detecting lead levels exceeding the level of 1 part per billion (ppb) recommended by the American Academy of Pediatrics to protect children from lead in school water fountains" (Fedinick, 2021). Importantly, being hydrated influences cognitive performance (Perry et al., 2015); chronic dehydration because of inadequate, insufficient, or habitual lack of water is expected to have persistent and long-term effects on cognitive development. It is a staggering failure that millions of children face a daily dilemma that if they stay hydrated, a feature that improves the ability to live life, they may suffer from the debilitating effects of lead poisoning.

4. Working memory is how much information an individual can hold in short-term memory during perceptual and linguistic processing; in other words, it is the number of different ideas bouncing around in your head when you are engaged in some sort of cognitive challenge. Fluid intelligence involves the ability to reason, think flexibly and critically, invent problem solving strategies, interpret information, and solve puzzles and abstract problems, among other things.

5. Of the individual fish consumed by orcas, 88% were salmon (genus Oncorhynchus) (Ford & Ellis, 2006).

6. Figure 2.10 shows one set of ideas about one type of sampling error that gives rise to uncertainty. There is another hierarchical structure that is part of a larger structure that includes uncertainty due to systematic sampling error.

7. DFW refers to the proportion of students in a particular course who were assigned grades of D or F, or withdrew from the course prior to the end of the semester.

8. The median number of months (National Center for Education Statistics, n.d.)

9. Zhang et al. (2024) wrote, "The internal rates of return (IRRs) for individuals with college degrees in 10 broad majors compared to high school graduates . . . shows significant differences in the age-earnings trajectories and IRRs across college majors. Specifically, Computer Science and Engineering majors have the highest IRRs, exceeding 13%, whereas Humanities & Arts and Education majors have the lowest IRRs, around 5% for male and 8–9% for female college graduates. Furthermore, the quantile regression analyses show that IRR is generally higher at the high end of the earnings distribution. Finally, we observed a slight decrease in IRR during the study period, which is consistent with the flattening and even decline in college wage premiums following the 2008 Great Recession.

10. The idea that student success in college is dependent on their parents' success in college is a question about cultural heritability. Heritability is a measure of how much variation in the traits of offspring can be predicted by the traits of their respective parents. The determinants of education attainment depend on cultural—not genetic—traits related to socioeconomic conditions, the equitability of access to educational opportunity, and the cultural fit between values of individuals and the characteristics of institutes of higher education.

11. Forced migration is defined as "movements of refugees and internally displaced people (those displaced by conflicts) as well as people displaced by natural or environmental disasters, chemical or nuclear disasters, famine, or development projects" (International Association for the Study of Forced Migration, IASFM.)

12. I have evidence from our large first-year introductory biology course that shows Black students have a demonstrable and statistically detectable lower probability of taking the high-stakes exams than white students.

Chapter 3

1. The prime and double prime mark different values for a dimension of the environment.

Chapter 4

1. A section is a separate group of enrolled students in the same course.

Chapter 5

1. Note that for this particular cohort, there was a pulse of immigration in the last year for MCDB; this was exceptional, because immigration into MCDB is typically low across all years in college.

2. "Tenure-track" refers to faculty who are on contracts that include tenure as a professional benchmark accomplishment; teaching professors are not eligible for tenure.

3. By the way, it was the literature focused on parental effects on students' choice of disciplinary focus where I came across a strategy of parental manipulation referred to as a "love withdrawal" parenting style. Mainly fathers manipulated the decision-making of their daughters by employing this strategy (Scott & Mallinckrodt, 2012).

4. During my time as a professor, I have witnessed more cases of the emergence of new disciplinary units through natural diversification than the consolidation of units.

5. Note that I am focusing on faculty who are in the classroom teaching and not simply the number of faculty. The faculty in the classroom directly interact with students on a regular basis.

Chapter 6

1. Data from observations using the COPUS confirm the pedagogy is didactic; moreover, on average, lecturing by the professor occupies more than 90% of the time. See Stains et al. (2018).

2. Shout out to the Clash.

3. Without getting into much detail, cognitive psychologists, generally, conceive of ideas as cognitive constructs encoded in the brain based on the presence or absence of neural activity in a complex neural network.

4. While Smith et al. (1994) described many relevant properties of misconceptions, they did so with the intention of invalidating the premise of misconception research. They wrote, "We identify a set of theoretical principles that represent a step beyond the epistemological premise of constructivism. These principles serve as a framework for reinterpreting and reevaluating the results of misconceptions research and of orienting future empirical studies. Most importantly, they provide multiple ways for explaining how novice conceptions, including common misconceptions, play productive roles in acquiring more advanced mathematical and scientific understanding" (p. 145).

5. According to Wikipedia, at his memorial, Rossiter Raymond was described as "one of the most remarkable cases of versatility that our country has ever seen—sailor, soldier, engineer, lawyer, orator, editor, novelist, story-teller, poet,

biblical critic, theologian, teacher, chess-player—he was superior in each capacity. What he did, he always did well." It's pretty clear that, for Raymond, the destruction of nature was a first step toward the creation of something useful for humans.

6. There is, as previously emphasized, a growing group of educators who view misconceptions as a foundational resource rather than as a detrimental thing that is best eliminated or eradicated in the context of the intellectual diversity and services possible without the effect of misconceptions (see Maskiewicz & Lineback, 2017).

7. Cognitive construal refers to the process by which individuals interpret and understand information, events, or experiences. It involves how people mentally represent and make sense of the world around them. Cognitive construal encompasses various aspects of cognition, including perception, attention, memory, reasoning, and decision-making.

References

Abney, A. K., Cook, L. A., Fox, A. K., & Stevens, J. (2019). Intercollegiate social media education ecosystem. *Journal of Marketing Education, 41*(3), 254–269.

Achike, F. I., & Ogle, C. W. (2000). Information overload in the teaching of pharmacology. *Journal of Clinical Pharmacology, 40*(2), 177–183.

Aguillon, S. M., Siegmund, G. F., Petipas, R. H., Drake, A. G., Cotner, S., & Ballen, C. J. (2020). Gender differences in student participation in an active-learning classroom. *CBE—Life Sciences Education, 19*(2), ar12.

Ahmed, F., & Fuge, M. (2018). Ranking ideas for diversity and quality. *Journal of Mechanical Design, 140*(1), 011101.

Ahn, C., Moser, K. F., Sparks, R. E., & White, D. C. (2007). Developing a dynamic model to predict the recruitment and early survival of black willow (Salix nigra) in response to different hydrologic conditions. *Ecological Modelling, 204*(3–4), 315–325.

Ahn, M. Y., & Davis, H. H. (2020). Four domains of students' sense of belonging to university. *Studies in Higher Education, 45*(3), 622–634.

Akin, S., & Winemiller, K. O. (2008). Body size and trophic position in a temperate estuarine food web. *Acta Oecologica, 33*(2), 144–153.

Alleyne, J. M. (2017). Adopting a sustainability framework in re-visioning library and information science education. *Journal of Bermuda College, 3*, 24–29.

Andrews, J. D. (1981). Teaching format and student style: Their interactive effects on learning. *Research in Higher Education, 14*, 161–178.

Ansari, R. A., & Landin, J. M. (2022). Coverage of climate change in introductory biology textbooks, 1970–2019. *PLoS One, 17*(12), e0278532.

Aplin, L. M., Farine, D. R., Morand-Ferron, J., Cole, E. F., Cockburn, A., & Sheldon, B. C. (2013). Individual personalities predict social behaviour in wild networks of great tits (Parus major). *Ecology letters, 16*(11), 1365–1372.

Archer, L., Dawson, E., DeWitt, J., Seakins, A., & Wong, B. (2015). "Science capital": A conceptual, methodological, and empirical argument for extending Bourdieusian notions of capital beyond the arts. *Journal of Research in Science Teaching, 52*(7), 922–948.

Archetti, M. (2009). The volunteer's dilemma and the optimal size of a social group. *Journal of Theoretical Biology, 261*(3), 475–480.

Ashton, I. W., Miller, A. E., Bowman, W. D., & Suding, K. N. (2010). Niche complementarity due to plasticity in resource use: Plant partitioning of chemical N forms. *Ecology, 91*(11), 3252–3260.

Astorne-Figari, C., & Speer, J. D. (2019). Are changes of major major changes? The roles of grades, gender, and preferences in college major switching. *Economics of Education Review, 70*, 75–93.

Aubusson, P. (2002). An ecology of science education. *International Journal of Science Education, 24*(1), 27–46.

Ausubel, D. P. (2012). *The acquisition and retention of knowledge: A cognitive view.* Springer.

Azmitia, M., Syed, M., & Radmacher, K. (2013). Finding your niche: Identity and emotional support in emerging adults' adjustment to the transition to college. *Journal of Research on Adolescence, 23*(4), 744–761.

Baken, E. K., Adams, D. C., & Rentz, M. S. (2022). Jigsaw method improves learning and retention for observation-based undergraduate biology laboratory activities. *Journal of Biological Education, 56*(3), 317–322.

Barack, D. L., Ludwig, V. U., Parodi, F., Ahmed, N., Brannon, E. M., Ramakrishnan, A., & Platt, M. L. (2024). Attention deficits linked with proclivity to explore while foraging. *Proceedings of the Royal Society B, 291*(2017), 20222584.

Barnett, R. (2017). *The ecological university: A feasible utopia.* Routledge.

Barnett, R., & Jackson, N. (2020). *Ecologies for learning and practice.* Routledge.

Bascompte, J., Jordano, P., Melián, C. J., & Olesen, J. M. (2003). The nested assembly of plant–animal mutualistic networks. *Proceedings of the National Academy of Sciences, 100*(16), 9383–9387.

Bascompte, J., & Stouffer, D. B. (2009). The assembly and disassembly of ecological networks. *Philosophical Transactions of the Royal Society B: Biological Sciences, 364*(1524), 1781–1787.

Bateson, G. (1972). *An ecology of mind.* Ballentine.

Bathory, E., & Tomopoulos, S. (2017). Sleep regulation, physiology and development, sleep duration and patterns, and sleep hygiene in infants, toddlers, and preschool-age children. *Current Problems in Pediatric and Adolescent Health Care, 47*(2), 29–42.

Bauters, M., Moonen, P., Summerauer, L., Doetterl, S., Wasner, D., Griepentrog, M., . . . & Verheyen, K. (2021). Soil nutrient depletion and tree functional composition shift following repeated clearing in secondary forests of the Congo Basin. *Ecosystems, 24*, 1–14.

Becker, S. O., & Ferrara, A. (2019). Consequences of forced migration: A survey of recent findings. *Labour Economics, 59*, 1–16.

Beckers, R., Van der Voordt, T., & Dewulf, G. (2016). Learning space preferences of higher education students. *Building and Environment, 104*, 243–252.

Beecham, J. A. (2001). Towards a cognitive niche: Divergent foraging strategies resulting from limited cognitive ability of foraging herbivores in a spatially complex environment. *Biosystems, 61*(1), 55–68.

Beggs, J. M., Bantham, J. H., & Taylor, S. (2008). Distinguishing the factors influencing college students' choice of major. *College Student Journal, 42*(2), 381–394.

Beghtol, C. (1998). Knowledge domains: Multidisciplinarity and bibliographic classification systems. *KO Knowledge Organization, 25*(1–2), 1–12.

Belkin, D. (2021, September 6). A generation of American men give up on college: "I just feel lost." *Wall Street Journal.*

Benner, A. D. (2011). The transition to high school: Current knowledge, future directions. *Educational Psychology Review, 23,* 299–328.

Berger-Tal, O., Embar, K., Kotler, B. P., & Saltz, D. (2015). Everybody loses: Intra-specific competition induces tragedy of the commons in Allenby's gerbils. *Ecology, 96*(1), 54–61.

Berkowitz, M., & Stern, E. (2018). Which cognitive abilities make the difference? Predicting academic achievements in advanced STEM studies. *Journal of Intelligence, 6*(4), 48.

Berry, W. (2002, November). Two minds. *The Progressive.*

Berry, W. (2021). *What I stand for is what I stand on.* Penguin UK.

Bertolotti, T., & Magnani, L. (2017). Theoretical considerations on cognitive niche construction. *Synthese, 194,* 4757–4779.

Bestelmeyer, B. T., Ellison, A. M., Fraser, W. R., Gorman, K. B., Holbrook, S. J., Laney, C. M., . . . & Sharma, S. (2011). Analysis of abrupt transitions in ecological systems. *Ecosphere, 2*(12), 1–26.

Bird, D. W., Bird, R. B., Codding, B. F., & Zeanah, D. W. (2019). Variability in the organization and size of hunter-gatherer groups: Foragers do not live in small-scale societies. *Journal of Human Evolution, 131,* 96–108.

Biro, P. A., & Adriaenssens, B. (2013). Predictability as a personality trait: Consistent differences in intraindividual behavioral variation. *American Naturalist, 182*(5), 621–629.

Block, J. H., & Burns, R. B. (1976). Mastery learning. *Review of Research in Education, 4,* 3–49.

Bourdieu, P. (2020). Outline of a theory of practice. In *The new social theory reader* (pp. 80–86). Routledge.

Bowler, D. E., & Benton, T. G. (2009). Variation in dispersal mortality and dispersal propensity among individuals: The effects of age, sex and resource availability. *Journal of Animal Ecology, 78*(6), 1234–1241.

Bradley, R. H., Caldwell, B. M., Rock, S. L., Ramey, C. T., Barnard, K. E., Gray, C., . . . & Johnson, D. L. (1989). Home environment and cognitive development in the first 3 years of life: A collaborative study involving six sites and three ethnic groups in North America. *Developmental Psychology, 25*(2), 217–235.

Bronfenbrenner, U. (1977). Lewinian space and ecological substance. *Journal of Social Issues, 33*(4), 199–212.

Bronfenbrenner, U. (1979). *The ecology of human development: Experiments by nature and design.* Harvard University Press.

Bronfenbrenner, U. (1994). Ecological models of human development. In *International encyclopedia of education* (2nd ed., vol. 3, pp. 37–43). Pergamon.

Brouwer, J., Flache, A., Jansen, E., Hofman, A., & Steglich, C. (2018). Emergent achievement segregation in freshmen learning community networks. *Higher Education, 76,* 483–500.

Brown, J. H., Gillooly, J. F., Allen, A. P., Savage, V. M., & West, G. B. (2004). Toward a metabolic theory of ecology. *Ecology, 85*(7), 1771–1789.

Brown, K. J., & Grunberg, N. E. (1995). Effects of housing on male and female rats: Crowding stresses males but calms females. *Physiology and Behavior, 58*(6), 1085–1089.

Brown, P. C., Roediger, H. L., & McDaniel, M. A. (2014). *Make it stick: The science of successful learning.* Harvard University Press.

Brown, S. P., Inglis, R. F., & Taddei, F. (2009). Evolutionary ecology of microbial wars: Within-host competition and (incidental) virulence. *Evolutionary Applications, 2*(1), 32–39.

BSCS. (2018). *Strategies for effective science teaching.* BSCS Science Learning.

Buchenroth-Martin, C., DiMartino, T., & Martin, A. P. (2017). Measuring student interactions using networks: Insights into the learning community of a large active learning course. *Journal of College Science Teaching, 46*(3), 90–99.

Buck, S., & Martin, A. P. (2023). Iterative drawing reveals diversity and change in student thinking about evolution. *International Journal of Higher Education, 12*(1), 17–35.

Bunge, S. A., & Crone, E. A. (2009). Neural correlates of the development of cognitive control. In J. M. Runsery & M. Ernst (Eds.), *Neuroimaging in developmental clinical neuroscience* (pp. 22–37). Cambridge University Press.

Burkart, J. M., Schubiger, M. N., & Van Schaik, C. P. (2017). The evolution of general intelligence. *Behavioral and Brain Sciences, 40,* e195.

Burrows, M. T., Schoeman, D. S., Buckley, L. B., Moore, P., Poloczanska, E. S., Brander, K. M., . . . & Richardson, A. J. (2011). The pace of shifting climate in marine and terrestrial ecosystems. *Science, 334*(6056), 652–655.

Bush, A. O., & Lotz, J. M. (2000). The ecology of "crowding." *Journal of Parasitology, 86*(2), 212–213.

Calder, W. A. (1983). Body size, mortality, and longevity. *Journal of Theoretical Biology, 102*(1), 135–144.

Capra, F. (1994). *Ecology and community.* Center for Ecoliteracy. https://sites.ffclrp.usp.br/ceb/arquivos/Fritjof%20Capra%20-%20Ecology%20And%20Community.pdf

Cardinale, B. J., Palmer, M. A., Ives, A. R., & Brooks, S. S. (2005). Diversity-productivity relationships in streams vary as a function of the natural disturbance regime. *Ecology, 86*(3), 716–726.

Carlquist, S. (1967). The biota of long-distance dispersal: V. Plant dispersal to Pacific Islands. *Bulletin of the Torrey Botanical Club, 94*(3), 129–162.

Carstensen, M. B. (2011). Ideas are not as stable as political scientists want them to be: A theory of incremental ideational change. *Political Studies, 59*(3), 596–615.

Carter, R. M., Bowling, D. L., Reeck, C., & Huettel, S. A. (2012). A distinct role of the temporal-parietal junction in predicting socially guided decisions. *Science, 337*(6090), 109–111.

Casari, M., & Tagliapietra, C. (2018). Group size in social-ecological systems. *Proceedings of the National Academy of Sciences, 115*(11), 2728–2733.

Caselle, J. E. (1999). Early post-settlement mortality in a coral reef fish and its effect on local population size. *Ecological Monographs, 69*(2), 177–194.

Chacoff, N. P., Resasco, J., & Vázquez, D. P. (2018). Interaction frequency, network position, and the temporal persistence of interactions in a plant–pollinator network. *Ecology, 99*(1), 21–28.

Chamberlain, P. (2020). Knowledge is not everything. *Design for Health, 4*(1), 1–3.

Chambers, J. Q., Negron-Juarez, R. I., Marra, D. M., Di Vittorio, A., Tews, J., Roberts, D., . . . & Higuchi, N. (2013). The steady-state mosaic of disturbance and succession across an old-growth Central Amazon forest landscape. *Proceedings of the National Academy of Sciences, 110*(10), 3949–3954.

Chan, W. P., Chen, I. C., Colwell, R. K., Liu, W. C., Huang, C. Y., & Shen, S. F. (2016). Seasonal and daily climate variation have opposite effects on species elevational range size. *Science, 351*(6280), 1437–1439.

Chandler, R. B., Hepinstall-Cymerman, J., Merker, S., Abernathy-Conners, H., & Cooper, R. J. (2018). Characterizing spatio-temporal variation in survival and recruitment with integrated population models. *The Auk, 135*(3), 409–426.

Chang, Y., & Brickman, P. (2018). When group work doesn't work: Insights from students. *CBE—Life Sciences Education, 17*(3), ar52.

Channon, S. B., Davis, R. C., Goode, N. T., & May, S. A. (2017). What makes a "good group"? Exploring the characteristics and performance of undergraduate student groups. *Advances in Health Sciences Education, 22*, 17–41.

Chapman, C. A. (1990). Association patterns of spider monkeys: The influence of ecology and sex on social organization. *Behavioral Ecology and Sociobiology, 26*, 409–414.

Charles, R. I., & Carmel, C. A. (2005). Big ideas and understandings as the foundation for elementary and middle school mathematics. *Journal of Mathematics Education, 7*(3), 9–24.

Chase, J. M. (2007). Drought mediates the importance of stochastic community assembly. *Proceedings of the National Academy of Sciences, 104*(44), 17430–17434.

Chen, H. Y., & Maklakov, A. A. (2012). Longer life span evolves under high rates of condition-dependent mortality. *Current Biology, 22*(22), 2140–2143.

Chi, M. T. (2005). Commonsense conceptions of emergent processes: Why some misconceptions are robust. *Journal of the Learning Sciences, 14*(2), 161–199.

Chi, M. T., & Roscoe, R. D. (2002). The processes and challenges of conceptual change. In M. Limon & L. Mason (Eds.), *Reconsidering conceptual change: Issues in theory and practice* (pp. 3–27). Kluwer Academic.

Christensen, B. T., & Schunn, C. D. (2007). The relationship of analogical distance to analogical function and preinventive structure: The case of engineering design. *Memory and Cognition, 35*, 29–38.

Christianou, M., & Ebenman, B. (2005). Keystone species and vulnerable species in ecological communities: Strong or weak interactors? *Journal of Theoretical Biology, 235*(1), 95–103.

Clark, J. S., Bell, D. M., Hersh, M. H., Kwit, M. C., Moran, E., Salk, C., . . . & Zhu, K. (2011). Individual-scale variation, species-scale differences: Inference needed to understand diversity. *Ecology Letters, 14*(12), 1273–1287.

Colautti, R. I., Maron, J. L., & Barrett, S. C. H. (2009). Common garden comparisons of native and introduced plant populations: Latitudinal clines can obscure evolutionary inference. *Evolutionary Applications, 2*(2), 187–199.

Colautti, R. I., Parker, J. D., Cadotte, M. W., Pysek, P., Brown, C. S., Sax, D. F., & Richardson, D. M. (2014). Quantifying the invasiveness of species. *Neobiota, 21*, 7–27.

Cole, D. G., Newman, C. B., & Wheaton, M. M. (2017). Learning communities and students' sense of belonging to their university: First results from a longitudinal study. AERA Online Paper Repository.

Coley, J. D., & Tanner, K. (2015). Relations between intuitive biological thinking and biological misconceptions in biology majors and nonmajors. *CBE—Life Sciences Education, 14*(1), ar8.

Colman, A. M. (2009). Lake Wobegon effect. In *A dictionary of psychology* (3rd ed.). Retrieved May 25, 2025, from https://www.oxfordreference.com/view/10.1093/oi/authority.20110810105237549

Colyvan, M., & Ginzburg, L. (2010). Analogical thinking in ecology: Looking beyond disciplinary boundaries. *Quarterly Review of Biology, 85*(2), 171–182.

Connell, G. L., Donovan, D. A., & Theobald, E. J. (2023). Forming groups in a large-enrollment biology class: Group permanence matters more than group size. *CBE—Life Sciences Education, 22*(4), ar37.

Connell, J. H. (1961). The influence of interspecific competition and other factors on the distribution of the barnacle Chthamalus stellatus. *Ecology, 42*(4), 710–723.

Connell, J. H. (1978). Diversity in tropical rain forests and coral reefs: High diversity of trees and corals is maintained only in a nonequilibrium state. *Science, 199*(4335), 1302–1310.

Connell, J. H. (1985). The consequences of variation in initial settlement vs. post-settlement mortality in rocky intertidal communities. *Journal of Experimental Marine Biology and Ecology, 93*(1–2), 11–45.

Connell, J. H., & Slatyer, R. O. (1977). Mechanisms of succession in natural communities and their role in community stability and organization. *American Naturalist, 111*(982), 1119–1144.

Cook, W. M., Yao, J., Foster, B. L., Holt, R. D., & Patrick, L. B. (2005). Secondary succession in an experimentally fragmented landscape: Community patterns across space and time. *Ecology, 86*(5), 1267–1279.

Cooper, K. M., Ashley, M., & Brownell, S. E. (2017). Using expectancy value theory as a framework to reduce student resistance to active learning: A proof of concept. *Journal of Microbiology and Biology Education, 18*(2).

Cooper, K. M., Downing, V. R., & Brownell, S. E. (2018). The influence of active learning practices on student anxiety in large-enrollment college science classrooms. *International Journal of STEM Education, 5*(1), 1–18.

Cooper, M. M. (2020). The crosscutting concepts: Critical component or "third wheel" of three-dimensional learning? *Journal of Chemical Education, 97*(4), 903–909.

Corkill, A. J., & Fager, J. J. (1995). Individual differences in transfer via analogy. *Learning and Individual Differences, 7*(3), 163–187

Corning, P. A. (2002). The re-emergence of "emergence": A venerable concept in search of a theory. *Complexity, 7*(6), 18–30.

Creel, S., Dantzer, B., Goymann, W., & Rubenstein, D. R. (2013). The ecology of stress: Effects of the social environment. *Functional Ecology, 27*(1), 66–80.

Dall, S. R., Bell, A. M., Bolnick, D. I., & Ratnieks, F. L. (2012). An evolutionary ecology of individual differences. *Ecology Letters, 15*(10), 1189–1198.

Dawkins, R. (1976). *The selfish gene.* Oxford University Press.

DeAngelis, D. L. (2018). *Individual-based models and approaches in ecology: Populations, communities and ecosystems.* CRC Press.

DeFaveri, J., & Merilä, J. (2013). Evidence for adaptive phenotypic differentiation in Baltic Sea sticklebacks. *Journal of Evolutionary Biology, 26*(8), 1700–1715.

Delamater, P. L., Street, E. J., Leslie, T. F., Yang, Y. T., & Jacobsen, K. H. (2019). Complexity of the basic reproduction number (R0). *Emerging Infectious Diseases, 25*(1), 1–4.

Dellantonio, S., & Pastore, L. (2021). Ignorance, misconceptions and critical thinking. *Synthese, 198*(8), 7473–7501.

Denice, P. A. (2021). Choosing and changing course: Postsecondary students and the process of selecting a major field of study. *Sociological Perspectives, 64*(1), 82–108.

Dewey, J. (1916). *Democracy and education: An introduction to the philosophy of education*. Macmillan.

Dewsbury, B. M. (2020). Deep teaching in a college STEM classroom. *Cultural Studies of Science Education, 15*(1), 169–191.

Dewsbury, B., & Brame, C. J. (2019). Inclusive teaching. *CBE—Life Sciences Education, 18*(2), fe2.

Dewsbury, B. M., Swanson, H. J., Moseman-Valtierra, S., & Caulkins, J. (2022). Inclusive and active pedagogies reduce academic outcome gaps and improve long-term performance. *PLoS One, 17*(6), e0268620.

DiSessa, A. A. (1993). Toward an epistemology of physics. *Cognition and Instruction, 10*(2–3), 105–225.

DiSessa, A. A. (2017). Conceptual change in a microcosm: Comparative learning analysis of a learning event. *Human Development, 60*(1), 1–37.

DiSessa, A. A. (2018). A friendly introduction to "knowledge in pieces": Modeling types of knowledge and their roles in learning. In G. Kaiser, H. Forgasz, M. Graven, A. Kuzniak, E. Simmt, & B Xu (Eds.), *Invited lectures from the 13th international congress on mathematical education* (pp. 65–84). Springer.

Dochtermann, N. A., Schwab, T., & Sih, A. (2015). The contribution of additive genetic variation to personality variation: Heritability of personality. *Proceedings of the Royal Society B: Biological Sciences, 282*(1798), 20142201.

Domino, G. (1971). Interactive effects of achievement orientation and teaching style on academic achievement. *Journal of Educational Psychology, 62*(5), 427–431.

Doyle, T., & Brady, M. (2018). Reframing the university as an emergent organisation: Implications for strategic management and leadership in higher education. *Journal of Higher Education Policy and Management, 40*(4), 305–320.

Drake, J. A. (1991). Community-assembly mechanics and the structure of an experimental species ensemble. *American Naturalist, 137*(1), 1–26.

Duffy, E. J., Beauchamp, D. A., Sweeting, R. M., Beamish, R. J., & Brennan, J. S. (2010). Ontogenetic diet shifts of juvenile Chinook salmon in nearshore and offshore habitats of Puget Sound. *Transactions of the American Fisheries Society, 139*(3), 803–823.

Dungan, M. L. (1985). Competition and the morphology, ecology, and evolution of acorn barnacles: An experimental test. *Paleobiology, 11*(2), 165–173.

Dunne, J. A., Williams, R. J., & Martinez, N. D. (2002). Network structure and biodiversity loss in food webs: Robustness increases with connectance. *Ecology Letters, 5*(4), 558–567.

Duran, D. (2017). Learning-by-teaching: Evidence and implications as a pedagogical mechanism. *Innovations in Education and Teaching International, 54*(5), 476–484.

Durden, G. C., & Ellis, L. V. (1995). The effects of attendance on student learning in principles of economics. *American Economic Review, 85*(2), 343–346.

Durham, M. F., Knight, J. K., & Couch, B. A. (2017). Measurement Instrument for Scientific Teaching (MIST): A tool to measure the frequencies of research-based teaching practices in undergraduate science courses. *CBE—Life Sciences Education, 16*(4), ar67.

Ebuara, V. O., Edet, A. O., & Okpa, O. E. (2020). Managing school carrying capacity for effective teaching and learning in public universities in Nigeria. *European Journal of Social Sciences, 60*(3), 174–183.

Economic Research Service, USDA. (2022). *Food security in the US—key statistics and graphics.* https://www.ers.usda.gov/topics/food-nutrition-assistance/food-security-in-the-u-s/key-statistics-graphics/#insecure

Eddy, S. L., & Hogan, K. A. (2014). Getting under the hood: How and for whom does increasing course structure work? *CBE—Life Sciences Education, 13*(3), 453–468.

Eddy, S. L., Brownell, S. E., Thummaphan, P., Lan, M. C., & Wenderoth, M. P. (2015). Caution, student experience may vary: Social identities impact a student's experience in peer discussions. *CBE—Life Sciences Education, 14*(4), ar45.

Edelman, A. J., & McDonald, D. B. (2014). Structure of male cooperation networks at long-tailed manakin leks. *Animal Behaviour, 97*, 125–133.

Edmonds, J. W., King, K. B., Neely, M. B., Hensley, R. T., Goodman, K. J., & Cawley, K. M. (2022). Using large, open datasets to understand spatial and temporal patterns in lotic ecosystems: NEON case studies. *Ecosphere, 13*(5), e4102.

Edwards, K. M., Peng, A., Miller, S. R., & Ahmed, F. (2022). If a picture is worth 1000 words, is a word worth 1000 features for design metric estimation? *Journal of Mechanical Design, 144*(4), 041402.

Elliott, S., & Davis, J. M. (2020). Challenging taken-for-granted ideas in early childhood education: A critique of Bronfenbrenner's ecological systems theory in the age of post-humanism. In A. Cutter-Mackenzie-Knowles (Ed.), *Research handbook on childhood nature: Assemblages of childhood and nature research* (pp. 1119–1154). Springer.

Emery, N., Maher, J. M., & Ebert-May, D. (2019). Studying professional development as part of the complex ecosystem of STEM higher education. *Innovative Higher Education, 44*, 469–479.

Englund, R. A., & Polhemus, D. A. (2001). Evaluating the effects of introduced rainbow trout (Oncorhynchus mykiss) on native stream insects on Kauai Island, Hawaii; Contribution No. 2001-012 to the Hawaii Biological Survey, Bishop Museum. *Journal of Insect Conservation, 5*, 265–281.

Epanchin-Niell, R. S., Hufford, M. B., Aslan, C. E., Sexton, J. P., Port, J. D., & Waring, T. M. (2010). Controlling invasive species in complex social landscapes. *Frontiers in Ecology and the Environment, 8*(4), 210–216.

Erdle, S., & Murray, H. G. (1986). Interfaculty differences in classroom teaching behaviors and their relationship to student instructional ratings. *Research in Higher Education, 24*, 115–127.

Estrada, M., Burnett, M., Campbell, A. G., Campbell, P. B., Denetclaw, W. F., Gutiérrez, C. G., Hurtado, S., John, G. H., Matsui, J., McGee, R. M., Okpodu, C. M., Robinson, T. J., Summers, M. F., Werner-Washburne, M., & Zavala, M. (2016). Improving underrepresented minority student persistence in STEM. *CBE—Life Sciences Education, 15*(3), es5.

Estrada, M., Young, G. R., Nagy, J., Goldstein, E. J., Ben-Zeev, A., Márquez-Magaña, L., & Eroy-Reveles, A. (2019). The influence of microaffirmations on undergraduate persistence in science career pathways. *CBE—Life Sciences Education, 18*(3), ar40.

Farrington, C. A. (2013). *Academic mindsets as a critical component of deeper learning.* University of Chicago: Consortium on Chicago School Research.

Fedinick, K. P. (2021, May 13). Millions served by water systems detecting lead. Natural Resources Defense Council. https://www.nrdc.org/resources/millions-served-water-systems-detecting-lead

Fokkema, R. W., Korsten, P., Schmoll, T., & Wilson, A. J. (2021). Social competition as a driver of phenotype–environment correlations: Implications for ecology and evolution. *Biological Reviews, 96*(6), 2561–2572.

Forrester, T. D., Casady, D. S., & Wittmer, H. U. (2015). Home sweet home: Fitness consequences of site familiarity in female black-tailed deer. *Behavioral Ecology and Sociobiology, 69*, 603–612.

Franco-Santos, M., Nalick, M., Rivera-Torres, P., & Gomez-Mejia, L. (2017). Governance and well-being in academia: Negative consequences of applying an agency theory logic in higher education. *British Journal of Management, 28*(4), 711–730.

Freeman, D. C., Klikoff, L. G., & Harper, K. T. (1976). Differential resource utilization by the sexes of dioecious plants. *Science, 193*(4253), 597–599.

Freeman, S., Haak, D., & Wenderoth, M. P. (2011). Increased course structure improves performance in introductory biology. *CBE—Life Sciences Education, 10*(2), 175–186.

Frith, C. (2007). *Making up the mind: How the brain creates our mental world.* Wiley.

Fu, K., Chan, J., Cagan, J., Kotovsky, K., Schunn, C., & Wood, K. (2013). The meaning of "near" and "far": The impact of structuring design databases and the effect of distance of analogy on design output. *Journal of Mechanical Design, 135*(2), 021007.

Fukami, T. (2015). Historical contingency in community assembly: Integrating niches, species pools, and priority effects. *Annual Review of Ecology, Evolution, and Systematics, 46*(1), 1–23.

Gal, S., & Irvine, J. T. (1995). The boundaries of languages and disciplines: How ideologies construct difference. *Social Research, 62*(4), 967–1001.

Gandhi, M. K. (2007). *Peace: The words and inspiration of Mahatma Gandhi.* Blue Mountain Arts.

Gardiner, C. L., & Smith, T. A. (2018). Student learning groups: Does group composition matter? *Journal of Criminal Justice Education, 29*(3), 349–369.

Gardner, H. E. (2011). *Frames of mind: The theory of multiple intelligences*. Basic Books.

Gentner, D. (1983). Structure-mapping: A theoretical framework for analogy. *Cognitive Science, 7*(2), 155–170.

Gentner, D. (2017). Analogy. In D. A. Balota, P. G. Chapin, M. J. Friedlander, & J. L. Kolodner (Eds.), *A companion to cognitive science* (pp. 107–113). Blackwell.

Godefroid, S., Piazza, C., Rossi, G., Buord, S., Stevens, A. D., Aguraiuja, R., . . . & Vanderborght, T. (2011). How successful are plant species reintroductions? *Biological Conservation, 144*(2), 672–682.

González-Forero, M., & Gardner, A. (2018). Inference of ecological and social drivers of human brain-size evolution. *Nature, 557*(7706), 554–557.

Goodale, J. G., & Hall, D. T. (1976). Inheriting a career: The influence of sex, values, and parents. *Journal of Vocational Behavior, 8*(1), 19–30.

Goulas, S., & Megalokonomou, R. (2019). Which degrees do students prefer during recessions? *Empirical Economics, 56*, 2093–2125.

Gould, S. J. (1989). *Wonderful life: The Burgess Shale and the nature of history*. Norton.

Gouvea, J. S., & Simon, M. R. (2018). Challenging cognitive construals: A dynamic alternative to stable misconceptions. *CBE—Life Sciences Education, 17*(2), ar34.

Gray, M. E., & Holyoak, K. J. (2021). Teaching by analogy: From theory to practice. *Mind, Brain, and Education, 15*(3), 250–263.

Green, S. J., & Grosholz, E. D. (2021). Functional eradication as a framework for invasive species control. *Frontiers in Ecology and the Environment, 19*(2), 98–107.

Green, A. E., Kraemer, D. J., Fugelsang, J. A., Gray, J. R., & Dunbar, K. N. (2012). Neural correlates of creativity in analogical reasoning. *Journal of Experimental Psychology: Learning, Memory, and Cognition, 38*(2), 264–272.

Greenstone, M. H., Payton, M. E., Weber, D. C., & Simmons, A. M. (2014). The detectability half-life in arthropod predator–prey research: What it is, why we need it, how to measure it, and how to use it. *Molecular Ecology, 23*(15), 3799–3813.

Guo, Q. (2003). Temporal species richness-biomass relationships along successional gradients. *Journal of Vegetation Science, 14*(1), 121–128.

Haak, D. C., HilleRisLambers, J., Pitre, E., & Freeman, S. (2011). Increased structure and active learning reduce the achievement gap in introductory biology. *Science, 332*(6034), 1213–1216.

Haddad, N. M., Holyoak, M., Mata, T. M., Davies, K. F., Melbourne, B. A., & Preston, K. (2008). Species' traits predict the effects of disturbance and productivity on diversity. *Ecology Letters, 11*(4), 348–356.

Hadwen, S., & Palmer, L. J. (1922). *Reindeer in Alaska* (No. 1089). US Department of Agriculture.

Hahn, R. D., & Price, D. (2008). *Promise lost: College-qualified students who don't enroll in college.* Institute for Higher Education Policy.

Halverson, A. (2010). *An entirely synthetic fish: How rainbow trout beguiled America and overran the world.* Yale University Press.

Hammar Chiriac, E. (2014). Group work as an incentive for learning—students' experiences of group work. *Frontiers in Psychology, 5,* 92652.

Han, C. S., & Dingemanse, N. J. (2017). You are what you eat: Diet shapes body composition, personality and behavioural stability. *BMC Evolutionary Biology, 17,* 1–16.

Hannan, M. T., & Freeman, J. (1977). The population ecology of organizations. *American Journal of Sociology, 82*(5), 929–964.

Hansen, Z. K., Owan, H., & Pan, J. (2006). *The impact of group diversity on performance and knowledge spillover: An experiment in a college classroom* (Working Paper No. 12251). National Bureau of Economic Research.

Hardin, G. (1968). "The tragedy of the commons." *Science, 162*(3859): 1243–1248.

Hasenjager, M. J., & Dugatkin, L. A. (2015). Social network analysis in behavioral ecology. *Advances in the Study of Behavior, 47,* 39–114.

Hausmann, L. R. M., Schofield, J. W., & Woods, R. L. (2007). Sense of belonging as a predictor of intentions to persist among African American and white first-year college students. *Research in Higher Education, 48*(7), 803–839.

Heddy, B. C., & Sinatra, G. M. (2013). Transforming misconceptions: Using transformative experience to promote positive affect and conceptual change in students learning about biological evolution. *Science Education, 97*(5), 723–744.

Hellmann, J. H., & Jucks, R. (2017). The crowd in mind and crowded minds: An experimental investigation of crowding effects on students' views regarding tuition fees in Germany. *Higher Education, 74,* 131–145.

Helmuth, B., Harley, C. D., Halpin, P. M., O'Donnell, M., Hofmann, G. E., & Blanchette, C. A. (2002). Climate change and latitudinal patterns of intertidal thermal stress. *Science, 298*(5595), 1015–1017.

Henke-von der Malsburg, J., Kappeler, P. M., & Fichtel, C. (2020). Linking ecology and cognition: Does ecological specialisation predict cognitive test performance? *Behavioral Ecology and Sociobiology, 74*(12), 154.

Hennessey, K. M., & Freeman, S. (2023). Nationally endorsed learning objectives to improve course design in introductory biology. *PLoS One, 19*(8), e0308545.

Herbert, T. B., & Cohen, S. (1993). Stress and immunity in humans: A meta-analytic review. *Psychosomatic Medicine, 55*(4), 364–379.

Herre, E. A., Knowlton, N., Mueller, U. G., & Rehner, S. A. (1999). The evolution of mutualisms: Exploring the paths between conflict and cooperation. *Trends in Ecology and Evolution, 14*(2), 49–53.

Hey, J. (2011). Regarding the confusion between the population concept and Mayr's "population thinking." *Quarterly Review of Biology, 86*(4), 253–264.

Hiddink, J. G. (2003). Modelling the adaptive value of intertidal migration and nursery use in the bivalve Macoma balthica. *Marine Ecology Progress Series*, *252*, 173–185.

Higashi, M., & Yamamura, N. (1993). What determines animal group size? Insider-outsider conflict and its resolution. *American Naturalist*, *142*(3), 553–563.

Hiron, M., Berg, Å., Eggers, S., Berggren, Å., Josefsson, J., & Pärt, T. (2015). The relationship of bird diversity to crop and non-crop heterogeneity in agricultural landscapes. *Landscape Ecology*, *30*, 2001–2013.

Holland, J. L. (1966). *The psychology of vocational choice*. Blaisdell.

Holyoak, K. J., & Thagard, P. (1996). *Mental leaps: Analogy in creative thought*. MIT Press.

Hood, S., Barrickman, N., Djerdjian, N., Farr, M., Magner, S., Roychowdhury, H., . . . & Hull, K. (2021). "I like and prefer to work alone": Social anxiety, academic self-efficacy, and students' perceptions of active learning. *CBE—Life Sciences Education*, *20*(1), ar12.

Horgan, F. G., Ramal, A. F., Villegas, J. M., Almazan, M. L. P., Bernal, C. C., Jamoralin, A., . . . & Arroyo, C. (2017). Ecological engineering with high diversity vegetation patches enhances bird activity and ecosystem services in Philippine rice fields. *Regional Environmental Change*, *17*, 1355–1367.

Hoskinson, A. M., Conner, L., Hester, S., Leigh, M. B., Martin, A. P., & Powers, T. (2021, August 20). Coevolution or not? Crossbills, squirrels and pinecones. CourseSource.

Howard, C., Marjakangas, E. L., Morán-Ordóñez, A., Milanesi, P., Abuladze, A., Aghababyan, K., . . . & Willis, S. G. (2023). Local colonisations and extinctions of European birds are poorly explained by changes in climate suitability. *Nature Communications*, *14*(1), 4304.

Howard, C., Stephens, P. A., Pearce-Higgins, J. W., Gregory, R. D., Butchart, S. H., & Willis, S. G. (2020). Disentangling the relative roles of climate and land cover change in driving the long-term population trends of European migratory birds. *Diversity and Distributions*, *26*(11), 1442–1455.

Hu, J., Amor, D. R., Barbier, M., Bunin, G., & Gore, J. (2022). Emergent phases of ecological diversity and dynamics mapped in microcosms. *Science*, *378*(6615), 85–89.

Huang, Y., Richter, E., Kleickmann, T., & Richter, D. (2022). Class size affects preservice teachers' physiological and psychological stress reactions: An experiment in a virtual reality classroom. *Computers and Education*, *184*, 104503.

Hubbard, L., & Mehan, H. (1999). Race and reform: Educational "niche picking" in a hostile environment. *Journal of Negro Education*, *68*(2), 213–226.

Huberth, M., Chen, P., Tritz, J., & McKay, T. A. (2015). Computer-tailored student support in introductory physics. *PloS One*, *10*(9), e0137001.

Hufbauer, R. A., Rutschmann, A., Serrate, B., Vermeil De Conchard, H., & Facon, B. (2013). Role of propagule pressure in colonization success: Disentangling the relative importance of demographic, genetic and habitat effects. *Journal of Evolutionary Biology, 26*(8), 1691–1699.

Hughes, B. B., Beas-Luna, R., Barner, A. K., Brewitt, K., Brumbaugh, D. R., Cerny-Chipman, E. B., . . . & Carr, M. H. (2017). Long-term studies contribute disproportionately to ecology and policy. *BioScience, 67*(3), 271–281.

Hughes, T. P. (1990). Recruitment limitation, mortality, and population regulation in open systems: A case study. *Ecology, 71*(1), 12–20.

Hugo, V. (1877). Chapter 10, conclusion. *The history of a crime* (T. H. Joyce & A. Locker, Trans.). Project Gutenberg.

Hutchinson, G. E. (1957). Population studies-animal ecology and demography—concluding remarks. *Cold Spring Harbor Symposia on Quantitative Biology, 22*, 415–427.

Ishizuka, W, & Goto, S. (2011). Modeling intraspecific adaptation of Abies sachalinensis to local altitude and responses to global warming, based on a 36-year reciprocal transplant experiment. *Evolutionary Applications, 5*(3), 229–244.

Jackson, S. T., & Blois, J. L. (2015). Community ecology in a changing environment: Perspectives from the Quaternary. *Proceedings of the National Academy of Sciences, 112*(16), 4915–4921.

Jakobsen, K. V., McIlreavy, M., & Marrs, S. (2014). Team-based learning: The importance of attendance. *Psychology Learning and Teaching, 13*(1), 25–31.

Jaramillo, J. A. (1996). Vygotsky's sociocultural theory and contributions to the development of constructivist curricula. *Education, 117*(1), 133–141.

Jimenez, J. C. (2011). *Factors affecting Hispanic high school students' plans to attend college: Student-perceived barriers and self-efficacy* [Doctoral dissertation]. University of Redlands.

Johnson, D. W., & Johnson, R. T. (1974). Instructional goal structure: Cooperative, competitive, or individualistic. *Review of Educational Research, 44*(2), 213–240.

Johnson, D. W., Johnson, R. T., & Smith, K. A. (2014). Cooperative learning: Improving university instruction by basing practice on validated theory. *Journal on Excellence in University Teaching, 25*(4), 1–26.

Johnson, D. W., Johnson, R. T., & Stanne, M. B. (2000, May). *Cooperative learning methods: A meta-analysis.*

Johnson, J., & Rochkind, J. (2009). *With their whole lives ahead of them: Myths and realities about why so many students fail to finish college.* Public Agenda.

Johnson, S. E. (2003). Life history and the competitive environment: trajectories of growth, maturation, and reproductive output among chacma baboons. *American Journal of Physical Anthropology, 120*(1), 83–98.

Jonassen, D. H. (2000). Toward a design theory of problem solving. *Educational Technology Research and Development, 48*(4), 63–85.

Jonassen, D. H., & Hung, W. (2015). All problems are not equal: Implications for problem-based learning. In A. E. Walker, C. E. Hmelo-Silver, H. Leary, &

P. A. Ertme (Eds.), *Essential readings in problem-based learning: Exploring and extending the legacy of Howard S. Barrows* (pp. 17–41). Purdue University Press.

Jones, J. M. (2022, January 10). Americans reading fewer books than in past. Gallup. https://news.gallup.com/poll/388541/americans-reading-fewer-books-past.aspx

Julliard, R., Jiguet, F., & Couvet, D. (2004). Common birds facing global changes: What makes a species at risk? *Global Change Biology, 10*(1), 148–154.

Jurado-Castro, J. M., Vargas-Molina, S., Gómez-Urquiza, J. L., & Benítez-Porres, J. (2023). Effectiveness of real-time classroom interactive competition on academic performance: A systematic review and meta-analysis. *PeerJ Computer Science, 9*, e1310.

Kahl, J. A. (1953) Educational and occupational aspirations of "common man" boys. *Harvard Educational Review, 23*, 186–203.

Kahmen, A., Renker, C., Unsicker, S. B., & Buchmann, N. (2006). Niche complementarity for nitrogen: An explanation for the biodiversity and ecosystem functioning relationship? *Ecology, 87*(5), 1244–1255.

Kahneman, D. (2011). *Thinking, fast and slow*. Macmillan.

Kanai, R., & Rees, G. (2011). The structural basis of inter-individual differences in human behaviour and cognition. *Nature Reviews Neuroscience, 12*(4), 231–242.

Keepers, K., Kane, N., & Martin, A. P. (2018). Following the fate of facilitated migration in a small desert spring. *Southwestern Naturalist, 63*(1), 8–16.

Kendra, J., & Wachtendorf, T. (2003). Creativity in emergency response to the World Trade Center disaster. In *Beyond September 11th: An account of post-disaster research* (pp. 121–146). Institute of Behavioral Science, Natural Hazards Research, and Applications Information Center, University of Colorado.

Keup, J. R. (2006). Promoting new-student success: Assessing academic development and achievement among first-year students. *New Directions for Student Services, 2006*(114), 27–46.

Khan, M. A., & Al-Jahdali, H. (2023). The consequences of sleep deprivation on cognitive performance. *Neurosciences Journal, 28*(2), 91–99.

Kiehl, K., Kirmer, A., Donath, T. W., Rasran, L., & Hölzel, N. (2010). Species introduction in restoration projects: Evaluation of different techniques for the establishment of semi-natural grasslands in Central and Northwestern Europe. *Basic and Applied Ecology, 11*(4), 285–299.

Kim, B. H., Armstrong, E., Freeman, M., Hughes, R., & Kajikawa, T. (with Kim, B. H., & Armstrong, E.). (2024, March 14). *Deadline updates, 2023–2024: First-year application trends through March 1*. Common App Data Analytics and Research.

Kimmerer, R. (2013). *Braiding sweetgrass: Indigenous wisdom, scientific knowledge and the teachings of plants*. Milkweed Editions.

Kimmerling, N., Zuqert, O., Amitai, G., Gurevich, T., Armoza-Zvuloni, R., Kolesnikov, I., . . . & Sorek, R. (2018). Quantitative species-level ecology of reef fish larvae via metabarcoding. *Nature Ecology and Evolution, 2*(2), 306–316.

King, M. L. (2013). *The relationship between African American high school students' desire to attend college, their perceived likelihood to attend college and actual college enrollment* [Doctoral dissertation]. University of Missouri–Kansas City.

Kirkwood, T. B., Kapahi, P., & Shanley, D. P. (2000). Evolution, stress, and longevity. *Journal of Anatomy, 197*(4), 587–590.

Klein, N. (2007). *The shock doctrine: The rise of disaster capitalism.* Macmillan.

Knapp, R. A., & Matthews, K. R. (2000). Non-native fish introductions and the decline of the mountain yellow-legged frog from within protected areas. *Conservation Biology, 14*(2), 428–438.

Knekta, E., Chatzikyriakidou, K., & McCartney, M. (2020). Evaluation of a questionnaire measuring university students' sense of belonging to and involvement in a biology department. *CBE—Life Sciences Education, 19*(3), ar27.

Knekta, E., & McCartney, M. (2021). What can departments do to increase students' retention? A case study of students' sense of belonging and involvement in a biology department. *Journal of College Student Retention: Research, Theory and Practice, 22*(4), 721–742.

Knowles, E. S., Kreuser, B., Haas, S., Hyde, M., & Schuchart, G. E. (1976). Group size and the extension of social space boundaries. *Journal of Personality and Social Psychology, 33*(5), 647–654.

Knudsen, E. S., & Lien, L. B. (2023). The half-life of knowledge and strategic human capital. *Human Resource Management Review, 33*(4), 100989.

Kolb, D. A. (1981). Learning styles and disciplinary differences. In A. W. Chickering (Ed.), *The modern American college* (pp. 232–235). Jossey-Bass.

Koppenhaver, G. D. (2006). Absent and accounted for: Absenteeism and cooperative learning. *Decision Sciences Journal of Innovative Education, 4*(1), 29–49.

Koski, S. E., & Burkart, J. M. (2015). Common marmosets show social plasticity and group-level similarity in personality. *Scientific Reports, 5*(1), 8878.

Kraft, N. J., Adler, P. B., Godoy, O., James, E. C., Fuller, S., & Levine, J. M. (2015). Community assembly, coexistence and the environmental filtering metaphor. *Functional Ecology, 29*(5), 592–599.

Krawczyk, D. C., Kandalaft, M. R., Didehbani, N., Allen, T. T., McClelland, M. M., Tamminga, C. A., & Chapman, S. B. (2014). An investigation of reasoning by analogy in schizophrenia and autism spectrum disorder. *Frontiers in Human Neuroscience, 8*, 517.

Krebs, C. J., Boonstra, R., & Boutin, S. (2018). Using experimentation to understand the 10-year snowshoe hare cycle in the boreal forest of North America. *Journal of Animal Ecology, 87*(1), 87–100.

Kucwaj, H., Ociepka, M., & Chuderski, A. (2022). Various sources of distraction during analogical reasoning. *Memory and Cognition, 50*(7), 1614–1628.

Kuh, G. D., Cruce, T. M., Shoup, R., Kinzie, J., & Gonyea, R. M. (2008). Unmasking the effects of student engagement on first-year college grades and persistence. *Journal of Higher Education, 79*(5), 540–563.

Lachner, A., Hoogerheide, V., van Gog, T., & Renkl, A. (2022). Learning-by-teaching without audience presence or interaction: When and why does it work? *Educational Psychology Review, 34*(2), 575–607.

Laland, K. N., Kendal, J. R., & Brown, G. R. (2007). The niche construction perspective: Implications for evolution and human behaviour. *Journal of Evolutionary Psychology, 5*(1), 51–66.

Laland, K. N., & Sterelny, K. (2006). Perspective: Seven reasons (not) to neglect niche construction. *Evolution, 60*(9), 1751–1762.

Lamba, S., & Mace, R. (2011). Demography and ecology drive variation in cooperation across human populations. *Proceedings of the National Academy of Sciences, 108*(35), 14426–14430.

Larkin, R. P. (2020). Effects of selected soil amendments and mulch type on soil properties and productivity in organic vegetable production. *Agronomy, 10*(6), 795.

Laughlin, D. C., Strahan, R. T., Moore, M. M., Fulé, P. Z., Huffman, D. W., & Covington, W. W. (2017). The hierarchy of predictability in ecological restoration: Are vegetation structure and functional diversity more predictable than community composition? *Journal of Applied Ecology, 54*(4), 1058–1069.

Laverty, J. T., Underwood, S. M., Matz, R. L., Posey, L. A., Carmel, J. H., Caballero, M. D., . . . & Cooper, M. M. (2016). Characterizing college science assessments: The three-dimensional learning assessment protocol. *PloS One, 11*(9), e0162333.

Lawson Handley, L. J., & Perrin, N. (2007). Advances in our understanding of mammalian sex-biased dispersal. *Molecular Ecology, 16*(8), 1559–1578.

Le, P. (2019). Facilitating inclusion and access of undergraduate students in large-enrollment science classrooms [Doctoral dissertation]. University of Colorado at Denver.

Leeson, P., Ciarrochi, J., & Heaven, P. C. (2008). Cognitive ability, personality, and academic performance in adolescence. *Personality and Individual Differences, 45*(7), 630–635.

Leopold, A. (1987). *Game management.* University of Wisconsin Press.

Leppel, K., Williams, M. L., & Waldauer, C. (2001). The impact of parental occupation and socioeconomic status on choice of college major. *Journal of Family and Economic Issues, 22,* 373–394.

Levchak, C. C. (2013). *An examination of racist and sexist microaggressions on college campuses* [Doctoral dissertation]. University of Iowa.

Leverich, W. J., & Levin, D. A. (1979). Age-specific survivorship and reproduction in Phlox drummondii. *American Naturalist, 113*(6), 881–903.

Levin, S. A. (1992). The problem of pattern and scale in ecology: The Robert H. MacArthur award lecture. *Ecology, 73*(6), 1943–1967.

Levins, R., & Lewontin, R. C. (1985). *The dialectical biologist.* Harvard University Press.

Levis, C., Flores, B. M., Moreira, P. A., Luize, B. G., Alves, R. P., Franco-Moraes, J., . . . & Clement, C. R. (2018). How people domesticated Amazonian forests. *Frontiers in Ecology and Evolution, 5,* 171.

Liao, H., Zhou, Z., Liu, Y., Luo, Y., Zhang, C., Feng, Y., . . . & Wang, J. (2024). "The Three Sisters" (maize/bean/squash) polyculture promotes the direct and indirect defences of maize against herbivores. *European Journal of Agronomy, 155,* 127118.

Licorish, S. A., Owen, H. E., Daniel, B., & George, J. L. (2018). Students' perception of Kahoot!'s influence on teaching and learning. *Research and Practice in Technology Enhanced Learning, 13*(1), 1–23.

Lima, S. L. (1995). Back to the basics of anti-predatory vigilance: The group-size effect. *Animal Behaviour, 49*(1), 11–20.

Lin, E. J. D., Sun, M., Choi, E. Y., Magee, D., Stets, C. W., & During, M. J. (2015). Social overcrowding as a chronic stress model that increases adiposity in mice. *Psychoneuroendocrinology, 51,* 318–330.

Loh, K. K., and Kanai, R. (2015). How has the internet reshaped human cognition? *Neuroscientist, 22*(5), 506–520.

Losapio, G., Jordán, F., Caccianiga, M., & Gobbi, M. (2015). Structure-dynamic relationship of plant–insect networks along a primary succession gradient on a glacier foreland. *Ecological Modelling, 314,* 73–79.

Lynch, M., Conery, J., & Burger, R. (1995). Mutation accumulation and the extinction of small populations. *American Naturalist, 146*(4), 489–518.

MacNulty, D. R., Tallian, A., Stahler, D. R., & Smith, D. W. (2014). Influence of group size on the success of wolves hunting bison. *PloS One, 9*(11), e112884.

Magurran, A. E., & Henderson, P. A. (2003). Explaining the excess of rare species in natural species abundance distributions. *Nature, 422*(6933), 714–716.

Main, M. B. (2008). Reconciling competing ecological explanations for sexual segregation in ungulates. *Ecology, 89*(3), 693–704.

Makuya, L., & Schradin, C. (2024). Costs and benefits of solitary living in mammals. *Journal of Zoology, 323*(1), 9–18.

Malgwi, C. A., Howe, M. A., & Burnaby, P. A. 2010. Influences on students: Choice of college major. *Journal of Education for Business, 80*(5), 275–282.

Mali, D., Lim, H. J., Roberts, M., & Fakir, A. E. (2023). An analysis of how a collaborative teaching intervention can impact student mental health in a blended learning environment. *International Journal of Management Education, 21*(3), 100853.

Manderino, L., Carroll, I., Azcarate-Peril, M. A., Rochette, A., Heinberg, L., Peat, C., . . . & Gunstad, J. (2017). Preliminary evidence for an association between the composition of the gut microbiome and cognitive function in neurologically healthy older adults. *Journal of the International Neuropsychological Society*, 23(8), 700–705.

Mann, S. (2012). Systems of creation: The emergence of life from nonliving matter. *Accounts of Chemical Research*, 45(12), 2131–2141.

Marshall, H. H., Sanderson, J. L., Mwanghuya, F., Businge, R., Kyabulima, S., Hares, M. C., . . . & Cant, M. A. (2016). Variable ecological conditions promote male helping by changing banded mongoose group composition. *Behavioral Ecology*, 27(4), 978–987.

Marshall, P. D., & Losonczy-Marshall, M. (2010). Classroom ecology: Relations between seating location, performance, and attendance. *Psychological Reports*, 107(2), 567–577.

Martin, A. P. (2018). A quantitative framework for the analysis of two-stage exams. *International Journal of Higher Education*, 7(4), 33–54.

Maskiewicz, A. C., & Lineback, J. E. (2013). Misconceptions are "so yesterday!" *CBE—Life Sciences Education*, 12(3), 352–356.

Matusov, E. (1999). How does a community of learners maintain itself? Ecology of an innovative school. *Anthropology and Education Quarterly*, 30(2), 161–186.

Matz, R. L., Fata-Hartley, C. L., Posey, L. A., Laverty, J. T., Underwood, S. M., Carmel, J. H., . . . & Cooper, M. M. (2018). Evaluating the extent of a large-scale transformation in gateway science courses. *Science Advances*, 4(10), eaau0554.

Matz, R. L., Koester, B. P., Fiorini, S., Grom, G., Shepard, L., Stangor, C. G., . . . & McKay, T. A. (2017). Patterns of gendered performance differences in large introductory courses at five research universities. *Aera Open*, 3(4), 2332858417743754.

Mayr, E. (1959). Darwin and the evolutionary theory in biology. In B. J. Meggars (Ed.), *Evolution and anthropology: A centennial appraisal* (pp. 1–10). Anthropological Society of Washington.

McCallum, H. (2012). Disease and the dynamics of extinction. *Philosophical Transactions of the Royal Society B: Biological Sciences*, 367(1604), 2828–2839.

McCoy, J. G., & Strecker, R. E. (2011). The cognitive cost of sleep lost. *Neurobiology of Learning and Memory*, 96(4), 564–582.

McEwen, B. S., & Sapolsky, R. M. (1995). Stress and cognitive function. *Current Opinion in Neurobiology*, 5(2), 205–216.

McKenzie, R. D. (1924). The ecological approach to the study of the human community. *American Journal of Sociology*, 30(3), 287–301.

Meeks, M. D., Knotts, T. L., James, K. D., Williams, F., Vassar, J. A., and Wren, A. O. (2013). The impact of seating location and seating type on student performance. *Education Sciences*, 3(4), 375–386.

Metcalf, J. L., Siegle, M. R., & Martin, A. P. (2008). Hybridization dynamics between Colorado's native cutthroat trout and introduced rainbow trout. *Journal of Heredity*, 99(2), 149–156.

Michaelsen, L. K., Knight, A. B., & Fink, L. D. (Eds.). (2023). *Team-based learning: A transformative use of small groups in college teaching.* Taylor and Francis.

Miele, V., Ramos-Jiliberto, R., & Vázquez, D. P. (2020). Core–periphery dynamics in a plant–pollinator network. *Journal of Animal Ecology, 89*(7), 1670–1677.

Miles, J. R., Anders, C., Kivlighan, D. M., & Belcher Platt, A. A. (2021). Cultural ruptures: Addressing microaggressions in group therapy. *Group Dynamics: Theory, Research, and Practice, 25*(1), 74–88.

Mintz, S. (2023, February 9). Rethinking the future of the humanities. *Inside Higher Education.*

Mittelbach, G. G., & Schemske, D. W. (2015). Ecological and evolutionary perspectives on community assembly. *Trends in Ecology and Evolution, 30*(5), 241–247.

Moakler, M. W., Kim, M. M. (2014). College major choice in STEM: Revisiting confidence and demographic factors. *Career Development Quarterly, 62*(2), 128–142.

Mooney, H. A., & Cleland, E. E. (2001). The evolutionary impact of invasive species. *Proceedings of the National Academy of Sciences, 98*(10), 5446–5451.

Moreira, P. A., Inman, R. A., Cloninger, K., & Cloninger, C. R. (2021). Student engagement with school and personality: A biopsychosocial and person-centred approach. *British Journal of Educational Psychology, 91*(2), 691–713.

Mure, L. S., Le, H. D., Benegiamo, G., Chang, M. W., Rios, L., Jillani, N., . . . & Panda, S. (2018). Diurnal transcriptome atlas of a primate across major neural and peripheral tissues. *Science, 359*(6381), eaao0318.

Nagar, D., & Pandey, J. (1987). Affect and performance on cognitive task as a function of crowding and noise. *Journal of Applied Social Psychology, 17*(2), 147–157.

Nathan, R. (2006). Long-distance dispersal of plants. *Science, 313*(5788), 786–788.

National Academies of Sciences, Engineering, and Medicine. (2025). *Transforming undergraduate STEM education: Supporting equitable and effective teaching.* National Academies Press. https://doi.org/10.17226/28268

National Center for Education Statistics. (n.d.). *Time to degree (Fast Facts).* https://nces.ed.gov/fastfacts/display.asp?id=569

Navarro Jover, J. M., & Martínez Ramírez, J. A. (2018). Academic performance, class attendance and seating location of university students in practical lecture. *Journal of Technology and Science Education, 8*(4), 337–345.

Nehm, R. H., Rector, M. A., & Ha, M. (2010). "Force-talk" in evolutionary explanation: Metaphors and misconceptions. *Evolution: Education and Outreach, 3,* 605–613.

Neumann, R. (2001). Disciplinary differences and university teaching. *Studies in Higher Education, 26*(2), 135–146.

Newfield, C. (2016). *The great mistake: How we wrecked public universities and how we can fix them.* Johns Hopkins University Press.

Nichol, K. L., Heilly, S. D., & Ehlinger, E. (2005). Colds and influenza-like illnesses in university students: Impact on health, academic and work performance, and health care use. *Clinical Infectious Diseases, 40*(9), 1263–1270.

Nichter, M., & Nichter, M. (1986). Health education by appropriate analogy: Using the familiar to explain the new. *Convergence, 19*(1), 63–71.

Niederle, M., & Vesterlund, L. (2010). Explaining the gender gap in math test scores: The role of competition. *Journal of Economic Perspectives, 24*(2), 129–144.

Niu, L. (2017). Family socioeconomic status and choice of STEM major in college: An analysis of a national sample. *College Student Journal, 51*(2), 298–312.

Noël, F., Prati, D., van Kleunen, M., Gygax, A., Moser, D., & Fischer, M. (2011). Establishment success of 25 rare wetland species introduced into restored habitats is best predicted by ecological distance to source habitats. *Biological Conservation, 144*(1), 602–609.

Nozawa, Y., & Harrison, P. L. (2007). Effects of elevated temperature on larval settlement and post-settlement survival in scleractinian corals, Acropora solitaryensis and Favites chinensis. *Marine Biology, 152*, 1181–1185.

Obama, B. (2012, March 23). Presidential proclamation—Cesar Chavez Day, 2012. White House.

Oda, R. (2021). Education as niche construction: Toward an evolutionary science of education. *Letters on Evolutionary Behavioral Science, 12*(1), 24–27.

O'Donoghue, M., Boutin, S., Krebs, C. J., & Hofer, E. J. (1997). Numerical responses of coyotes and lynx to the snowshoe hare cycle. *Oikos, 80*(1), 150–162.

Odum, E. P. (1969). The Strategy of Ecosystem Development: An understanding of ecological succession provides a basis for resolving man's conflict with nature. *Science, 164*(3877), 262–270.

Olesen, J. M., Stefanescu, C., & Traveset, A. (2011). Strong, long-term temporal dynamics of an ecological network. *PloS One, 6*(11), e26455.

Olson, A. M., Frid, A., dos Santos, J. B. Q., & Juanes, F. (2020). Trophic position scales positively with body size within but not among four species of rocky reef predators. *Marine Ecology Progress Series, 640*, 189–200.

Olssen, M., & Peters, M. A. (2005). Neoliberalism, higher education and the knowledge economy: From the free market to knowledge capitalism. *Journal of Education Policy, 20*(3), 313–345.

Ors, E., Palomino, F., & Peyrache, E. (2013). Performance gender gap: Does competition matter? *Journal of Labor Economics, 31*(3), 443–499.

Osman, R. W., Whitlatch, R. B., & Zajac, R. N. (1989). Effects of resident species on recruitment into a community: Larval settlement versus post-settlement mortality in the oyster Crassostrea virginica. *Marine Ecology Progress Series, 54*(1–2), 61–73.

Özdemir, G., & Clark, D. B. (2007). An overview of conceptual change theories. *Eurasia Journal of Mathematics, Science and Technology Education, 3*(4), 351–361.

Paine, R. T. (1966). Food web complexity and species diversity. *American Naturalist, 100*(910), 65–75.

Paine, R. T., & Levin, S. A. (1981). Intertidal landscapes: Disturbance and the dynamics of pattern. *Ecological Monographs, 51*(2), 145–178.

Palameta, B., & Brown, W. M. (1999). Human cooperation is more than by-product mutualism. *Animal Behaviour, 57*(2), F1–F3.

Palmer, M. A., Ambrose, R. F., & Poff, N. L. (1997). Ecological theory and community restoration ecology. *Restoration Ecology, 5*(4), 291–300.

Parker, K. (2021, November 8). What's behind the growing gap between men and women in college completion? Pew Research Center. https://www.pewresearch.org/short-reads/2021/11/08/whats-behind-the-growing-gap-between-men-and-women-in-college-completion/

Parker, K., Horowitz, J. M., Brown, A., Fry, R., Cohn, D., & Igielnik, R. (2018, May 22). What unites and divides urban, suburban and rural Communities. Pew Research Center. https://www.pewresearch.org/social-trends/2018/05/22/what-unites-and-divides-urban-suburban-and-rural-communities/

Parsons, J. D., & Davies, J. (2022). The neural correlates of analogy component processes. *Cognitive Science, 46*(3), e13116.

Paulson, E. L. (2012). *Invasive crayfish in a desert spring system: Using landscape genetics to inform ecological restoration* [Doctoral dissertation]. University of Colorado at Boulder.

Paulson, E. L. (2016). *Community ecology and restoration of desert springs* [Doctoral dissertation]. University of Colorado at Boulder.

Paulson, E. L., Chaudoin, A., & Martin, A. P. (2021). Ecological divergence of a habitat constructed to harbor an endangered species. *Conservation Science and Practice, 3*(8), e471.

Paulson, E. L., & Martin, A. P. (2014). Discerning invasion history in an ephemerally connected system: Landscape genetics of *Procambarus clarkii* in Ash Meadows, Nevada. *Biological Invasions, 16*, 1719–1734.

Paulson, E. L., & Martin, A. P. (2019). Inferences of environmental and biotic effects on patterns of eukaryotic alpha and beta diversity for the spring systems of Ash Meadows, Nevada. *Oecologia, 191*(4), 931–944.

Pearson, J. A. (n.d.). How to build a tree. https://jamesapearson.com/how-to-build-a-tree/

Peay, K. G., & Bruns, T. D. (2014). Spore dispersal of basidiomycete fungi at the landscape scale is driven by stochastic and deterministic processes and generates variability in plant–fungal interactions. *New Phytologist, 204*(1), 180–191.

Peng, L., Deng, Y., & Jin, S. (2022). The evaluation of active learning classrooms: Impact of spatial factors on students' learning experience and learning engagement. *Sustainability, 14*(8), 4839.

Peniston, J. H., Backus, G. A., Baskett, M. L., Fletcher, R. J., & Holt, R. D. (2024). Ecological and evolutionary consequences of temporal variation in dispersal. *Ecography, 2024*(2), e06699.

Perkins, D. N., & Salomon, G. (1992). Transfer of learning. In *International encyclopedia of education* (vol. 2, pp. 6452–6457).

Perkins, K. K., & Wieman, C. E. (2005). The surprising impact of seat location on student performance. *Physics Teacher, 43*(1), 30–33.

Perry, A. L., Low, P. J., Ellis, J. R., & Reynolds, J. D. (2005). Climate change and distribution shifts in marine fishes. *Science, 308*(5730), 1912–1915.

Perry, C. S., Rapinett, G., Glaser, N. S., & Ghetti, S. (2015). Hydration status moderates the effects of drinking water on children's cognitive performance. *Appetite, 95*, 520–527.

Petersen, C. I., Baepler, P., Beitz, A., Ching, P., Gorman, K. S., Neudauer, C. L., Rozaitis, W., Walker, J. D., & Wingert, D. (2020). The tyranny of content: "Content coverage" as a barrier to evidence-based teaching approaches and ways to overcome it. *CBE—Life Sciences Education, 19*(2), ar17.

Peterson, A. T. (2001). Predicting species' geographic distributions based on ecological niche modeling. *The Condor, 103*(3), 599–605.

Pielou, E. C. (1974). *Population and community ecology: Principles and methods.* CRC Press.

Pike, T. W., Samanta, M., Lindström, J., & Royle, N. J. (2008). Behavioural phenotype affects social interactions in an animal network. *Proceedings of the Royal Society B: Biological Sciences, 275*(1650), 2515–2520.

Pinker, S. (2010). The cognitive niche: Coevolution of intelligence, sociality, and language. *Proceedings of the National Academy of Sciences, 107*(suppl. 2), 8993–8999.

Piola, R. F., & Johnston, E. L. (2006). Differential tolerance to metals among populations of the introduced bryozoan *Bugula neritina. Marine Biology, 148*, 997–1010.

Pittman, L. D., & Richmond, A. (2007). Academic and psychological functioning in late adolescence: The importance of school belonging. *Journal of Experimental Education, 75*(4), 270–290.

Pleasant, J. (2016). Food yields and nutrient analyses of the Three Sisters: A Haudenosaunee cropping system. *Ethnobiology Letters, 7*(1), 87–98.

Pleasant, J., & Burt, R. F. (2010). Estimating productivity of traditional Iroquoian cropping systems from field experiments and historical literature. *Journal of Ethnobiology, 30*(1), 52–79.

Pocheville, A. (2015). The ecological niche: History and recent controversies. In T. Heams, P. Huneman, G. Lecointre, & M. Silberstein (Eds.), *Handbook of evolutionary thinking in the sciences* (pp. 547–586). Springer.

Pompea, S. M., & Russo, P. (2020). Astronomers engaging with the education ecosystem: A best-evidence synthesis. *Annual Review of Astronomy and Astrophysics, 58*, 313–361.

Popielarz, P. A., & McPherson, J. M. (1995). On the edge or in between: Niche position, niche overlap, and the duration of voluntary association memberships. *American Journal of Sociology, 101*(3), 698–720.

Porcel, S., Fogel, M. L., Izaguirre, I., Roesler, I., & Lancelotti, J. L. (2022). Effect of rainbow trout introductions on food webs in lakes of the arid Patagonia. *Hydrobiologia, 849*(9), 2057–2075.

Posselt, J. R., & Lipson, S. K. (2016). Competition, anxiety, and depression in the college classroom: Variations by student identity and field of study. *Journal of College Student Development, 57*(8), 973–989.

Pride, R. E. (2005). Optimal group size and seasonal stress in ring-tailed lemurs (Lemur catta). *Behavioral Ecology, 16*(3), 550–560.

Priestley, M., Hall, A., Wilbraham, S. J., Mistry, V., Hughes, G., & Spanner, L. (2022). Student perceptions and proposals for promoting wellbeing through social relationships at university. *Journal of Further and Higher Education, 46*(9), 1243–1256.

Ptacnik, R., Andersen, T., Brettum, P., Lepistö, L., & Willen, E. (2010). Regional species pools control community saturation in lake phytoplankton. *Proceedings of the Royal Society B: Biological Sciences, 277*(1701), 3755–3764.

Pugh, K. J. (2011). Transformative experience: An integrative construct in the spirit of Deweyan pragmatism. *Educational Psychologist, 46*(2), 107–121.

Pulliam, H. R., & Danielson, B. J. (1991). Sources, sinks, and habitat selection: A landscape perspective on population dynamics. *American Naturalist, 137*, S50–S66.

Pulliam, H. R., & Dunning, J. B. (1987). The influence of food supply on local density and diversity of sparrows. *Ecology, 68*(4), 1009–1014.

Pulliam, H. R., & Haddad, N. M. (1994). Address of the past president: Human population growth and the carrying capacity concept. *Bulletin of the Ecological Society of America, 75*(3), 141–157.

Pywell, R. F., Bullock, J. M., Hopkins, A., Walker, K. J., Sparks, T. H., Burke, M. J., & Peel, S. (2002). Restoration of species-rich grassland on arable land: Assessing the limiting processes using a multi-site experiment. *Journal of Applied Ecology, 39*(2), 294–309.

Quillin, K., & Thomas, S. (2015). Drawing-to-learn: A framework for using drawings to promote model-based reasoning in biology. *CBE—Life Sciences Education, 14*(1), es2.

Quinn, J. A. (1939). The nature of human ecology: Reexamination and redefinition. *Social Forces, 18*(2), 161–168.

Rankin, D. J., Bargum, K., & Kokko, H. (2007). The tragedy of the commons in evolutionary biology. *Trends in Ecology and Evolution, 22*(12), 643–651.

Rasmann, S., Pellissier, L., Defossez, E., Jactel, H., & Kunstler, G. (2014). Climate-driven change in plant–insect interactions along elevation gradients. *Functional Ecology, 28*(1), 46–54.

Reeves, M., Ibáñez, I., Blumenthal, D., Chen, G., Guo, Q., Jarnevich, C., . . . & Boyte, S. (2021). Tools and technologies for quantifying spread and impacts of invasive species. In Poland, T. M., Patel-Weynand, T., Finch, D. M., Miniat,

C. F., Hayes, D. C., & Lopez, V. M. (Eds.), *Invasive Species in Forests and Rangelands of the United States: A Comprehensive Science Synthesis for the United States Forest Sector* (pp. 243–265). Springer.

Refinetti, R., Wassmer, T., Basu, P., Cherukalady, R., Pandey, V. K., Singaravel, M., . . . & Piccione, G. (2016). Variability of behavioral chronotypes of 16 mammalian species under controlled conditions. *Physiology and Behavior, 161*, 53–59.

Richter-Heitmann, T., Hofner, B., Krah, F. S., Sikorski, J., Wüst, P. K., Bunk, B., . . . & Friedrich, M. W. (2020). Stochastic dispersal rather than deterministic selection explains the spatio-temporal distribution of soil bacteria in a temperate grassland. *Frontiers in Microbiology, 11*, 1391.

Ridley, M. (2010). *The rational optimist: How prosperity evolves* (1st US ed.). Harper.

Risch, S. J., & Hansen, M. K. (1982). Plant growth, flowering phenologies, and yields of corn, beans and squash grown in pure stands and mixtures in Costa Rica. *Journal of Applied Ecology, 19*(3), 901–916.

Rittschof, D., Forward, R. B., Cannon, G., Welch, J. M., McClary, M., Holm, E. R., . . . & Van Dover, C. L. (1998). Cues and context: Larval responses to physical and chemical cues. *Biofouling, 12*(1–3), 31–44.

Roberts, P., Hunt, C., Arroyo-Kalin, M., Evans, D., & Boivin, N. (2017). The deep human prehistory of global tropical forests and its relevance for modern conservation. *Nature Plants, 3*(8), 1–9.

Roche Allred, Z. D., Santiago Caobi, L., Pardinas, B., Echarri-Gonzalez, A., Kohn, K. P., Kararo, A. T., . . . & Underwood, S. M. (2022). "Big ideas" of introductory chemistry and biology courses and the connections between them. *CBE—Life Sciences Education, 21*(2), ar35.

Roderick, M., Coca, V., & Nagaoka, J. (2011). Potholes on the road to college: High school effects in shaping urban students' participation in college application, four-year college enrollment, and college match. *Sociology of Education, 84*(3), 178–211.

Romanuk, T. N., Hayward, A., & Hutchings, J. A. (2011). Trophic level scales positively with body size in fishes. *Global Ecology and Biogeography, 20*(2), 231–240.

Roos, C. I., Guiterman, C. H., Margolis, E. Q., Swetnam, T. W., Laluk, N. C., Thompson, K. F., . . . & Whitehair, L. (2022). Indigenous fire management and cross-scale fire-climate relationships in the Southwest United States from 1500 to 1900 CE. *Science Advances, 8*(49), eabq3221.

Rosati, A. G. (2017). Foraging cognition: Reviving the ecological intelligence hypothesis. *Trends in Cognitive Sciences, 21*(9), 691–702.

Roth, W. M., & Roychoudhury, A. (1993). The concept map as a tool for the collaborative construction of knowledge: A microanalysis of high school physics students. *Journal of Research in Science Teaching, 30*(5), 503–534.

Roughgarden, J. (1972). Evolution of niche width. *American Naturalist, 106*(952), 683–718.

Rozumko, A. (2017). Adverbial markers of epistemic modality across disciplinary discourses: A contrastive study of research articles in six academic disciplines. *Studia Anglica Posnaniensia, 52*(1), 73–101.

Ruedas-Gracia, N., Jiang, G., & Maghsoodi, A. H. (2023). Is belonging stable over time? A four-year longitudinal examination of university belonging differences among students. *Emerging Adulthood, 11*(4), 1022–1038.

Russell, I. J., Hendricson, W. D., & Herbert, R. J. (1984). Effects of lecture information density on medical student achievement. *Academic Medicine, 59*(11), 881–889.

Ryoo, J., & Winkelmann, K. (Eds.). (2021). *Innovative learning environments in STEM higher education* (Springer Briefs in Statistics). https://doi.org/10. 1007/978-3-030-58948-6_2

Saavedra, S., Reed-Tsochas, F., & Uzzi, B. (2009). A simple model of bipartite cooperation for ecological and organizational networks. *Nature, 457*(7228), 463–466.

Sabo, A. E., Frerker, K. L., Waller, D. M., & Kruger, E. L. (2017). Deer-mediated changes in environment compound the direct impacts of herbivory on understorey plant communities. *Journal of Ecology, 105*(5), 1386–1398.

Savage, V. M., Allen, A. P., Brown, J. H., Gillooly, J. F., Herman, A. B., Woodruff, W. H., & West, G. B. (2007). Scaling of number, size, and metabolic rate of cells with body size in mammals. *Proceedings of the National Academy of Sciences, 104*(11), 4718–4723.

Schaafsma, S. M., Pfaff, D. W., Spunt, R. P., & Adolphs, R. (2015). Deconstructing and reconstructing theory of mind. *Trends in Cognitive Sciences, 19*(2), 65–72.

Schaeffer, K. (2022, April 12). 10 facts about today's college graduates. Pew Research Center. https://www.pewresearch.org/short-reads/2022/04/12/10-facts-about-todays-college-graduates/

Scharf, I., Feldman, A., Novosolov, M., Pincheira-Donoso, D., Das, I., Böhm, M., . . . & Meiri, S. (2015). Late bloomers and baby boomers: ecological drivers of longevity in squamates and the tuatara. *Global Ecology and Biogeography, 24*(4), 396–405.

Schmidt, C., Collette, F., Cajochen, C., & Peigneux, P. (2007). A time to think: Circadian rhythms in human cognition. *Cognitive Neuropsychology, 24*(7), 755–789.

Schmidt, K. A., & Massol, F. (2019). Habitat selection and the value of information in heterogenous landscapes. *Oikos, 128*(4), 457–467.

Schulze, P. (Ed.). (1996). *Engineering within ecological constraints.* National Academies Press.

Scott, A. B., & Mallinckrodt, B. (2005). Parental emotional support, science self-efficacy, and choice of science major in undergraduate women. *Career Development Quarterly, 53*(3), 263–273.

Seidl, R., & Turner, M. G. (2022). Post-disturbance reorganization of forest ecosystems in a changing world. *Proceedings of the National Academy of Sciences, 119*(28), e2202190119.

Seymour, E., & Hewitt, N. M. (1997). *Talking about leaving*. Westview Press.

Shaw, R. G., & Antonovics, J. (1986). Density-dependence in Salvia lyrata, a herbaceous perennial: The effects of experimental alteration of seed densities. *Journal of Ecology, 74*(3),797–813.

Sih, A., & Del Giudice, M. (2012). Linking behavioural syndromes and cognition: A behavioural ecology perspective. *Philosophical Transactions of the Royal Society B: Biological Sciences, 367*(1603), 2762–2772.

Singh, A., & Roy, S. (2017). High altitude population of Arabidopsis thaliana is more plastic and adaptive under common garden than controlled condition. *BMC Ccology, 17*, 1–16.

Sladek, M. R., Doane, L. D., Luecken, L. J., & Eisenberg, N. (2016). Perceived stress, coping, and cortisol reactivity in daily life: A study of adolescents during the first year of college. *Biological Psychology, 117*, 8–15.

Slavin, R. E. (1977). Classroom reward structure: An analytical and practical review. *Review of Educational Research, 47*(4), 633–650.

Slish, D. F. (2005). Assessment of the use of the jigsaw method and active learning in non-majors, introductory biology. *Bioscene, 31*(4), 4–10.

Smith, A. B., Godsoe, W., Rodríguez-Sánchez, F., Wang, H. H., & Warren, D. (2019). Niche estimation above and below the species level. *Trends in Ecology and Evolution, 34*(3), 260–273.

Smith, J. P., DiSessa, A. A., & Roschelle, J. (1994). Misconceptions reconceived: A constructivist analysis of knowledge in transition. *Journal of the Learning Sciences, 3*(2), 115–163.

Smith, M. D., Knapp, A. K., & Collins, S. L. (2009). A framework for assessing ecosystem dynamics in response to chronic rescurce alterations induced by global change. *Ecology, 90*(12), 3279–3289.

Solomon, N. L., & Zeitzer, J. M. (2019). The impact of chronotype on prosocial behavior. *PloS One, 14*(4), e0216309.

Soravia, C., Ashton, B. J., Thornton, A., & Ridley, A. R. (2022). General cognitive performance declines with female age and is negatively related to fledging success in a wild bird. *Proceedings of the Royal Society B, 289*(1989), 20221748.

Sosa, S., Jacoby, D., Lihoreau, M., & Sueur, C. (2021). Animal social networks: Towards an integrative framework embedding social interactions, space and time. *Methods in Ecology and Evolution, 12*(1), 4–9.

Sousa, W. P. (1984). The role of disturbance in natural communities. *Annual Review of Ecology and Systematics, 15*(1), 353–391.

Springer, L., Stanne, M. E., & Donovan, S. S. (1999). Effects of small-group learning on undergraduates in science, mathematics, engineering, and technology: A meta-analysis. *Review of Educational Research, 69*(1), 21–51.

Stains, M., Harshman, J., Barker, M. K., Chasteen, S. V., Cole, R., DeChenne-Peters, S. E., . . . & Young, A. M. (2018). Anatomy of STEM teaching in North American universities. *Science, 359*(6383), 1468–1470.

Stamps, J. A., Briffa, M., & Biro, P. A. (2012). Unpredictable animals: Individual differences in intraindividual variability (IIV). *Animal Behaviour, 83*(6), 1325–1334.

Stander, P. E., Haden, P. J., Kaqece, I. I., & Ghau, I. I. (1997). The ecology of asociality in Namibian leopards. *Journal of Zoology, 242*(2), 343–364.

Stanley, K. O., & Lehman, J. (2015). *Why greatness cannot be planned: The myth of the objective.* Springer.

Stocking Jr., G. W. (1995). Delimiting anthropology: Historical reflections on the boundaries of a boundless discipline. *Social Research, 62*(4), 933–966.

Stommel, J. (2017, October 26). Why I don't grade. *Jesse Stommel.* https://www.jessestommel.com/why-i-dont-grade/

Stratford, R. J. (2024). Towards ecological everything: The ecological university, ecological subjectivity and the ecological curriculum. *Policy Futures in Education, 22*(7), 1338–1356.

Sundrud, R. B., & Hueftle, K. (2009). Essential analogies in human anatomy and physiology. *American Biology Teacher, 71*(9), 554–557.

Survivorship curve. (n.d.). *Wikipedia.*

Sutherland, J. P. (1990). Recruitment regulates demographic variation in a tropical intertidal barnacle. *Ecology, 71*(3), 955–972.

Szolnoki, A., & Chen, X. (2021). Cooperation and competition between pair and multi-player social games in spatial populations. *Scientific Reports, 11*(1), 12101.

Taylor, D. L., Young, M., & Bashet, A. Z. (2021). Personalized and adaptive learning. In J. Ryoo & K. Winkelmann (ds.), *Innovative learning environments in STEM higher education* (Springer Briefs in Statistics). https://doi.org/10.1007/978-3-030-58948-6_2

Tenenbaum, J. B., Kemp, C., Griffiths, T. L., & Goodman, N. D. (2011). How to grow a mind: Statistics, structure, and abstraction. *Science, 331*(6022), 1279–1285.

Terborgh, J. (1973). Chance, habitat and dispersal in the distribution of birds in the West Indies. *Evolution, 27*(2), 338–349.

Terenzini, P. T., Cabrera, A. F., Colbeck, C. L., Bjorklund, S. A., & Parente, J. M. (2001a). Racial and ethnic diversity in the classroom: Does it promote student learning? *Journal of Higher Education, 72*(5), 509–531.

Terenzini, P. T., Cabrera, A. F., Colbeck, C. L., Parente, J. M., & Bjorklund, S. A. (2001b). Collaborative learning vs. lecture/discussion: Students' reported learning gains. *Journal of Engineering Education, 90*(1), 123–130.

Theobald, E. J., Eddy, S. L., Grunspan, D. Z., Wiggins, B. L., & Crowe, A. J. (2017). Student perception of group dynamics predicts individual performance: Comfort and equity matter. *PloS One, 12*(7), e0181336.

Thomas, L. (2012). *Building student engagement and belonging in higher education at a time of change.* Paul Hamlyn Foundation. https://www.phf.org.uk/wp-content/uploads/2014/10/What-Works-report-final.pdf

Thomas, L., & Jones, R. (2017). *Student engagement in the context of commuter students*. The Student Engagement Partnership. http://lizthomasassociates. co.uk/projects/2018/Commuter%20student%20engagement.pdf

Tilman, D., Knops, J., Wedin, D., Reich, P., Ritchie, M., & Siemann, E. (1997). The influence of functional diversity and composition on ecosystem processes. *Science, 277*(5330), 1300–1302.

Tinker, M. T., Guimarães, P. R., Novak, M., Marquitti, F. M. D., Bodkin, J. L., Staedler, M., . . . & Estes, J. A. (2012). Structure and mechanism of diet specialisation: Testing models of individual variation in resource use with sea otters. *Ecology Letters, 15*(5), 475–483.

Tooker, J. F., & Frank, S. D. (2012). Genotypically diverse cultivar mixtures for insect pest management and increased crop yields. *Journal of Applied Ecology, 49*(5), 974–985.

Townsend, C. R. (1989). The patch dynamics concept of stream community ecology. *Journal of the North American Benthological Society, 8*(1), 36–50.

Townsend, L. (1994). How universities successfully retain and graduate Black students. *Journal of Blacks in Higher Education* (4), 85–89.

Trauernicht, C., Brook, B. W., Murphy, B. P., Williamson, G. J., & Bowman, D. M. (2015). Local and global pyrogeographic evidence that indigenous fire management creates pyrodiversity. *Ecology and Evolution, 5*(9), 1908–1918.

Trompf, L., & Brown, C. (2014). Personality affects learning and trade-offs between private and social information in guppies, Poecilia reticulata. *Animal Behaviour, 88*, 99–106.

Tucker, J., & Friedman, S. T. (1972). Population density and group size. *American Journal of Sociology, 77*(4), 742–749.

Turcotte M. 2011. Intergenerational education mobility: University completion in relation to parents' education level. Component of Statistics Canada Catalogue no. 11-008-X (pp. 37–43).

Twyman, J. S., & Hockman, A. (2021). You Have the Big Idea, Concept, and Some Examples . . . Now What? *Behavior Analysis in Practice, 14*(3), 802–815.

Ullen, F., Hambrick, D. Z., & Mosing, M. A. (2016). Rethinking expertise: A multifactorial gene–environment interaction model of expert performance. *Psychological Bulletin, 142*(4), 427.

Ulrich, W., Zaplata, M. K., Winter, S., Schaaf, W., Fischer, A., Soliveres, S., & Gotelli, N. J. (2016). Species interactions and random dispersal rather than habitat filtering drive community assembly during early plant succession. *Oikos, 125*(5), 698–707.

University of Colorado Boulder IR. (2024). CU Boulder undergraduate admissions counts and academic preparation of first-year students. Tableau Public. https://public.tableau.com/app/profile/university.of.colorado.boulder.ir/viz/ QualComp/AdmissionsCounts

Vance, R. R. (1988). Ecological succession and the climax community on a marine subtidal rock wall. *Marine Ecology Progress Series, 48*(2), 125–136.

Van Rooij, S. W., & Lemp, L. K. (2010). Positioning e-learning graduate certificate programs: Niche marketing in higher education. *Services Marketing Quarterly, 31*(3), 296–319.

Vehrencamp, S. L. (1983). Optimal degree of skew in cooperative societies. *American Zoologist, 23*(2), 327–335.

Venezia, A., & Jaeger, L. (2013). Transitions from high school to college. *The Future of Children, 23*(1), 117–136.

Vittoz, P., & Engler, R. (2007). Seed dispersal distances: A typology based on dispersal modes and plant traits. *Botanica Helvetica, 117,* 109–124.

Vosoughi, S., Roy, D., & Aral, S. (2018). The spread of true and false news online. *Science, 359*(6380), 1146–1151.Wakefield, E. D., Cleasby, I. R., Bearhop, S., Bodey, T. W., Davies, R. D., Miller, P. I., . . . & Hamer, K. C. (2015). Long-term individual foraging site fidelity—why some gannets don't change their spots. *Ecology, 96*(11), 3058–3074.

Walker, L., & Warfa, A. R. M. (2017). Process oriented guided inquiry learning (POGIL®) marginally effects student achievement measures but substantially increases the odds of passing a course. *PLoS One, 12*(10), e0186203.

Wang, A. I., & Tahir, R. (2020). The effect of using Kahoot! for learning—A literature review. *Computers and Education, 149,* 103818.

Ward, A. F., Duke, K., Gneezy, A., & Bos, M. W. (2017). Brain drain: The mere presence of one's own smartphone reduces available cognitive capacity. *Journal of the Association for Consumer Research, 2*(2), 140–154.

Wardle, D. A., Karban, R., & Callaway, R. M. (2011). The ecosystem and evolutionary contexts of allelopathy. *Trends in Ecology and Evolution, 26*(12), 655–662.

Wiens, J. A. (1989). Spatial scaling in ecology. *Functional Ecology, 3*(4), 385–397.

Wigfield, A., & Eccles, J. S. (2002). The development of competence beliefs, expectancies for success, and achievement values from childhood through adolescence. In A. Wigfield & J. S. Eccles (Eds.), *Development of achievement motivation* (pp. 91–120). Academic Press.

Wiggins, B. L., Eddy, S. L., Grunspan, D. Z., & Crowe, A. J. (2017). The ICAP active learning framework predicts the learning gains observed in intensely active classroom experiences. *AERA Open, 3*(2), 2332858417708567.

Wilkins, A. (2012). Push and pull in the classroom: Competition, gender and the neoliberal subject. *Gender and Education, 24*(7), 765–781.

Williams, J. L., Auge, H., & Maron, J. L. (2008). Different gardens, different results: Native and introduced populations exhibit contrasting phenotypes across common gardens. *Oecologia, 157,* 239–248.

Wilmer, H. H., Sherman, L. E., & Chein, J. M. (2017). Smartphones and cognition: A review of research exploring the links between mobile technology habits and cognitive functioning. *Frontiers in Psychology, 8,* 605.

Wingfield, J. C., Hunt, K., Breuner, C., Dunlap, K., Fowler, G. S., Freed, L., & Lepson, J. (1997). Environmental stress, field endocrinology, and conservation biology. In J. R. Clemmons & R. Buchholz (Eds.), *Behavioral approaches to conservation in the wild* (pp. 95–131). Cambridge University Press.

Wolbring, T., & Treischl, E. (2016). Selection bias in students' evaluation of teaching: Causes of student absenteeism and its consequences for course ratings and rankings. *Research in Higher Education, 57,* 51–71.

Woolley, A. W., Chabris, C. F., Pentland, A., Hashmi, N., & Malone, T. W. (2010). Evidence for a collective intelligence factor in the performance of human groups. *Science, 330*(6004), 686–688.

Ulrich, W., Zaplata, M. K., Winter, S., Schaaf, W., Fischer, A., Soliveres, S., & Gotelli, N. J. (2016). Species interactions and random dispersal rather than habitat filtering drive community assembly during early plant succession. *Oikos, 125*(5), 698–707.

University of Colorado Boulder IR. (2021, February 6). Historical enrollment since 1877. Tableau Public. ttps://public.tableau.com/app/profile/university. of.colorado.boulder.ir/viz/HistoricalEnrollment-1877/Enrollment

Väljataga, T., Poom-Valickis, K., Rumma, K., & Aus, K. (2020). Transforming higher education learning ecosystem: Teachers' perspective. *Interaction Design and Architecture(s) Journal, 46*(46), 47–69.

van de Heyde, V., & Siebrits, A. (2019). The ecosystem of e-learning model for higher education. *South African Journal of Science, 115*(5–6), 1–6.

Xiao, H., Carney, D. M., Youn, S. J., Janis, R. A., Castonguay, L. G., Hayes, J. A., & Locke, B. D. (2017). Are we in crisis? National mental health and treatment trends in college counseling centers. *Psychological Services, 14*(4), 407–415.

Yang, X., Yan, C., Zhao, Q., Holyoak, M., Fortuna, M. A., Bascompte, J., . . . & Zhang, Z. (2018). Ecological succession drives the structural change of seed-rodent interaction networks in fragmented forests. *Forest Ecology and Management, 419,* 42–50.

Yazedjian, Y., Toews, M. L., & Navarro, A. (2009). Exploring parental factors, adjustment and academic achievement among white and Hispanic college students. *Journal of College Student Development, 50*(4), 458–467.

Yu, D. W. (2001). Parasites of mutualisms. *Biological Journal of the Linnean Society, 72*(4), 529–546.

Zaret, T. M., & Rand, A. S. (1971). Competition in tropical stream fishes: Support for the competitive exclusion principle. *Ecology, 52*(2), 336–342.

Zerwin, S. M. (2020). *Point-less: An English teacher's guide to more meaningful grading.* Heinemann.

Zhang, L., Liu, X., & Hu, Y. (2024). Degrees of return: Estimating internal rates of return for college majors using quantile regression. *American Educational Research Journal, 61*(3), 577–609.

Zhu, Y., Queenborough, S. A., Condit, R., Hubbell, S. P., Ma, K. P., & Comita, L. S. (2018). Density-dependent survival varies with species life-history strategy in a tropical forest. *Ecology Letters, 21*(4), 506–515.

Zografou, K., Swartz, M. T., Tilden, V. P., McKinney, E. N., Eckenrode, J. A., & Sewall, B. J. (2020). Stable generalist species anchor a dynamic pollination network. *Ecosphere, 11*(8), e03225.

Zwolak, J. P., Zwolak, M., & Brewe, E. (2018). Educational commitment and social networking: The power of informal networks. *Physical Review Physics Education Research, 14*(1), 010131.

Index